THE POWER GAME IN BYZANTIUM

The Power Game in Byzantium

Antonina and the Empress Theodora

James Allan Evans

continuum

Continuum International Publishing Group

The Tower Building	80 Maiden Lane
11 York Road	Suite 704
London	New York
SE1 7NX	NY 10038

www.continuumbooks.com

British Library Cataloguing-in-Publication Data
A catalogue record for this book is available from the British Library.

ISBN: 978-1-4411-4078-4 (hardcover)

Library of Congress Cataloging-in-Publication Data
A catalog record for this book is available from the Library of Congress.

Typeset by Fakenham Prepress Solutions, Fakenham, Norfolk NR21 8NN
Printed and bound in India

For Eleanor

Contents

List of Illustrations

Preface

Why in the world do we need another book on the empress Theodora? A querulous portion of the reading public will ask that question – and some reviewers as well – and reasonably enough. The simple answer is that we don't, though if only books that were necessary were written, library stacks would be half empty. Authors write books on well-worn subjects either because they imagine that they can shift the focus, and present a familiar picture with new background lighting, or because they are self-important enough to think that somewhere, there exist readers for their publication. Often both motives are at work. In my defence, however, I would argue that this is not simply a book about Theodora, or even about the imperial couple, like Robert Browning's superb *Justinian and Theodora*, which combines an unparalleled grasp of history with a splendid literary style. It is about two women who knew how to use political power to advance their interests, lead lives outside contemporary social norms and influence the workings of the government. They lived in a period when most women lived lives circumscribed by social convention, and their example shows that women – even if they were born into the lowest ranks of society – could play the power game as well as men. They were also outsiders in a new age of intolerance.

Labelling the reigns of Justin I and Justinian a new age of intolerance is a harsh judgement, but it can be justified. The Late Roman Empire had evolved into the Christian state of Romania,[1] where the emperor's mandate from Heaven was to rule as God's deputy on earth. The angels in Heaven hated heterodoxy; so also should God's deputy. Heretical belief was dangerous not only to a Christian's salvation but to the wellbeing of the empire as well, and it followed that ever since Constantine I embraced Christianity, emperors had been embroiled in doctrinal disputes.[2] Yet, from 482 until the accession of the old soldier, Justin I, Justinian's adoptive father, the religious policy of the eastern Roman Empire was regulated by the *Henotikon*, a 'Unity Creed' formulated in the emperor Zeno's reign by the patriarch of Constantinople, Acacius, and his strategy for dealing with the bitter quarrel about the nature of the Trinity was to anoint it with the healing oil of imprecision. The *Henotikon*, which Acacius crafted, was a masterpiece of artful vagueness, with the result that it satisfied no one, which was an impossible goal anyway, but it did allow the peaceful co-existence of those Christians who believed in the Chalcedonian Creed and those who could not stomach it. It represented official willingness to separate church and state just far enough to allow freedom to choose. Yet it was a compromise; and for Rome, and the Latin bishoprics of what was once the western Roman Empire, there could be no compromise with ultimate truth, which only Rome had the mandate to pronounce.

The *Henotikon* would not do. In 484, the pope in Rome excommunicated Acacius, thus beginning the 'Acacian Schism', which lasted until the emperor Anastasius died and his successor, Justin I, egged on by his wife, a convinced Chalcedonian like himself, surrendered to Rome's demands. Pope Hormisdas in Rome insisted that opposition to the decision of Chalcedon must be suppressed. The view of old Anastasius, who was no Chalcedonian himself, had been that it was not worth spilling blood to enforce what Rome considered orthodoxy. Justin and his nephew Justinian thought otherwise.

This was the Indian summer of the classical world, when the Greek classics were still the foundation of a cultivated man's education. Constantinople, founded by Constantine in 324, was the new Rome, and the language of law was still Latin, but the language of communication and culture was Greek. The Byzantines saw themselves as citizens of Romania, and though they might speak Greek, they called themselves 'Romans', not *Graikoi*, which had connotations of spinelessness.[3] Nor did they call themselves 'Hellenes', for 'Hellene' now meant 'pagan'. Hellenism was a culture that endangered the Christian soul.

Yet paganism was by no means dead, though it was outlawed, and sacrifices had been forbidden for two centuries. An anti-pagan pogrom in Constantinople in 545–6 swept up a great number of the city's educated elite, who were assembled in churches to be taught the truth of Christianity,[4] and as late as 14 years after Justinian's death, a secret pocket of pagan worshippers was discovered at Baalbek in Syria; under torture they revealed the names of many fellow worshippers, particularly in Antioch.[5] Paganism had become a bootleg religion, surviving underground among the educated upper crust as nostalgia for the intellectual traditions of the past and, on the popular level, as sorcery and superstition and inherited awe for the ancient holy sites where the gods of Greece and Rome were once worshipped. Neoplatonic philosophy was still taught in the schools of Alexandria and Athens and, in Athens at least, where Justinian terminated the school, it made no compromise with Christian thought. Classical culture that was the mark of an educated person had been purely pagan and historians of the Late Empire, who wrote their histories in self-conscious classical Greek and took Herodotus and Thucydides as their models, seem like dual citizens, acknowledging their allegiance to the pagan past almost as much as to the Christian present-day world. Paganism still had room to breathe under Anastasius. In his reign, the pagan apologist Zosimus could still produce a history of Rome that drew a connection between Rome's decline and its adoption of Christianity. Freedom to express publicly views like that disappeared when Justinian's uncle, Justin, appropriated the imperial throne and, once Justinian himself became emperor, he re-enacted the old laws outlawing paganism and initiated his first pagan witch-hunt. More of them would follow.

The intolerance extended to the anti-Chalcedonians. 'Monophysite', the label generally applied to them, came into popular usage as a pejorative term only in the eighth century, long after Justinian was dead, though the Monophysites themselves were already using its antonym 'diphysite' or 'diaphysite' for their rivals. But 'Monophysite' has become an umbrella term for all Christians who believe that Christ's humanity was subsumed by his divine nature, and I shall go along with the same convenient anachronism. 'Monophysite' in this book means simply 'anti-Chalcedonian'. In the reign of Anastasius, who was a Monophysite himself, it would have been inappropriate to call Monophysitism a heresy. Whatever the Church of Rome thought, in the eastern provinces, most Christians – but not all – considered Monophysitism the correct faith and for them Justinian's wife, the Monophysite empress Theodora, would be 'the believing queen', defender of true orthodoxy. Yet, once Justin I took hold of the imperial throne and a new regime began, Monophysitism became officially a heresy that was to be suppressed by force if necessary. A line was drawn in the sand – if we may make an analogy between theological controversy and sand. Chalcedonian Catholicism became the authorized religion, the imperial faith of Romania, and Monophysitism became the 'other'. In the east, the Chalcedonians were labelled 'melkites', the emperor's men – 'melkite' was derived from the Syriac word for 'king', in Greek, *basileus*. It would be Melkite churchmen who coined the label 'Monophysite' for the anti-Chalcedonians. The Monophysites were not disloyal to the emperor, nor to the idea of the Roman Empire, but there were limits to their loyalty. With a helping hand from the empress Theodora they would develop into a separate denomination with its own priests and bishops and, whether or not its founders intended it, Monophysitism became a separatist movement.

Theodora's role has always been fascinating. Her nearest modern equivalent is Eva Perón, the second wife of President Juan Perón of Argentina. Like

Theodora, Eva Perón was an actress. She married Juan Perón in 1945, the year
before he was elected president. Like Theodora she championed the rights of
women. She headed ministries in Perón's government, which Theodora never
did officially, though she knew how to make her influence felt in the imperial
bureaucracy. Eva was Perón's partner in power and was even nominated for the
office of Vice-President, though she withdrew from the race before the election.
Like Theodora, she died of cancer. Like Theodora, too, she left a reputation
behind her that provokes widely different reactions. Was she a saint or a
trouble-maker? Did she follow a consistent policy of outreach to marginalized
groups, whether they were women, the *demi-monde* of the theatre, or religious
dissidents?

One thing seems certain: Theodora bore some responsibility for the growing
absolutism of the age. How much we cannot say. It was Justinian who was the
basileus, the ruler who issued the imperial edicts. One of them states baldly
that the emperor, not the people, was the source of law, for the emperor was
law incarnate.[6] Theodora may have encouraged the growth of court ceremony
which was a symbol of the increasing autocracy, and no doubt she enjoyed
seeing the aristocratic notables of Constantinople prostrating themselves before
her, and kissing her shoe, but it was Justinian who formulated the legal
definition of despotism. Justinian certainly listened to his wife; in letters to
Theodahad, king of the Ostrogoths[7] and to Khusro, shah of Persia,[8] she actually
claimed that Justinian did nothing without consulting her, but only in one
of his laws does Justinian himself state that he sought Theodora's advice. But
she did know her way around the corridors of power, and we find her acting
independently almost to the point of subverting her husband's policies. She had
her own network of agents to keep her informed, some of them, no doubt, her
old contacts in the theatre whom she welcomed into the imperial palace, to the
immense distaste of imperial upper-crust society. Antonina was one of them.
We know nothing of Theodora's private conversations with her sister Comito,
or Indaro or Chrysomallo, all of them former actresses, but we do know a great
deal about Antonina, thanks to Procopius of Caesarea.

He is our chief source for Antonina, whom he knew well, for she accompanied Belisarius on his campaigns in Africa and Italy and Procopius had plenty
of opportunity to see her in action. Whether or not he ever met Theodora we
do not know. If so, it was probably a formal audience, where he was required
to kiss her shoe. But our second important source did know Theodora on a
personal level. He was John of Amida, better known as John of Ephesus,[9] for
he was the titular Monophysite bishop of Ephesus, though he never lived there.
He had no interest in Antonina, but he knew Theodora well as the defender

of the Monophysite faith, whom the Chalcedonians, even with all the weight of the papacy behind them, could not silence. The reliability of Procopius and John as sources is a question that I shall discuss in an appendix. Without their evidence this book could not have been written, though there is enough information from other sources to provide a check on their veracity. Yet, we must supplement them with a degree of learned speculation, which I admit without apology. Speculation is the disreputable brother of imagination, without which we cannot construct a picture of the historical past, but the disreputable brother taints legitimate imagination only when it crosses the boundaries of reasonable probability. It stumbles into mere speculation when it produces an unlikely portrait of the past, informed by the author's personal biases, and I have tried to avoid that. I have presented Justinian, Theodora, Belisarius and Antonina as plausible characters within the historical tapestry of their own day: not always admirable – often, in fact, quite the opposite – but shapers of history nonetheless. They are figures compatible with the evidence.

Late Antiquity tends to fall between two academic disciplines: ancient history, which is dominated by classical scholars and ends when the Mediterranean world abandoned Christianity, and mediaeval studies which takes over the field once classicists abandon it. I was fortunate enough to spend ten years of my university career as an historian in a history department, where the boundaries between ancient and mediaeval history were blurred. So my first venture into the age of Justinian was on a panel at the 1968 annual conference of the Canadian Historical Association, along with the late Tom Carney who was working at the time on the structure of the imperial bureaucracy in the Justinianic period.[10] The Canadian Historical Association publishes a small number of the papers presented each year, and mine was among those chosen for the 1968 volume. It was an effort that seems naïve to me now, to show how and why the outlook of Procopius changed from apparent optimism at the start of Justinian's reign to bitterness at its end. I floated the idea that there was a clear connection between Procopius' *Secret History*, and his encomium on Justinian's building programme, for they were the obverse and reverse of the same coin. The one presents Justinian as the true emperor who built for the glory of God and cared for the welfare of his subjects; in the other he is evil incarnate who brought disasters upon the state. I still clung this hypothesis when I published a slim volume on Procopius four years later, where I suggested that it was for artistic reasons alone that the *Secret History* indicates four times[11] that, when it was written, the Byzantines had endured 32 years of Justinian's rule, counting the years of Justin's reign as part of it, and thus pretending that it was a covert palinode composed when the *History of the Wars* was published. I imagined that Procopius really wrote his clandestine invective as a commentary on his *History* in his old age, when he found it politic, for whatever reason, to produce a panegyric on Justinian. In reality, the 32 years of Justinian's rule counted from his accession in 527 and the *Secret History* was actually his outlet for the bitterness that haunted the recesses of his mind as he produced his formal praises of an emperor whom he equated with the Antichrist.[12]

But that hypothesis will not do. It is a product of the disreputable brother of imagination. The question of when Procopius wrote his *Secret History* has been finally settled now, thanks to Anthony Kaldellis' recent article, 'The Date and Structure of Prokopios' *Secret History* and his Projected Work on Church History'.[13] The *Secret History* dates to 550. The first book of the panegyric on Justinian's building programme must have been completed before the partial collapse of the dome of Hagia Sophia in 558, but it was perhaps as much as three years later that this odd encomium reached its present form. For the date of the eighth book that concludes the *History of the Wars*, I favour 557 rather than 554, but I cannot prove that I am right, nor, I think, can anyone prove that I am wrong. However, for the most part, the question of when Procopius wrote his various works is no longer a matter of debate.

I began this book hoping that it would be academically respectable and accessible as well to the reading public who have minimal interest in footnotes. I came to the study of the Justinianic age as an historian of the classical and Hellenistic world, drawn to it by the connection between Procopius and his mentors, Herodotus and Thucydides. Academic interest in Late Antiquity has exploded since I ventured into the field, and now advancing age will prevent me from pursuing my interest in Late Antiquity much further. For what I have learned about the period I owe a great debt to the many scholars, and two I should mention by name: Anthony Kaldellis who responded to a request of mine with a sheaf of his offprints, and Geoffrey Greatrex of the University of Ottawa, who has made an enormous contribution to our understanding of the age of Justinian. A file in my office labelled with his name is overflowing with copies of his articles. I am very grateful to Jonathan Bardill, too, who supplied the photographs in this book. I should also mention two recent books that have done much to make me rethink my view of the period: *The Ruin of the Roman Empire*, by James J. O'Donnell, who subtitles his book, *A New History*. The other is Bryan Ward-Perkins' *The Fall of Rome and the End of Civilization*. Both present viewpoints which I respect, even when I disagree.

I must also thank my wife Eleanor, for whose patience I am forever grateful. And I am also grateful to Procopius, one of the great Greek historians, who has been a companion of mine for the last 40 years.

Abbreviations

BASOR – *Bulletin of the American School of Oriental Research*
BMGS – *Byzantine and Modern Greek Studies*
BZ – *Byzantinische Zeitschrift*
CAH – *Cambridge Ancient History*
CIC – *Corpus Iuris Civilis*, eds T. Mommsen, P. Krueger et al., 3 vols. (Berlin, 1928–9)
CSCO – Corpus scriptorium christianorum orientalium
DOP – *Dumbarton Oaks Papers*
GRBS – *Greek, Roman and Byzantine Studies*
Hdt. – Herodotus, *The Histories*
JRS – *Journal of Roman Studies*
LA *Guide* – *Late Antiquity. A Guide to the Postclassical World*, eds G. W. Bowersock, Peter Brown and Oleg Grabar (Cambridge, MA and London: Harvard University Press, 1999)
ODB – *The Oxford Dictionary of Byzantium*, ed. Alexander P. Kazhdan (New York and Oxford: Oxford University Press, 1991)
OHBS – *The Oxford Handbook of Byzantine Studies*, ed. Elizabeth Jeffreys, with John Haldon and Robin Cormack (Oxford: Oxford University Press, 2008)
PLRE – *The Prosopography of the Later Roman Empire*, eds A. H. M. Jones, J. R. Martindale and J. Morris (Cambridge: Cambridge University Press, 1971)
PO – *Patrologia Orientalis*
REB – *Revue des Études Byzantines*
TTH – *Translated Texts for Historians* (Liverpool University Press)

The Background to the Story

At Meydani, the 'Square of the Horses', the great rectangle of turf that lies in the south-east corner of modern Istanbul, still marks the heart of the city. One end of it reaches south toward the Sea of Marmora, and the other stretches northwards towards Hagia Sophia, Constantinople's cathedral built by the emperor Justinian, and now his most conspicuous monument. The Turks who captured Constantinople in 1453 transformed it into a mosque, and in the twentieth century, it became a museum. *At Meydani* is all that remains of the great Hippodrome of the 'Royal City', that once accommodated up to 100,000 spectators. Its seats have vanished long ago, and the racecourse itself lies buried under three metres of earth, heaped over it by the passage of time. Yet if we stand in its midst, and employ only a small morsel of imagination, the years drop away and we can conjure up the scenes that once took place here: teams of sweating horses bursting out of the starting gates, whipped to a hard gallop by their drivers as they teetered on their flimsy chariots, racing down one lane of the course, wheeling around the turning post and then racing up the other lane, while the spectators cheered, and the sovereign of the Roman Empire, God's deputy on earth,[1] surveyed the scene from his seat high above in the *kathisma* – the imperial loge, connected to the palace by a private passageway. Twenty-five races filled up a day of fun.

Little remains now of Constantinople's great Hippodrome. Four gilded bronze horses from above the starting-gates, once belonging to a four-horse chariot, now adorn the cathedral of San Marco in Venice, where they were taken after the Fourth Crusade in 1204 plundered the city. The *spina* – the low wall which divided the racecourse into two lanes, once bristled with monuments appropriated from assorted sites in the empire. Constantine, the founder of Constantinople, set the example: before he died, the *spina* bore no fewer than 20 filched monuments, and Constantine's successors followed his example up until the time of Justinian. Two are still to be seen. One is a bronze column of three serpents intertwined, which was filched from the sanctuary of Apollo's oracle at Delphi.[2] It commemorated a moment of glory

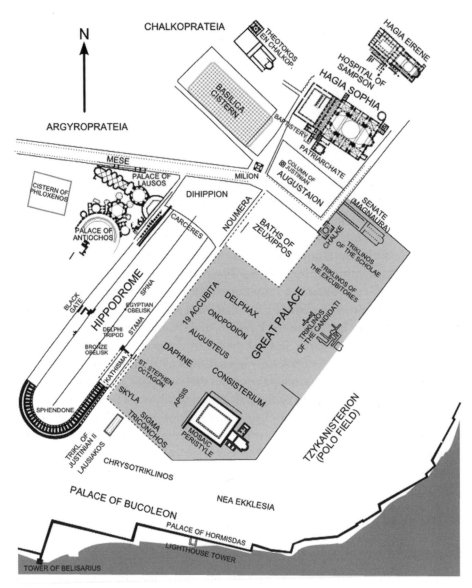

Great Palace, Constantinople.

in the history of classical Greece, when the Greeks defeated a Persian invasion at Plataea in 479 BCE. In modern Istanbul, the column sits in a shallow well, for the ground level has risen and the column base is now far below the surface of the earth. The other is an obelisk which the Pharaoh Thutmose III erected three and a half millennia ago in Egypt. The emperor Theodosius I, brought it to Constantinople and erected it on a new base to mark the centre of the Hippodrome. On the four sides of the base are sculptured reliefs, one of which shows Theodosius himself and his courtiers watching the races from the *kathisma*. Fast forward a century and a half from Theodosius' reign, and we can imagine the great emperor Justinian himself sitting in immobile splendour in the same *kathisma*, which he remodelled early in his reign to make loftier and more impressive.[3] His partner-in-power, Theodora, an ex-actress who played her most famous role as empress of Romania, would not be at his side, for women did not attend the races; in fact, a wife who went to the races gave her husband a lawful cause for divorce.[4] Yet Theodora knew the Hippodrome well. As a child she had come there as a suppliant, along with her two sisters, to beg for the compassion of the fans.

These monuments are poor remnants of a splendid past. Only a few of the buildings that were once Justinian's pride survive in Istanbul of today. The mosque of Sultan Ahmet, the so-called 'Blue Mosque', stands where the imperial palace once sprawled over the south-east corner of the city. Archaeologists have recently begun to unearth some of its remains, including remarkable floor mosaics which hint at what its grandeur must have been. Justinian's Hagia Sophia has endured the vicissitudes of time, though it no longer confronts the imperial palace across the *Augustaeum* square, so named after Constantine's mother, Helena Augusta, whose image once stood on a column there. This was the heart of Rome's successor city, Constantinople, capital of eastern Romania that survived the decline of the western empire. Here in the Hippodrome the great emperor, heir to a line of emperors that began with Imperator Caesar Augustus, came face to face with his subjects.

There was a rough-and-ready democracy in the Hippodrome. The crowd gathered there to acclaim new emperors, for the concept that the emperor was a magistrate elected by the Roman people was not yet dead. Many centuries had passed since the assemblies of the ancient Roman republic passed laws and elected magistrates; yet the populace of New Rome still exercised its ancient right to make its will known to the emperor as he sat in his imperial loge. There might be direct dialogues between the people gathered in the Hippodrome and the emperor, who communicated with them using a herald trained to project his voice. Nor did the mob hesitate to howl protests and maledictions up at the emperor if his policies displeased it. Between 491 and 565 we know of at least 30 riots there.[5] One erupted in 507, when the emperor Anastasius refused to free some prisoners whom the people favoured, and they hurled rocks at him as he sat in his imperial loge. Once again, in 512, a wrathful mob in the Hippodrome almost toppled the same Anastasius from his throne. Twenty years later, the emperor Justinian saved his regime by butchering rioters that packed the Hippodrome to acclaim a replacement emperor. It must have been in this same Hippodrome, one day in the reign of Anastasius, that the little girl who would later become the *Augusta* Theodora made her first appearance before people of Constantinople.

Chariot racing and, for that matter, most public spectacles in the cities of the empire, were managed by production companies, or 'factions', that took their names from the ribbons worn by their horses. There were the Reds, Whites, Blues and Greens, and each colour had its own party or group of fans which sat together in separate sections of the Hippodrome. The tradition went back to the great Circus Maximus of Rome on the Tiber – the 'elder Rome' – but in the fifth century, the factions had developed into production companies in the entertainment industry, responsible for the performances in the hippodromes and theatres of the empire. The Blue and the Green factions were the dominant ones and the Reds and Whites were paired with them, White and Blue teams racing together against Greens and Reds. Each faction's aficionados cheered on their teams and howled curses at their rivals. The Blues and the Greens in particular had companies of loyal supporters who were as passionate as the fans of modern football teams.[6]

Every race was moment of wild exhilaration. The trumpet sounded, the starting gates opened, and the horses plunged forward, hoofs pounding. A roar of applause mingled with jeers and taunts for the losers thundered from the seats. Here was where the young males of Constantinople sublimated their testosterone rush, for they had few other outlets: the gymnasiums and the ephebate culture that was once an important part of the classical city had not survived the fifth century.[7] In his imperial box the emperor surveyed the scene with regal dignity. Emperors were above crass displays of emotion. Yet it was the imperial stables that provided some of the race horses – perhaps by Justinian's reign, all of them – and the emperors were expected to be aficionados of one team or another. The emperor Zeno (474–91) sided with the Greens; his successor, the Anastasius (491–518) who was no great supporter of public spectacles, was nonetheless a fan of the Reds, and Justinian and his empress Theodora were both fervent partisans of the Blues – especially Theodora, and the reason for her partiality went back to her childhood.

SOMETIME IN THE OPENING YEARS OF THE SIXTH CENTURY, WHILE ANASTASIUS WAS EMPEROR, ACACIUS, THE BEAR-KEEPER OF THE GREEN FACTION DIED. The factions maintained a supply of wild beasts, some of which were destined for the wild beast hunts (*venationes*), which were a favourite Roman spectacle, pitting wild animals and huntsmen against each other in the arena. The beasts were slaughtered to the delight of the spectators as they watched toreadors perform tricks such as vaulting over the back of a frantic animal as it charged, and sometimes they had the additional amusement of seeing one of them disembowelled. Unlike the fake ferocity and the improbable stunts of professional wrestlers on television, the acrobatics of the toreadors endangered life and limb, and the blood in the arena was real. Anastasius outlawed these extravaganzas of butchery in 498, but they soon made a comeback, probably even before Anastasius died.[8] When Justinian inaugurated his consulship in 521, he presented games that featured the slaughter of 20 lions and 30 panthers in wild animal hunts. He was doing nothing unusual, for consuls regularly presented costly inaugural games that included wild beast hunts, and Justinian promulgated a law ordering the consuls to make proper arrangements for them.[9] Some of the money lavished on the games trickled down to the poor, among them entertainers from the theatre. Tastes change, however; the year 537 saw the last *venatio* in Constantinople. The consulship itself was abolished in 541 and the name of the consul of the year no longer appeared on Roman laws. Costs had to be cut; the empire was gearing up for renewed war with Persia and consular inaugurations, which cost 2,000 gold pounds, most of it supplied by the imperial treasury, were a waste of money.[10] At any rate, if someone lusted after the title of consul, honorary consulships were still for sale.

Yet bears were also performers: dancing, or taking part in acrobatic acts. Our only source for the story of Acacius describes him as the 'keeper of the wild beasts used in the hunt' with the title 'Caretaker', or 'Master of the Bears'.[11] Since Anastasius' ban on the hunts was probably still in force when Theodora was a young girl, Acacius probably trained the bears that performed in the Hippodrome for the crowd in the *entr'actes* between chariot races. A mob left without entertainment could become a dangerous thing, and while the Hippodrome attendants were removing splintered chariots and injured horses and bringing the teams for the next race into the starting gates, the factions that managed the races provided distractions – acrobatic acts, mimes, dances and performing bears. The speech-writer, Choricius from the school at Gaza,[12] a contemporary of Theodora's youth, who wrote a defence of mimes, remarked that chariot races fired the passions and spectators with their passions aroused could be dangerous to public order; but mimes gave pleasure without passion. It was an example of judicious crowd control and Acacius' job was to provide bears that could perform tricks or, should the entertainment industry require it, be slaughtered for the amusement of the spectators.

In Constantinople's class structure a bear-keeper's rank was at the bottom of the ladder and history would never have noticed Acacius' death, except that he was the father of the future empress Theodora. He left behind him his widow and three small daughters. Comito, the eldest, was not yet seven years old, and Theodora hardly more than five. The youngest, Anastasia, must have been only a toddler and, since she fades out of the story, she may have died young. Sons generally followed their father's trade, and if Acacius had had an adult son, probably he would have taken over the job that his father left vacant. But he had no son. However his widow, who belonged to the Constantinople theatre crowd, was not without resource. She quickly found another husband, thus acquiring a man to assume Acacius' post and support her little family into the bargain. Or so she hoped. But her scheme failed.

The job of bear-keeper must have been a coveted one, for in a pre-industrial city like Constantinople, demand for steady employment fell far short of supply. Constantinople's main economic activity was the business of governing and there was no industrial base to absorb surplus labour. Tradesmen belonged to guilds where a son followed his father's occupation, and outsiders could not break in without an *entrée*. A post in the imperial bureaucracy was a road to wealth for men with the proper education, but for the untrained worker there was only occasional employment. Life for the unskilled masses – at least if they were young and male with only strong muscles to offer for hire – consisted of temporary jobs, punctuated by street fighting, church services and the chariot races in the Hippodrome. A bear-keeper had steady employment; perhaps he even had a slave or two at his command, which allowed him a morsel of self-importance. More than one man coveted the vacancy created by Acacius' death.

It was the lead pantomime dancer of the Green faction who had the right to make the choice. Factions were business organisations and the lead dancers also served as administrative officers who oversaw staffing and discipline. It appears that their responsibilities even extended to crowd control in the Hippodrome, for three times in Anastasius' reign, when the demes[13] were unruly, the emperor exiled the lead dancers of both factions.[14] Byzantine bureaucrats, as a matter of course, supplemented their salaries with bribes, and the lead dancer of the Greens was no better or worse than any other official with a crumb of power. Bribery greased the wheels of Byzantine officialdom. Asterios, the lead dancer of the Green faction, took a substantial inducement from another candidate and rejected the new husband of Acacius' widow.

The rejection had one unintended consequence: it ensured that history would remember Asterios' name; but, at the time, his decision spelled utter disaster for this little family. Theodora and her two sisters were left with a stepfather, but no income. They were destitute. Their mother played her final card. When the next show took place in the Hippodrome, she dressed her little daughters as suppliants, with wreaths on their heads and garlands in their hands, and had them sit in the dust in front of the section reserved for the Green fans. They begged for compassion. But the Greens had none to give. No one cared to challenge Asterios' right to select the new Master of the Bears. The Green fans would not interfere. Stars of the theatre and the hippodrome had claques[15] to lead the applause for their performances, and mock their rivals, and Asterios' claque may have led the jeers for this first public performance of Theodora and her sisters. Theodora did not forget the rejection.

But the Blues were more sympathetic. As luck would have it they had a vacancy, for their Master of the Bears had just died and their faction needed a bear-keeper. They took pity on Theodora's little family, and gave her stepfather the job. We hear no more about Theodora's stepfather, nor about her mother either except that she put her daughters on the stage as soon as they were old enough. But the Blues had rescued the little family from penury and the family reciprocated by transferring its loyalty to them. Theodora remained a devoted Blue as long as she lived.

THERE ARE TWO OPPOSING TRADITIONS ABOUT THEODORA, ONE A DARK LEGEND AND THE OTHER, A SAINTLY ONE. In the dark legend, Theodora was the temptress who led Justinian astray and persuaded him to challenge the authority of the pope, the heir of St Peter. In the saintly legend, she was the 'believing queen', the defender of the persecuted Monophysites and co-founder of the Syrian Orthodox and Coptic churches, where she is still revered to this day. John of Ephesus, whose language was Syriac, helped to lay its foundations and it did not matter to him that she had been an actress who, like all actresses of the day, was a part-time prostitute, for he calls her at one point, 'Theodora from the brothel'. He must have been repeating an epithet from the streets of Constantinople, for the words 'from the brothel' (*ek tou pourneiou*) appear in Greek in the Syriac text of one of his *Lives of the Eastern Saints*,[16] which are short biographies of Monophysite believers who suffered persecution. John did not intend to vilify. In his status hierarchy a reformed actress ranked high and, if she was Monophysite, so much the better.

But the saintly legend developed a life of its own as the Monophysites separated from the Chalcedonians and formed their own hierarchy of clergy. Theodora was equipped with a pious background and a birthplace in the east in a centre of Monophysite faith. In the year 2000, the approximate fifteen hundredth anniversary of Theodora's birth, the patriarch of the see of

Mosaic from the Great Palace, Constantinople, showing a wild beast hunt.

Antioch issued an encyclical from his patriarchal house in Damascus, urging his followers to 'beatify the righteous Queen Theodora who preferred the disgrace of Christ, that is, the bearing of the Holy Cross, to all the glories of the world, that our names may be inscribed, as was hers, with the names of the Saints in the Church of the first born in Heaven'.[17] The patriarchal encyclical named the Syrian city of Mabbug, present-day Manbij, as her birthplace. Mabbug had always been a holy place; when the empire was pagan, it was Hierapolis, the 'sacred city', centre of the cult of the 'Syrian Goddess', Atargatis. The patriarch was following the tradition put forward by a twelfth-century patriarch of his see, Michael the Syrian,[18] who had pointed to Mabbug as her birthplace. But other places claimed her, too. A nameless monk[19] from the monastery of Qartmin in south-east Turkey, writing in the ninth century, made her birthplace Callinicum on the Euphrates River, on the edge of the Persian Empire, and reported that her father was an anti-Chalcedonian priest. The chronicler of Qartmin was the first to tell the tale of how Justinian and Theodora met: once upon a time, Justinian, while on a military mission in Syria, was passing through Callinicum, where he saw her and fell desperately in love. But her father refused consent to their marriage until Justinian swore he would never require her to accept the 'accursed creed', that the Council of Chalcedon adopted in 451. The story is unlikely. Justinian emerges into history only in 518, when his uncle Justin became emperor, and by that time he was already a member of the imperial guard. After 518, he never strayed far from Constantinople. Yet before we dismiss the chronicler of Qartmin, we must admit that we do not know what Justinian's travels may have been in his early years.[20] He could have visited Callinicum, or Mabbug for that matter, while he was still a relatively obscure young army recruit, which would have given some flesh to the legend.

There are other tales as well from late sources: one related that she was a poor girl from Paphlagonia in modern Turkey and that when Justinian met her she was living virtuously in a little house in Constantinople, spinning wool to eke out a living.[21] Still another tale claimed her for Cyprus.[22] But the tradition that Mabbug was her birthplace, which may have begun with Michael the Syrian, is the one that has found ecclesiastical sanction. In 1956 the bishop of Iraq, a distinguished scholar named Gregorius Bulus Behnam, wrote a play in Arabic about Theodora.[23] Her home was Mabbug and she was the daughter of a priest. Historical proof the legend may lack, but it has found theological favour.

The dark legend has its roots in the theological controversies of the sixth century but the chief authority for it now is the greatest historian of Justinian's reign, Procopius of Caesarea, a slippery source that is not easy to pin down. He mentions Theodora only eight times in his *History of the Wars of Justinian* but one of them is a great scene at the crisis point in the *Nika* riots of 532, when Justinian and his court were about to flee for their lives. She rallied the frightened men around her and told them that she, at least, would not run and live a life in exile: the imperial purple, she said, would make a good winding sheet. She appears as a dramatic figure: a courageous and ruthless woman with the virility of a warrior, and this episode has coloured our perception of her. But the drama has a sour aftertaste for Procopius, for whom the past was never a foreign country, borrows from the story of an uprising against an iniquitous tyrant in Sicily, Dionysius of Syracuse, who was on the point of fleeing when an advisor reminded him that tyranny made a good winding sheet.[24] Procopius substituted 'kingship' for 'tyranny' in the empress's speech, knowing that a reader with a good knowledge of the classics like his own, might pick up the ambiguity, but not hoi polloi. It was his private touch of denigration.

In his *Secret History* he throws all ambiguity aside, and pours out his bile on four chief targets, Justinian and Belisarius and their wives, Theodora and Antonina. The *Secret History* is an invective – an inverse panegyric, composed with some literary polish, and it pretends to be a supplement to the first seven

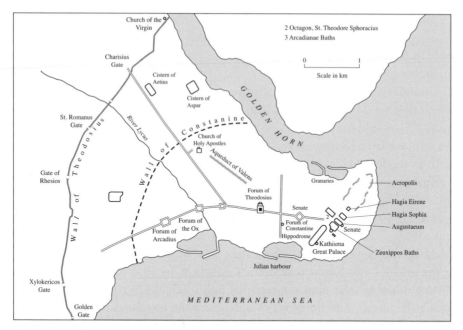

Constantinople in the Justinianic Period.

books of the *History*, published in 550–1. It would be possible to write a life of Theodora without using the *Secret History*, though there is no good reason to do so.[25] It is invaluable for the glimpses it gives of the private lives of its victims and the bureaucratic chicanery behind the scenes, and it allows us to see two shrewd and ruthless women who exercised political clout.

The dark legend of Theodora's past began as malicious gossip reflected in the *Secret History*, and it flourished. The author of the *Frankish Chronicle* in seventh-century France had heard it[26] and much later Cardinal Baronius, the historian of the Counter-Reformation, contributed mightily to it in his *Annales Ecclesiastici*.[27] He likened Theodora to all the Furies of Hell. She was the temptress who lured Justinian into sin; without her, the anti-Chalcedonian sectarians would have withered away, and the church would have been united.[28]

Baronius wrote before a copy of the *Secret History* was discovered in the Vatican Library; if he had known it, he would have liked its portrayal of Theodora, for it shows her as a meddler in theology, which should have been a masculine pursuit. There was nothing genuine to her beliefs. She connived with Justinian to stir up strife by appearing to oppose her husband's confession of faith, while all the time they worked as allies to wreak havoc upon the empire. They turned the imperial office into the antithesis of what it should have been.

Theodora was a destroyer. She attacked the foundations of the social order and fomented strife in the theological arena.[29] She surrounded the imperial office with the trappings of oriental despotism and became a symbol of the growing absolutism of the age.

However, we cannot convict the *Secret History* of fabrication. Its reportage may have been venomous but, where we can check it against independent evidence, it seems to be soundly based. The *Secret History* must have had readers, for otherwise it could not have survived, and some of the men who read it could have seen Theodora on stage. They would have recognized invented tales about her early career. So we can accept the story that Theodora was 'white trash', belonging to the beating heart of the entertainment industry in Constantinople where the popular name of the street leading to the theatre was 'Harlot's Row'.[30] She was reared there, and probably born there, too. Her story was a rags-to-riches tale: a survivor who rose from the dregs of society to become an empress, to help found a church and dethrone a pope.

The same *demi-monde* produced the woman who was to be her collaborator and – with some qualifications – her lifelong friend, Antonina, the wife of the great field marshal Belisarius, and his companion on his campaigns to reconquer North Africa and Italy for the Roman Empire. Antonina's mother was a dancing girl.[31] As for Theodora's mother, no tradition reports that she was an actress herself, but she put her children on the stage as soon as she could, and that speaks for itself. She was a tough survivor, determined to launch her daughters on careers which might bring them a comfortable life, and in any case it was the best she could do. By law, trades passed from father to son. The offspring of a parent who practised a heritable trade was required to follow the same one and the first Christian emperor, Constantine, extended the law to the theatre by enrolling stage and other performers among the hereditary professions. The daughter of an actress was expected to become an actress, too.[32]

What the fate of Theodora's mother was, we do not know. She was probably already dead before Theodora met Justinian. Very likely she died without the last rites of the church, with all her sins upon her soul, for the law forbade priests to administer the sacraments to an actress except when death was imminent, and even then only if a bishop approved and the appropriate public official was satisfied that this was a *bona fide* supplication. An actress who wanted to retire might feign mortal illness and, once she was absolved of her sins and had received the sacraments, she could never return to her indecent profession; thus she might abandon the stage without breaking the law.[33] Yet she would have to live out her remaining years in virtuous retirement. With due penance for her sins, she might attain a small degree of respectability.

When little Theodora and her sisters appeared as suppliants in the Hippodrome, kneeling in the dust before the Green section, her fellow alumna of the theatre, Antonina, was already old enough to know the ways of the world. It cannot have been later than the year 520 that she gave birth to an unloved son by her first husband and she also had one daughter, and possibly two, before she met Belisarius and captivated him. She, too, belonged to the entertainment business. Perhaps, like her mother,[34] she was one of the chorus girls who danced in theatre orchestras, the semi-circular dancing floor in front of the stage, where they danced to the music of a piper. Some orchestras could be flooded so that the girls might present water-play shows, clad in scanty bathing suits. Even in the old theatre of Dionysus in Athens, excavators in the nineteenth century found an intake pipe in the orchestra which connected to a water tank higher up on the south slope of the Acropolis. In the status hierarchy, chorus girls who danced in the orchestras ranked beneath the *mimae*, the female mime players who acted out slapstick burlesque on stage, performing skits based on mythology, or mocking characters from everyday life, not excluding priests and nuns, to the annoyance of the church. Even among theatre trash, chorus girls like Antonina's mother were bottom feeders. Everyone believed that actresses practised the sex trade – the laws assumed it as a matter of course – but there was a world of difference between the courtesan, whose patrons were men of standing and wealth, and a prostitute who might be a country girl sold by a needy father to a whoremonger. Dancers in theatre orchestras were only a step above these poor harlots who solicited customers on the streets of Constantinople and Antonina's mother was probably no exception.

Antonina's father and her grandfather were both charioteers who had driven teams in the hippodromes of Constantinople and Thessalonica. When Antonina's father competed at Thessalonica, its hippodrome was already falling into disrepair, for the citizens of Thessalonica had already begun to use it as a stone quarry, filching hewn blocks from it to build the city wall. But apparently chariot racing still went on there.[35] Charioteers followed a dangerous trade but with luck and skill they could have long careers, sometimes lasting 30 years or more. They might become celebrities: darlings of the urban masses with stage names which have been preserved both on honorific monuments and on curse tablets, which were thin sheets of lead with maledictions inscribed on them then folded, pierced with a nail and buried. But for all the popularity a chari-oteer might win, his social status was no better than an actor's.

We do not know what acclaim Antonina's father enjoyed nor, for that matter, if her father and mother were man and wife, joined in a marriage blessed by the church. We need not assume that they were for, like Theodora, Antonina came from a background that placed her beyond the pale. They were not like respectable women in Constantinople who spent their days spinning wool or weaving; and even empresses were expected to be expert needlewomen. Reputable women did not attend the spectacles in the Hippodrome or the theatres.[36] It was not done. When actresses appeared in public, perfumed and bare-headed, respectable women who met them on the streets or marketplaces, looked away.

Well-bred women in Constantinople would live in houses two stories high, though by the time Theodora was a young girl, taller houses were being built. On their upper floors were rows of windows and balconies jutting out over the streets below. Balconies became so popular that the emperor Zeno regulated them by law: they were to be at least 15 feet above the ground so as not to obstruct traffic and at least 10 feet should separate them from the house across the street. The sitting-rooms on the main floor were a male preserve and on the storey above were the quarters of the women, which they shared with the children and the serving maids. Respectable ladies did not mix freely with men. When they attended church services, they sat or stood in the women's section in the balcony or in a special area on the main floor.[37] The empress herself was no exception. In the great church of Hagia Sophia, she and her attendants occupied part of the gallery.

Life on the bottom rungs of society was a great deal less comfortable. The tenements of sixth-century Constantinople were fire traps, between five and nine stories tall, where the working poor eked out a living. If a tiny flat in a tenement was beyond their means, they lived on the streets, making hovels for themselves wherever there was space. Some of the worst slums bordered the sprawling palace complex which spread along the sea front from the Sea of Marmora to the Golden Horn, taking in the whole area east of the Hippodrome and south of the palace that the Ottoman sultans later occupied. This was a noisome, dangerous region where human life was cheap. Yet it was a section of the city which both Theodora and Antonina must have known well as children. The circuit wall of the Great Palace in the south-east corner of the city separated wealth and luxury from abject destitution. Theodora as a child must have looked at the splendid bronze gates at the main entrance to the palace and never guessed in her wildest dreams that she would ever pass through them.

What was it like to be a little girl in sixth-century Byzantium? The mosaics found in the remains of the imperial palace in Constantinople do show children, but they are mostly boys. How did Theodora learn to read and write? Only some 10 per cent of the populace were literate, even if we count as literate those who could only write their names. But Theodora could read, if the letters were large enough, for she was short-sighted. Did she ever learn to speak Latin, Justinian's native tongue? What of Syriac? She could carry on conversations with Syriac-speaking Monophysites after she became empress. Did they speak Greek to each other, or was there a translator present? Were her mother and her stepfather Chalcedonians or Monophysites, or were they Christians at all? The sources provide no answers.

ALMOST TWO CENTURIES HAD PASSED SINCE THE FIRST CHRISTIAN EMPEROR, CONSTANTINE, founded Constantinople in 324, after defeating his rival Licinius and reuniting the Roman Empire.[38] The city's history had begun almost a thousand years earlier as the Greek colony of Byzantium but it was still a modest city when Constantine, attracted by its strategic site on the threshold of Asia, chose it as his new capital. On the landward side he built a new defensive wall, enclosing more space to give his 'New Rome' room to expand, but the urban area soon outgrew it and, under Theodosius II, the huge Theodosian Walls were constructed further west to protect the landward approach. The forum of the pre-Constantinian city became the central square of Constantinople, the *Augustaeum*, and on its northern side was the great basilica of Hagia Sophia, built by Theodosius II, which would be reduced to ashes in the *Nika* riots of 532. The same fate befell the monumental entrance to the imperial palace, known as the 'Brazen House', across the square. Further west were the Baths of Leucippus, built by the emperor Severus but embellished by Constantine with statues purloined from across the empire. Running northwest from the *Augustaeum* was the 'Middle Street' (*Mese*), the great main thoroughfare of the city: the *Divanyolu*, its successor in modern Istanbul, is still the main street of the city. It was a bustling thoroughfare, lined at street level with colonnades and shops that were full of exotic sights and smells and seething with the cut and thrust of commerce. Nearest the imperial palace were the stalls of the perfumers and spice merchants, for the fragrance of their wares went well with the sacred presence of the emperors, and further along were the silversmiths and money-changers. The road continued past the *Praetorium*, the residence of the urban prefect or city governor, which had the city gaol in its basement, and it emerged into the Oval Forum, or the Forum of Constantine, where the fur-traders bought and sold furs.

Marking the centre of the Oval Forum was a great column of porphyry, the hard, reddish-purple granite quarried in Egypt that was reserved for imperial use. Rising over a hundred feet high, it supported an effigy of the city's founder, Constantine – which was a recycled statue of Apollo, with the emperor's head substituted for the pagan god's. The monument from the pagan past had been recycled for a new Christian age. In present-day Istanbul the stump of the pillar is still to be seen, blackened by fire and reinforced with iron bands: all that remains of a monument which once dominated what the people of Constantinople called *ho phoros*: 'the Forum'. The Forum *par excellence.*

Beyond the Oval Forum, the *Mese* continued westwards, past the slave market and a row of bakeries, through three more forums, the largest of which was the Forum of Theodosius (modern *Beyazit*), which was meant to rival the great Forum of Trajan in Rome. It was Constantinople's swine market. Nearby was the Capitolium, where the emperor Theodosius II founded the University of Constantinople in 425, with professors of Greek and Latin grammar, rhetoric, philosophy and law. The road forked at Theodosius' Forum, with one branch heading north-west past Constantine's church of the Holy Apostles, with the imperial mausoleum beside it, and then on to the city gate which opened on to the road to Adrianople. The other, southern fork continued to the Golden Gate, the monumental entrance into the city from the west. It gave on to the great Roman *Via Egnatia*, that crossed the Balkan peninsula, past Thessaloniki to Durazzo, ancient Dyrrachium on the coast of the Adriatic Sea. From there a short voyage took the traveller to Brundisium on the heel of Italy.

By the time Theodora was born, Constantine's foundation had recycled much of its pagan past, and grown into a very Christian city. This was a society permeated by religion, where the sacraments of the Christian church imprinted a person's life span from birth to death: baptism, confirmation, confession, the Eucharist, marriage and holy unction. They marked the milestones of life. Services were held in the city's churches every day. At sunrise, thanks were given for the new dawn. At the third hour there was the celebration of the descent of the Holy Spirit at Pentecost, and at the sixth hour Christ's Crucifixion was commemorated. At the ninth hour there was the celebration of His Death. The Eucharist was held every Sunday, and it had its own pageantry. The liturgy began with the 'Little Entrance', a procession of deacons and priests bearing the Gospel, symbolizing the Incarnation of Christ; then, during Holy Communion, there was a second procession, when a deacon bearing a paten with the Eucharistic bread and a priest carrying a chalice of wine processed from the sacristy into the nave and then to the altar.[39] The ritual was imbued with the symbolism of the birth and death of Christ.

These were merely the regular services: there were the great festivals marking the chief events in Christ's life as well. The Annunciation fell on 25 March; then

the Nativity on 25 December, the Circumcision on 1 January and Epiphany on
6 January, which was also the day of the Blessing of the Waters. During the 40
days of Lent services were held to honour the dead and celebrate the triumph
of the Christian faith. Lent climaxed with Holy Week when there were special
services every day, starting with Palm Sunday and ending with Good Friday
and, finally, Easter Sunday, which was the greatest festival of the church. Then
followed the feasts of the Ascension, Pentecost and Transfiguration.

These were merely festivals that celebrated the episodes of Christ's life on
earth. The Virgin Mary, whose cult had burgeoned in the fifth century, had
her own cycle of festivals too and the faithful hailed her as the *Theotokos*, the
'Mother of God'. The most venerated relics in Constantinople were the Virgin's
girdle and her veil. Then, in addition, there were the festivals of the apostles, the
saints and the martyrs whose lives earned commemoration. Christian worship
left little space for secularism in this society. To be non-Christian was to be an
outsider.

The economic consequences of all this business of Divine Worship was
immense. The church was an economic powerhouse. It absorbed a greater
share of the Gross National Product than any other single activity, including
the constant wars that the empire waged. In Constantinople, in 535, Justinian
fixed the staff of the great church of Hagia Sophia to 60 priests, 100 deacons, 40
deaconesses, 110 readers, 25 singers and 100 door-keepers, not to mention the
grave-diggers, and that represented a reduction from its previous size.[40] Hagia
Sophia's clergy served only four churches in Constantinople, and the city was
full of churches that had to be staffed. Bishops were well-paid. Their stipends
compared well with those of senior officials in the imperial bureaucracy. But
it was not only generous stipends that made ordination attractive. There was
also exemption from military service and, if the ordinand belonged to the
curial class, freedom from the duties that *curiales* (town councillors) had to
perform.[41]

Yet there were still pagan survivals, for the ancient gods were not forgotten.
The wine festival of Dionysus called the *Brumalia* was still celebrated from
24 November to the winter solstice, and even the imperial court took part.
In Antioch, there was a month-long May festival called the *Maiouma*, which
featured bathing in the nude. Sacrifices had long since been forbidden but it
seems that, at the *Brumalia*, a goat was sacrificed nonetheless.[42] In Athens, the
Neoplatonic School was still an intellectual stronghold of pagan philosophy;
in fact, philosophy was Athens' main export, and after the Neoplatonic School
was closed down in 529, the city faded into unimportance. Paganism's death
was slow and lingering and Justinian renewed the laws against it to make sure

that they were enforced. Christianity was triumphant, but there were many who conformed to it while at the same time looking back at paganism with a mixture of nostalgia and superstition. Well-educated men who could read the Greek classics and took them as their literary models must have recalled the past with equivocal feelings, for there was no Christian God in Homer or Thucydides. Many of them appear to have been cultural dual citizens, owing allegiance to contemporary Christianity, but at the same time maintaining a secret loyalty to the ancient traditions.

Yet the Christian religion could hardly fail to penetrate all sectors of society, even the world of the theatre, however much the church might treat it as a pariah. Men discussed the finer points of theology in the marketplace, for without theological correctness there could be no salvation. Suspicious changes in church liturgy could provoke riots. In 512, the emperor Anastasius tampered with the *Trisagion*: 'Holy God, holy and mighty, holy and immortal'. Suddenly, one Sunday, the congregation at the service in Hagia Sophia heard the coda, 'who was crucified for us', added to it: they were appalled. 'Who was crucified for us' was used in the eastern churches that opposed the Chalcedonian Creed! It implied that it was Jesus, the very God rather than Jesus the human being who was crucified, and no supporter of the Chalcedonian Creed could accept that![43] The Sleepless Monks, self-appointed guardians of Chalcedonian orthodoxy, who took shifts endlessly praising God in their monastery on the east shore of the Bosporus, caught a whiff of heresy and set off like bloodhounds in pursuit. They had a branch plant in the Stoudion monastery within Constantinople, where they kept vigilant watch to nip any deviation from Chalcedonian orthodoxy in the bud. Anastasius' addition to the *Trisagion* aroused a surge of holy paranoia in their breasts, and they whipped up revolt. Marinus, the praetorian prefect, was a Syrian and since Syrians were known to be Monophysite partisans, the mob rushed off to find him. Marinus[44] himself escaped, but his house was ransacked and burned and an unfortunate Syrian monk, who was found there, had his head removed from his shoulders and exhibited on a pole. Anastasius saved his throne, and probably his life, too, only by presenting himself bareheaded to the mob in the Hippodrome, and when the people saw the old man without his crown, bearing the Scriptures in his hands, they had a change of heart, and begged him to put on his crown again. Anastasius resumed control, and once it was safe for him to act he punished the ringleaders of the riot without mercy.

THE GREAT THEOLOGICAL BONE OF CONTENTION IN LATE ANTIQUITY began with the first chapter of the *Gospel According to St John*. 'In the beginning was the Word, and the Word was with God and the Word was God.' The 'Word' was the *Logos*, and *Logos* has nuances of meaning which no English translation can convey. It was the divine, yet indefinable element of godhead, which emperors reflected so long as they were true representatives of God, ruling the empire with Heaven as their model. True emperors were friends and comrades of the *Logos*.

Then, in the fourteenth verse, the author of the *Gospel* writes:

'And the Word was made flesh, and dwelt among us, and we beheld his glory, the glory as of the only begotten of the Father, full of grace and truth.'

The meaning seems clear. During the sojourn of Jesus on earth, he was the incarnation of the *Logos*, with the flesh and blood of a human being. But did that mean that He was a human being infused with the *Logos*? Or was He a divine being, no less than God himself? Or was He, somehow or other, both man and God, possessing both a divine and a human nature?

The question had already spawned a major heresy in Egypt by the time Constantinople was founded. In Alexandria, Arius, a mere presbyter, quarrelled with his archbishop, Alexander, who headed the see of St Mark. Arius maintained that Jesus Christ was lesser than God the Father, who had existed since time immemorial, whereas His son, Jesus, was created at birth and hence was not co-eternal with the Father. Alexander rebuked him but Arius was not easily awed by any archbishop; instead of withdrawing meekly, he took his doctrine directly to the masses. He spread his doctrine with popular songs which travellers sang on the roads and roustabouts in the dockyards, and he brought the fascination of theological controversy to the man on the street.

Alexander tried to nip this heresy in the bud, but Arius fled to Nicomedia in Bithynia, where he won the support of its bishop, Eusebius. The learned bishop of Caesarea in Palestine, also named Eusebius, fell under Arius's spell too, and the heresy soon attracted wide support. Constantine, having just reunited the empire, found Christendom rent by angry controversy. His acquaintance with the dark alleyways of theology was still slight; if he had been better informed he might have realized that Christians had always disagreed about theology, and it was not altogether wise to insert the imperial state into their long tradition of controversy. It would mean that the concept of Christian orthodoxy would become inextricably tangled with the idea of a united Roman Empire. But Constantine was a forthright soldier and he dealt with the Arian problem as a soldier would. He postponed an intended pilgrimage to Jerusalem, and instead summoned a church council to gather at Nicaea, modern Iznik in Turkey, to iron out the dispute.

What emerged from the council was the Nicene Creed, defining the relationship between God the Father and Christ the Son in words that Constantine himself suggested. It asserted that Christ was 'of joint substance with the Father' – and hence it followed that he was co-eternal with the Father. The Greek word translated as 'of joint substance' is *homoousios*. The word that the Arians wanted was *homoiousios*, meaning 'of similar substance', a more ambiguous adjective that allowed for a Son who was not co-eternal with the Father. Only one letter separated the Nicene and Arian definitions, and it was the smallest letter of the Greek alphabet, 'iota'. But this was an 'iota' that conveyed a world of difference. The Arians had lost the first round.

Arius himself came to a bad end. The Catholics put about a story that he was struck dead in a latrine as he evacuated his bowels. However, Arianism remained a force. There were still Arian worshippers in the eastern empire when Justinian came to the throne and their churches were wealthy. It was Arian missionaries who were the first to reach the barbarian tribes on the imperial frontiers and convert them, hence the Visigothic kingdom in Spain, the Ostrogoths in Italy and the Vandals in North Africa were all Arians. The Ostrogoths allowed the Italian Catholics freedom of worship and if Arianism resulted in a kind of apartheid between Goths and Italians that suited both of them well enough. But the Vandal kingdom was intolerant; Gaiseric and his successor Huneric inflicted harsh persecutions on the Catholics, which were described in lurid detail and bad Latin by the contemporary bishop Victor of Vita. However, one barbarian realm was not Arian: the Frankish kingdom in Roman Gaul. The Franks were still pagans when they appropriated Gaul, and when they converted to Christianity, they chose Catholicism.

Arian theology had ceased to roil the empire by the time Theodora was born. The emperor Theodosius the Great ended any chance that it might have had of winning the stamp of orthodoxy. He gathered an ecumenical council at Constantinople in 381 which reasserted the Nicene Creed's definition of Christ as 'of joint substance' with the Father. *Homoousios*, not *homoiousios*. So much for Arianism. It lived on in the barbarian kingdoms but not within the empire. The same council made a cautious statement about the Holy Spirit. It asserted that whereas the Son was *begotten* by the Father, the Holy Spirit *proceeds* from the Father, thus setting the stage for a long-lived controversy between the Greek Orthodox east and the Latin west, where the Catholics inferred that, since Father and Son were 'of joint substance', then the Holy Spirit should proceed from both of them, and in 1014, they emended the Latin liturgy to say so.

The Council of Constantinople ratified another canon, too, which raised hackles. It ruled that the bishop of Constantinople should have second rank after the Bishop of Rome because it was the New Rome. Rome refused to recognize the canon, and the other great patriarchates of the church were not amused. The wealthy see of Alexandria, founded by St Mark, had always claimed to be second to Rome, and the see of Antioch, like Rome, could claim St Peter as its founder.[45] Byzantium had been a mere suffragan bishopric before the emperor Constantine transformed the city into an imperial capital, and the patriarch of Constantinople was a comparative upstart, too close to the centre of imperial power to be independent of political influence. The Roman church was more fortunate: it developed a tradition of independence, for as long as Italy was under Ostrogothic rule, it was beyond the coercive power of any emperor in Constantinople. That happy situation would change with Justinian.

THE PATH FROM THE FIRST COUNCIL OF CONSTANTINOPLE IN 381 to the Council of Chalcedon in 451, that produced the Chalcedonian Creed defining orthodoxy, is full of acerbic saints, wily church politicians and court intrigues. Heresies spawned new heresies. Arianism begot Apollinarianism, which was created by Apollinaris, bishop of Laodicea in Asia Minor. It was a mirror image of Arianism: Arius stressed the human element in Christ; Apollinaris the divine element. The Council of Constantinople was even-handed: it condemned the doctrines of both Arius and Apollinaris. But Apollinarianism in turn provoked a rejoinder. Two churchmen from the see of Antioch pushed the concept of Christ's dual nature to its limits. We shall hear their names again, for they became the centre of a spat that would roil the theological arena in the mid-sixth century and pit Justinian against the pope. They were Diodore, bishop of Tarsus in the late fourth century and his later contemporary, Theodore, bishop of Mopsuestia, present-day Misis near Adana in Turkey. They founded what we may call the Antiochene School of theologians, one of whom was Ibas, bishop of Edessa, whom we shall meet again. The Antiochene School of theologians agreed that Christ was both God and man during his sojourn on earth, and they did not dispute the *homoousios* doctrine that the Council of Constantinople had made orthodox. But His divine nature, they claimed, never absorbed his human nature. On that point, Apollinaris had grievously erred. Christ, they argued, possessed two natures: one divine, the other human, and both remained intact and separate within Him. Jesus born of Mary, a mother of flesh and blood, was a man of flesh and blood like any other man.

In 428, the teachings of Diodore and Theodore migrated from Antioch to Constantinople, when Nestorius arrived there as archbishop. The emperor at the time was Theodosius II, a pious, pacific man, intellectually limited, and dominated by the women of his house for most of his reign. He was still a boy when he became emperor and at first it was his elder sister Pulcheria who controlled him. But, once he reached the age of 20, he wanted a wife and Pulcheria chose the beautiful Athenais, an Antiochene by birth but the daughter of a professor of philosophy in Athens, and a pagan.[46] Athenais embraced Christianity` and was fitted out with a new name, Eudocia, and she eased Pulcheria out of power. Both Theodosius and Eudocia wanted an effective preacher as archbishop of Constantinople and their choice fell on Nestorius, a monk from Antioch and a disciple of Diodore and Theodore, whose doctrine he brought with him.

On one score Nestorius did not disappoint: he was indeed a fiery preacher. But he soon made deadly enemies. Eudocia liked him, but the emperor's virgin sister, the *Augusta* Pulcheria, nursed a deadly hatred. She conceived of herself as the living image of Mary, the mother of Jesus, the *Theotokos* whose cult was growing in popularity at this time. She had wheedled a concession out of Nestorius' predecessor on the patriarchal throne, who had allowed her to take communion at Easter within the sanctuary of Hagia Sophia, where no women were admitted. But when the first Easter service where Nestorius presided rolled around, on 15 April 428, she had an unpleasant surprise. As she was about to enter the sanctuary, Nestorius stopped her. Why? demanded the *Augusta*, for had she not given birth to God? Nestorius would have none of it. Not God, he said, but Satan. Pulcheria, who lived and died a virgin and bore no offspring, either holy or satanic, retreated with what dignity she could muster.

She did not forget or forgive. The gynaecocracy that ran the imperial court split into warring factions that made the emperor Theodosius' life miserable. But Pulcheria was not the only person whom Nestorius infuriated. He also antagonized the pious rank and file of Constantinople by downgrading the cult of the *Theotokos*, the 'Mother of God', who had replaced the mother goddess Hera, queen of the Olympians, who soothed a woman's pains of childbirth and watched over newborn babes. Nestorius, taking his doctrine to its logical conclusion, preached that it was wrong to call the Virgin the Mother of God, for her son was not God, but a human being, and her proper title was *anthro-potokos*, 'mother of a man', not *Theotokos*. Nestorius would compromise enough to accept the epithet *Christotokos*, 'Mother of the Messiah', but he would countenance nothing that suggested that Jesus was anything other than a human being while he lived on earth. The people of Constantinople were affronted, for they loved the Virgin. Some remembered, perhaps, that the heretic Arius had also denied the Virgin the title *Theotokos*.

The patriarch of Alexandria, Cyril, smelled heresy, and at the same time, recognized a chance to humiliate the upstart patriarchate of Constantinople, which was a cause close to his heart. Cyril combined the dangerous talents of a brilliant theologian and an intolerant zealot. He hated pagans, Jews and heretics, more or less in that order of intensity, and his mob of *parabalani* – hospital orderlies who doubled as thugs – dominated the streets. Pagans were still prominent in the intellectual life of Alexandria and the most famous of them, whom Cyril particularly abominated, was Hypatia, a mathematician and philosopher with a wide circle of disciples. In 415, when Cyril's patriarchate was only in its third year, a mob of *parabalani* pulled her from her carriage, dragged her to the cathedral church and tortured her, and then carried off her mangled body to burn it on a pyre of brushwood.[47] It cannot be shown that Cyril was directly responsible for the murder but the savage bigotry animating the mob that slew Hypatia owed much to his instigation. He was not a man to shrink from a contest with Nestorius.

Cyril destroyed him at the First Council of Ephesus in 431. Nestorius went back to his monastery, but he was not allowed to remain there in peace. Four years later, he was arrested and banished to an oasis in the desert of Egypt, where he ended his life in misery. The same council also settled, once and for all, the Virgin's right to the title 'Mother of God', and in Rome, Pope Sixtus III marked the decision by building the basilica of Santa Maria Maggiore, which still stands. But Cyril had to make compromises, too. He came to Ephesus prepared to argue that Christ, as the Word of God made Flesh, was a single entity, but the formula he had to accept asserted that Jesus Christ was at the same time 'perfect God and perfect man … of one substance with the Father in his godhead, and of one substance with us in his manhood, so that there is a union of two natures …'. Thus the doctrine of Christ's double nature survived Nestorius' downfall; it had merely been modified. Nestorius had allowed only for contact between the two natures of Christ, whereas the formula of Ephesus called it union. The compromise did not please Egypt, where the desert was full of monks and solitaries who took the complete unity of God for granted. God, they believed, was One, never Two. Yet as long as Cyril lived, he kept to the settlement reached at Ephesus, but he left an ambiguous legacy, for both the orthodox and the Monophysites claimed him, the former because he accepted the double nature of Christ, and the latter because Cyril's writings went so far in their emphasis on the single nature of Christ that he seemed to be a Monophysite at heart.[48] Yet Cyril's compromise at Ephesus defined Christian orthodoxy in the eastern empire for three-quarters of a century.

Nestorianism did not die. Rather, it moved east. At Edessa, present-day Urfa in Turkey, the Edessene School of Theology taught Nestorian doctrine, though with some nuances. For instance, Ibas, bishop of Edessa and leader of the school until his death in 457, accepted the Virgin's right to the title *Theotokos* and attacked Nestorius for rejecting it. When Ibas died one of his pupils, Barsauma, left Edessa and founded an academy at Nisibis across the Persian frontier and, after 489, when the emperor Zeno expelled the Nestorian Edessene School from the Roman Empire, it followed Barsauma and joined his academy. At Nisibis the Antiochene School survived.

But within the boundaries of the Roman Empire, the Nestorians were anathematized, though the empress Theodora's policy of outreach extended even to them, for in 532, when she was pressing Justinian to try dialogue with the Monophysites instead of harassing them, she also received an emissary from the Persian church and explored the possibility of an *entente* of some sort.[49] Outside the Empire, however, Persian missionaries spread far and wide, founding bishoprics in Merv, Herat, Samarkand and further east, in China. In the west they were less successful; yet a missionary from the Persian Church made his way as far Cornwall in Britain and gave his name to St Ives.[50] The theology of the Antiochene School is still taught by the Assyrian Church of the East.

THE REPRESSED DISCONTENT ERUPTED AT A SECOND CHURCH COUNCIL THAT WAS ALSO HELD AT EPHESUS, IN AUGUST, 449. Cyril was by then dead, and his successor Dioscorus would have nothing to do with any doctrine that recognized two natures in Christ, one human and the other divine, even with the qualification that the two were united in Him. The empress Eudocia had by now fallen under a cloud, for she had been indiscreet with a court official and had left Constantinople for the Holy Land. Pulcheria, however, had not regained power; instead Theodosius had fallen under the influence of a shrewd court eunuch, Chrysaphius. Flavian, who was now the patriarch of Constantinople, was an upright man but neither eloquent nor politically supple. When he was elected in 446, Chrysaphius intimated to him that he expected a *douceur* in return for his support. Flavian sent him a piece of consecrated bread. Chrysaphius sent it back. He had no use for prelates who practised rigorous integrity, and Flavian would find him a dangerous enemy.

Chrysaphius' godfather was Eutyches, the head of the monastery of Job in Constantinople where, for some 30 years, he had directed the lives of more than three hundred monks. He took the teachings of the great Cyril of Alexandria to their logical limit. Cyril had accepted the proposition that, within Christ, a human and a divine nature were joined but, once the union had taken place, the result was a single nature. Thus, as he put it, there was 'one incarnate nature in the Word of God'. Eutyches went a step further and claimed that Christ's divine nature completely absorbed his human nature, and thus it was wrong to assert that Christ ever had two natures, one human and another divine. Nestorius had taken an extreme position, arguing that Christ had two natures that were completely separate, whereas Eutyches' position was at the opposite end of the spectrum. Eutychianism opened a theological dispute that would roil the fifth and sixth centuries and remained still without a resolution when the new religion of Islam arose to challenge Christianity in the east.

EUTYCHES THREW DOWN THE GAUNTLET AT A LOCAL SYNOD IN CONSTANTINOPLE IN NOVEMBER OF 448, WITH AN OPEN ATTACK ON THE TWO-NATURES CREDO. Lurking in the background were two powerful allies: his godson Chrysaphius, and Dioscorus, Cyril's successor as patriarch of Alexandria. Dioscorus had a double objective. One was to demolish the Two-Natures Credo and the second – equally important in his eyes – was to make it clear that Alexandria, not Constantinople, was rightfully the second see of Christendom. Flavian of Constantinople had already recognized that Eutyches was reviving the heretical doctrine of Apollinaris and condemned him for it, but Eutyches appealed and won on a technicality. Now Dioscorus joined the battle. He accused Flavian of deviating from the Nicene Creed and the malleable emperor, Theodosius II, summoned a second church council to Ephesus in the hot summer month of August 449 to consider the question. The delegation from Alexandria came prepared for a brawl.

The council was a rowdy, violent fracas, but it was a triumph for Dioscorus, with Chrysaphius manipulating behind the scenes. Eutyches' doctrine emerged victorious. The three legates that Pope Leo the Great sent from Rome raised objections but they spoke Latin, which most of the Greek clergy could not understand. Perhaps it was just as well, for they avoided a cudgelling. Flavian was condemned, and banished. He died on his way to exile, perhaps as a result of the manhandling he had received, for a legend grew up that his enemies murdered him. The battling mob of monks who supported Dioscorus turned the council into a riot, but this was only the opening volley in the battle. Dioscorus' success was short-lived.

In Rome, Pope Leo was dismayed and angry. But history has not called him 'Leo the Great' for nothing. He was no man to be trifled with. He had been invited to attend the Council of Ephesus but declined, and instead instructed his secretary to draft a definition of the faith and send it to Flavian. This was the famous *Tome* of Leo, a papal statement of correct belief that cut to the heart of the problem, and its imperial tone recalled the grandeur that was ancient Rome. Its subtext was that Rome, and the successors of St Peter, had the right to establish Christian doctrine, not ecumenical church councils. Leo asserted in forthright terms that, within Jesus Christ, there were two natures that were distinct and always remained so. He turned his back on the decision of the First Council of Ephesus of 431, and moved so close to Nestorian doctrine that Nestorius himself, who was living out the final months of his life in miserable exile in Egypt, read the *Tome* and found nothing in it with which he could disagree.

Flavian never presented Leo's *Tome* to the Second Council of Ephesus for he thought it would stoke the flames of controversy. But the pope's anger was not directed at Flavian; rather it was the iniquitous council itself that roused his fury. It was a den of thieves, he fumed, a '*latrocinium*'. He fiercely rejected its definition of orthodoxy. But then, suddenly, before a schism could develop, the political climate changed. The emperor set out on a hunt and fell off his horse; the accident proved fatal. Before the end of July 449 he was dead. His sister Pulcheria seized the levers of power but, since public opinion was not ready to accept a female ruler, she found a husband, though not a bed-partner. But she did go through a marriage ceremony with an old soldier, Marcian, a protégé of the Master of the Soldiers in Constantinople, Aspar, who controlled the German troops in the capital but, as an Arian heretic, was not eligible himself for the imperial office. Chrysaphius was put to death on Pulcheria's orders and Eutyches was banished to northern Syria. The cadaver of poor Flavian, who had been a casualty of the '*latrocinium*', was brought tenderly to Constantinople.

On 8 October 451 some 520 bishops gathered at the church of St Euphemia just outside Chalcedon, where a silver sarcophagus held the mortal remains of St Euphemia, that once each year exuded blood that was distributed to the faithful. The bishops had come to undo the damage of the '*latrocinium*'. Pulcheria and the new patriarch of Constantinople, Anatolius, kept tight control of the agenda. Anatolius had been one of Dioscorus' creatures in the past but, once he replaced Flavian as patriarch, he seized his first chance to turn on his old patron. Dioscorus was deserted by everyone except for six bishops from Egypt. It was his turn to go into exile, condemned not for his doctrines but for his conduct at the Council of Ephesus. Leo's *Tome* was approved, but the unfortunate Nestorius, who had just died, was once again condemned. So were Eutyches and Eutychianism. A new creed emerged which affirmed the Two Natures of Christ in almost legal terminology. It was a victory for Pope Leo and for Rome, and the price that Christendom would pay for it was high.

The battle lines were drawn. In Egypt in particular the reaction to the Creed of Chalcedon was absolute fury. Dioscorus' successor at Alexandria, Proterius accepted it, and consequently it was only with the support of the imperial army that he clung to the episcopal throne. When news of the emperor Marcian's death reached Egypt in 457, the Alexandrian mob celebrated by seizing Proterius and tearing him limb from limb. The decision of Chalcedon split the empire. Yet, for Pope Leo's successors on the throne of St Peter, Chalcedon represented not only the orthodox faith but also the supremacy of Rome, and they refused to budge. The prestige and authority of the popes were bound up in the Chalcedonian Creed. Heirs to the imperial traditions of Rome, and often scions of aristocratic families themselves, the bishops of the Latin west saw it as their duty to impose their creed on the unregenerate world.[51] In the east, the opposition to Chalcedon was more nuanced – there was never any anti-Chalcedonian creed which all anti-Chalcedonians accepted – but the passions of the masses were roused. The fabric of Christendom was in danger of unravelling.

TO UNDERSTAND THE DEPTHS OF POPULAR FEELING, we must set this theological fracas against the background of the monastic movement, which spread like wildfire through the eastern empire in Late Antiquity and then passed to the west.[52] It fed on an epidemic urge to abandon the norms of classical civilization. The pattern was set by St Anthony, the son of well-to-do peasants in Egypt, who sought a life of ascetic solitude in the desert about the year 269. By the time he died at the age of 105 he had a host of imitators, both men and women. This was a grassroots movement which cut across the class and language barriers of the multicultural empire, and it gave a voice to an underclass that had been voiceless before. St Anthony was a Coptic-speaking Egyptian; so, too, was the founder of the first cenobitic monastery, St Pachomius, who established communities of monks and nuns that lived a life in common, their daily rounds governed by a rule which assigned them a rota of tasks and ordained prayers at specific times. But it was the great ascetics who inspired the most awe and reverence.

Ascetics sought rewards in Heaven by mortifying the flesh with a zeal which seems outlandish to the twenty-first century, but this was a time when true believers regarded their bodies as prisons for their souls. By denying the needs of the flesh for food and sex, and even sleep, a devout Christian believed he could free his spirit from the bonds of this polluted earth and attain life everlasting. An ascetic who attained renown won enormous admiration, and the pilgrim trade that he attracted brought prosperity to his home town. In Syria, St Symeon the Stylite (ca. 389–459) carried the mortification of the flesh to a new height: he tried first to live in a dry cistern which he soon exchanged for a small cell, and then he moved to an enclosure on a mountainside where he chained one leg to a stone. When the local bishop protested that his self-abuse was far too extreme, he allowed the chain to be cut off. But then he hit upon a satisfactory hermitage where he could have both seclusion and celebrity. He perched on a pillar which grew higher and higher until it reached 16 metres, and there he dwelt, preaching to crowds of pilgrims as the spirit moved him. He had many imitators. The modern century may see the stylite saints as filthy, lice-ridden scarecrows, but to the masses of Late Antiquity they were charismatic witnesses to the faith, holy men who could heal the sick and defend the downtrodden. In the lifetime of Theodora and Justinian another St Symeon, known as St Symeon the Younger, perched on a column outside Antioch and, when the pandemic of bubonic plague smote the Antiochenes in 541, they eagerly sought his wisdom. To ascetics and saints such as these, the nature of Christ was an issue that wrenched their guts and seared their souls.

Not all monks were solitary ascetics. Large numbers lived in the towns and villages and built their monasteries there. The first cenobitic monastery in Constantinople, the Dalmatou, was founded by a Syrian monk in 382 and by the time of Justinian, the number of monasteries in the city had reached 70. In addition there was a population of devout men and women: day labourers, tradesmen, teachers, or spinsters who devoted a part of their wages to good works. These were all passionate partisans of their own brands of theology, and they added their muscle to the doctrinal disputes. Pagans were their favourite target and they also thought it a holy task to inflict discomfort on Jews and Samaritans. But what truly aroused their hearts and minds was heresy. Violence was the muscular expression of theological debate.

Under the emperor Zeno, Acacius, the patriarch of Constantinople, tried to bridge the gulf between the Chalcedonians and their opponents. He produced a neutral declaration of faith, which Zeno then issued as an official statement of doctrine. This was the *Henotikon*: the 'edict of unity', which attempted to dispose of the differences between the two camps by ignoring them, and banning further debate.[53] The *Henotikon* left the Creed of Chalcedon unmentioned, and the critical question of Christ's nature, whether single or dual, was glossed over. Zeno tried to move the issue from the public arena to the realm of private belief and accept the fact that, in a multicultural Christian empire, emperors could legislate only the broad principles of faith. The details had to be left to the individual Christian. The *Henotikon* signalled that, in matters of religious belief, it was prudent to place limits on state control.

The *Henotikon* gave no one complete satisfaction. Some die-hard Monophysites[54] objected that it did not explicitly condemn the Council of Chalcedon, but the moderates, the 'Hesitants', as they were called, were willing to live with it. So could the papal legates whom Pope Felix III sent to Constantinople to examine it. It complied with the formula that the patriarch of Alexandria, Cyril, had accepted at the First Council of Ephesus in 431 and Cyril's memory was generally respected. But the Sleepless Monks howled a protest, accusing the legates of accepting bribes, and Pope Felix convoked a synod of bishops in Rome that condemned the *Henotikon* and issued a ukase deposing Acacius from his patriarchal throne.

Acacius ignored the pope's decree, though a diehard Sleepless Monk slipped into the chancel of Hagia Sophia, where Acacius was celebrating mass, and pinned on his robe a papal letter listing his sins. The monk was seized and put to death for his pains, and the pope and the patriarch excommunicated each other. The Acacian Schism, as the split between the churches of Rome and Constantinople was called, endured until 518, when Justinian's uncle, Justin I, became emperor and put an end to it.

Thus Theodora grew up in a Christian milieu that was deeply divided. The emperor Anastasius who succeeded Zeno on the throne, was no friend of the Chalcedonian Creed. He appointed his protégé Severus as patriarch of Antioch, and the see which had once produced the Antiochene School that defended the doctrine of the Two Natures of Christ became a hotbed of anti-Chalcedonianism. History books call them Monophysites, though contemporaries did not use the label.[55] Yet it is a convenient umbrella under which to group the many varieties of anti-Chalcedonians, who poured their resentments into this controversy. This was a quarrel nourished by the ancient ethnic divisions of the Roman Empire. In Egypt, Monophysitism was defended by a horde of fanatic monks whose native tongue was Coptic, descended from the language of the pharaohs, and for them their Monophysite faith was partly a symbol of Egyptian self-definition. Into this quarrel they poured all the hurt and bitterness of a people whose ancient civilization had been submerged by the conquering Greeks ever since Alexander the Great's Macedonian army entered the Nile Valley. In Syria, the language of Monophysitism was Syriac, the Edessene dialect of Aramaic, and the Monophysites took over the Syrian villages where Hellenistic culture had always been a thin veneer, while in the cities, where the way of life was Greek, Chalcedonianism held its own.

In Rome, however, Chalcedonian doctrine and the primacy of the papacy were yoked together. To be anti-Chalcedonian was to be a heretic who should be destroyed. Rome had two objections: first, the *Henotikon* did not uphold the Chalcedonian Creed though, admittedly, it did not contradict it; and, second, it was an attempt by a secular ruler to define Christian belief. Pope Felix III's successor, Gelasius, wrote to the emperor Anastasius boldly asserting the entitlement of the church within the sphere of theology. Two powers governed the world, he claimed, the royal power of the emperors and the authority of the consecrated bishops of the church, and of these the second was the more weighty, for emperors were accountable at the Judgement Seat of God. Anastasius, an anti-Chalcedonian himself, tried to reach some sort of *modus vivendi* with Rome without abandoning the *Henotikon*. But Rome was adamant, and Anastasius would not spill blood on the streets to impose Roman orthodoxy. By the end of his reign, he had broken off relations with the pope.

Yet he could not coerce Rome, for the long arm of imperial power did not extend so far. Italy was occupied by the Ostrogoths and though Theoderic the Goth recognized the suzerainty of the emperor, he was not sorry to see a doctrinal dispute driving a wedge between Italy and Constantinople. He knew that his Italian subjects saw him as a barbarian king, a *rex* and not a true *imperator*. Their Gothic conquerors, who had appropriated one-third of the land of Italy for themselves,[56] spoke an incomprehensible language, worshipped in their own churches which preached the Arian heresy, and wore moustaches. They were uneasy and sometimes rapacious neighbours of the Italian Catholics. So much the better for Theoderic if the popes in Rome regarded the emperor as heretical.

How far did theological controversy penetrate the *demi-monde* of the theatre? It was beyond the pale; it even dared to burlesque priests and nuns on the stage. Christian piety would appear to have no place in the theatre. Pagan myths still supplied the plots for some of the most popular mimes produced on stage. Yet the Christian religion was pervasive, and actors and actresses must sometimes have feared the fires of Hell. Did Theodora's anti-Chalcedonian sympathies date back to her childhood? She may have been brought up in a household that had no great respect for the stiff-backed Chalcedonians, for in Constantinople Monophysite faith must have marked one as an outsider, and the *demi-monde* of the theatre was full of outsiders. If an actress fell ill and sought the help of a holy man or woman, would she turn to a Chalcedonian or a Monophysite?

We can only conjecture, for theology in Theodora's world could divide families, and the division between the two sides did not coincide with class boundaries.[57] At some point, Theodora became an outright partisan of anti-Chalcedonianism, and her background in the theatre may supply part of the reason why.

WHILE THE CHRISTIAN CHURCH WAS SQUABBLING OVER THE FINE POINTS OF THEOLOGY, CONVINCED THAT ETERNAL SALVATION WAS AT STAKE, the Roman Empire grew feebler. In 378 CE it suffered a calamitous defeat at Adrianople, uncomfortably close to Constantinople, where a horde of Visigoths destroyed a

Roman army and the emperor Valens along with it. It fell to Valens' successor, Theodosius I, to reconstitute the Roman military in the eastern empire as an effective force and secure the frontiers. When he died in 395, he divided the imperial rule between his two sons, with the elder, Arcadius governing the east and his younger brother, Honorius, ruling the west, with his capital at Milan. The division proved permanent. The city of Rome was defended by a great circuit wall that was begun by the emperor Aurelian (270–5) but the city no longer had military importance. The imperial palace on the Palatine Hill still had a staff of ornamental retainers,[58] but emperors rarely visited and the city itself had become a vast museum, packed with the monuments of a long and illustrious history. Rome was a magnificent symbol of past imperial greatness, but it no longer had an economic or strategic role to play.

As the sixth century dawned, the western empire had only a shadowy existence. The invaders had proved unstoppable. The Vandals possessed the grain fields in Roman Africa that once fed Rome and their fleet controlled the western Mediterranean. Not even Greece was safe from raids and an effort by the emperor Leo in 468 to counterattack ended in a disaster, which still haunted Constantinople 70 years later. In Italy, Theoderic had established his kingdom by 493. Life in Italy continued as before, with tenant farmers still bound to work the fields belonging to the great landowners, some of the greatest of whom were now Goths. Romans and Goths lived side by side with little intermingling. The Goths were Arians, the Italians Chalcedonians who still recognized the Roman emperor as their rightful ruler, even if he no longer lived in Italy but far away in Constantinople.

In the east, the empire survived. It was a near thing but it had turned the corner by the time that Anastasius became emperor in 491. On the eastern frontier Anastasius fought a war with Persia which lasted from 502 to 506 and when it ended with a truce, Rome had the upper hand.[59] Before the truce was signed, Anastasius started building the great fortress of Dara on the Euphrates River where the duke of Mesopotamia would be stationed, in command of the troops on the Persian frontier, and though the Persian king, Kavadh, resented it bitterly, he accepted it.[60] The frontier had peace for 20 years. Along the Danube River, Anastasius began constructing a string of forts which re-established Roman control of the Balkan frontier, and even though the Bulgars and Slavs continued to make raids across it year after year, some of them major invasions, none had resulted yet in any permanent settlement. The raiders took their loot and retreated, avoiding battle with the imperial forces if they could, and the peasants returned from the forts where they had taken refuge and carried on with their lives.

But geography shielded the wealthiest regions of the eastern empire from the barbarian inroads that ravaged the Balkans. Egypt in particular was profitable: one estimate suggests that three-fifths of all imperial revenues came from there.[61] There was a wary peace on the eastern frontier. The eastern empire was generally prosperous. The imperial treasury was full and the population was increasing. Society was remarkably mobile; in spite of laws that tried to bind men to hereditary occupations, a poor man might rise to power through the army, the church or the imperial bureaucracy. The emperor Zeno's family came from a village in Isauria in Asia Minor, which was barely touched by Roman culture. The emperor Justin I began his career as a peasant recruited into the army and his empress Euphemia was a former slave, whom Justin freed and made his wife.[62] Theodora, a mime actress from the theatre, at the very bottom of the social scale, married Justin's heir and, as she rose to the top rung of society, she brought her family and friends from the theatre with her. One of them was Antonina, and though she was not the only friend of Theodora to benefit from her rise to power, she is the one we know best.

The Scum of Society

THEATRES ATTRACTED CROWDS OF SPECTATORS IN CONSTANTINOPLE WHEN THE FUTURE EMPRESS THEODORA WAS A CHILD, but they were for men only. They were no place for respectable women. The theatre workforce was the scum of society, so much a pariah class that the law forbade the display of pictures of popular actors or charioteers in porticoes or other public areas where the portraits of the emperor and the imperial family might be exhibited. If posters advertising actors were discovered befouling such respectable locations, they were to be ripped down immediately. Pictures of such riffraff might be put on view on the gates of a circus, or below the raised stage of theatre, but they could not be posted on reputable buildings. Entertainers of all sorts, not excluding charioteers, were on the very bottom rung of the social ladder, lower even than the infirm or feeble-minded, who were considered worthless.[1]

The church regarded the theatre with immense disapprobation, all the more because it was a rival, a place where a man might, for a brief hour or two, escape the constraints of respectable society. Yet, the strictures of the law and the censure of the church notwithstanding, the man on the street loved the theatre and the chariot races. To keep the masses content the shows had to go on and the law tried to make sure they did. Persons registered as mime artists were expected to live out their lives in the theatre. There was even an imperial official with the title 'tribune of pleasures' (*tribunus voluptatum*)[2] who regulated the shows in the theatre as well as actors, actresses and prostitutes, for it was assumed that actresses practised the sex trade and, like other tradespeople, they paid an onerous value-added tax called the *chrysargyron* until the emperor Anastasius put an end to it. Theodora was only a youngster then, but she must have known women who had paid the tax and blessed the old emperor for abolishing it. Theodora was learning what a woman of her class had to do to succeed.

Some did succeed. A law of the emperor Constantine prevented actresses from marrying into the senatorial class, but they could become courtesans, and some won well-born admirers who made no secret of their passion for the women they loved. Take, for instance, a romance immortalized in a poem of Agathias, a poet as well as an historian who continued Procopius' *Wars*. 'I was a courtesan in Constantinople', it reads, 'and offered my love for purchase to all comers. I am Callirhoe, famous for my wit. Smitten with desire, Thomas has set up this portrait of me, thus putting on display all the ardour flaming in his heart …'[3] The social norms allowed 'Thomas' to commission an epigram to advertise his love, but marriage was out of the question. Yet a courtesan like Callirhoe was a world removed from the common whores who lived out dreary lives, plying their trade on the streets of Constantinople, never far from destitution. A courtesan was an *hetaira*, a 'companion' or 'paramour', whereas a prostitute was a *porné*, a common harlot, the property of a whoremonger who kept a stable of whores and lived off their earnings. They had little hope of escape. Theodora, as a teenager, must have known women who prowled the streets, offering their bodies for hire. She knew the sort of life they lived. They existed on the margins of society, where they were exploited and then cast off. The efforts of Justinian and Theodora to put an end to prostitution once they became emperor and empress reflect Theodora's experience.

As soon as Theodora and her sisters were old enough, their mother introduced them to the theatre. Comito, the eldest, was the first to go on stage. She can have been only in her early teens, but she was a pert beauty and quickly became a well-known *hetaira*. She went to banquets where men met for conversation, fun and sometimes business. Probably she sang and danced and perhaps played a musical instrument like the cithara, the ancestor of the guitar. Theodora went along as Comito's attendant, dressed as a slave girl, carrying a stool on her shoulders for Comito to use as a prop when she needed it as part of her act on stage. It was Theodora's first dramatic rôle.

She soon got her chance in the theatre, starting first in supporting roles. She could play neither the flute nor the harp, and she was at best a third-rate dancer, but she had a flair for comedy. Modesty never restrained her. Without hesitation, she would strip herself almost naked before a theatre audience, leaving a mere wisp of cloth to cover her groin, and that only because the law required a minimum of decency. Mime actresses usually never appeared completely naked on stage,[4] and Theodora kept within the legal minimum. Good striptease artists tease as much as they strip, and Theodora, it seems, knew her trade well. Her favourite vehicle was the pantomime of 'Leda and the Swan', which told how Zeus, disguised as a swan, raped Leda, the mother of Helen of Troy, as she was bathing in a stream. Theodora interpreted the myth with minimal choreography. Removing her clothes with appropriate gestures, she sprawled on her back on stage and mimed a bath in a shallow pool. Slave attendants sprinkled her groin with barley. Enter a gaggle of geese which picked the barley off her body and ate it. The rape scene was left to the imagination but Theodora went as far as convention allowed. A purist might object that the myth mentioned a swan, not a gaggle of geese, but geese were more reliable on stage, for if one failed to perform as it should, another would. Once the act was over, Theodora got to her feet and acknowledged the applause of the crowd with apparent delight. She seemed proud of her performance. Her business was to pleasure her audience, and she knew how.

Her notoriety went beyond the theatre. She was easily recognized on the streets and in the marketplace respectable people shrank from her. The theatre belonged to the realm of the devil, for there was something demonic about the spell it cast over its all-male audience. Good Christians feared it, and perhaps the fear was reciprocated among the theatre *demi-monde*, for the church held the keys to salvation. Given Theodora's later devotion to theology, we may suspect that she looked forward with anxious hope to finding an escape from her profession.

We can borrow some details of an actress's life from the story of St Pelagia the Harlot, an imaginary saint saved from a life of infamy by the good, but equally legendary, bishop Nonnos. Pelagia, the story goes, was the lead dancer in the theatre at Antioch. As she rode her donkey through the streets, perfumed and bejewelled, her head uncovered, and followed by a throng of boys and girls, she passed by Nonnos and his disciples. The good bishop's disciples averted their eyes, but Nonnos watched her and prayed for her. His prayers were heard. They turned Pelagia away from her wicked existence and toward a holy life. She gave away her wealth, went to Jerusalem and eventually died there in a lonely cell on the Mount of Olives, disguised as a eunuch hermit named Pelagius. The story underlined the truth that rescuing an actress from her sinful life was a peculiarly holy deed.[5]

Theodora was no *prima ballerina assoluta* like Pelagia, but she and her sister Comito must have been well known in the small world of the Constantinople theatre. Decent Christian women averted their eyes when they spotted her in the marketplace, and men stared. Perhaps the adoptive son of the Count of the Excubitors, the future emperor Justinian, was one of those who stared and, for all we know, he may have worshipped her from afar, but he was only a *candidatus* at the time, one of the emperor's 40 elite bodyguards, conspicuous in their white uniforms. A liaison with an unsuitable consort, who may already have been known for Monophysite sympathies, would have damaged his chances of advancement.

The harsh disapproval of reputable society must have hurt. It forced the *demi-monde* of the entertainment industry into a quasi-ghetto. Theodora must sometimes have raged at the confines of her life, where she could win the applause in the theatre, but never respect. She was quick to lose her temper, Procopius claims, and sometimes burst out wrathfully against her fellow actresses.[6] Antonina was a close friend but Theodora, once she became empress, would upbraid her bitterly for her sexual adventures and Antonina feared her.[7] Yet she did not abandon her old friends in the theatre once her own fortunes rose. Her fellow actresses might arouse her anger, but she never turned her back on them. Among Justinian's laws there is a group that improved the status of women, actresses included,[8] and probably Theodora inspired them.

Pregnancy was an occupational hazard for women who sold their bodies. Abortions were frequent and Byzantine pharmacology knew a number of abortifacients. In the fourth century Oribasios, the emperor Julian's personal doctor, collected a recipe book of potions that made pregnant women abort, many of which he in turn had borrowed from the great physician Soranus of Ephesus, who practised in Rome under the emperors Trajan and Hadrian. But advanced pregnancy could never be safely terminated and Theodora gave birth to a bastard daughter when she cannot have been much more than 15 years old.[9] We do not know the daughter's name, and we have no hint of who her father was, but he was not Justinian,[10] for he never acknowledged the girl as his and she was conceived before he and Theodora began to live together. She was the fruit of an affair that took place while Theodora was a young soubrette on the stage, perhaps no more than 14 or 15 years old, for Theodora had a grandson of marriageable age when she died in 548.

She may have had a bastard son, too. Procopius relates a tale that while Theodora was on stage, she conceived a child, and having tried every abortifacient she knew without success, willy-nilly she gave birth to an unwanted boy. The father, seeing that Theodora's post-partum depression was so severe that he feared she might kill the child, took him up in his arms, thereby acknowledging him as his son, and named him John. When he left Constantinople, he took the boy with him.

The story goes on to relate that the boy's father brought him up in Arabia and only years later, when he was on his deathbed, did he reveal to his son who his mother was. Young John did not set out to find the empress right away, but when he came to Constantinople some time after his father's death, he was indiscreet enough to let out the secret of his mother's identity. The gossip reached the palace, where Theodora learned of it. She ordered the youth brought to her and after seeing him, handed him over to one of her domestics and he was never seen again. Procopius thought that she ordered him killed, for she feared Justinian's wrath if he learned about the boy.

The report seems implausible. Why should Justinian resent Theodora's son when he accepted a bastard daughter? The tale sounds like malicious gossip, intended to illustrate not merely the immorality of Theodora's youth but also her ruthlessness once she became empress. Yet, it is possible that an impostor did turn up, whose name was John, who spread a rumour about his illustrious birth to bolster his self-importance, and found that there were unforeseen consequences. If that was the case, and if Theodora actually did confront a 'son', whether he was an imposter or not, the encounter must have left a sour taste in her mouth. Once Theodora was Justinian's wife, she wanted badly to have a son, but the abortions she had undergone in her early life had exacted a price. The marriage of Justinian and Theodora remained childless.

At last Theodora found a patron who took her from the theatre. Hecebolus of Tyre, presumably a Phoenician, whose sole claim to fame is that Theodora was briefly his concubine, had purchased the governorship of Cyrenaica, known as the 'Pentapolis' or 'Five Cities' because within it were five Greek foundations: Berenice, Arsinoe, Ptolemaïs, Apollonia and Cyrene. The emperor Hadrian had added a sixth but the old name, Pentapolis, persisted. The law[11] forbade a man such as Hecebolus to abduct a woman from the theatre and keep her in his own house, but it was an old law and probably not enforced. Hecebolus may have been no better or worse than most provincial governors. They bought their appointments, borrowing money to pay for them, and they expected to make a profit large enough to pay off their debts and return home well-to-do men. A hundred years before Justinian, the metropolitan bishop of Ptolemaïs, Synesius, wrote with delicate irony to a lackadaisical correspondent in Constantinople, chiding him that he had no excuse for failing to write more often, for the postal service was excellent: letters could always be entrusted for delivery to newly appointed governors departing for Cyrenaica and their departures were frequent, for the turnover of governors was constant. New appointees were easy to recognize by the swarms of creditors crowding around them, each demanding a share of the wealth that the governors would fleece from the unfortunate provincials.

A governor's profit came largely from administering justice, for while their verdicts in the law courts were in theory not for sale, money always greased the cogwheels of equity. It is significant that years later, when Justinian promulgated a law designed to curb provincial maladministration; he acknowledged that he had consulted Theodora, 'our most pious consort given us by God'.[12] Only once, as far as we know, did she have direct experience of provincial government and that was during her brief sojourn in Cyrenaica. Theodora's advice was to ban the sale of governorships, which Justinian did – and then, according to the baleful evidence of Procopius' *Secret History*,[13] he disregarded his own ban and sold offices to entrepreneurs who bought them with money borrowed at staggering rates of interest.

In the century that followed Synesius, the metropolis of the province had moved from Ptolemaïs to Sozousa, formerly Apollonia, named after the pagan god Apollo. The name change reflected the Christian present. Theodora moved into the governor's palace there as Hecebolus' concubine, but not for long. They quarrelled. We can only guess why, but by this time, Theodora may already have been a mother and if she had brought her baby with her Hecebolus might have found it a nuisance that should be exposed to die, as unwanted girls often were.[14] At any rate, Hecebolus discarded her and she was left to make the journey home on her own. Sozousa had no place for her.

She travelled to Alexandria, probably on board a coastal trading vessel. There something happened to her which we do not entirely comprehend. Her spiritual life was awakened. Theodora still belonged to the dregs of society, all the more so once she was now Hecebolus' discarded concubine. Yet everyone's life in the sixth century was touched by religion in some way or other. Perhaps Theodora sought help from the church and found the Monophysite clergy in Alexandria more approachable than the Chalcedonians in Constantinople. There must have been plenty of opportunity for her to meet and talk to Monophysite refugees who had been driven from their churches and convents by persecution and took shelter in Alexandria. Yet Theodora the comedienne of Constantinople was no St Pelagia, the star dancer of Antioch. She never felt any desire to abandon the world. The ascetic life had no appeal for her. Yet her spiritual awakening in Alexandria made a deep and lasting impression. To understand why, we should look at what was taking place in the see of St Mark where the patriarch of Alexandria, Timothy III, presided during Theodora' brief sojourn there.

ON THE NIGHT OF 9 JULY, 518, THE OLD EMPEROR ANASTASIUS DIED. A great storm was raging over Constantinople and the palace was struck with lightning, frightening Anastasius to death, or so it was rumoured.[15] If so, it served the emperor right, said the Catholics who held to the Chalcedonian Creed, for Anastasius was no favourite of theirs. But whether or not God intervened to terminate Anastasius' life, his death provoked a crisis. There was no obvious heir. Nor was there any empress to take charge, as there was when Zeno died, and Zeno's widow, Ariadne, selected Anastasius. The senate and the people deferred to her and Ariadne ratified her choice by marrying Anastasius soon after she chose him as emperor. But by 518, Ariadne was dead and Anastasius was childless.

It fell to the senate, meeting in the palace with the patriarch of Constantinople, John II Cappadox, and the senior bureaucrats to select the next emperor and it was not used to making decisions on such important matters. An expectant crowd gathered in the Hippodrome and waited restively. Had there been more time and if the crowd had been more patient, the choice might have gone to Anastasius' nephew Hypatius,[16] a general with a thoroughly undistinguished military career during which no army under his command ever won a victory. Yet, his family connections were impeccable and they might have outweighed his mediocrity. But when his uncle died he seems to have been in Antioch, serving as 'Master of the Soldiers' in command of the troops in the East. The senators needed someone who was on the spot in Constantinople, for the noisy crowd waiting in the Hippodrome was becoming more and more impatient as the hours passed and, as the dickering and haggling dragged on, the senate grew nervous.

We can guess the struggle behind the scenes from the evidence of John of Ephesus and the chronicle of John Malalas, or John the Barrister. We know almost nothing about this author except that his chronicle reveals familiarity with the workings of the government in both Antioch and Constantinople.[17] It seems that the late emperor's chamberlain, the eunuch Amantius,[18] whom the Monophysites considered a friend, wanted the throne himself, but his lack of gonads was a disqualification that could not be rectified. So he put forward one of his staff, Count Theocritus, whom he intended to manipulate, and he entrusted Justin with a sum of money to buy the necessary votes. Justin was the Count of the Excubitors, the palace guard made up of effective soldiers, unlike the ornamental *scholarii*, who were once effective when they were founded by Constantine, but no longer. Justin was a rough old soldier, too old and uneducated to be ambitious, or so Amantius may have thought. He miscalculated. Justin went about the task of winning support for Theocritus and the army and the people took the money willingly but, as Malalas put it without irony, 'by the will of God' they chose Justin himself as emperor.

The 'will of God' received some direction from Justin and, probably too, from his nephew and adopted son, Justinian, who recognized a vacuum of power and was adroit enough to exploit it. Justin, Procopius[19] reported, 'shoved aside all the kinsmen of Anastasius, though they were numerous and very distinguished'. His accession was evidently a Chalcedonian *coup d'état*, and he began his reign with a political murder: he put the ambitious eunuch Amantius to death. The ostensible reason was that Amantius had quarrelled with the patriarch John Cappadox.[20]

Justin was 65 years old and barely literate – a stupid donkey too incompetent to do his subjects either harm or good, if we can believe Procopius' *Secret History*.[21] But he was a man with a mind of his own and deep religious convictions and if he was illiterate, so were most of his subjects. He came from a Latin-speaking region of the Balkans and he was loyal to the pope and a convinced Chalcedonian. So was his wife, which was not unimportant. Moreover, he had a very capable nephew, Justinian – to give him his full name: Flavius Petrus Sabbatius Justinianus. Though no one guessed it at the time, the senate's frightened decision to choose Justin as emperor would mark the end of an era.[22]

Justin's career was a remarkable example of social mobility. He was born in the village of Bederiana in the province of Dardania, near the capital of modern Bulgaria, Sofia. His family probably belonged to the Romanized Thraco-Illyrian people, who fled to the mountains for security in the sixth and seventh centuries, settling there, and reappearing in the eleventh century as the Vlachs. The province of Dardania had been in a danger zone ever since the Visigoths annihilated a Roman army at Adrianople in 378. From 440 on, the Huns had raided and pillaged it; in 447, Attila led his horde as far south as the Pass of Thermopylae in central Greece, laying waste the land along the way. Attila died in 453 and his horde fell apart, but that only cleared the way for the Ostrogoths to invade. The peasants in the Balkans lived only one step ahead of destitution. For Justin, there was no future on the family farm and so, not long after 465, he set out for Constantinople, accompanied by two other young men with names that sound Thracian, Dityvistus and Zimarchus. They walked all the way, taking with them only some toasted bread in their cloaks to eat along the road.

When the three reached Constantinople, they found that the emperor Leo (457–74) was recruiting a new imperial bodyguard, the Excubitors, intended to counterbalance the muscle of the German troops in the capital, and for that he needed a guard which knew how to fight. The three arrivals were healthy, strong young men and they were immediately enrolled. We hear no more of Dityvistus and Zimarchus. But Justin rose through the ranks until the emperor Anastasius appointed him Count of the Excubitors.

As his fortunes rose, he acquired a wife. He purchased a slave woman from a man who had used her as his concubine and then put her up for sale when he grew tired of her. Justin bought her, freed her and married her. The wedding must have taken place before Justin rose to senatorial rank, for otherwise the law would not have countenanced marriage between a senator and an ex-slave.[23]

She was called Lupicina, which was a common name among whores, and when she became empress she chose to be called Euphemia, after Saint Euphemia, who had been thrown to wild beasts in the arena during the great persecution unleashed by the emperor Diocletian in 303. But her marriage to Justin was childless.

Yet men without children could adopt and, as Justin rose through the ranks, he remembered the family that he had left behind him. He brought two of his nephews to Constantinople and saw to it that they got an education. One of them, Germanus, was to make an acceptable marriage and become a brilliant general, though he seems to have been an easy-going man with no great ambition. The other, Flavius Petrus Sabbatius, the child of Justin's sister Vigilantia, became Justin's son by adoption, and would become his successor as emperor, and Theodora's husband.

Vigilantia had married Sabbatius from the neighbouring village of Tauresium, now Cariçin Grad, which Justinian rebuilt once he became emperor, renaming it 'Justiniana Prima', and making its archbishop the primate of Illyricum.[24] It was a small place even after Justinian's reconstruction. According to Roman custom, an adopted son added his new father's name in adjectival form to his own; thus when Justin adopted Flavius Petrus Sabbatius, he assumed the name 'Justinianus', by which he would be known in history. He received a proper education – Justin saw to that – and he acquired the veneer of classical learning that marked him as an educated man. His mother tongue was Latin and he was proud of it, but Greek was now the lingua franca of the eastern empire. The great *Corpus* of Roman law which Justinian commissioned was written in Latin, which was still the language of law when Justinian became emperor, but after the publication of its second edition[25] Justinian broke with tradition and when he addressed edicts to his Greek-speaking subjects, he wrote in Greek. Only when they were addressed to Latin-speaking parts of his empire did he continue to use Latin.

The subtleties of theology were beyond old Justin's comprehension, but he came from a Latin-speaking enclave in the Balkans where the religion was Roman Catholic and his heart told him that the pope in Rome was the supreme arbiter of orthodoxy. The pope upheld the Chalcedonian Creed; so then would Justin. His was an uncomplicated faith, untroubled by the quiddities of theology. He was determined to end the tolerance that Anastasius had shown the anti-Chalcedonians and close the Acacian Schism that divided the bishoprics of Rome and Constantinople. Anastasius had tried to find some grounds for compromise, but the popes were intransigent and Pope Hormisdas, who occupied the papal throne when Anastasius died, was insulting into the bargain. Justin inherited a yawning chasm between pope and emperor.

Anastasius had belonged to an aristocratic family that agreed to disagree on religious dogma: some of its members were Chalcedonians but Anastasius himself favoured the Monophysites. In Antioch he had removed the patriarch Flavian from his see and replaced him with his protégé Severus. Severus was a moderate anti-Chalcedonian whose faith was based on the teachings of Cyril of Alexandria: like Cyril, he did not deny that Christ possessed both human and divine natures, but he held that after the incarnation, when the 'Word' became flesh, the two natures fused to form one – in Greek, a *mia physis* – and this one nature was divine.[26] The bald definition of Christ's two natures in the Chalcedonian Creed was more than Severus could swallow. 'Miaphysite', that is, Single-Nature Believer, is a convenient label for the Monophysitism of Severus, though it was not a contemporary one. However its use is defensible, for Severus used the term 'Diaphysite' (Two-Nature Believer) to label his Chalcedonian opponents.[27]

Severus' Miaphysite teachings found sympathetic listeners in Egypt. But in Palestine, and even within Severus' own patriarchate of Antioch, there were dissenters. A Palestinian monk named Nephalius argued for an interpretation of the Chalcedonian Creed which softened its hard edges and brought it closer to the teachings of the great Cyril of Alexandria. Two other Palestinians, John of Scythopolis and John the Grammarian, also tried to use Cyril to bridge the gap between Chalcedonian and Monophysite. Severus rejected them both, though to do so he had to impose his own interpretations upon Cyril's writings. Cyril's language, he argued, did not convey exactly the meaning that Cyril intended, whereas Severus knew what Cyril really meant. Or so he claimed.[28]

The Palestinian monasteries looked on Severus with alarm, and rightly so, for he was hardening the theological battle line and opposing Rome's rigidity with rigidity of his own. The doughty abbot of the lauras in Palestine, Mar Saba, whose monastery still exists in modern Israel, was a Chalcedonian champion and would not accept Severus' theology without a fight. The struggle of Chalcedonian with Monophysite would eventually bring the West and the East into collision and split it in two. But not yet. Compromise still seemed possible.

But with Justin's accession, imperial policy veered sharply towards the Chalcedonians. Anastasius' cronies were eliminated quickly; the eunuch chamberlain Amantius who would have continued Anastasius' anti-Chalcedonian policy if his candidate had become emperor, was the first to go. There was no place now for a defender of the *Henotikon* like Amantius. Justin was determined to terminate the schism with Rome. It was a ham-fisted move with fearful consequences.

IF JUSTIN WAS TO END THE ACACIAN SCHISM, HE HAD TO TURN BACK THE CLOCK and nullify the *Henotikon*, the politically correct formula which the emperor Zeno hoped that both the Chalcedonians and the Monophysites could accept. The *Henotikon* had lasted for 36 years and it was a masterpiece of discretion. It evaded the controversial question of Christ's nature and ended with a blanket condemnation of all heresy, whether it was put forward at Chalcedon or any other church council. In the east, a large cohort of the faithful on both sides of the theological rift was prepared to live with it. But Rome was not. It broke off communion with Constantinople and excommunicated Acacius. If Justin was to heal the schism with Rome, the price would be ending the toleration of the anti-Chalcedonians.

Justin was ready. He was an old soldier used to issuing and receiving orders. The dark corridors of theology were beyond his comprehension. He could not know that once he tossed the *Henotikon* into the dustbin of history, his successors would search in vain to find a replacement, until the rise of Islam made the search no longer important. As a peasant boy on the hardscrabble farm where his family eked out a living, Justin had learned to think of the pope as the final authority on Christian dogma and he accepted the pope's terms like any good soldier receiving orders from the high command.

Justin invited Pope Hormisdas to Constantinople and his adopted son, Justinian, reinforced Justin's invitation with a personal letter; but Hormisdas declined. Instead he sent legates, who arrived in 519 to an impressive welcome. Three envoys from the emperor met the pope's legates at the tenth milestone outside Constantinople. One of them was Justinian and another was a stout champion of the Chalcedonian Creed, Vitalian, a commander of the federate troops on the Danube, who had led a rebellion against the Monophysite-sympathizer, Anastasius, and was still a renegade lurking in Dobruja at the mouth of the Danube River when Anastasius died.[29] Justin recalled him to Constantinople, made him a Master of the Soldiers and selected him as consul for the year 520. Vitalian was a man to watch, a potential rival for Justinian. The pope's legates, whom Justin's envoys welcomed, came with instructions to accept the surrender of the Eastern Church and nothing less. Pope Hormisdas was not ready to argue questions of faith with his inferior, John II Cappadox, the patriarch of Constantinople. John could either accept Rome's terms for ending the schism or remain excommunicate.

The terms were humiliating. Pope Hormisdas was an ungenerous conqueror.

He demanded that John anathematize all the patriarchs who preceded him back to Acacius who had formulated the *Henotikon*, all the bishops who had accepted their authority, and all the emperors as far back to Zeno. In the liturgy of the church, while the Eucharist was being celebrated, a deacon would read aloud the names of persons, living or dead, who deserved commemoration. Henceforth, all clergy who had accepted the *Henotikon* would have their names erased from the list, and be consigned to oblivion. The demand was extreme; it implicitly rejected the doctrines of the great patriarch of Alexandria, Cyril, which were still the touchstone of orthodox belief in the Eastern Empire, and John was understandably unhappy. He had become patriarch only the year before and his rawness must have added to his distress. But Justin was determined to make peace with Rome and his wife, the empress Euphemia, was as determined as he was.[30] The surrender was made, and the schism between pope and emperor was closed, if not healed.

Then Pope Hormisdas insisted that anti-Chalcedonians be eliminated. Justin should use whatever force was necessary. He was a new broom that should sweep clean. With Justin, ideology triumphed over politic tolerance, and a wave of persecution engulfed the holy men and women of the eastern provinces who opposed the Chalcedonian Creed. Monophysite clergy were ejected from their churches and monks turned out of their monasteries. The Monophysite laity was not harmed, but they were left without priests to administer the sacraments unless they accepted them from the hands of Chalcedonian clergy, which they would not do. Orders came to the Count of the Orient in Antioch to arrest the patriarch Severus and cut out his tongue. The command came from Vitalian, who hated Severus for personal reasons: Flavian, the patriarch of Antioch of suspect loyalty, whom Anastasius had turned out of office in 512 and replaced with Severus, was Vitalian's godfather. But Severus was warned in time and boarded a ship sailing to Egypt, where the patriarch of Alexandria offered refuge.

He was joined there by an old supporter, Julian of Halicarnassus, who had been Severus' ally in the past against the Chalcedonians, but in Egypt the two men soon quarrelled bitterly over an abstruse theological point: was Christ's human body subject to corruption? Severus believed that it was, but Julian claimed it was not, for if one pushed Monophysite doctrine to its extreme, which Julian did, then Christ's human nature was completely subsumed by his divinity and divine substance cannot decay.

At Mabbug, a little more than 100 miles east of Antioch, the bishop was less fortunate than Severus. Mabbug was a centre of Syriac culture and its bishop, Aksenaya, better known by his Greek name, Philoxenos, was a notable exponent of it. He was also the chief partisan of the anti-Chalcedonian resistance in Syria. He was arrested and died a horrible death, shut up in a room above the kitchen of an inn where he suffocated in the smoke, for chimneys were not yet invented. But anti-Chalcedonian belief lived on. Persecution only made it stronger among Syriac-speaking Christians.

Pope Hormisdas was remorseless. He urged Justin to tighten the screws of oppression and at first Justin was willing enough. In Severus' place as patriarch of Antioch he appointed an implacable cleric who was recommended by the pope and the cleric lived up to his reputation. He rooted out the Monophysite clergy ruthlessly. But within a year, Justin and his nephew Justinian were having second thoughts. Justinian began to try to find some compromise formula – a new *Henotikon* – which would satisfy the moderates of both camps. It was a quest he would continue throughout his life, with little real success.

As for the emperor Justin, he did not understand such things. He was no theologian but he knew the limits of military power. No matter what the pope ordered, he declined to press home the attack on the anti-Chalcedonian stronghold of Egypt, where the Alexandrian mob was a fearsome thing, and the soldiers on whom the imperial government relied to control it were Egyptian recruits. Justin's persecution spared Egypt, and Alexandria became a haven for refugee anti-Chalcedonian clergy.[31]

WHEN THEODORA REACHED ALEXANDRIA, THE FERMENT THERE WAS PALPABLE. Alexandria had always been unruly, and relations between the patriarch and the Augustal Prefect who headed the civil administration in Egypt were often uneasy. The city knew its importance to the empire. The grain grown in the Nile valley fed Constantinople, and the cargoes shipped from the port of Alexandria were essential for peace and order there, for if the populace went hungry, it rioted. Egypt was anti-Chalcedonian but support for anti-Chalcedonian doctrine was never unanimous. For instance, the great Pachomian monastery called the *Metanoia* (Penitence) at the Canopic mouth of the Nile was a Chalcedonian stronghold, as were the other monasteries elsewhere in Egypt that followed the rule of St Pachomius, the founder of coenobitic monasticism. The monks of the *Metanoia* were skilful seamen, crewing the river boats that carried grain down the Nile to Alexandria and even voyaging north across the Mediterranean to Constantinople. It must have been reassuring to the imperial government to have the grain shipments in the hands of such good Chalcedonians.

Did Theodora meet the patriarch of Alexandria, Timothy III, himself? There is a tradition, reported by a chronicler[32] living a century and a half later, that she looked on Timothy III as her spiritual father. Yet she could not have been baptized for she was still a theatre wench and it was only later, after she became empress, that she received the rite of baptism. However, she could have become a catechumen in the church, receiving instruction in Christian doctrine so that she might some day be admitted to baptism. Catechumens were excluded from the Eucharist. Early churches had an anteroom at the end of the nave where catechumens were admitted for the first part of the Eucharistic service but after the sermon, when the time came for the Eucharist mystery, the priest cried out three times: 'Ye catechumens depart! No catechumens!' Theodora may have been among the catechumens in the Alexandria cathedral who were asked to leave before the Holy Eucharist. It was as much as she could hope for.

Yet Alexandria left a lasting impression on her.[33] It provided the second formative influence in her life. The first was her adventure as a little girl, appealing to the Greens in the Hippodrome to hire her stepfather as bear-keeper and facing the terrible disappointment of refusal. That had left her with a lasting loyalty to the Blues, who had saved her little family from destitution. Then, in Alexandria she encountered a spiritual awakening. If she took instruction as a catechumen, it would be the Miaphysite doctrine of Severus that she was taught. So, at least, we would surmise. At any rate, if she were not anti-Chalcedonian before her visit to Egypt, her experience there left her one. It was hardly a politically correct step to take in the empire of Justin I and his ambitious nephew, Justinian.

FROM ALEXANDRIA THEODORA MADE HER WAY TO ANTIOCH. Probably she went by ship, though Procopius supposed that she made her way along the road up the Syrian coast, practising her ancient profession as she went. Procopius is a prurient witness, ready to put a malevolent interpretation on whatever Theodora did, but she must have supported herself somehow. Possibly she did visit cities like Gaza and Caesarea in Palestine and may have used her connections with the Blue faction to perform at their theatres. At any rate, when she reached Antioch, she made contact with a dancing girl named Macedonia. Like Antonina's mother, Macedonia was an *orchestris* – a dancer in the chorus line of the Antioch theatre, performing in the orchestra rather than on stage. She belonged to the Blue faction, and since Theodora was also a Blue they shared the same management. Theodora, it appears, had by this time returned to her acting career.

Macedonia provides us with a possible clue to one of the mysteries surrounding Theodora's life during this period.[34] How did she, a mime and a dancer with no great talent, meet Justinian, the adoptive son of the emperor who expected to inherit the throne? Justinian may have seen Theodora on stage earlier, in Anastasius' reign, and admired her, but they did not move in the same social circles. How did they meet? Macedonia may provide the missing link.

Like Theodora, Justinian was a partisan of the Blues. This was a period when violence on the streets was increasing, both in Constantinople and other cities of the empire. The root cause was a surfeit of unemployed youth who identified with either the Blue or the Green party in the Hippodrome, and divided themselves into rival gangs. Like all street gangs, they could be politicized, but the view which historians once held that the Blues were Chalcedonians and the Greens Monophysites has been abandoned.[35] Theodora could be both a Blue and a Monophysite. The Greens and Blues were divided by small differences, but they sufficed to envenom the political atmosphere. Blue and Green hoodlums made the streets dangerous after dark. The Blue party was the smaller of the two and may have had fewer extremists in its ranks, which may have been the reason why Justinian thought that he could secure its loyalty by supporting it, for at this point in his career, he was building up a cadre of allies. He considered himself Justin's heir, but his succession was by no means certain. Many members of the Chalcedonian elite must have thought that Vitalian, who held the consulship in 520, was a more likely candidate, for he was a hardened soldier, whereas Justinian had no military record worthy of notice. When ruffians attacked Vitalian on the streets in 520 and killed him, Justinian was suspected, since the murder removed a dangerous rival. The senators who chose Justin as emperor never intended him to start a dynasty. Anastasius' sudden death had caught them off-guard and, frightened by the clamour of the mob in the Hippodrome, they agreed to choose the old man as emperor, but they did not expect his reign to be long, for he was already 65. The Constantinople Establishment looked on this new imperial family sprung from Balkan peasant stock with distaste. Justin's election as emperor did not make Justinian his automatic successor, and he knew it.

Macedonia was more than a girl in the chorus line of the theatre. She was also one of Justinian's secret agents. She belonged to the long list of actress-spies in history: if she fingered someone as a potential threat, she informed Justinian and appropriate action was taken. The intelligence that she forwarded secretly to Justinian had already brought destruction on a number of notables in Antioch. Macedonia took an interest in Theodora, a Blue like herself; perhaps she already knew her by reputation. The world of the theatre was not large, and Theodora had won a modest degree of celebrity as a comedienne in Constantinople before her adventure with Hecebolus. It was Macedonia's business to observe and report.

One day, Theodora seemed dejected. Macedonia noticed and asked why.

Theodora described her misadventure with Hecebolus, and how he had discarded her. Macedonia must have heard similar stories before. Still, in her side-line as an intelligence agent, all information of this sort could be useful. But Theodora had a more immediate misfortune: she had been robbed. Macedonia comforted her, telling her that *Tyche* – Lady Luck – would smile on her in the future, and make her a rich woman. That sounds like an implied hint that Macedonia had an offer for her. Then Theodora recalled that only the previous night, she had dreamed that when she reached Constantinople she would share her bed with the Lord of the Demons and he would marry her and shower her with wealth. She need not worry about money. The dark lord would be Justinian, though Theodora did not yet know it. Only later would his identity be revealed. It is a curious story, fabricated long after Theodora met Justinian, when victims of Justinian's rule speculated, more than half-seriously, that Justinian was the Antichrist.[36]

What really happened must have been that Macedonia recruited Theodora into Justinian's secret service. She was the go-between who brought Justinian and Theodora into contact. Their encounter took place in Constantinople: that much we can infer from the prophecy that it was there she would meet the Prince of Evil. For Justinian, a bachelor approaching 40, it was love at first sight. He was probably a man of limited sexual experience and no doubt he found Theodora's aptitude entrancing. In a law[37] that he issued ten years before Theodora's death, he remarked, as if from personal experience, 'for we know that nothing is more vehement than the fury of love'. But if it was the 'fury of love' which sparked the life-long alliance between this oddly matched couple, it was mutual respect that made it last.

The Rise to Power

HOWEVER IT WAS THAT JUSTINIAN MET THEODORA AND FELL UNDER HER SPELL, by 522 at least the two of them were living together in the Palace of Hormisdas beside the Sea of Marmora, or the Propontis as the Greeks called it, close by the precincts of the sprawling Imperial Palace. So close, in fact, that once Justinian himself became emperor he joined the two with a private passageway. Theodora was not yet welcome in the palace, nor would she be as long as Justin's wife was alive, for the empress Euphemia disapproved of her; but Justin yielded to Justinian's urging and Theodora's charm was enough to grant her patrician status, an ancient distinction that the emperor Constantine had revived. Justinian had been given the status himself only in 523, and it advertised his liaison with Theodora when she was elevated to the same status so soon after him. Theodora might not yet be Justinian's wife but she received a wife's esteem, for ordinarily when a woman held the rank of patrician it was because her husband held it. We may wonder what old Euphemia thought about it all, but at least she need not have witnessed this heretic fugitive from the theatre receiving the distinction, for patrician status was conferred in a ceremony that the emperor attended but not the empress. Her absence made no difference to the distinction conferred on Theodora, which signalled that she was the confidante of Justinian, who in turn had Justin's ear, and she was rapidly becoming known as a woman of influence.

It was no secret that she did not support the Chalcedonian Creed and the Monophysite clergy, harassed as they were by Justin's police, quickly recognized her as a friend willing to lobby on their behalf even before she became empress. John of Ephesus records what may have been her first intervention when Mare, the abbot of John's monastery at Amida, and his monks were driven into the desert by the imperial police, and were starving, and he sent two of his followers to Constantinople to beg Theodora for help.[1] Theodora did not disappoint them. She won over Justinian and, at his urging, Justin granted leave to Mare and his little group of refugees to make their way to Egypt. When Mare died there, Theodora saw to it that his body was returned to Amida for burial.

Justin was prepared to tolerate Theodora's religious convictions but not so his empress. Lupicina had taken the respectable name of Euphemia when she became empress, and her choice was significant, for St Euphemia was the Chalcedonian Creed's patron saint. It was in her church, just outside the city of Chalcedon, that in the year 451, the famous council met which drew up the Chalcedonian Creed. Legend had it that the church fathers allowed the saint herself to choose the true definition of Christ's two natures. They opened her coffin and placed two scrolls within it, one bearing the Monophysite credo and the other the Catholic one. When they reopened the coffin they found the Monophysite scroll trampled beneath the saint's feet, while in her hands she clutched the Catholic statement of faith. It was adopted forthwith as the orthodox creed. The empress Euphemia was an uneducated woman but she believed that she knew what orthodoxy was and she was as staunch a defender of it as the saint whose name she adopted. Theodora was not only a former actress, but what was worse: a heretic! Euphemia could never countenance her marriage to her adopted son, Justinian.

Theodora must have known many snubs of this sort and no doubt they hurt. We would like to know what her private thoughts were but she kept them to herself. The elderly emperor would not override Euphemia's veto and though Euphemia doted on her adoptive son, Justinian, and could refuse him nothing, on this one point she would not yield. But she had not long to live. We do not know the exact date of her death but she had probably departed this life to meet her – presumably Chalcedonian – maker before the end of 523 and without her Justin was malleable. He modified the legal barrier standing in the way of marriage between an actress and a man of the senatorial class to allow Justinian and Theodora to marry and the wedding took place, perhaps in 525, the year when Justin gave his nephew the rank of 'Caesar', thereby designating him clearly as his heir.[2]

By then, Justinian and Theodora had been living together for five years or more in the Palace of Hormisdas and they did not have to wait much longer before they had the imperial office in their grasp. Justin still clung to power but his health was failing. An old wound that had never properly healed was sapping his strength and he reluctantly agreed to share his throne with Justinian. On 1 April 527 the coronation ceremony took place in the Triclinium of the Nineteen Couches, the great banqueting hall within the palace compound that could accommodate 228 guests, who ate lounging Roman style on 19 couches, 12 per couch. We can picture the scene: at the high table, the ailing emperor reclined with his high-ranking 'friends'; and on his right hand was Justinian. The other tables were assigned to guests according to rank and, while they watched with due respect, the ancient title of Augustus was conferred on Justinian and he became co-emperor.

Was Theodora present? Probably not: neither women nor children attended banquets such as this one, though Theodora may have had a banquet of her own in the Hormisdas Palace and it is possible that among her guests were old acquaintances from the theatre. But Theodora would have been present three days later, on Easter Sunday, when the patriarch performed the coronation ceremony in the basilica of Hagia Sophia and administered the oath of office.

It was a magnificent occasion. The day belonged to Justinian and Theodora, for old Justin was too ill to take part in ceremonies. Once the coronation was done, the new emperor and empress made their way in solemn procession, accompanied by the notables, ecclesiastical and secular, to the Hippodrome. Theodora was splendidly robed in garments of silk, every inch an empress. The palace guards, both the Scholarians and the Excubitors, lined the road. Trumpets sounded as Justinian and Theodora entered the imperial loge, which was a sumptuous stage-set for the theatre of power. The ever-triumphant vicegerent of God, his empress at his side, presented himself to the people of Constantinople, who crowded below them in the Hippodrome, hailing them with shouts of 'Send you victorious!' The late Robert Browning, who wrote one of the most attractive books on Justinian and Theodora, allowed his imagination full play as he conjured up the scene on that first day of April:

> What were the thoughts that passed through Theodora's mind as she stood, stiff and hieratic in the glittering brocades and jewels of a Roman empress, in that very circus where she had begun her strange career? Did she exchange a wink of complicity with her brooding and unsmiling spouse? Or with her sister Comito, soon to be a general's wife? We shall never know. But we may be sure that on this day she gave the finest performance of her life.[3]

Four months later to the day, on 1 August, old Justin, who had yielded power with little enthusiasm, died and his sarcophagus joined his wife's in the church of St Euphemia. The empire was now in the hands of Justinian and Theodora. The little girl who had once begged the Greens in the Hippodrome to save her family from destitution had become empress. She was determined to make her mark in history.

THEODORA POSSESSED POWER AT LAST, AND THE WEALTH THAT WENT ALONG WITH IT. She revelled in it. As a child she had known what it meant to be poor and helpless and now she relished the opulence and luxury that her

Mosaic of Justinian from S. Vitale, Ravenna.

Mosaic of Theodora from S. Vitale, Ravenna.

new rank conferred on her. She slept late and took long, voluptuous baths before breakfast, for warm baths were considered good for the health. She was beautiful woman and knew it and she took care never to become overtired, which might have etched unwelcome wrinkles on her face. For lunch and dinner her table was loaded with gourmet foods. Justinian ate little and worked long hours, but Theodora followed her own agenda. She would escape the summer heat in Constantinople by retiring to a seaside villa in Hieron, at the northern exit of the Bosporus where there was an imperial customs house. The villa could be supplied only by boat and the voyage was difficult, made all the more perilous because a rogue whale patrolled the Bosporus and attacked cargo ships. Theodora did not care. One of the fruits of power was the right to expect service from lesser mortals.

She was rich. Justinian showered gifts on her while she was still his mistress, living with him in the Palace of Hormisdas. When they married, Justinian settled on her the customary donation which bridegrooms gave their brides to counterbalance the bride's dowry. Theodora had no dowry but Justinian's prenuptial donation was generous nonetheless. Once Theodora became empress the properties that were the empress's portion became hers. She acquired estates in the provinces of Pontus, Paphlagonia and Cappadocia, all in Asia Minor. Transfers of property between an emperor and an empress should have been subject to public scrutiny but transfers between Justinian and Theodora were exempt. They laboured night and day for the good of their subjects, Justinian asserted, which gave them a right to privacy. It was only just.

Constantinople was a city where buildings and monuments made statements, and the proudest of them all were made by the House of Theodosius, descended from Theodosius I, the emperor who saved the empire after the disaster at Adrianople in 378, when imperial power teetered on the edge of catastrophe. The male line of the Theodosian House ended when Theodosius II died in 450, but the monuments of Constantinople still proclaimed its importance. In the *Augustaeum* in front of the imperial palace there stood a column bearing a silver statue of the great Theodosius. Justinian replaced it with an equestrian statue of himself, made of the finest polished brass which gleamed like gold. Yet, the Constantinople Establishment remained in the shadow of the Theodosian legacy even after the upstarts Justinian and Theodora took over.

It was not the lowly birth of this imperial couple that gave offence. The aristocracy of culture was open to anyone with the right education and the right attitude to Byzantium's traditions. In Byzantium, the concept of Heaven had fused with the idea of the earthly kingdom, which was an imitation of Heaven, and since it had achieved such a degree of perfection it followed logically that

Church of Hagia Sophia.

reform was not merely unnecessary: it was wrong, not to say dangerous. In Heaven, the great reformer had been Lucifer and he came to a bad end, as everyone knew.[4] Justinian and Theodora were reformers who wanted to change traditions that long usage had sanctified. Theodora in particular, with her emphasis on pomp and circumstance and all the other trappings of despotism, became a symbol of a slippage towards tyranny.

Shortly before Justinian became emperor, one of the richest of the *grandes dames* of the old Constantinople Establishment, Anicia Juliana, great granddaughter of the Empress Eudocia, granddaughter of the western emperor Valentinian III and daughter of another western emperor, Anicius Olybrius, built the largest church in Constantinople as her palace chapel, and dedicated it to St Polyeuctus; or to be more correct, she rebuilt it, for an earlier St Polyeuctus was dedicated by her great-grandmother, Eudocia. Juliana's father, Olybrius had been emperor for only a few months but at least he died in his bed of natural causes, which was an achievement of sorts for emperors in fifth-century Italy where imperial reigns were brief. Anicia Juliana had the ambiguous distinction of being offered in marriage by the emperor Zeno to Theoderic the Ostrogoth and being rejected. Yet she combined the wealth and prestige of the old Theodosian imperial lineage with that of one of the richest families in Rome, the Anicii, and may even have been an ambiguous role model for Theodora: she built and embellished churches and was a player in the clash of competing theological doctrines that roiled the empire – she was a devout Chalcedonian. Buildings conveyed messages and when Anicia Juliana began to build her church for St Polyeuctus at the end of her life she intended to proclaim her status and wealth and, probably too, disdain for the occupants of the imperial throne in her own time: Anastasius, whose background was modest and his theology Monophysite, and Justin I, a Chalcedonian to be sure, but an uncultured peasant nonetheless. Back when Justin was still new on the throne Anicia had imperial ambitions for her son, Olybrius, and the succession remained uncertain until Justin reluctantly made Justinian 'Caesar' in 525, at the urging of the senate which wanted no dynastic disputes when Justin died. But the great church of St Polyeuctus remained as a symbol of rival claims to the throne and a reference point to the good old days.

No wonder, then, that as soon as he could Justinian built an even greater church to replace the old basilica of Hagia Sophia and, on the capitals surmounting its columns, Theodora's monogram appears as well as Justinian's. Its splendid dome overshadowed St Polyeuctus, which had a wooden roof. The old Constantinople Establishment was fading, full of impotent rage, and in its place was a new Establishment made up of new men who owed their placement to Justinian. Justinian's Hagia Sophia still stands in modern Istanbul, whereas St Polyeuctus' church collapsed in an earthquake in the twelfth century and was almost forgotten until its chance discovery in 1960. It is now a neglected archaeological site.[5]

Theodora was now a *grande dame* herself, greater than Anicia Juliana ever was, and determined to act the part. Even before Justin died, she gave money to rebuild the church of the archangel Michael in Antioch which had collapsed in a terrible earthquake that nearly destroyed the city. She also used her new-found wealth to supply columns from Constantinople for a basilica in Antioch where the law courts functioned.[6] Great emperors and empresses were benefactors and patrons and though Theodora's donations were less munificent than her husband's she was determined to play the role of philanthropist to the full.

The lowly untouchable from the theatre had become a magnificent patron, surrounded by extravagant pomp and circumstance. In 529, only two years after she became empress, she made a procession of 80 km from Constantinople to Python,[7] where there was – and still is – a famous spa with healing waters, and her progress gave her a chance to flaunt her status and riches.[8] She travelled with a staff of 4,000, made up of ladies of the bedchamber, patricians, eunuchs and others, including the Count of the Sacred Largesses to facilitate her expenditures. As she went she made donations to churches, monasteries and hospices and with each donative she manifested her wealth and power. Justinian was generous with the taxpayers' money. Since Theodora developed a liking for the waters of Pythion, Justinian built a palace for her comfort and presented Pythion with an aqueduct to supply it with water.[9] Nothing was too good for Theodora.

The old Establishment that still dominated the Constantinople senate was made to learn a lesson in humility. The notables who bought the services of courtesans such as Theodora once was, now had to pay her homage. A senator with the status of patrician in time past would to salaam to the emperor when he entered his presence, bending to touch his lips to the emperor's right breast. The emperor in turn kissed the patrician's head and dismissed him. Ordinary senators merely genuflected and withdrew. Usually they did not salute the empress at all. But that was before the new regime of Justinian and Theodora reformed protocol. Now all the senators, whether patricians or not, prostrated themselves face downwards on the floor with their hands outstretched, and kissed the crimson shoes of the imperial partners. One shoe each would do, so long as both the emperor and empress received a kiss. Then they struggled to their feet, breathless and humiliated, and withdrew. Justinian, who was affable and approachable, may have watched the performance with detached amusement. But for Theodora it was a perquisite of imperial power and she valued it. It signalled that there was now a new Establishment in Constantinople, and Theodora belonged.

Petitioners seeking an audience with Theodora had to crowd into a small antechamber and await her pleasure. It did not matter if they belonged to Constantinople's upper crust which thought it had a right, if not an absolute duty, to look with disdain on trash like Theodora. Snobbery of that sort was no longer prudent, now that power was firmly in the hands of this parvenu couple, one sprung from Balkan peasant stock and the other from the theatre riff-raff. A Monophysite holy man, his clothes in tatters, exuding the stink of unwashed sanctity, might go to the head of the queue and enter the empress's presence with no delay, while decent citizens had to linger in the antechamber awaiting the empress' pleasure. Time would pass and when, at long last, they were admitted into her presence they had to prostrate themselves before her before they presented their petition. It was a foolish petitioner who failed to observe due protocol. A law preserved in Justinian law code stated 'that the imperial office be subject to the laws is more important than the imperial power'.[10] But that was a legal concept of an earlier time. Justinian took a different view. He was above the law. He was the imperial lawgiver, the very incarnation of Law,[11] sent by God to rule mankind, as he describes himself in one of his decrees.[12] Theodora was his partner in power and her behaviour reflected the rising despotism of the age. Citizens had genuflected to emperors before Justinian – Diocletian at the end of the third century had surrounded the imperial office with ceremony – but no previous emperor had gone as far as Justinian nor had they made their wives associates in this panoply of tyranny.

The *Secret History* reports a sad tale that sounds authentic. A patrician, grown old in the imperial service, sought Theodora's help. The old man had loaned money to one of her cronies, who refused to repay it. Theodora arranged a reception for the old patrician that was a parody of a church service. He made his entreaty with the appropriate tears and pleas of poverty and the empress intoned a reply, like a priest leading a liturgy, and her eunuch attendants chanted a mantra in response. 'It's a great hernia you have!' Men with hernias had been objects of ridicule in the classical world, particularly in comic mimes. When the old patrician tried again to press his case, he received the same response. The cruel antiphony continued until at last, he made the required obeisance and departed, empty-handed.[13]

Great families chose their marriage alliances shrewdly and it was hardly remarkable that Theodora, as the greatest doyenne of the new order, took a particular interest in who married whom. Matrimony was too important to be left to dewy-eyed romantics. Justinian legislated in one of his laws that mutual love was the prerequisite of wedlock,[14] not dowries or other such considerations, but Theodora did not allow the sovereign power of love to overrule her whim of iron. She saw herself as a shrewd and unsentimental *yia-yia*[15] of people who mattered, and never hesitated to arrange betrothals when it suited her, or even undo marriage contracts. For her own daughter, born out of wedlock before she married Justinian, she chose a husband from the house of the old emperor Anastasius. For her niece Sophia, she arranged a marriage with Justin, the son of Justinian's sister, Vigilantia. Her concern extended even to her old friends from the theatre. Living in the imperial palace as Theodora's guest was a retired dancing girl whose stage name was Chrysomallo, meaning 'golden-haired', for blondes were preferred by the all-male theatre patrons and if nature did not provide an actress with golden hair, art could create it. Theodora found a suitable marriage partner for Chrysomallo's daughter, a young bachelor of impeccable parentage named Saturninus, whose late father, Hermogenes, was a former Master of Offices. Saturninus had been betrothed to his first cousin's daughter, evidently a respectable girl, and the mating of the two would have conserved the family's wealth. The marriage arrangements were progressing towards their anticipated conclusion when Theodora intervened. Saturninus was snatched from the arms of his first cousin once removed and wed, willy-nilly, to Chrysomallo's daughter. She was no longer a virgin, as Saturninus discovered on their wedding night and imprudently grumbled about it to a friend. His complaint reached Theodora's ears and she took offence. She ordered him tossed in a blanket and his backside was whipped as if he were a naughty schoolboy. What right had Saturninus to worry about such considerations as virginity? Justinian himself had not.[16]

Her niece by marriage, Preïecta, the daughter of Justinian's sister Vigilantia, was not spared her attention. Preïecta's first husband had been a well-born senator, Areobindus, who became governor of Africa, and lost his life when the army mutinied. He was a man with no military experience and put up only a pitiful resistance when the Byzantine commander in Numidia, Gontharis, rose in revolt with the support of the Moors. Gontharis forced Preïecta to write Justinian that he was innocent of her husband's murder and had treated her well, for he fancied Preïecta as his own wife. He was already reckoning up the dowry she would bring him when an Armenian soldier named Artabanes slew him and recovered Africa for Justinian. Gontharis had lasted a mere 36 days.

Artabanes was an Arsacid, belonging to the ancient royal house of Armenia, which was still a powerful clan, though Armenia no longer had kings. He had once served in the Persian army and fought well for the Persian shah before he deserted to Byzantium. Now he had become Preïecta's saviour. She fell in love with this strong, handsome Armenian of royal descent and Artabanes returned her affection, attracted equally by her beauty and her dowry. When Preïecta returned to Constantinople, Artabanes contrived a recall for himself as well.

Their wedding was fast approaching when a woman arrived from Armenia and appealed directly to Theodora: she was, she claimed, Artabanes' wife, whom he had married while he was still very young. She had lived quietly in Armenia while Artabanes pursued his career in the imperial army but, now that he had risen to eminence, she wanted the perquisites that the wife of a successful general had the right to expect.

By this time, Theodora had little more than a year to live but the distress of Artabanes' wife touched her heart and perhaps her family pride, too, for Preïecta's brother was her son-in-law. She insisted that Artabanes remain faithful to his wife. For her niece Preïecta, she found another husband, who was the great-nephew of the emperor Anastasius. He was suitably rich, and his marriage to Preïecta would unite the wealth of the old imperial family of Anastasius with the new family that replaced it. Artabanes, seething with impotent rage, settled into marital discomfort with his unwanted Armenian wife.[17]

Theodora wasted no sympathy on him. Nearly ten years before, in 538, her sister Comito's husband, Sittas, had been killed in a skirmish with the Persians in Armenia. Sittas had been one of the best generals who served Justinian, steadier than Belisarius and his equal in military expertise, and the Armenian who struck the fatal blow was Artabanes. He was at the time in the service of Khusro, shah of Persia. The trooper who struck down Theodora's brother-in-law cannot have been her preferred choice as the husband of her niece, even though he had since become a valued soldier of Justinian. Once Theodora was dead, Artabanes divorced his unwanted wife but by then Preïecta had remarried. Artabanes, embittered by his treatment, took part in an abortive conspiracy after Theodora's death but Justinian, who may have had some covert sympathy for him, pardoned him and sent him off to fight the Goths in Sicily.[18]

TWO YOUNG WIDOWED SISTERS IN CONSTANTINOPLE ATTRACTED THEODORA'S NOTICE. We do not know their names. If we did, we might understand Theodora's intervention into their lives better than we do. She chose second husbands for them, alleging that they were living dissolute lives in their widowhood. These two merry widows were of ancient and distinguished lineage, which cannot have endeared them to a *parvenue* like Theodora, and the mates she selected for them were louts dredged up from the lower classes, or at least that is what the two widows thought and so, too, did Procopius, who relates the tale in his *Secret History*.[19] The unwilling brides abhorred their prospective mates so much that they fled for refuge to the baptistery of Hagia Sophia and clung to the font for refuge. But Theodora knew how and where to apply pressure, and it was effective enough to persuade the widows to accept the loutish husbands that Theodora had chosen for them. Then, having presided over this mismatched wedding which shocked all the upper crust of Constantinople, Theodora secured appointments for their husbands as magistrates, thereby conferring respectability upon them. But very soon everyone who had dealings with them had reason to share the repugnance of their unwilling wives.

That is the story as Procopius relates it and the reader cannot help but feel that some important details are missing. Who were these two young widows of impeccable ancestry who enjoyed their widowhood without thought of remarriage? No doubt they were rich. Their fathers, grandfathers and great-grandfathers had all been consuls and consuls were never poor men. The husbands whom Theodora chose for them were not wealthy. They were probably men whom Theodora had found useful in the past, or they may even have been old family friends. In any case, Theodora decided that they should become respectable, and so they did, once they were fitted out with rich wives and appointed to high offices. Theodora was generous with her patronage.

Yet the forced marriage of these two widows was an assault on the pride and property of the old ruling class in Constantinople, which was proud of its traditions and anxious to conserve its wealth. Whoever these two were, we can be sure that Theodora took some pleasure from humbling their pride, even if the whole affair sounds like a violation of women's rights, which generally Theodora upheld.

Justinian and Theodora were innovators in a traditional society that reviled change and some of the changes that were especially dear to Theodora were innovations in society and family life. She wanted to alter the balance of power in marriage, shifting greater clout to the wife. Women in distress could look to her for support. Traditionalists complained that wives ran amok because Theodora undercut a husband's authority in the family.[20] But Theodora knew what it was to be defenceless in Byzantine society and she made it her business to help those who lacked the power to help themselves. She shared some of the tenets of modern feminism but her main concern was not the status of women.[21] Marrying well, and maintaining the social standing of her family remained a woman's proper aim in life. This was the age before 'the pill' and modern hygiene, when propagating the population at the replacement rate was an overriding concern of society. Theodora would have been an uncomfortable member of the feminist sisterhood. Rather, she worked within the traditions of Christianity, which taught that it was a righteous deed to help the helpless. She had herself sprung from the powerless stratum of society, and had witnessed at first hand the exploitation of poor women. She did not forget it.

IT WAS NEVER WISE TO CROSS THEODORA, FOR SHE WAS A VENGEFUL ENEMY WHO DID NOT FORGET SNUBS. There were stories circulating on the streets of Constantinople about the implacability with which she pursued anyone she considered an enemy. Men who thwarted her, or failed to hide their contempt, learned to regret it. Her agents kept her informed of the gossip on the streets and if it was reported that someone was slandering her, he would disappear. He would be secretly arrested and incarcerated and he might wait a long time before Theodora released him, if ever. One of the 'disappeared' was an ex-consul who was a secretary of Justinian's, Priscus, who made the error of disdaining Theodora and failing to conceal his condescension. He was pretentious and corrupt and used his public offices to amass a large fortune. Yet he was not alone in that. What irked Theodora was not so much his dishonesty as his evident scorn for her background. She complained to Justinian. But Justinian was on good terms with Priscus and shut his ears. Then, suddenly, in 529 when a general purge of pagans was in full swing, Priscus was arrested, and though it was mid-winter when sailing was dangerous, he was put on board ship and sent off to Cyzicus, modern Balky-Kale on the Hellespont. There his head was shaved and he was transformed into a reluctant clergyman. Justinian dismissed Priscus' fate from his mind without further ado, though he did not forget to confiscate what was left of Priscus' fortune.[22]

Partisans of the Green party in the Hippodrome were particularly likely to attract Theodora's wrath, for she was a devoted Blue and always quick to help any Blue who transgressed the law. She prosecuted two Greens, Basianus and Diogenes on the charge of homosexuality. Both of them were men about town and great purveyors of gossip, well-known for their malicious wit. Theodora's early career in the theatre must have been no secret to men like these two. Basianus spread scandalous tales about her. But it seems that Theodora could also recall equally disreputable tales about Basianus' private life and when she learned about his scandal-mongering she instructed the chief of police to lay a charge of sodomy against him. Theodora's early life in the theatre had made her familiar with the seamy underside of Constantinople society and Basianus was not unknown. He took sanctuary in a church but the police chief removed him and inflicted a punishment which more than fitted his crime. Basianus was castrated and his property confiscated.

Diogenes was a witty fellow and popular at court. Even Justinian liked him. It is not clear why he incurred Theodora's wrath, except that he was a Green partisan, which may have been reason enough. Yet she went to considerable pains to prove a charge of homosexual intercourse against him. She persuaded two boys who were in Diogenes' service to act both as accusers and witnesses. There was a public trial and the judges decided that the testimony of the two boys was not credible. Then Theodora tried to make one of Diogenes' friends bear false witness against him but he refused. He was tortured but still refused to co-operate and the court acquitted Diogenes. The lawsuit was evidently a *cause célèbre* for there was widespread rejoicing when Diogenes was exonerated,[23] at least in the circles frequented by our source for this tale, Procopius.

THEODORA WAS CAREFUL TO SCOTCH ANY RUMOURS THAT SHE WAS UNFAITHFUL TO HER HUSBAND. 'It is Our wish that everyone lead chaste lives, so far as is possible', Justinian wrote in the preface of one of his laws.[24] Theodora knew that the one thing which could alienate Justinian was evidence that she had not forsaken her disreputable past. She was unhappy about her crony Antonina's philandering, for Antonina never made quite the same break with her unchaste past that Theodora did, and sometimes Theodora would upbraid her angrily; but Antonina was a useful friend, who knew what the limits were. There was scuttlebutt, however, that Theodora actually did fall in love with a handsome young domestic of hers who served as one of her stewards.[16] His name was Areobindus, and he was a 'barbarian', probably an Armenian from the Persian-controlled part of Armenia. But once Theodora learned that people were gossiping about a love affair, she made a point of treating poor Areobindus atrociously. Then he disappeared suddenly from court. Procopius, who reports the tale, hints slyly that he ended up in the palace dungeon or worse. The story is probably pure fiction. However a favourite drama of the great actress, Sarah Bernhardt was *Théodora*, by Victorien Sardou, a playwright who is now generally forgotten. It told a tale of an illicit affair between Theodora and a young lover named Andreas, rather than Areobindus, who was a fan of the Greens in the Hippodrome, which should not have recommended him to the Theodora of history. Yet the rumour of the Areobindus affair is the wisp of evidence which Sardou used to construct his romantic drama.

JUSTINIAN AND THEODORA SEEMED LIKE ILL-MATCHED PARTNERS AND CONTEMPORARIES WERE AMAZED AND EVEN SHOCKED. Procopius[25] expressed the indignation of the respectable circles to which he belonged when he averred that Justinian could have had his choice of refined women for his wife and yet he was so lacking in shame that he selected Theodora. On the all-important issue of religion they disagreed, though how great their disagreement was puzzled their contemporaries. Justinian opposed the anti-Chalcedonians and persecuted them, whereas Theodora supported them, gave refuge to the victims of the persecution and made no secret of it. Yet Justinian made it clear that he accepted Theodora as his partner in power. Newly-appointed provincial governors, before they set out for their provinces, took oaths of fidelity to both Justinian and Theodora. Even when their policies differed they remained loyal to each other as if some peculiar power bound them together. What was it? Mutual respect? A 'good cop-bad cop' routine? Or a malign alliance to keep their subjects divided so that they would not unite against them? Could it be sorcery?[26]

It was rumoured that Theodora was a witch and the suspicion must have appealed particularly to the Chalcedonians. Gossip had it that witchcraft was the secret of her strange domination of Justinian.[27] It was said that she had rubbed shoulders with magicians and sorcerers ever since she was a child and she knew how to summon up evil spirits to bend her husband to her will. Some of the men who shared Theodora's bed while she was still on the stage told stories of how a demon would descend on them out of the darkness and drive them headlong from her bedroom.[28] To the Monophysites she might be a God-fearing queen but to the Chalcedonians she was a whelp of the Devil, who had taught her the black arts belonging to Satan's hellish crew.

She had her own network of agents and informants. Among them were old friends from the theatre whom she welcomed into the imperial palace. We know of an Indaro, and two called Chrysomallo, but they are only names. But one we know well: Antonina, the wife of Justinian's general, Belisarius. Procopius' *History of the Wars* gives more space to Antonina than it does to Theodora and what he wrote about her was based on personal knowledge, at least for as long as he was Belisarius' legal secretary. Our information is good enough to chart the interaction of these two women, and to get a glimpse of how they worked together to manipulate the levers of power. Theirs was an ambiguous friendship, sealed by self-interest on both sides, but together, they played the power game skilfully and ruthlessly.

4

The Remarkable Career of the Young Belisarius

DID ANTONINA WATCH THE CORONATION OF JUSTINIAN AND THEODORA? If she did, she may have reflected how abruptly Theodora's fortune had changed, with happy consequences both for Theodora's family and her friends, particularly herself. Like Theodora, the world she knew when she was young was beyond the perimeter wall of the great Imperial Palace. She was the older of the two and when they first met she must have already been experienced in the ways of the world. Before she married Belisarius she was the 'mother of many children', according to the unkind reportage of Procopius.[1] We know of two for certain and possibly a third. By her first marriage she had a son named Photius, born shortly before her first husband died. He was a teenager in 535 when his mother and he accompanied Belisarius on the expedition against the Ostrogoths in Italy,[2] but wise beyond his years. He had been a delicate child whom Antonina neglected and he bore the psychological scars of her treatment all his life. A daughter became the wife of a high-ranking officer in Constantinople named Ildiger.[3] Antonina also had a granddaughter who may or may not have been Ildiger's child. She was wooed by Sergius, a general whose minimal competence was outweighed by the fact that he was the nephew of Solomon who succeeded Belisarius as commander in Africa, once it was conquered from the Vandals. Sergius was put in charge of the military forces in Tripolitania, where he stirred up a Berber revolt by murdering some Berber envoys who came to him on a diplomatic mission. But Theodora favoured him for Antonina's sake, and Sergius survived to display his ineptitude once again in 559, long after Theodora's death, when a horde of Kutrigur Huns swept into northern Greece and defeated and captured him.

With Belisarius Antonina had one child, a daughter, Joannina, who attracted Theodora's attention because she was Belisarius' heir and should have inherited his considerable wealth. When Joannina was ripe for marriage, Theodora had a bridegroom ready and waiting. He was her own grandson, the child of her bastard daughter whose name is lost. Antonina regarded the match with a notable lack of enthusiasm, though she recognized that Joannina was a

bargaining chip in her relations with Theodora. But that belongs to the end of
Theodora's life and, coincidentally, also the end of Belisarius' remarkable career.

WHEN THE EMPEROR JUSTIN DIED ON THE FIRST DAY OF AUGUST 527, Belisarius
had just been given his first major command. He was appointed commander of
the great fortress of Dara on the Persian frontier and the historian Procopius
was assigned to his staff as his legal secretary and advisor. He tells us what little
we know about Belisarius' youth. His birthplace was Germania, now the village
of Sapareva Banya in western Bulgaria, and he was perhaps of mixed German
and Thracian stock. His background may have recommended him to Justinian,
for it bore a certain similarity to his own. Belisarius enrolled in Justinian's corps
of *bucellarii*, retainers that generals and important state officials maintained as
bodyguards, who swore fidelity both to their paymasters and to the emperor.[4]
Justinian's *bucellarii* corps was also a school for officers; there he enrolled and
tested the recruits whom he would entrust with high command, for Justinian
made a point of spotting talented young men while he was still waiting for his
uncle to die, and at that early point in his career he was a shrewd judge of a
man's potential. Unfortunately, it was an ability that faded as the years went by.
But as a new emperor, Justinian felt the audacity of hope keenly and reform was
his agenda. Belisarius was one of the youths who appeared to have potential.

Probably Antonina noticed him, too, and we would probably be right to
discern the fine hand of Theodora behind the scenes. The handsome young
guardsman and Antonina did not ordinarily move in the same circles but
Theodora liked to play matchmaker, and once she became empress she did
not forget her old friends from the theatre. A late and not overly trustworthy
source, the *Patria of Constantinople*, reports that Antonina was Theodora's *zosté
patrikia*: a 'belted patrician', or 'Mistress of the Robes'. Perhaps 'lady-in-waiting'
is the nearest modern equivalent. The office was purely honorary. The *Patria*
is a miscellany of texts mixing history and fiction and if the report is true that
Antonina was a 'belted patrician', she was the first on record. We must wait until
the ninth century before we find another.[5] But the *Patria* has this much right:
there was a bond between the two women which was generally acknowledged
and it was Theodora who brought Antonina into the circles where she and
Belisarius could meet. Perhaps Theodora encouraged the match and Belisarius
was willing. In fact, he fell passionately in love.

Love was the icing on the cake but Belisarius must have known that
a partnership with Antonina was also an astute career move, for she was
Theodora's crony and hence a woman with influence. It may have been just
before his marriage to Antonina that his first opportunity opened up, while

he was still in the pride of youth – 'wearing his first beard', as Procopius put it, making an implicit comparison with the young god Hermes, who bore the same epithet in Homer's *Iliad*[6] – and all educated Byzantines knew Homer. In 526, while Justin I was still emperor, he and his equally young comrade-in-arms, Sittas, were sent on a raid into Persarmenia, the Persian-controlled portion of Armenia, which was by far the larger portion. The object of the raid was seize captives for the slave market and find recruits for the imperial army for, like the Byzantines, the Armenians were Christians and supplied the Byzantine Empire with some of its best soldiers.

Sittas' own background may have been Armenian, though his name has a Gothic ring to it. He, like Belisarius, was a promising young soldier and Justinian had his eyes on them both. So did Theodora, but she saw them not merely as soldiers with successful careers ahead of them and the wealth that would go along with it, but as marriageable young men who needed suitable wives. Theodora's older sister, Comito, got Sittas, and Antonina took Belisarius.

ON THEIR FIRST RAID, BELISARIUS AND SITTAS WERE SUCCESSFUL. They pillaged a large area, took many captives and withdrew safely, which qualified as success. They were not so lucky with their second raid. Two brothers, Narses and Aratius, belonging to one of the great Armenian feudal families, the Kamsarakan, mustered their retainers and met Belisarius and Sittas in battle. The Byzantines got the worse of it. The Kamsarakan brothers proved their worth as soldiers of the Persian shah, but allegiances in the frontier regions could shift easily. A couple years after this victory, the brothers defected to Byzantium and became officers in the imperial army.

Yet in spite of the defeat, Belisarius received a promotion. At the same time as Belisarius and Sittas made their fruitless raid, the commander of the military forces in the East (*Magister Militum per Orientem*), a mediocrity named Libelarius, made a foray across the Persian frontier, accomplished nothing and withdrew in the sweltering heat to the fortress of Dara. Libelarius was a cautious officer who avoided a defeat by the Persian army by keeping well clear of it. Justinian was not impressed. He replaced Libelarius and promoted Belisarius to Duke of Mesopotamia, commanding the troops at Dara.[7]

The fortress-city of Dara on the eastern frontier was a thorn in the side of Kavadh, the Persian shah. Anastasius began building it in 505, while Persia and the Byzantines were at war, and even though Kavadh agreed next year to a truce which ushered in two decades of peace, construction continued and the emperor named his new city after himself: Anastasiopolis. It contravened an old treaty dating to 422 and Kavadh complained, but he was too occupied elsewhere to do more than protest.[8] Persia was under attack by migrants from Mongolia whom we know under various names: Ephthalites, White Huns, Chionites, Kidarites, Ye-Ta or Hayatila. They first appeared in Iran in the fourth century and in the fifth century they defeated a Persian king in battle and took him prisoner. Kavadh himself as a youth spent some years as a hostage at the court of the Ephthalite khan.

It was not only the Ephthalite menace that distracted Kavadh. Within Persia there was a religious revolt against the orthodox Zoroastrianism, which was Persia's state religion, and internal politics of the kingdom were in turmoil. The leader of the revolt was a Persian heresiarch named Mazdak who preached a doctrine with a communist flavour. No Byzantine author mentions Mazdak and, within the borders of Romania, Mazdakism seems to have been confused with Manicheanism, which was prohibited. But in Persia, Kavadh supported it and may even have become a convert himself. He soon changed his mind: once the Mazdakite movement began to threaten the Iranian class system and the property of the nobility, Kavadh scented danger and slaughtered the Mazdakite leaders. His brutal suppression failed to annihilate the Mazdakites but as a political threat their power was spent. When Justinian came to the throne Persia's interval of weakness was past and war on the eastern frontier had already started again.

Justinian moved first. Once he became sole emperor on old Justin's death he ordered Belisarius to build a fort right on the Persian boundary.[9] Belisarius moved swiftly. The fort was half-built before a Persian force arrived and demanded that construction cease. Justinian refused to back down. Instead he dispatched a detachment of troops from Lebanon under two rash young commanders to drive off the Persians. There was a fierce battle and the Byzantines were badly beaten. One of the young generals was taken prisoner and led away in chains. Belisarius did not distinguish himself. One source reports that he took to his heels and fled. In any case he retreated, destroying his half-completed fort, and pulled back.

Yet the setback did not harm his career. He received another promotion. The Master of the Soldiers in the East, the generalissimo commanding the army in the great prefecture of *Oriens* which stretched from Constantinople to the eastern frontier, was Hypatius,[10] the nephew of the old emperor Anastasius, which was his chief qualification for high command, for he never in his long career led an army to victory. However, he had the virtue of lack of ambition, though it must have occurred to him that, as Anastasius' nephew, he had some right to the throne. Now he was removed as Master of the Soldiers and sent back to his mansion in Constantinople to enjoy his retirement, which would be briefer than he expected. In his place, Justinian appointed Belisarius, who cannot have yet been 30 years old.[11]

This was indeed a meteoric career and we may wonder what Belisarius had done to deserve it. He had made one successful raid into Persarmenia, partnered with Sittas, followed by another that ended in defeat and flight. He had shown competence but no outstanding brilliance. Yet back at Constantinople both Belisarius and Sittas had women of influence who supported them. It was probably in 528 that Sittas married Theodora's older sister, Comito, and the wedding celebration was a brilliant festivity. It was held near the Hippodrome in a magnificent palace that had been built by a eunuch named Antiochus, who had made himself wealthy in the service of the emperor Theodosius II; now, apparently, it was gifted to Theodora's sister. It may have been about the same time that Belisarius married Antonina. At any rate, these two young soldiers whose wives had Theodora's ear were promoted at the same time. When Belisarius became Master of the Soldiers in the East, Sittas was appointed Master of the Soldiers in Armenia.

This was a new office. Hitherto there had been a Count of Armenia who protected the portion of Armenia that was under Roman control. But now Sittas, with the rank of Master of the Soldiers, commanded the northern sector of the frontier facing Persarmenia; Belisarius, with the same rank, defended the central sector. Further south, Justinian relied on Arab allies to protect the marches of Palestine: sometime before 531, he recognized the sheik of the Ghassanid tribe, al-Harith, as supreme phylarch or tribal leader, gave him the title of king and entrusted him with the defence of the frontier from the Red Sea to the Euphrates River.[12] But the two critical sectors were further north and there the defence of the frontier was entrusted to the husbands of Comito and Antonina, Sittas and Belisarius, young officers making their way up the career ladder.

Sittas did not disappoint. In 530 he inflicted a sharp defeat on one of Persia's ablest generals and soon after he was promoted to the rank of Master of the Soldiers in the Presence, stationed in Constantinople close to his wife but still with responsibility for the army in Armenia. He left behind an officer named Dorotheus with the rank of Master of the Soldiers in Armenia, but Dorotheus reported to Sittas and they carried out an offensive together in 531. In the same year, Belisarius won his first great victory, outside the walls of Dara.

IT IS A FLUKE OF HISTORY THAT WE KNOW A GREAT DEAL ABOUT BELISARIUS' VICTORY AT DARA but much less about the brilliant campaign that Sittas and Dorotheus waged in their sector of the frontier. Belisarius' staff included

Procopius of Caesarea as *assessor* or legal advisor, who was well-trained in the classics and realized that he had the opportunity to emulate the great Thucydides for, like him, he was witnessing great events in history. Belisarius could not have asked for a better public-relations man. Quite possibly he presented his flattering report of the battle of Dara as a public reading to a select audience in Constantinople. At this point he was still a loyal admirer of his young commander, though later his admiration would turn to bitterness, but that was in the future. Yet Justinian himself must have had a few misgivings about Belisarius' competence, for he did not allow him complete independence. The powerful Master of Offices, Hermogenes, was attached to his staff and he had a supervisory role even though Procopius glosses over the fact. Hermogenes kept a watchful eye. But Belisarius acquitted himself well. The Persian commander had 40,000 troops whereas Belisarius had merely 25,000, including a skimpily-trained infantry corps which Belisarius wisely posted behind a trench to protect it from a charge by the dreaded Persian horsemen.[13] The battle ended with a Persian defeat. This was no Battle of Waterloo, for though the Persian army fell back it continued to menace Dara. An unkind reporter who looked only at the long-term results of the battle might have labelled the whole conflict a draw.

Yet the success at Dara was the first victory Byzantium had won over Persia for over a hundred years. The last one had been in 422, when the shah of Persia, angry because the emperor Theodosius II refused to surrender Christian refugees fleeing persecution in Persia, launched an attack and was soundly defeated. The victory at Dara was a return to the triumphant mode. It was great enough for the praetorian prefect to celebrate it by setting up an equestrian statue of Justinian in the Hippodrome. Overnight Belisarius acquired a reputation as a commander to watch. His glory paled only slightly a few weeks later when a band of Bulgar prisoners, including a captured king, was also paraded through the Hippodrome, sent there by Mundo, the Master of Soldiers in Illyricum. Mundo[14] was the son of a king of the Gepids, barbarians settled in the Danube region, who had joined Theoderic the Ostrogoth, serving him in Italy, but when Theoderic died in 526, he offered his services to Justinian, who welcomed him. Mundo served Justinian well. In 530, he won a double victory: first he routed a horde of Slavs, and then crushed a Bulgar horde that had already defeated two Byzantine armies and was terrorizing the Balkans.[15] Yet Mundo's victories could not eclipse the first victory over a Persian army in a century, or dim the glory of the commander who won it.

Next year, when Belisarius was defeated at Callinicum (Raqqa, on the Euphrates River), his in-house historian found it a challenging task to spin a favourable report. The Persians had launched a raid across the Euphrates into northern Syria where the Byzantine cities were only lightly fortified, and no danger was expected. The Persians had some 20,000 troops, including a detachment of Arabs belonging to the Lakhmid tribe, led by their sheikh al-Mundhir. News reached Antioch that Persian raiders were approaching and the city was panic-stricken. But Belisarius with 3,000 men, reinforced by al-Harith and some 5,000 of his Ghassanid tribesmen, caught up with the Persians and barred their approach to Antioch. The Persians retreated with Belisarius dogging their heels. Meanwhile the available Byzantine forces mustered for battle and by the time the Persian invaders reached the Euphrates and encamped on its right bank opposite the city of Callinicum, Belisarius' army had grown to some 20,000 troops, all over-confident and spoiling for a fight. Easter Sunday fell on the following day and Belisarius' men had been fasting but, even so, they lusted for battle. The Persians, they knew, would break camp on Sunday and retreat with their plunder into the desert that lay beyond Callinicum. The Byzantines could not follow them there. It seemed that a chance for a victory was about to vanish.

Yet Belisarius was cautious. He had driven the Persians out of imperial territory without a battle and would have preferred not to risk one now that his objective was won. But his troops could see the Persians bivouacked on the Euphrates river bank and they wanted to fight. Belisarius' caution looked to them like cowardice and they began to mock him openly until he gave way. Perhaps he thought he was facing a mutiny if he opposed his fire-eating troops, who would engage the Persians whether he wanted it or not. Possibly, too, Hermogenes, the Master of Offices who was with him, supported the demands of the soldiers. In any case, Belisarius failed to assert his authority, made a right-about-face, and abandoned caution. On Sunday morning, he drew up his army at a right angle to the river bank and, with a cold wind blowing in the faces of his troops, he offered battle.[16]

The result was a sharp defeat. The story of the debacle that we have from Procopius, which may reflect a report that he drew up for the emperor's eyes, shifts much of the blame on to the shoulders of the Ghassanid sheikh. It alleged that al-Harith and his Arabs fled when the Persians attacked and opened the way for them to break through the Byzantine battle line, whereas Belisarius himself acted with exemplary courage. He dismounted from his horse, and joined his infantry, fighting off one onslaught after another until the Persians withdrew to their camp. Not until then did Belisarius and his men embark on a barge and cross to the safety of an island in the river.

Next day a small flotilla of barges set out from Callinicum to evacuate the Byzantines and the Persians departed with their spoils. Yet when the shah of

Persia counted up the casualties his army had suffered, he thought Callinicum was a Pyrrhic victory. He was not pleased by the outcome.

But we have a different story from the chronicler John Malalas,[17] which may have been based on the investigation that Justinian ordered into the defeat. According to it, some of the Arabs did flee but al-Harith and his Ghassanids fought well and did not turn tail and run at a critical juncture. Malalas reports Belisarius' conduct as less than heroic. When he saw that his army was getting the worse of it, he embarked in a boat and crossed the river to safety. His army retreated with him, except for two dukes, Sounikas and Simmas whose brave action Procopius fails to mention. They dismounted and continued to fight shoulder to shoulder with their men. Malalas assigns no credit either to Belisarius' tactics or his leadership.

Justinian had expected better. He dispatched a field commander named Constantinus[18] to take command of the troops at Dara. Sittas was assigned the overall defence of the eastern frontier. Belisarius was recalled to Constantinople, and Mundo replaced him briefly for a few months before being reassigned to Illyricum in the Balkans. Belisarius was under a cloud and if he had been a general with no connections at court his career might have suffered real damage. But Antonina and Theodora were friends and so long as that was true Antonina's husband continued to be welcome at court. He remained a 'Teflon general' while he had Theodora's support and his disappointing performance at Callinicum did not change that. Hence he was in the imperial palace when Justinian and Theodora faced the Nika riots at the beginning of the year 532, which nearly cost them their thrones.

IT CAN BE DEBATED WHETHER OR NOT BELISARIUS WAS ONE OF THE GREAT FIELD MARSHALS OF HISTORY, but he was lucky: opportunities opened up for him when he was ready for them. The violent riot that exploded in Constantinople on 13 January 532 was unexpected and it frightened Justinian so much that he was ready to board ship and flee the city. Belisarius was on hand, awaiting the emperor's orders but still in command of his personal bodyguard of troops whose loyalty was unquestionable. Without Belisarius and his men the rioters would almost certainly have toppled the regime of Justinian and Theodora then and there.

As for Sittas, Comito's husband, his star was rising while Belisarius remained under a cloud. Comito was Theodora's sister and her husband had proved his ability. But in January of 532 he was still on the eastern frontier, repairing the damage to imperial prestige caused by the defeat at Callinicum. He was not in Constantinople to defend Justinian's regime in this time of crisis. Mundo was on hand; he had returned from the eastern frontier and had not yet left to take charge of the defence of Illyricum. His presence was fortunate for he had a bodyguard of barbarian Heruls: tough, merciless warriors who were loyal to their leader, a barbarian himself. They would be indispensable. Yet it was Belisarius whose mettle was tried and proved in the Nika riots.

JANUARY IN ISTANBUL IS COLD AND UNPLEASANT and it cannot have been much different in Justinian's day. The New Year of 532 must have found many homeless men on the streets trying to keep warm and poor families huddled in wretched dwellings which could not keep out the dank chill. The unemployed urban population had been growing. The city streets were heartless and no less so were the imperial tax collectors whose zeal for their task swelled the number of the destitute. Justinian's new praetorian prefect, John the Cappadocian, the minister of finance and much else, preferred efficiency to humanity. Taxes were collected without pity, by fair means or more often foul, for John's agents were cruel and duplicitous.[19] Small landowners were ruined. The poor and dispossessed in the provinces flocked to the capital, partly out of a forlorn hope that their wrongs might be redressed there, partly because they thought that life in Constantinople might be easier.[20] The authorities responded by enforcing law and order with stiffer penalties, which only increased the discontent that was already simmering. Add to that the alienation of the old ruling elite that looked on Justinian and Theodora as upstarts; Theodora in particular, white trash risen to the imperial purple, must have stuck in their collective craw.

The antagonism between the Blue and Green parties was the catalyst, supplying an outlet for popular resentment. Street violence in the large cities of the empire had peaked in the early years of old Justin's reign and it was past its peak by 532, but it was still a fact of life in Constantinople. It was an outlet for general discontent, fuelled by the anomie of the youth culture in the cities, for this was a pre-modern society where half the population is usually under 20 years old.[21] There were many semi-employed young men who had been surplus labour in the rural villages, where relentless taxation was emptying the small farms, and they migrated to the large cities looking for jobs and excitement. Wealth had passed them by and no doubt they resented men whose lives were more fortunate. They added their muscle to the Blue and Green gangs. They cultivated a look that identified them as beyond the norms of everyday respectable life for they wore beards and moustaches, trimmed their hair after the fashion of the Huns with foreheads shaved and ponytails at back, and wore shirts with puffed sleeves as if to allow space to flex their impressive biceps. When night fell in the city gangs of husky youths waylaid men whose clothes marked them as comfortably prosperous and sometimes they left their victims dead or dying. Boys were buggered by gang members and their fathers could not protect them. The propertied classes grew nervous. Money lenders thought it wise to cancel debts and men who were well-to-do believed it was prudent to wear shabby clothes in public. It was dangerous to flaunt wealth.

Justinian was blamed for the violence, for he protected the Blues from punishment. The streets of Constantinople believed, rightly or wrongly, that the Blue youth gangs were Justinian's men. The word on the street was that if a sodomite who was a Green was caught he was castrated, but if he was a Blue he would get off scot-free.[22] While Justin I was still on the throne and Justinian's succession was not entirely certain, he recruited agents and supporters among the Blues and he may have imagined that the growing disorder on the streets brought him some advantage. But finally the gangs went too far and murdered a citizen of high rank in the Great Church of Hagia Sophia itself. Word of what was going on at last reached the old emperor Justin and he commanded the city prefect Theodotus to restore order. The prefect acted vigorously and some gang members were executed for their crimes; others were forced into hiding. Justinian was sick at the time and could not interfere.

When Justinian recovered from his illness, he wreaked vengeance on poor Theodotus. He accused him of sorcery and magical arts, which was a very serious charge, but it failed to stick. So Theodotus was abducted to Jerusalem where he sought asylum in a church, for he feared that the gangs would send assassins to kill him. Theodotus was nicknamed the 'Pumpkin', which may have been an unflattering reference to the amplitude of his waistline or possibly tribute to his good health, for pumpkins symbolized physical well being. If that was the import of Theodotus' sobriquet it was out-of-place after Justinian was finished with him. But he had done his job: order in Constantinople was restored, at least for the time being, and once Justinian himself became emperor one of the first prescripts that he sent to all the cities in the empire was an order that all rioters and murderers should be punished, no matter whether they were Blues or Greens.[23] Justinian was still a fan of the Blues and the *Augusta* Theodora was an ardent supporter, well-known as a protector of Blue malefactors, but the regime took a hard line against street violence and it was past its peak when the *Nika* riots took place.

The opening scene of the *Nika* uprising was a demonstration by the Greens in the Hippodrome on Sunday 11 January. We have what appears to be an official log of it, created perhaps by a stenographer who was present in the Hippodrome and made a record of it in shorthand for the imperial archives. It was available for the chronographer Theophanes the Confessor[24] at the end of the eighth century. The Green fans entered the Hippodrome prepared to voice a complaint: they took their seats in the Green section and recited it in unison to the emperor who sat aloft in the imperial loge. The emperor replied through a herald, a man whose voice was trained to project over a great distance. This was a remarkable example of Hippodrome democracy: the Greens, led by a precentor named Antlas, chanted a rhythmic protest and the herald intoned a reply, acting as the emperor's mouthpiece. The cadence must have had an almost hypnotic effect, organizing and amplifying crowd emotion as it did. The Greens chanted that they were being oppressed by a *spatharius*, that is, the officer who was in charge of the eunuch attendants of the imperial bedchamber, the *cubicularii*. The Greens' *bête noir* was a man they called Calopodius, probably a derisive nickname for it means 'Pretty Foot' or perhaps 'Dainty Feet'; or the 'guy with nice shoes'. The *spatharius* at this time was Narses, a eunuch from Armenia whose ability made up for his lack of formal education; he would eventually emerge as a rival of Belisarius and a more effective general.[25] At this time he was still at the beginning of a long career, though he may have already been Theodora's protégé, and for all we know he may have worn fine boots which gave him his nickname. At any rate, whoever this Calopodius was, Justinian denied that he had done the Greens any harm.[26]

A Green gang member had been murdered, it seems. It was the twenty-sixth in a series of such murders. The Greens thought that Justinian was implicated and said so. The Blues broke in to shout that only the Greens committed murder and the herald hurled back an accusation that the Greens were responsible for two recent homicides. The Greens responded with a bitter rejoinder, crying out that it was better to be a Jew or a pagan than a Blue. They filed out of the Hippodrome leaving the Blues and the emperor to watch the chariot races by themselves.

This is a puzzling dialogue. If we knew all the circumstances behind it we might understand what connection it had with the *Nika* riots, but we do not.[27] What the dialogue does indicate, however, is how bitter the Greens had become because of the emperor's hard-line policy against them and the favour that they perceived was still bestowed upon the Blues, notwithstanding the imperial decree that all murderers and rioters should be punished alike, whether Blues or Greens. The Blues remained partisans of Justinian, and Theodora's support for them must have been well-known. Yet the situation was more volatile than anyone at court Justinian imagined and when the revolt broke out, Justinian quite unready for its extreme violence. If the idea ever crossed his mind that by provoking a little riot he could bring the secret foes of his regime out into the open where he could deal with them, he miscalculated. The insurgency was a near thing, and when it burst out Justinian dithered. His weakness was not simulated to encourage his enemies to expose themselves. He appeared weak because his position *was* weak.

The tinder was dry; all that was needed was a spark. It came when Justinian forgot the old 'Divide and Conquer' rule of statecraft, which had served him in the past, and began to apply the rule of law to Blue and Green malefactors alike.

On the evening after the Hippodrome dialogue the city prefect, Eudaemon, who had already arrested a number of gang members, both Blues and Greens, ordered that seven of them who were convicted of murder should be put to death. Four were to be beheaded and three hanged. But the hangman was incompetent. The three felons destined for the noose were taken to a gallows near the monastery of St Conon and there they were strung up; but the rope broke and two of them tumbled to the ground still alive. The hangman tried again with no better luck. Then the monks rushed out from St Conon's monastery, grabbed the felons and carried them off bodily across the Golden Horn to the church of St Lawrence, to seek asylum there. The city prefect set a guard around the church to prevent the two criminals from escaping. One was a Green and the other a Blue.

Church of Hagia Eirene.

The news spread like wildfire and two days later, when Justinian presented himself at the races in the Hippodrome on Tuesday 13 January, the Blues and the Greens joined to beseech him to pardon the two criminals. Justinian paid no heed. Then, as the teams were pounding down the track on the twenty-second race of the day and there were only three races left to run, the Blues and Greens raised a great cry in unison, 'Long live the merciful Greens and Blues!' The unexpected had happened – unexpected at least by Justinian and his ministers. The Blues and the Greens had joined forces against the regime.

This alliance cannot have been accidental. The leaders of the Greens and the Blues must have talked beforehand and both parties knew that they shared a common grievance. The Blues had been Justinian's favourites and they were reluctant to turn against him. Yet one of the felons cowering in the church of St Lawrence was a Blue gang member, and Justinian's obduracy had come as a shock to his Blue partisans. When the Green leaders raised the cry of revolt the Blue claqueurs rose to their feet and joined them, and suddenly a great roar of fury rolled across the Hippodrome and up to the imperial loge. Justinian and his court were taken by surprise. The watchword that the rioters adopted was 'Nika', the imperative of the word 'to win', which was the cry raised to acclaim a new emperor, and in this context it was full of menace. The people of Constantinople had reclaimed their right to select their ruler and he would not be Justinian.

The Blues and Green exited the Hippodrome, while the party in the imperial loge scuttled back to the palace along the private passageway linking the two. That evening, the mob made its first move.

A gang of rioters surged down the main street of the city, led by Constantinople's equivalent of lager louts, with their pony tails, shaved hairlines and biceps rippling under their tunics. They demonstrated outside the Praetorium, the official residence of the city prefect with the city gaol in the basement, and demanded that the two felons in the church of St Lawrence be released. The prefect gave no reply. Thereupon they burst into the Praetorium, released the prisoners that they found incarcerated there and set fire to the building. The gaol keepers and the Praetorium staff had their throats cut.

Then the mob poured along the *Mese* towards the *Augustaeum*, which had the basilica of Hagia Sophia on one side, and on the other the monumental entrance to the Great Palace, the so-called Brazen House. They set fire to them both. The blaze spread, whipped to fury by a wind blowing across the Bosporus, and as it moved westwards it grew into a wildfire, devouring whatever was in its path. The great Baths of Zeuxippos went up in flames. Hagia Sophia burned to the ground and from Hagia Sophia the blaze spread to the old church of Hagia

Eirene[28] close by. The Hospice of Samson standing between the two churches caught fire and the patients inside were incinerated as they lay in their beds. The flames spread along the *Mese*, jumping from colonnade to colonnade, until it reached the Forum of Constantine. There was little that anyone could do to stop it. Wild fervour took over the streets and even women, who did not attend the chariot races, joined the rioters.[29]

On Wednesday Justinian, hoping to distract the mob, ordered another day of races in the Hippodrome. But the Blues and the Greens had developed a taste for arson. The objective of the rioters had changed in 24 hours. We hear no more of the felons in the church of St Lawrence. The mob was now politicized. It demanded the ousting of three unpopular ministers: the city prefect Eudaemon, the praetorian prefect John the Cappadocian, and Tribonian, a brilliant but corrupt jurist who held the office of quaestor. These men were movers and shakers in Justinian's regime. John, who had only recently been appointed praetorian prefect, could not produce a well-turned sentence in elegant Greek, much less Latin, but he knew a great deal about efficiency and cutting costs and his reforms threatened the beloved perquisites of many of the ruling class, not least the senators. Tribonian headed a juridical commission that was working on the *Digest* of Roman law, codifying the verdicts of past Roman jurists. In retrospect the *Digest* appears as a landmark in jurisprudence but in 532 the legal community was watching his work with apprehension. The *Digest* represented innovation.

Justinian yielded. Eudaemon, John and Tribonian were dismissed. Their replacements were men whom the senators should have respected. By now Justinian recognized clearly that the riot was drawing on a deep well of hostility among the upper classes that despised him and hated the *Augusta* Theodora with her imperial airs. The Blue and Green lager louts may have started the uprising but it was becoming a popular insurrection and the old Establishment saw a chance to use it for their own ends. They moved to transform it into a revolt against the regime.

Justinian attempted appeasement. But by now the mob recognized its power. No effective attempt had been made to curb it. Having forced out three unpopular ministers, it began to think of replacing the emperor himself. The emperor Anastasius had not been universally popular – certainly not among the poor, for his reform of the bronze coinage had hit them hard[30] -- but he was remembered now with nostalgia, particularly among those whose support of the Chalcedonian Creed was tepid at best, and though he was dead his family was still rich and influential. It represented continuity with the good old days. Two of Anastasius' nephews, Hypatius and Pompeius, were shut up in the Great Palace with Justinian along with a number of the other senators but there was one, Probus, who was not. The mob rushed to his house to proclaim him emperor. It was too late: Probus had prudently left Constantinople for the country, and in frustration the mob set fire to his house. After the revolt was over Justinian exiled Probus in spite of his adroit retreat from the scene of danger and seized his property, but a year later he relented, recalled him and returned the property he had confiscated.

On Thursday, Justinian tried to use force to restore order. Belisarius led out a contingent of his guards against the mob. But the narrow streets of Constantinople put them at a disadvantage and though the battle was fierce and bloody it achieved nothing. Belisarius pulled back and the rioting and arson continued. An onlooker standing on the enclosure wall of the palace grounds would have viewed a city in flames. Justinian and his court were under siege and by Saturday Justinian was beginning to panic. Fearing treachery from within, he ordered those senators who were shut in the palace with him to leave at nightfall and go and defend their own homes. There were only a few exceptions and the two nephews of Anastasius, Hypatius and Pompeius, were not among them.

They both begged to stay behind in the palace, for they must have known by now that the mob had gone to the mansion of their cousin Probus and tried to make him emperor. Only his absence had saved him. But their protests only increased Justinian's paranoia and he would not listen. He ordered them out. His rationale is hard to understand, and perhaps there was none, for he was a frightened man and possibly imagined that disaffected troops within the palace itself might shift their loyalty to either Hypatius or Pompeius if they remained behind. He was no longer sure whom he could trust.[31]

Next morning, early on Sunday, Justinian tried to copy the stratagem that old Anastasius had used in 512, when he pacified a howling mob in the Hippodrome that accused him of abetting heresy by entering the *kathisma* without his crown, bearing the Scriptures in his hands. Following Anastasius' example, Justinian presented himself to the crowd in the Hippodrome, clutching the Gospels. Speaking through a herald, he swore an oath that he would grant amnesty to the malefactors for the damage done and meet the people's demands. There were a few friendly voices raised, for imperial agents had been trying hard to buy support among the mob. But the friendly shouts were soon drowned out. The rioters remained angry and hostile. They jeered Justinian and called him a liar. He made a hasty retreat.

Meanwhile the news spread that Hypatius had left the palace and was at his home. Hypatius' abilities were mediocre but he was a man of breeding and no innovator. Unlike his uncle, he was a Chalcedonian, but probably not a hard-edged one. The disaffected senators, who were by now steering the revolt, must have thought him a sound choice for the throne. The mob surged to Hypatius' house. Hypatius was terrified and his wife Maria cried out in anguish that he was being taken to his doom, but he was carried willy-nilly to the Oval Forum and there, at the foot of the column bearing Constantine's statue, a golden chain was placed on his head as a substitute crown.

Then the senators who wanted to oust Justinian met in council in the Senate House which adjoined the Oval Forum and debated. What should be done next? A senator named Origenes spoke up, and advised prudence. The senate should do nothing rash. But then a rumour spread that Justinian had fled, and Hypatius recovered his courage. He began to feel the fatal allurement of the imperial crown and went willingly enough to the imperial loge in the Hippodrome to be acclaimed emperor. The mob crowded into the great building and loudly reviled Justinian and Theodora, though the insults were not quite unanimous for the *spatharius*, Narses, the shrewd eunuch from Persarmenia who had Theodora's confidence, had been spreading bribes in the crowd, buying support for Justinian, and many of the Blues were still loyal. Yet as Hypatius looked down from the lofty *kathisma* to the crowd milling below, he must have thought that nothing now stood between him and the throne.

Within the palace a council was taking place. Justinian was there, and Theodora, and John the Cappadocian – even though he had just been dismissed as praetorian prefect, he was still within the inner circle. Belisarius was there, too, and Mundo, who had just been reappointed Master of the Soldiers in Illyricum but had not yet left Constantinople to take up 'his command. It was simple luck that he was in the palace at this juncture, with a corps of loyal Heruls at his back. Years earlier, in 267 CE, the Heruls had burst into Greece and sacked Athens, but since then they had settled in the Balkans on the borders of the empire and supplied recruits for the imperial army. Both Belisarius and Mundo led dependable troops and their loyalty was vitally important, for the palace guards were no longer reliable. The Scholarians were decorative soldiers, never of much use in a fight at the best of times, and the allegiance of the Excubitors was doubtful. Some may have sympathized with Hypatius for unlike Justinian, who had never commanded an army on a battle-field as far as we know, Hypatius was an old veteran and though his military career had been singularly inglorious, the imperial guardsmen may have felt some partiality for him.

Belisarius' legal secretary, Procopius, could have been present at this council;[32] if not, he could easily have heard a first-hand report. We owe a large share of what we know about the riot to him and it was probably based on the account of a witness, though Procopius retold it with the skill of a literary master. We can be reasonably certain that Antonina was not there, though she would not have been too far from her husband's side. She might have been in a palace corridor talking, perhaps, to her friend Vigilantia, who was Justinian's sister, and quietly calculating what the chances were that the regime would survive. Vigilantia's sons, Boraïdes and Justus, were there ready for action. The situation was desperate and the atmosphere crackled with panic. Both John the Cappadocian and Belisarius agreed that Justinian should flee. Then, while Justinian sat silently, indecisive and unnerved, Theodora rose to her feet.

Our only source for what she said is Procopius,[33] and he reports this little drama with all the tools of rhetoric. There are echoes of Euripidean drama in the tale. First Procopius reports that about the same time as Theodora was speaking to the frightened men in the imperial palace, a measured debate was going on in the senate house, where Origenes advised caution. Do not storm the palace, he urged; leave Justinian free to flee the city, and all would be well. Take no risks. Meanwhile, within the palace, Theodora delivered her bold speech, saying what she would have said if she were playing the role of a proud, defiant heroine on stage.[34] The contrast between her and Origenes was sharp; not only was there a difference in gender but it was the empress who was bold and Origenes, the senator, who was unheroic. Yet Theodora, as Procopius told the story, still remembered the rules of rhetoric. She began with a conventional apology for speaking at all: she was only a female in the midst of men. Yet, mere woman though she was, she invoked a masculine hardihood. All men must die sometime, she pointed out, but all men need not live out their lives in exile. Let Justinian flee if he wished! The ships were ready and there was still time to abscond with a good portion of the imperial treasury. But as for her, she would rather die than live on in a world where no one addressed her any longer as 'Your Majesty'. She preferred to live by the old adage that the imperial purple made a good burial shroud.[35]

It was a plucky speech, full of the stubborn pride of a woman who had risen from the trash heap to the peak of the social order and would rather die than slide down again. If Theodora had gone to a good school, she might have uttered something like the words that Procopius put in her mouth. But since her school had been the theatre and the mean streets of Constantinople her speech was probably less elegant, if equally dramatic. It may well have been she who pointed out to the unnerved men in the council that they had a golden opportunity to fall upon the mob, while it was packed into the Hippodrome acclaiming Hypatius emperor and never expecting an assault. In fact, there was a rumour that Hypatius himself sent a message to Justinian suggesting to him that he attack the mob in the Hippodrome, but the imperial secretary who received the message replied that Justinian had already fled. The rumour was probably untrue. It was based on the pitiful defence which Hypatius himself put forward after the riot was over when he was brought before Justinian and Theodora. Yet someone in this anxious council realized that while the troops led by Mundo and Belisarius could not get the upper hand in street fighting, they would be deadly if they were directed against a throng of rioters crowded close together in the Hippodrome, and that 'someone' could well have been the cool-headed empress. Kill or be killed was the order of the day, and if massacre was necessary to save the regime, Theodora would not shrink from it.

Belisarius first tried to force his way along the private passageway from the palace into the imperial loge. But the door was shut and the soldiers guarding it refused to open it. They wanted to be on the winning side and it was not yet clear what side that would be. For the moment, Belisarius lost his nerve; he returned to report to Justinian that all was lost. But Justinian ordered him to make his way directly through the smouldering ruins of the Brazen House, then across the *Augustaeum* to the Hippodrome and invade the imperial loge by the small door that opened into it from a colonnaded room called the Blue Stoa. His target was Hypatius; Belisarius was to seize him and take him prisoner and all might be well. Belisarius set forth again, but he found Hypatius' soldiers standing guard at the Blue Stoa and he knew better than to join battle with them in narrow quarters. Desperate now, he ordered his troops to draw their swords and charge the mob. Pressed tightly together, it was defenceless.

Meanwhile Mundo and his troops had exited the palace by another gate, which gave on to a winding path that evidently descended around the substructures of the Hippodrome which can still be seen at its south end, and entered by the gate which was used to remove dead horses and the broken bodies of unlucky charioteers during the races. His Heruls fell on the mob with savage glee. Hypatius, in the imperial loge high above the crowd, heard the shouts of acclaim turn to cries of rage and wails of anguish. Thirty thousand men were reportedly killed, some massacred by the soldiers, others trampled under foot in the panic. By contrast, the Chinese Communist government's repression of the uprising in Tiananmen Square in Beijing on the night of 3–4 June 1989 cost upwards of seven thousand lives. By any standard, the incident in the Hippodrome in January 532 came to a bloody conclusion.

Justinian may have been a little appalled by the bloodshed which he did not intend; but Theodora wasted no sympathy on the rioters. Hypatius and

Pompeius were seized as they stood in the imperial loge and dragged before the emperor and empress. Pompeius blubbered with fright but if military experience had failed to show Hypatius how to win victories it had at least taught him dignity in the face of death. The two men pleaded that they had acted under compulsion and that they had even helped Justinian by bringing the mob into the Hippodrome where they could be slaughtered. Justinian might have forgiven the two men, but Theodora took a tougher line. When she sensed that Justinian was inclining towards mercy she broke in with an angry rebuke and Justinian heeded.[36]

Hypatius and Pompeius were put to death and their cadavers hurled into the sea. Yet Justinian's revenge was temperate. He exiled 18 senators and confiscated their property but later, when he was secure, he let them return. He gave them back their possessions, or at least what remained of them, for he had already given away a portion. The assets of Hypatius and Pompeius were returned to their children and, when the sea washed Pompeius' body up on the shore, Justinian allowed his kin to inter him in the family sepulchre in the church of St Maura.[37] A son of Pompeius would eventually marry Justinian's niece. That would be years later, only shortly before Theodora's death.

Belisarius had proved his loyalty. Not only had he been in the right place at the right time but he had been steady and even courageous in a time of crisis. Justinian's power was now secure and he had great plans for the future. Belisarius and Antonina would be part of them. First, the damage which the *Nika* revolt had inflicted on Constantinople had to be mended. Burned-out buildings had to be demolished and reconstruction begun. But the following year there would be an expedition against the Vandal kingdom in North Africa. Belisarius would lead it and Antonina would accompany him. Henceforth she would be Belisarius' companion on his campaigns.

Antonina in Love

ANTONINA HAD FALLEN IN LOVE. Regrettably, the object of her lust was not her husband. This was not, it seems, an altogether unusual state of affairs, for neither marriage nor the onset of respectability had dulled Antonina's appetite for sexual adventure. Belisarius was blind to his wife's roving eye, though the empress Theodora was not and she sometimes reprimanded Antonina severely; but Antonina was too useful for the empress to discard. In this case Antonina's lover was her own stepson – at least he was a stepson adopted by the rites of the church, if not in law. His name was Theodosius and, like Belisarius himself, he came from Thrace.

There must have been a story behind this adoption which we can only guess from a brief reference from Procopius.[1] Theodosius belonged to Belisarius' household, which implies family relationship; at least it was kinship that gave Theodosius a claim on Belisarius. That gives rise to an interesting question: what was Belisarius' own background? Had he been brought up in the orthodox faith? For Theodosius' immediate family belonged to the Anomoian sect, which was an offshoot of the Arian heresy. The Council of Constantinople of 381, which condemned Arianism, condemned the Anomoians as well. The founder of the sect, Eunomius, who began his career as the stenographer of a bishop, had pushed Arian doctrine to its logical limit: Arius asserted that God the Father and Christ the Son were not of the same substance, whereas Eunomius emphasized the difference so much that he refused to accept the notion of the Trinity; it followed logically that the Anomoians could not baptize in the name of the Trinity. Instead Eunomius developed his own rite: a single immersion in the name of Christ's crucifixion.

Presumably Theodosius was baptized according to the Anomoian rite, with Belisarius standing by the baptismal tank. The baptism took place shortly before he set out on his expedition against the Vandal kingdom in North Africa in 533 and he acted as Theodosius' sponsor and godfather, performing the ceremony of single immersion in the baptismal tank and lifting him out in his arms. He became Theodosius' *koumbaros*, with all the obligations the word implies. Did

Belisarius' family also belong to this splinter neo-Arian sect? As far as we know, Belisarius was brought up in the Chalcedonian faith but perhaps his childhood and family connections left him with no great respect for the imperial papacy of Rome. The clues are inconclusive and the mystery remains unsolved.

Antonina became Theodosius' godmother and whatever maternal feelings she had for her godson soon began to quicken into sexual passion. Antonina liked eager young men. Belisarius was younger than she, but Theodosius was still a mere neophyte and very willing to learn. When Belisarius set out to conquer the Vandal kingdom in Africa, Antonina and Theodosius both sailed with him.

A great deal had happened in the 18 months before the Vandal expedition set sail. The *Nika* revolt of the previous year, which nearly toppled Justinian and Theodora, was crushed in a bloodbath and the victory was complete. The senatorial opposition was crushed. The old Constantinople Establishment that hated Justinian and despised Theodora might grind their teeth in rage as they prostrated themselves before them and kissed their shoes, but they were impotent and could grumble only in secret. Theodora must have enjoyed seeing them humbled. They had disdained her as the trash of the theatre; now let them grovel!

The conflagration had burned out the city centre but it prepared the way for a new building programme which would transform Constantinople and, as a by-product, give employment to the city's construction workers. We know of 34 churches in the city that Justinian built or rebuilt. Much of the construction would have happened anyway, for Justinian erected buildings to proclaim his greatness, but some of it replaced casualties of the *Nika* revolt, including the greatest church in the city, Hagia Sophia. The old basilica of Hagia Sophia, built by Theodosius II, had been reduced to ashes and so too, close by it, had the church of Hagia Eirene ('Holy Peace'), which the patriarch used for his daily services when he was not officiating at Hagia Sophia. A new Hagia Sophia was begun right away with breathtaking speed. On 23 February, only 40 days after the old basilica burned to the ground, the construction of the new church started and thousands of labourers – around ten thousand, we are told – set to work on it. The turnaround was so swift that Justinian must have been using architectural plans for a new church drawn up before the flames of the *Nika* revolt prepared the site for it.

Peace was purchased with Persia. The old shah, Kavadh had died on 13 September after a stroke, but before his death he placed the crown on the head of his son Khusro to mark him as his chosen heir. He made a wise choice: Khusro was to become the greatest of Persian kings of the Sassanid dynasty but, at the start of his reign, he needed time to consolidate his position. He was Kavadh's third male child and his two older brothers were not happy at being passed over by their father. The eldest was suspected of Mazdakite sympathies, while Kavadh's second son had lost an eye, which should have barred him from the throne, but he might have emerged as a rival nonetheless. Khusro was ready for peace with Byzantium. The negotiations lasted a year and what resulted was a peace without term. This Endless Peace came into effect in 533. Justinian agreed to pay Khusro 11,000 pounds of gold. It was an expensive accord but war was even more expensive and this peace was to last forever. Probably no one at the imperial court really believed that, but neither did they dream that war would break out again a mere seven years later.

The campaign against the Vandal kingdom in Africa was Justinian's first war of reconquest to restore the Roman Empire. There is a notion floating about the academic world that the recovery of the lost imperial provinces in the west was always Justinian's aim, and that he harboured this ambition from the moment he took the throne.[2] The notion is not without some merit, for Justinian belonged to the last imperial family of Byzantium whose native language was Latin, and the ancient grandeur of Rome no doubt gripped his imagination. As he saw it, it was the negligence of previous emperors that had allowed the western provinces to slip away. But let us not think that he made peace with Persia in order to divert resources westwards, so as to reconquer Roman Africa, Italy and even a slice of Spain, and by so doing, fatally weakened Byzantine strength in the very eastern provinces that provided most of the empire's revenue. The evidence for such a perception is weak.

Instead, the reconquest began because a golden opportunity dangled before Justinian's eyes and he could not resist it. But he was careful to limit the risk. The Vandal kingdom was a century old, and was showing its age. The Vandals had once been tough warriors when they were led into Roman Africa by their king, Gaiseric (428–77), but under his successors they slipped easily into the role of rich landowners, developing a taste for luxury in the process. Gaiseric, who was an immensely talented general, made his kingdom into a naval power and swept the Romans out of the western Mediterranean. He sacked Rome in 455, and his plunder included the daughter of the western Roman emperor, Valentinian III, who married Gaiseric's son and successor Huneric (477–84). It was their child, Hilderic, who was king when Justinian came to the throne. Hilderic, a grandson of a Roman emperor and proud of it, wanted good relations with Constantinople. He went so far as to abandon the Arianism of his Vandal forebears and become a Catholic. The Vandal nobles were not amused. They overthrew him and installed his cousin Gelimer on the throne instead.

When the Vandals conquered Roman Africa, many of the large landowners who could emigrate did so, but most must have had no choice but to stay and adapt to life as an underclass.[3] The Vandals made up only a minority of the population, and on the local level, not much changed. Roman legal and administrative traditions continued as before. But the Catholics found the religious climate very chilly. Gaiseric had been an occasional persecutor, but his two successors tightened the screws. Stubborn Catholics were harassed and sometimes put to death. In the town of Tipasa there were Catholics whose tongues were cut out by a Vandal officer because they refused conversion to Arianism. The story was well-known, for the victims could still speak after they lost their tongues, which everyone considered a marvel. In Constantinople a vocal lobby of exiled churchmen, merchants and dispossessed landowners from Africa cried out for help and, in 468, the emperor Leo made an effort on their behalf. He dispatched a great fleet against Carthage but the command was entrusted to the empress Verina's incompetent and corrupt brother, Basiliscus, and he was no match for Gaiseric. The Roman armada was utterly destroyed, with a loss of perhaps 400,000 men. It was crippling disaster; some 60 per cent of the imperial armed forces perished, and years later, people still shuddered when they remembered it.[4]

So, when Justinian announced his plan for a new expedition, there was consternation. Except for the African lobbyists, no one at court could muster any enthusiasm for it. The bureaucrats in charge of revenues and expenses were shocked and the army officers were fearful, for none of them had any experience in naval warfare. Yet no official dared protest, except one. The praetorian prefect John the Cappadocian had been removed from office by popular demand during the *Nika* revolt but by now he was back at his old desk. Theodora hated him and John returned the odium in equal measure, but Justinian valued his ability, for John knew how to raise revenue and save money by cutting corners. Now he spoke up to warn Justinian of the perils of an African campaign. The distances were great, communication was slow and even if the Byzantines took Africa, it would be difficult to retain it so long as Sicily and Italy were ruled by the Ostrogoths. They, like the Vandals, adhered to the Arian heresy and the Byzantines could expect little co-operation from them. Justinian listened and had second thoughts. He decided against the expedition.

And then he changed his mind again. A bishop arrived in Constantinople 'from the east', and told Justinian that God had sent him a message in a dream to go to Justinian and chide him for his hesitation, for He would bring him victory. In fact, in 531, the year when Belisarius won his great victory at Dara, a holy man had come to Constantinople from the east. Not a bishop but the abbot of the monastery of Mar Saba outside Jerusalem, the great St Sabas himself, whose loyalty to the Chalcedonian cause approached bigotry. He met the empress Theodora while he was in Constantinople and the encounter was brief and hostile. She asked for his prayers that she might conceive and have a son. The saint's reply was brusque. He would never pray God that Theodora give birth, for her whelp might be a heretic as ruinous to the empire as herself. Holy men had inherited the right of the Cynic philosophers in the pagan past to speak bluntly to the powerful, and St Sabas knew how to exercise it.

The main purpose of the saint's journey was to seek relief for Palestine, which had suffered dreadfully from the Samaritan revolt in 529 and even more from the harsh measures taken to suppress it, but while he was in the emperor's presence he urged him to extinguish the Arian heresy that lived on in Africa and Italy. Was St Sabas the model for the 'bishop from the east', who put iron into Justinian's resolve to invade the Vandal kingdom by reminding him that it was an emperor's duty to succour the faithful?

Possibly so, for Procopius, who tells the story, was not above fudging strict accuracy in order to recycle a story pattern that he found in the Father of History, Herodotus,[5] who told how the Persians arrived at their ill-fated decision to invade Greece a thousand years before Justinian's expedition against Africa. The Great King, Xerxes, summoned his nobles to announce his invasion and no one dared object until his uncle, Artabanus, spoke up to advise against it. Xerxes reacted wrathfully but later, when his anger cooled, he decided that his uncle was right. Then at night as he slept he had a dream that rebuked him for changing his mind. It was a malevolent dream, for Xerxes' great expedition was crushed. As Procopius recycled the story, John the Cappadocian took the role of Artabanus and the dream came to an anonymous bishop, whose archetype was perhaps St Sabas. Yet, unlike Xerxes' invasion of Greece, Justinian's Vandal expedition would be a stunning success. John the Cappadocian's advice was wrong as well as negative, which may have been the reason why Procopius made a point of putting it on the record.

Yet Justinian took only a limited risk. He committed a very modest army to the venture: some 10,000 infantry and 5,000 horse: about standard size for a small Byzantine expeditionary force. This would be no armada such as the ill-fated one that the emperor Leo dispatched against Africa in 468. The roustabouts on the docks of Constantinople who saw the fleet set sail must have wondered if they would ever see it again. Yet its departure was a splendid sight. Five hundred troop transports were mobilized, with 92 fast war galleys as escort vessels. The patriarch Epiphanius came down to the Sea of Marmora to give the fleet his blessing as it lay off the Julian harbour. Justinian and Theodora watched from the walls of the imperial palace as the ships spread sail, heading for the Hellespont and the Aegean Sea beyond.

Belisarius was in command and with him were Antonina and Theodosius. So also was Belisarius' legal advisor, Procopius, who was prepared to apply his well-honed literary skill to the subject of the Vandal war in Africa.

ANTONINA TOOK CHARGE OF SUPPLIES FOR THE FLAGSHIP. It was a pity that she was not the chandler for the whole fleet, for food poisoning almost wrecked the expedition before it crossed the Adriatic Sea. When the fleet reached Methone on the south-west tip of the Peloponnesus and lay there, becalmed, the men disembarked; but while they waited for a favourable wind they began to fall ill with dysentery. The ship's biscuit should have been twice-baked but John the Cappadocian, in his unceasing quest to skimp and save, had ordered it toasted in the hypocaust of a public bath. Since the baking was not thorough enough, it crumbled and began to stink. It was midsummer; the temperature soared, and the combination of heat and mouldy biscuit made the troops sick. The death-toll reached five hundred. John had made a costly blunder, which might have aborted the whole expedition. Belisarius restored his men to health by buying supplies of locally-baked bread, but he made a point of letting the emperor know how John had put the expedition in jeopardy. Antonina knew, if Belisarius did not, that Theodora would be happy to have any instances of John's maladministration reported. But John escaped punishment.

From Zacynthus, the fleet headed out into the Adriatic Sea. The wind was light and the crossing was slow: only on the sixteenth day did the fleet sight Sicily. The drinking water that the ships carried began to smell from algae forming in the tanks but thanks to Antonina, the flagship was spared. While the fleet was still at Zacynthus, she had taken precautions to preserve the flagship's water supply by bottling it in glass containers, burying them in sand to prevent breakage and then keeping them in the dark to inhibit the growth of algae. Thus while the rest of the fleet suffered, the flagship's drinking water remained wholesome until fresh supplies were available in Sicily.

When the fleet reached Syracuse Procopius disembarked, and while he was visiting the city he met an old acquaintance from his native Caesarea. He had just come from Carthage and could report that the Vandals had no inkling that the expedition was on its way. The Byzantine attack would come as a complete surprise. The captains and crews of the vessels that carried trade goods between Carthage and Constantinople must have learned something about the armada that was bearing down on the Vandal kingdom but apparently there was little or no transfer of intelligence between the Vandal overlords of North Africa and the traders calling at the port of Carthage. Belisarius was lucky and his luck held. Some three months after the fleet left Constantinople it reached Africa and landed without meeting resistance at Caput Vada, modern Ras Kaboudia, halfway between Sfax and Sousse. From there the army advanced overland towards Carthage and in four days reached Decimum, the Tenth Milestone outside the city. About four miles from Decimum, Belisarius found a good site for a stockaded camp where he left all his infantry under the command of Antonina. He himself rode forward with his cavalry.

Belisarius' career might have ended then and there if the defence of Africa had gone as the Vandal king Gelimer planned. He was at his country estate some distance outside Carthage when he learned that the Byzantine force had landed. He moved swiftly. He planned a three-pronged counterattack and had he been a steadier commander he might have routed the Byzantines. But his brother Ammatas, who was leading the spearhead advancing from Carthage against the invaders, attacked too early and fell in a skirmish with an advance force of Bulgars from Belisarius' army. As Gelimer pressed forward to the attack, he came upon his brother's corpse lying on the battlefield and was overcome with grief. He waited long enough to bury Ammatas and, while he delayed, lost his chance for victory. The clash at the Tenth Milestone ended with the Vandals fleeing in disorder.

Next day Antonina brought up the infantry and the whole army moved forward as far as Carthage, though for the first night it bivouacked outside the city, for Belisarius feared an ambush in the dark. But the following day his army entered Carthage and he ate lunch in Gelimer's magnificent palace. The meal had been prepared the previous day for Gelimer himself but Gelimer had fled and now Antonina, with Belisarius and his staff, feasted on Gelimer's food. The Catholics immediately reclaimed their churches from the Arians. In the great basilica of St Cyprian, Arian priests were preparing to celebrate the 'Cypriana', the festival of St Cyprian, bishop of Carthage, who was martyred in 257; but when the news of the Vandal defeat reached them, they made a swift exit and the Catholics repossessed the church.

It was now mid-September and winter lay ahead. Gelimer had suffered a defeat but he had not yet lost the war. He camped at Bulla, a journey of four days to the west of Carthage, where he offered a reward for the head of every Roman soldier brought to him. He summoned his brother Tzazon back from Sardinia, where he had sent him to put down a revolt while he was still blissfully unaware of the peril approaching from Constantinople. In the meantime his agents were active, cultivating the Berber tribes and offering bribes. Belisarius recognized danger ahead if he let Gelimer gain the initiative and in mid-December he forced Gelimer to battle by threatening his camp. The engagement was fought 30 miles west of Carthage, at a place called Tricamarum, and it was a complete victory. The Vandal army disintegrated. Gelimer fled to the mountains of south Numidia where the local Berbers gave him refuge.

The transmutation from king to hunted fugitive was more than Gelimer could bear. He composed a poem in Latin on his tribulations and, when it was finished, he sent a message to the Roman commander who was blockading him in his mountain hideout, asking for three gifts: a lyre so that he might make music to accompany his poem, a sponge to wipe away his tears, and a loaf of bread, for he had not laid eyes on one ever since the blockade began. He was a broken man. At the end of March the next year, 534, he surrendered.

Antonina spent the winter in Carthage and her alluring young godson Theodosius was with her.

On the voyage from Constantinople to Africa, quarters were cramped on the flagship and in the pressure cooker below deck Antonina's affection for young Theodosius flowered into infatuation. She cannot have been much less than 40 years old and had been sexually active for some 25 years, whereas Theodosius was an inexperienced youth with a young male's testosterone rush. Their attachment ripened into a classic affair of a young man with an older, practised woman whose husband was absorbed in his job. Belisarius was leading a risky campaign and his whole career hung upon the outcome. He was oblivious to the affair developing between his wife and his godson.

Yet while both Antonina and Theodosius were on board ship the opportunities for fornication must have been limited. Antonina was not incautious and Theodosius was no bold lover. However, while they were wintering in Carthage, the limitations which shipboard life imposed on the romance vanished. Belisarius was wrapped up in the business of war. The walls of Carthage had to be strengthened, for until the Vandals were finally defeated at the battle of Tricamarum there was a real danger of a counterattack, particularly after Tzazon returned from Sardinia with his troops. Antonina had plenty of opportunity to introduce young Theodosius to the joys of coitus. At first they were circumspect; then less so. Soon the affair was an open secret among the maids and man-servants. Yet Belisarius remained unaware.

Once he almost stumbled on the truth. He went into a storage room in the cellar of the palace in Carthage and there found his wife and Theodosius together. Theodosius had put on his clothes so quickly that he had no time to adjust his belt. It looked as if Belisarius had interrupted a tryst, as no doubt he had, and his suspicions were aroused. But before his anger boiled over,

Antonina explained that she had brought the lad down to this cellar room to help her conceal some valuable spoils which she wanted to sequester for her husband and herself. Belisarius understood; possibly he had even entered the cellar room himself intent on a similar mission. The Vandal kingdom was rich and the royal treasure of the Vandal kings belonged to Justinian and should go back to Constantinople. But the Byzantine soldiers were mostly poor men and expected some booty as the reward of war and the risks they had taken. Belisarius was no exception: the Vandal campaign would lay the basis for his vast personal fortune – and also for Justinian's suspicions about his integrity. If Antonina was trying to keep some valuable items out of the imperial treasury's clutches, so much the better as far as Belisarius was concerned. He approved. The Belisarius-Antonina enterprise believed in large bonuses for itself, as did all the officers in Justinian's armies, though they lacked equal opportunity. Belisarius accepted Antonina's explanation and forgot his misgivings.

In Constantinople, Justinian waited anxiously for news from Africa and at last, by the third week in November, word finally reached him. The Vandals had been defeated in the battle at the Tenth Milestone and Carthage had been captured and occupied. News of the final victory over the Vandals at Tricamarum must have been slow to arrive, for sailing in winter was always risky, but when it did, it was followed not much later by a report from some of Belisarius' officers that their general's loyalty was questionable and Justinian should beware. Jealousy and backbiting were endemic in the general staff but Belisarius seems to have encountered more of it during his career than Justinian's other generals and Antonina's presence in the army camp cannot have helped the situation. As it happened, the disaffected officers sent two copies of their slanderous dispatch to Justinian in two separate ships to make sure that at least one survived the perils of the voyage to Constantinople. One did and the dispatch was delivered to Justinian, but the ship that carried the other was captured and the message fell into Belisarius' hands and alerted him to the treachery that lurked in the path ahead. At least he was forewarned.

Justinian acted circumspectly. He decided to replace Belisarius and, as his successor, he sent out a eunuch named Solomon, a competent military officer but not, like Belisarius, a star general. Solomon owed his castration to an accident rather than a trader who gelded boys for the slave market, but his condition meant that no wife would share the commander's headquarters. Belisarius was given the choice of returning to Constantinople with Gelimer and the treasure he had captured at Carthage or remaining in Africa. Belisarius realized that Justinian was testing his loyalty and that it was time to return home and scotch the rumours which were floating about in court circles. Antonina and he set out together for Constantinople and Theodosius went with them.

WHATEVER JUSTINIAN'S PRIVATE SUSPICIONS MAY HAVE BEEN, he gave Belisarius a magnificent welcome when he returned to the capital. For almost six centuries, no one other than an emperor or member of the imperial family had celebrated a Victory Triumph. Triumphs for victorious generals belonged to the Roman republic, when conquerors such as Julius Caesar and his great rival Pompey paraded their captives and loot through the streets of Rome, ending their procession with a parade down the Sacred Way, through the Forum and up the Capitoline Hill to the Temple of Jupiter. For Belisarius the tradition was revived.

However the ancient rituals of the Roman triumph which went back to the Roman Republic needed modification. The Byzantine Empire was an autocracy where the emperor ruled as the vicegerent of God on earth. Though the old republican office of the consulship continued to exist and two consuls were still chosen each year, one in Rome and the other in Constantinople, their sole remaining function was to produce and contribute, in a small way, to the cost of their inaugural celebration at the start of the consular year. Belisarius did not ride in a chariot like a *triumphator* in ancient Rome. Instead he set out from his own house on foot and walked to the Hippodrome. Once there, he entered by the starting gates at the north end and strode forward until he stood below the imperial loge. There he prostrated himself before Justinian and Theodora, who looked down on him from their lofty thrones. Belisarius might be a conquering hero but in the sacred presence of the emperor and empress he was still a lowly subject and the ceremony was designed to emphasize the point.

Yet the victory parade of booty was magnificent. The tall, fair-haired Vandal captives made a vivid impression. Conspicuous among them were the Hasdings, the Vandal royals, including Gelimer himself who wore a cloak of purple cloth which was stripped from his shoulders before he, like Belisarius, prostrated himself before Justinian and Theodora. Over and over again he muttered the words from the book of *Ecclesiastes*, 'Vanity of vanities: all is vanity'.[6] What thoughts, we may wonder, were going through his mind at this time? Did he perhaps recall another verse from *Ecclesiastes* too, as he gazed up at the imperial loge, 'I saw under the sun the place of judgment, that wickedness was there; and the place of righteousness, that iniquity was there'?[7]

Among the treasures which Belisarius brought to Constantinople was the booty that Gaiseric had carried off to Carthage when he sacked Rome in 455. All of it was put on public display so that the citizens of the capital could behold it, and marvel at the fruits of victory. They could look at the loot from old the imperial palace on the Palatine Hill, which now Belisarius had found in Carthage. Also on display was the plunder from Jerusalem which was brought to Rome after a Roman army under the future emperor Titus took Jerusalem and destroyed the Second Temple in the year 70, more than four and a half centuries earlier. The Temple Treasure had been displayed in Titus' triumph in Rome and then lodged in the Forum of Peace, where the Vandals found it and brought it as plunder to Carthage. Now, less than a century later, Belisarius brought it to the New Rome, Constantinople. But the Temple Treasure did not remain in the Great Palace for long, for a spokesman for the Jewish community in Constantinople told Justinian that the only fitting place for it was in King Solomon's city. Whenever it was elsewhere, he said, it brought only misfortune: while it was in Rome, the Vandals had sacked the imperial palace; when it was removed to Carthage, the royal palace had fallen to the Byzantines. The Temple Treasure should go home.

Justinian accepted the warning. This was an age which heeded any intimations of the wrath of God. He sent the Treasure to Jerusalem and lodged it in various Christian churches. But Justinian and Theodora were not unkind to their defeated foes. Gelimer, the last of the Hasding royals, was granted an estate in Galatia in Asia Minor where he could live with his family, and the captive Vandal warriors were enrolled in the Byzantine army to fight for Justinian in the future. For Belisarius, there was a further honour in store: he was chosen consul for the following year. In his inauguration ceremony Vandal captives lifted him as he sat in the curule chair of office, high above their heads, and the bounty that he bestowed on the people of Constantinople to mark the occasion was plunder taken from the Vandals. His star was at its zenith. He was ready for a new theatre of war and he had not long to wait.

In Africa, Justinian created a third praetorian prefecture with seven new provinces out of the old Vandal kingdom and he legislated a new bureaucracy into being to govern it, with all the details spelled out in full, including even the salaries of the officials. The royal estates of the Vandal kings were confiscated and Africans whose property was seized by the Vandal occupiers were given five years to reclaim it. Tax receipts from the new prefecture should be more than enough to pay for the costs of administering and defending the new prefecture, or so Justinian imagined.[8] Yet all was not well. The Berber tribes were restless, for though Justinian was slow to realize it he had inherited a native problem in Africa. The Vandals had been fighting a losing battle against the Berber nomads, who raided the farming settlements on the fringes of the desert, and it was not long before they challenged the Byzantines who replaced the Vandals. An insurgency was waiting to happen. The war to pacify Africa had just begun.

MEANWHILE ANTONINA HAD THEODOSIUS. He was no longer poor, for some of the booty from Carthage had stuck to his fingers. He could thank Antonina for that, as well as Belisarius' gullibility. But Antonina's son, Photius, was watching his mother with a vigilance that was anything but benevolent. He was Antonina's unwanted child, the living evidence that she was no longer young and had lost her virginity at an early age. Moreover, he worshipped his stepfather, Belisarius, who gave him the affection that his mother denied. How soon he learned of his mother's adultery we do not know, but he quickly became aware that Theodosius' influence was growing and he resented it. He was being shoved aside. Yet it was not Photius, but Theodora whom Antonina really feared. Theodora was not easily deceived and in spite of her own background, or perhaps because of it, she had little patience with adulterous women.

She was waging a jihad against the human trafficking in young girls that went on outside the palace walls. In 528, only a year after she was crowned empress, she summoned the whoremongers and other entrepreneurs in the Constantinople sex trade, who toured the countryside to find impoverished peasants willing to sell their daughters. They then rented out the services of these poor girls in the city brothels. When the whoremongers were brought before Theodora with their stables of girls, she demanded that each of them declare upon oath what price he had paid the girls' parents. They chorused that they had paid five gold coins each,[9] which was no small investment. Theodora refunded their money, freed the girls and gave each of them one gold coin and new clothes. Henceforth all of Constantinople's brothels were to be closed.[10]

If Theodora thought that was the end of the problem, she was naïve, for what would the poor girls do once their new clothes became shabby and their gold coins spent? Harlots continued to ply their trade in the marketplace, selling their bodies for only enough to live on. Theodora had them rounded them up and sent them off to a convent named the *Metanoia*: the 'Convent of Repentance', where not all the ex-prostitutes found their new life of chastity to their liking. Procopius, who gives us a cynical version of Theodora's crusade against harlotry,[11] reports that some of the girls found a pious life so unbearable that they killed themselves, leaping to their deaths from the convent walls. Procopius relates the tale with a barely suppressed sneer.[12]

Yet, after Theodora was dead, Procopius produced an encomium on Justinian's building programme and in it, as we would expect, he presents the story of the *Metanoia* with a different spin. He reports that Justinian and Theodora together closed the brothels and remodelled a palace on the eastern shore of the Bosporus as a refuge for harlots, thus delivering them from their degrading

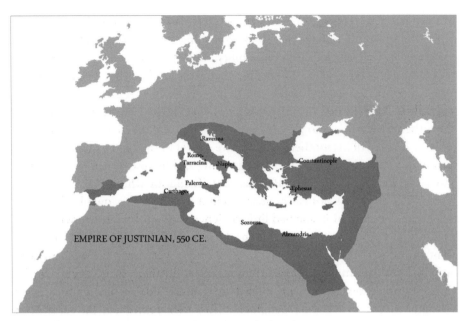

The Empire of Justinian, 550 CE.

profession. The imperial couple supplied their convent with an endowment and added subsidiary buildings. Here women rescued from the brothels were given comfortable surroundings and were left without any reason to abandon a life of virtue.[13] The panegyric mentions no suicides, though its avowal that the ex-harlots could not reasonably abandon a life of legislated virtue hints that some of them may have been unreasonable. The *Metanoia* foundation was perhaps the only convent that Theodora and Justinian built as partners, but it was not the only one that Theodora founded as a shelter for women who needed refuge. The persecution of the Monophysites in the western provinces brought an influx of nuns into Constantinople, from nunneries in Asia Minor and Syria, and Theodora built convents for them.[14] They go unmentioned in Procopius' panegyric.

Theodora had turned her back on the immorality of her early life, and as for Justinian, he always had a streak of puritanism. 'It is Our wish that everyone should lead chaste lives, so far as is possible', wrote Justinian in the preamble to a law,[15] dating to 535, outlawing procurers and panders who exploited girls for prostitution. Theodora must have heartily agreed with the law – she may have inspired it, for seven years had passed since she paid off Constantinople's whoremongers, and the problem was still far from solved. Yet Theodora did not stop trying, for she had seen at first hand the hard life of the common harlot who worked the streets. A nunnery was at least a refuge; in fact it was the only one.

In the same year as Justinian's edict expressed his desire for universal chastity, Belisarius opened the campaign against the Ostrogothic kingdom by invading Sicily. Antonina and Theodosius were in his entourage and their relationship was anything but chaste. Photius, Antonina's unwanted son, accompanied them and watched with all the resentment of a rejected child as their illicit love affair developed.

THERE WAS STILL TROUBLE IN AFRICA, BUT JUSTINIAN LEFT THAT IN THE HANDS OF SOLOMON, Belisarius' successor. Justinian expected Africa to bring in revenue enough to support the troops stationed there and he did not worry about their pay.[16] He turned his attention to a new project: an offensive against Ostrogothic Italy. Always the opportunist, Justinian saw a chance for conquest with little risk and he could not let it slip. In 526, Theoderic the Ostrogoth died and was interred in his little domed mausoleum which is still to be seen in Ravenna. His last years were gloomy and paranoid, as if he realized that time and tide had turned against his kingdom. Four years before his death, his son-in-law died, leaving his daughter Amalasuntha a widow and her son Athalaric the heir to the Gothic throne.[17]

When his father died, Athalaric was only 4 years old and only 8 when he became king himself. Amalasuntha was an able woman, quite capable of acting as regent for her son, but she had two counts against her. First, her gender: the Gothic warrior culture had no place for a female ruler. Second, she admired Roman culture and was herself half-assimilated into it. She was a woman between two cultures and she wanted her son to have a Roman education, which did not sit well with Theoderic's old retainers, who believed that a Gothic king should have a Gothic upbringing, with emphasis on fighting, drinking and wenching. These were the sort of pastimes that made a Goth into a real man, not the deracinated way of life that Amalasuntha wanted for her son. She was forced to give way and watch as her son degenerated into a drunken lecher. He died in 534, the same year that Constantinople witnessed Belisarius' victory triumph over the Vandal kingdom.

Amalasuntha was left isolated. Even before her son died, she learned that some Gothic malcontents were conspiring against her. She planned a counterplot to eliminate the three ringleaders and contacted Justinian to request asylum in case her plot failed. She even sent a ship with a cargo of money to Dyrrachium, modern Durazzo on the Adriatic coast, for if she had to flee she intended to take with her as much gold as she could. But her counterplot turned out as well as she hoped. The ringleaders were killed and Amalasuntha remained in Ravenna.

Yet she knew that she could not remain regent once her son was dead and she was not the sort of woman to relinquish power easily. There was one last remaining male scion of the Amal royal house and she thought that she could use him for her purposes. Theodahad was no warrior but, compared to most of the Goths, he was an educated man who had had a brush with Neoplatonic philosophy, though his neighbours knew him better as a rapacious landowner who had acquired most of Tuscany at their expense by fair means or, more often, foul. He already had a wife, which precluded marriage with Amalasuntha, but he readily accepted the alliance which she proposed: it would be a model of mutual assistance. Theodahad would be king in name but Amalasuntha would do the ruling. Her praetorian prefect, Cassiodorus, drafted an elegant letter to the senate which reported the partnership in glowing terms, likening it even to celestial mechanics. 'The very stars in the heavens are governed by mutual help, and order the world with their light by sharing, and exchanging toil', he asserted.[18] Another dispatch went to Justinian to ask for his congratulations. But before it reached Constantinople, Theodahad had deposed Amalasuntha and thrown her into prison.

It had all happened quickly. Athalaric died on 2 October 534, and Justinian had not yet heard the news when he dispatched a suave diplomat and Theodora's client, Peter the Patrician, as his envoy to the Gothic court. Theodora appreciated Peter's talents. He was an adroit servant of the regime as well as a man of learning who wrote a history of the times and also a book on court protocol and etiquette, which was near to Theodora's heart. Neither has survived. The reason why Justinian dispatched him to Italy was to negotiate the transfer of Lilybaeum, modern Marsala, in Sicily. Years before, Theoderic had ceded it to the Vandals as part of the dowry of his sister when she married the Vandal king Thrasamund and, now that Justinian had conquered the Vandals, he claimed it as his. The Goths thought otherwise. Peter was also instructed to assess the lie of the land and report back. But as he journeyed along the Via Egnatia from Constantinople to Italy, the situation kept changing.

On reaching Thessaloniki, he met Amalasuntha's envoys making their way to Justinian with the news that Athalaric was dead and Amalasuntha was partnered with a new king, Theodahad. When he reached Valona on the Adriatic shore and waited there for a fair wind to cross to Italy he met another embassy from the Gothic court. Theodahad informed him that Amalasuntha was in prison. Peter continued on his way to Ravenna but before he arrived there Amalasuntha was already dead, strangled in her prison on an island in Lake Bolsena. Theodahad claimed that the murder was done without his consent but he rewarded Amalasuntha's murderers. His action belied his words.

The account of Amalasuntha's death seems straightforward enough. But was the empress Theodora was involved in it in some way? She was taking a special interest in Italian affairs at this point in time. In the spring of 535 Theodahad addressed a letter[19] to Theodora in reply to one he had received from her. In it Theodahad mentions his receipt of instructions from Theodora to inform her first of anything he wants to ask from Justinian, for if he did Theodora intimated that she would be his advocate. Justinian, she assured him, did nothing without consulting her. Theodahad also made it clear that he fully understood Peter the Patrician's position: he was Theodora's client, chosen by her as her go-between. The letter is straightforward enough, remarkable only for Theodahad's acknowledgement of Theodora's authority. But at the same time as Theodahad wrote this letter, his wife Gudeliva wrote a shorter one to Theodora which was full of fulsome rhetoric and compliments, but it ended with a mysterious remark: '... though there should be no quarrel between the Roman realms, just the same an affair has arisen which should make me still dearer to your justice'. Some 'affair' had taken place which Queen Gudeliva believed Theodora would find not unwelcome. What was it?

Procopius' *Secret History*[20] provides a possible answer. He tells a tale of intrigue that implicates Theodora in Amalasuntha's murder. Peter had travelled alone on his way to meet Theodahad, with some menservants to be sure but without any colleagues to report on his intrigues. Nonetheless, the *Secret History* claims to report inside information. Theodora instructed Peter to see to it that Amalasuntha was killed and Peter carried out orders. According to Procopius' informant, Amalasuntha was still alive when Peter reached Ravenna and it was he who told Theodahad to have her strangled. As a reward for his services Theodora saw to it that Peter got the powerful post of Master of Offices and that much is true: Peter did get the promised appointment and as such became master of a small army of bureaucrats known as *magistriani*, whose tentacles reached even into the office of the praetorian prefect. If this tale is true, the 'affair' which Queen Gudeliva thought would please Theodora may have been the murder of Amalasuntha.[21]

And Theodora's motive? Jealousy, reports the *Secret History*. Amalasuntha was well-educated and nobly born, whereas Theodora knew that she was neither. She was also aware that the Gothic queen was beautiful, intelligent and accustomed to wielding power. She was no doubt a natural blonde too, unlike the blonde stars of the theatre with stage names like 'Chrysomallo' (Blondie).

She might acquire undue influence at Justinian's court and Theodora feared Justinian's wayward eye.

Most historians think that Justinian did *not* have a wayward eye: he respected and loved Theodora too much. But not all contemporaries would have agreed. Among the Ethiopic and Coptic stories told about the saintly monk, Daniel of Scetis, there is a legend about the patrician Anastasia,[22] where Justinian appears as a monarch with a well-developed sexual appetite and a taste for beautiful women who were well-read and clever. He admired Anastasia's intelligence and prudence so much that he wanted her to make her home in the imperial palace. Theodora was incensed, and to avoid her wrath Anastasia departed Constantinople for Egypt, where she founded a convent. After Theodora died, Justinian discovered Anastasia's whereabouts and tried to entice her back to the capital but she fled into the wilderness and lived there as a solitary for the last 28 years of her life. Daniel did not believe that Justinian had eyes only for Theodora, and he was a contemporary.

However, Theodora had another reason for intense interest in Italian affairs at this point in time and it had nothing to do with Amalasuntha.

She had just scored a triumph, a new *Henotikon* acceptable both to the patriarch of Constantinople, Anthimus, and Severus, the Monophysite patriarch of Antioch whom the persecution that Justin I initiated had ousted from his see. Justinian was supportive. But everything depended on Rome, where a new pope had just been chosen: an elderly cleric, Agapetus, son of Gordian.[23] What would his reaction be? Theodora was anxious to know. She had written to Agapetus and to the Roman senate and her agent, Peter the Patrician, let Theodahad know that a reply was expected. Theodahad passed on her command to the pope. The Ostrogothic kings never held the popes in awe and Theodahad was ready to press Agapetus hard if Theodora wanted it. The mysterious 'affair', which Queen Gudeliva mentions in her letter to Theodora, may have been the service Theodahad had done for her, acting as a go-between with Agapetus. Still, suspicion remains.

Amalasuntha's murder cannot have been entirely unwelcome to Justinian, for it gave him a pretext for invading Italy. Now he had a just cause for war: he could play the part of the avenger of Amalasuntha, the daughter of the great and good Theoderic the Amal. It was a cause that should appeal to the Franks on the north border of the Ostrogothic kingdom, for Amalasuntha's mother was a Frankish princess and Justinian was working to persuade the Franks to threaten the Goths from the north while Belisarius attacked from the south. Yet it is one thing to take advantage of a murder and another to instigate it. If a Scottish court were trying either Justinian or Theodora on a charge of inciting murder, it would have to bring down a verdict of 'Not Proven'.

So, in 535, Belisarius set forth on an expedition to Sicily with a modest force, barely half as strong as the army he had led against the Vandals, for the Gothic kingdom looked like a ripe plum ready to fall. A report was circulated in Constantinople that Belisarius was on his way back to Carthage but that was deliberate disinformation. Once he reached Sicily, he disembarked at Catania and occupied the island. Only at Panormus, modern Palermo, was there any significant resistance. The Gothic garrison there put up a fight but it lost heart when Belisarius' fleet entered the harbour and sailed so close to the city walls that archers swinging from the tops of the ships' masts could shoot arrows down on the Gothic troopers. They surrendered quickly.

At the end of December 535 Belisarius laid down his consulship in Syracuse. Sicily had fallen with amazing ease. At the end of the same year, Peter the Patrician was in Ravenna once again, negotiating a secret pact with Theodahad, who became pitifully anxious to please once he saw the Gothic will to resist crumbling in Sicily. He ordered Pope Agapetus to go to Constantinople to intercede for him and the pope knew better than to refuse, even though he had to pawn some of the Holy See's treasures to pay his travel expenses.[24] Peter found the irresolute king ready to surrender. In return for a guaranteed income of 1,200 gold pounds a year and a dignified exile in Constantinople he would hand over Italy to Justinian.

Peter journeyed back to Constantinople with the offer and Justinian was happy to agree. He dispatched Peter again to Ravenna to implement the bargain and ordered Belisarius in Sicily to prepare to receive the surrender of Italy. But when Peter returned to Ravenna he found the mood changed. The Goths had won a small success over the Byzantines in Dalmatia where they had killed Mundo, the Master of Soldiers in Illyricum, in a skirmish. Theodahad recovered his courage. He repudiated his pact with Peter and arrested him and his party. Justinian reacted by sending a new force out to Dalmatia led by Constantinian, who bore the title of 'Count of the Stables', and he quickly drove the Goths back to Ravenna. In Sicily, Belisarius received orders to launch his little army against the Gothic kingdom.

IT WAS IN SYRACUSE, WHERE BELISARIUS LAID DOWN HIS CONSULSHIP, THAT HE FIRST LEARNED about his wife's affair with his godson Theodosius. He was the last to know, for it seems that the romance was common knowledge within Belisarius' household. Two slave boys, who were assigned to the bedchamber where the trysts took place, had seen everything and they were not prudent enough to remain silent about them. They snickered that Belisarius' wife and his godson were copulating in the great commander's own headquarters. The gossip soon spread. It was unusual enough for a general to bring his wife along with him on a campaign, but a great deal more unusual for the wife to bring along her lover! The rumours reached the ears of two generals who were Belisarius' immediate subordinates, Constantine and Bessas, and even though they were men of the world they must have raised their eyebrows at this scandal. Yet the busybody who finally tattled to Belisarius was a slave girl named Macedonia, who admired her master and disliked Antonina. Perhaps she was even jealous of her. The consequence of her revelation, however, would give her cause to dislike Antonina even more.

Macedonia approached Belisarius with her secret after the conquest of Sicily, while he was still in Syracuse. She knew what the fallout would be if Antonina learned that she had tattled and so, before she revealed what she knew to Belisarius, she made him swear an oath on the Holy Writ never to betray her. Then, thinking he would never break an oath so sacred, she told him the whole story about his wife and her lover, Theodosius. Belisarius was beside himself with fury. He ordered Theodosius seized and killed. It is not clear whether the men he picked for the killing were his slaves or his guardsmen but, whichever they were, they knew Belisarius' mettle and how easily Antonina dominated him. They saw to it that Theodosius was not guarded too closely and he escaped to Ephesus.

The voyage from Sicily to Ephesus was long and Theodosius' flight probably took place early in the navigation season, while sailors could still encounter bad weather. Theodosius could hardly have made his journey without help. Possibly he escaped while Belisarius was otherwise engaged in Africa, for just after Easter, which in 536 fell on 23 March, an unexpected fugitive brought alarming news from Carthage. Solomon, the praetorian prefect and commander-in-chief of the army in Africa, reached Syracuse, having just escaped with his life from a mutiny of his troops. He needed help desperately. Belisarius took one hundred of his guardsmen, sailed to Africa, won a victory over the mutineers which saved Carthage but did not end the mutiny, and then was recalled to Syracuse by news that there was unrest among his own soldiers. Had they lost respect for their cuckolded commander? Or did they harbour some sympathy for young Theodosius whom Antonina had seduced? The general Constantine, who saw that his commander was downcast and pitied him, told him forthrightly what he himself would have done if he were the wronged husband. 'I would have killed your wife rather than the lad', he said. Antonina learned what Constantine said, and she resolved that he would pay dearly for it.

Belisarius may have considered an honour killing, as Constantine suggested, and Antonina must have been a little apprehensive; but if Belisarius had tried it, he would have made Theodora an enemy and in any case he was still deeply in love with his wife. Antonina managed to persuade him that Macedonia was lying. She coaxed him to hand over to her both Macedonia and the two young bedchamber attendants for punishment and, in spite of the sacred oath he had given Macedonia, he yielded. The penalty which the meddlesome trio paid for their betrayal was terrible. With help of a trusted retainer named Eugenius, Antonina cut out their tongues and then chopped them up into chunks of flesh which she stuffed into sacks and hurled into the sea. Even in a ruthless age when slaves had no rights, Antonina's vengeance was horrific.

Belisarius' household took note from the sidelines. Among those who must have been impressed was Antonina's own son, Photius. He had watched while his stepfather, whom he adored, was cuckolded and at the same time he learned the perils of revealing secrets that his mother wanted concealed. For the time being, he held his peace.

CONSTANTINE'S PUNISHMENT FOLLOWED IN DUE TIME. ANTONINA HAD TO WAIT MORE THAN A YEAR FOR HER REVENGE. Her chance came during the terrible siege of Rome in the abnormally cold winter of 537–8, when the Ostrogoths blockaded Belisarius and his army in the city for a year and nine days. Belisarius accused Constantine of making an attempt on his life and put him to death, to the consternation of his general staff. If we can believe the *Secret History*, Antonina was the cause of it.[25] The affair that led to his execution was a tempest in a teapot which got out of hand.

To understand what happened we need to comprehend how it was that tension had grown between Belisarius and Constantine. Before the siege of Rome began Praesidius, a citizen of Ravenna, had ridden south with a few attendants to join the Byzantine forces. The only valuables he brought with him were two daggers with sheaths made of gold and studded with gems. He made a rest stop at a church outside Spoleto, which Constantine held at the time. Somehow Constantine learned about Praesidius' daggers and sent one of his guardsmen to the church to seize them. Praesidius continued to Rome, followed soon afterwards by Constantine, and the long siege got underway. Praesidius chose not to report the theft right away but he did not forget it and, when the Byzantines began to get the upper hand and the Goths sought a truce, he thought the time was ripe to make his move. He complained about Constantine to Belisarius, who urged Constantine to make restitution. Constantine refused. He knew that soldiers of armies of occupation usually did 'liberate' valuable items as a matter of course and he had done nothing that any Byzantine officer would not do.

Finally, Praesidius brought the matter to a head. As Belisarius was riding in the Roman forum one day, Praesidius approached him and grabbed his horse by the bridle. Did the laws of the emperor allow a suppliant to be robbed? he cried out in a loud voice. Belisarius' attendants threatened him but he refused to loosen his hold on the bridle until Belisarius promised that his daggers would be returned.

Next day Belisarius summoned Constantine before his general staff and urged him again to restore the daggers; Constantine replied indignantly that he would rather fling them into the Tiber. Belisarius lost his temper. Didn't Constantine know that he was subject to his commander's orders? Yes, he was, answered Constantine, in everything save this. Then Belisarius ordered his guards to enter and when Constantine saw them approaching he cried out in alarm that Belisarius was going to have him killed. Belisarius retorted angrily that he had no such intention but Constantine drew his dagger and lunged forward to stab Belisarius in the belly. But Belisarius stepped adroitly behind Bessas, who shielded him with his body while two officers, Ildiger, who was Antonina's son-in-law, and Valerian caught Constantine by the arms and held him back. Belisarius' guards wrested the dagger from Constantine's hands and led him off to confinement in another chamber. Time passed and tempers cooled. Then, in cold blood, Belisarius had Constantine put to death. Procopius, who reports the story, judged his action 'unholy'.[26]

So Antonina had her revenge. Constantine's fellow officers would have acquitted him but Antonina intervened and insisted that Constantine die. It was an unpopular decision, for Belisarius had flown into a rage when he confronted Constantine and Constantine had good reason to think that Belisarius' guards intended to cut him down. His lunge at Belisarius was self-defence. No doubt he deserved some sort of punishment; yet Belisarius waited until all danger was past, and then made a cold, calculated decision to execute him. The general staff suspected Antonina's hand and, when Justinian learned how Constantine died, he was annoyed and the sparkle of Belisarius' star grew a little dimmer.

IF IT WAS ANTONINA WHO DEMANDED CONSTANTINE'S DEATH, BELISARIUS WAS IN NO GOOD POSITION TO REFUSE HER. The empress Theodora was in Antonina's debt, for she had just done her a great favour. She had shoved Pope Silverius off his papal throne and installed another pope who promised to be more amenable to Theodora's wishes. Theodora realized what an able ally Antonina could be. She was efficient, ruthless and untroubled by any religious scruples that might get in the way of what she wanted to do. Theodora forgot her disapproval of Antonina's wanton behaviour. Antonina became her trusted agent in Rome. Theodora needed a person of her mettle to unseat a pope from his throne.

To understand why Theodora was determined to remove Pope Silverius and replace him with a pope that she chose, we must turn our attention to the theological battlefront where Chalcedonian jousted with anti-Chalcedonian for the Holy Grail of orthodoxy. We need to pick up the thread in 527, when Justinian succeeded Justin to the throne and inherited Justin's policy of enforcing Chalcedonian belief by persecution.

Victory and Defeat in the Ecclesiastical Arena

WHEN JUSTINIAN BECAME EMPEROR IN 527 SEVERUS, THE ANTI-CHALCE-
DONIAN PATRIARCH OF ANTIOCH whom Justin I had replaced when he made
peace with the pope, was past 60 and had been living for eight years as an exile
in Egypt where the patriarch of Alexandria gave him refuge. Severus had by now
emerged as the leader of the Miaphysites,[1] who rejected the Creed of Chalcedon
as Nestorianism with a different label but never denied that Christ did have a
human nature. The bone of contention was whether His two natures remained
distinct after the incarnation, as the Chalcedonians believed, or united in Him
to form a single nature – a *mia physis*. That, the Miaphysites could claim, was
what the great patriarch of Alexandria, Cyril, had argued a century earlier.

In the modern secular world, this controversy might have been solved by
recognizing two distinct Christian sects that agreed to disagree over some
details. The *Henotikon* that caused the Acacian Schism had attempted a cautious
step in that direction. But the Byzantine emperor was God's representative ruling
over an imitation of Heaven on earth, and this earthly facsimile of Heaven had
room for only one correct belief. In the Byzantine thought-world, there was
one empire and one orthodox faith, and it was a mark of loyalty to accept it.
Severus considered himself a faithful subject of Justinian. He valued the unity of
Christendom and was reluctant to make any move to found a separate church.
Yet, once old Justin launched the persecution that Pope Hormisdas demanded
as the price for ending the Acacian Schism, the anti-Chalcedonian clergy found
themselves in deadly peril. Severus himself escaped to Alexandria only hours
before troops arrived to arrest him with orders to cut out his tongue. In Egypt
he was safe, for though the pope urged Justin to oust Timothy III, the patriarch
of Alexandria, and replace him with a stout Chalcedonian, Justin was too
prudent for that and Egypt remained a secure asylum.

In Severus' stead, Justin appointed a patriarch who had Hormisdas' *impri-
matur*, a stiff-necked prelate named Paul, who had been the superintendent of
a hospice in Constantinople. He was tough and his Chalcedonian credentials
were impeccable. He ordered that whenever the churches in his see celebrated

the Eucharist, the names of all the 630 bishops who had attended the Council of Chalcedon should be read out aloud to the congregation, thereby rubbing salt into the ecclesiastical wounds, which was Paul's intention. The Monophysites were incensed, for they considered that the very name of Chalcedon was the spawn of the Devil. They broke off communion with Paul and shunned his Eucharist, for they would not receive the Body and Blood of Christ from a Chalcedonian. Severus, exile in Egypt though he was, remained in their eyes the rightful patriarch of Antioch.

Severus had been born in Sozopolis in the province of Pisidia in Asia Minor, where his parents were members of the curial class, possessing enough property to make them eligible to sit on the local town council and assume the obligations that went along with membership. The most burdensome of these was to collect the taxes. In earlier centuries, when the Empire was prosperous and taxes relatively light, it was an honour to serve on the town council but now it was a duty that well-to-do persons were desperate to escape. The empire had grown hungry for revenue and taxes were hard to collect. If a town failed to meet its quota, councillors had to make up the shortfall and family fortunes could disappear into the tax-collector's maw. Joining the senatorial class was one way of escape but that was a path open only to the elite few. Joining the ranks of the clergy was another, for Christian clergy and Jewish rabbis were exempt from curial duties, and so it is not surprising that great numbers of men with property felt the calling to become clergymen. Justinian had to put a ceiling on the number of clergy attached to Hagia Sophia in Constantinople. Severus' grandfather had been bishop of Sozopolis, which must have helped to preserve the family fortune.

Severus' mother (his father was by then dead) sent Severus and his two older brothers to Alexandria and Beirut for their education. Alexandria's schools of philosophy were famous and Beirut possessed one of the great law schools of Late Antiquity. Severus graduated from his course in legal studies and had already purchased a toga to wear when he pleaded cases before a judge; but before he began his legal career, he first made a pilgrimage to Jerusalem. There he met Peter the Iberian, the son of the king of Iberia, modern Georgia – Peter was his baptismal name; his native Iberian name was Murvan. As a 12-year-old boy he had been taken as a hostage to Constantinople but he escaped to Jerusalem, where he became a monk and founded a monastery at Maiuma near Gaza, which carried on the theology of the patriarch of Alexandria, Cyril.

Severus became Peter's disciple. He abandoned his legal career, instructed a friend to sell his clothes and furniture and give the money to the poor and, sending his slaves back home to Sozopolis, he became a monk at

Interior, SS. Sergius and Bacchus Church.

Maiuma. His first meeting with the emperor Anastasius was in 508, when he journeyed to Constantinople to plead for the anti-Chalcedonian monks in Palestine who were suffering persecution, for most of the Palestinian monasteries were firmly on the side of the Chalcedonians and wasted no love on Monophysites. Anastasius took his measure and liked what he saw. A coalition of Neo-Chalcedonian monks[2] in Palestine at this point in time was trying hard to show that Cyril's teachings were compatible with the Chalcedonian Creed and the arguments that they put forward were attractive; but Severus, who was a formidable researcher, demolished them with a barrage of erudition. Anastasius invited Severus to remain in Constantinople but Severus declined and returned to Maiuma.

In 512 the patriarch of Antioch, Flavian, was deposed under suspicion of treason, for he was a friend and ally of the patriarch of Constantinople who was accused of plotting rebellion against Anastasius. Then, as one of Severus' biographers[3] put it, 'The emperor and God approved the choice of Severus'. A deputation arrived at his monastery when most of the monks were away and knocked on the door. No answer. They knocked again, more urgently. Finally Severus heard them and came down from an upper chamber, opened the door and was handed a summons to a church council at Sidon. Once there, he learned the reason for the deputation. He was the emperor's choice as the new patriarch of Antioch. At first he was reluctant to accept but he let himself be persuaded and journeyed to Antioch, where he discovered a new vocation as a popular, charismatic preacher. There he remained until Justin made peace with Rome. One of the conditions for peace that Pope Hormisdas demanded was the suppression of the anti-Chalcedonian clergy. Severus fled Antioch for Egypt, narrowly escaping capture.

Justinian's accession in 527 brought no immediate relief. He abhorred heterodoxy of any sort. 'I hate heresy', he states flatly in one of his laws.[4] He began his reign with a flurry of measures directed against both those who did not embrace Christianity and those whose version of it was incorrect. Paganism was given no quarter. Earlier laws that targeted pagans were renewed and reinforced. The last stronghold of pagan philosophy, the Neoplatonic Academy in Athens, was closed down and the so-called 'House of Proclus' on the south slope of the Acropolis where the head of the Academy lived was abandoned – hurriedly, it would appear, from the evidence of its remains that have been excavated. Its close neighbour, the temple of Asclepius, became a Christian pilgrimage site.[5] The Neoplatonic Academy looked back to the Academy that Plato had founded almost nine centuries earlier and, though there was no direct line of descent from it down to the Academy of Justinian's day, the closure marked the concluding chapter of a philosophical tradition in Athens which went back a thousand years.

But the Monophysites were too numerous to be legislated out of existence. If Justinian failed to grasp that fact himself, he had Theodora at his elbow to remind him. By 531 it was clear even to Justinian that the anti-Chalcedonian persecution, which old Justin had initiated, was not working. Monophysite monks and nuns from the eastern provinces who were driven from their convents were filtering into Constantinople seeking shelter, but they remained stubbornly anti-Chalcedonian.[6] Justinian changed course. Active persecution ceased for the time being and he decided to try the approach that Theodora urged upon him: dialogue. Theodora and Justinian sponsored a conference in the Palace of Hormisdas between the Chalcedonians and the Monophysites. They invited Severus to attend but he refused, thinking that nothing could come of it. The conference went ahead anyway and it began a new chapter in the conflict in which Theodora would take a hand; she came within a smidgen of winning peace.

PAUL, WHO HAD REPLACED SEVERUS AS PATRIARCH OF ANTIOCH, DID NOT LAST LONG. A Monophysite archdeacon of his was killed and Paul fell under suspicion of homicide. The slain archdeacon's son escaped and got word of his father's death to Theodora, who was already living with Justinian, and she saw to it that it reached her lover. Our source for this story is the twelfth-century Monophysite patriarch of Antioch, Michael the Syrian,[7] who may have borrowed it from John of Ephesus, who could in turn have learned it from Theodora, for he was one of her friends. Paul retired from the patriarchal throne with an imperial nudge in the direction of the exit and died soon afterwards. His successor, Euphrasius, was a more kindly man but his theology was equally Chalcedonian. He lost his life in 526 in one of the numerous earthquakes that devastated Antioch: the floor of his palace collapsed and Euphrasius tumbled down into the cellar beneath, where vintners were sealing wine jars with boiling pitch and Euphrasius fell into the seething cauldron. The pitch cooked Euphrasius' body until the flesh fell off the bones and his remains would have been unidentifiable, except that his head hung over the rim of the cauldron and enough of his face survived to be recognizable. So related the Monophysites,[8] who thought that his death was a manifestation of God's justice. There was a less grisly Chalcedonian report that Euphrasius was simply killed by falling debris and some Chalcedonians tried to claim that he was snatched up to Heaven, like the prophet Elijah.

While Justinian and Theodora were waiting for Justin to die they lived in a mansion built two centuries earlier for a prince of the Persian royal house,

Hormisdas, who had defected to the Romans when the first Constantine was emperor. In 519 Justinian started construction of a palace chapel there and dedicated it to SS Peter and Paul. Like most imperial buildings it made a statement: that Justinian, like his uncle, was a worthy Chalcedonian, even more so than the *grande dame* Anicia Juliana whose great church of St Polyeuctus was also arising at this time. The year 519 was when Justin made peace with Rome and ended the Acacian Schism. Justinian's new church commemorated the mending of the split and the Chalcedonian victory and he wrote Pope Hormisdas to request relics of SS Peter, Paul and Lawrence for it.[9] It was clearly intended as a Chalcedonian place of worship. Justinian had as yet no doubts about the Chalcedonian faith. But not two years later Justinian and his Monophysite paramour set up their household in the Hormisdas palace.

Once Justin was dead and Justinian and Theodora moved into the Great Palace, Justinian turned the Hormisdas Palace over to Theodora. She made it a place of refuge for Monophysite clergy and monks who had been expelled from their churches and monasteries. They came from all over the eastern provinces: stylite saints who were driven off the pillars where they kept their lonely vigils, hermits who were thrust out of their cells and bishops expelled from their bishoprics. By the mid-530s the religious community that Theodora organized in the Hormisdas Palace held no less than five hundred of these fugitive Christians whose faith was now outlawed.[10] They crowded all the available space. One who knew the Hormisdas Palace well was John of Ephesus, for he spent a couple of years there himself and he reports that visitors marvelled at the numbers of these blessed men and their venerable appearance.[11] Some stood without moving a muscle as they raised their voices in holy songs and canticles that filled the rooms and courtyards of the palace. Every chamber and hallway was crammed with tiers of planks where the holy men might recline in the discomfort appropriate to sanctity. For the pillar saints and solitary hermits and for the hallowed old men who merited great honour Theodora had private cells built. There was no effort at concealment. Everyone in Constantinople knew that there was a refuge for anti-Chalcedonian holy men in the Hormisdas Palace, under Theodora's patronage, and many visitors, including Chalcedonians, were awed and dumbfounded by what they saw.

Among them was Theodora herself. She came regularly every two or three days to receive the blessings of these holy men and pay them reverence. Justinian built a passageway connecting the Palace of Hormisdas and the Great Palace to make her visits easy, for Theodora disliked physical exertion. Sometimes Justinian came with her and was impressed by the sanctity of these men of God, much as he rejected their definition of the Trinity. Little by little she brought him over to the view that these were persons who deserved the blessing of Heaven, even though they could not stomach the Chalcedonian Creed.

John relates a story that illustrated how greatly God cared for the refugees in the Hormisdas Palace. Monophysite worshippers would gather there from the city to take communion with the refugees and once, when an immense congregation had crowded into a great hall of the palace which housed a martyr's shrine, the floor collapsed. The palace echoed with the cries and wails of the injured. But God saved his pious believers. Not one of them was killed. Clearly they were saved by a miracle. Justinian and Theodora were astonished.[12]

It was probably after this near-disaster that Justinian and Theodora jointly built a church adjoining SS Peter and Paul, which may have been for the use of the anti-Chalcedonians[13] for it was dedicated to two saints that were dear to them. They were Sergius and Bacchus and the building still survives in present-day Istanbul. Sergius and Bacchus, the story goes, were guardsmen serving a pagan emperor named Maximianus, whom we cannot identify. They were favourites of this unknown emperor, so much so that their comrades grew jealous of them and denounced them as Christians, for Maximianus was a bitter persecutor and would not take the accusation lightly. He ordered them to take part in a sacrifice to Zeus and, when they refused to eat the flesh of the sacrificial victim, they were sent off to be martyred. The site where Sergius was beheaded was at the Roman fort of Rusafa in the Syrian steppe and there, in 431, the bishop of Mabbug built a church dedicated to the saint. It became a great pilgrimage shrine which the emperor Anastasius renamed Sergiopolis and made a metropolitan bishopric. The church of SS Sergius and Bacchus is now Küçük Ayasofya Camii, the Little Hagia Sophia mosque, separated from the seashore by a railway track. The vibrations from the passing trains are slowly cracking the dome and the building no longer treasures the heads of SS Sergius and Bacchus and other Christian relics. But inside it a great dedication inscription below the dome still calls upon God to guard 'the rule of the sleepless sovereign and increase the power of the God-crowned Theodora whose mind is adorned with piety, whose unceasing toil lies in unsparing efforts to nourish the destitute'.

Piety and compassion for the needy and helpless were virtues which Theodora cultivated. But now the 'God-crowned' empress was about to launch a new initiative in the theological battlefield.

THE PERSECUTION OF THE ANTI-CHALCEDONIAN CLERGY THAT THE OLD EMPEROR JUSTIN INITIATED had not worked. The anti-Chalcedonian clergy were driven from their churches and found refuge wherever they could. Monks were driven from their monasteries and nuns fled from their convents, many of them to Constantinople. Severus, the acknowledged Monophysite leader, fled to Egypt. But the Monophysite congregations remained faithful; persecution fostered a sense of community among them and the theological battle lines grew more rigid. Oppression only added to the charisma of the monks and holy men who were forced out of their retreats, some of whom took refuge in the country villages where they spread their doctrines. The unity of the empire was threatened. In the minds of men the church was still one, with its five great archbishoprics, chief of them Rome, and it was still unthinkable that there should be two divergent paths to salvation. But the unthinkable could happen and Justinian was aware of it. He decided to abandon persecution and try dialogue.

Dialogue was what Theodora had been advocating and now we begin to recognize her fine hand behind imperial policy. Justinian began to heed his wife's advice. An invitation went out to the exiled bishops in their places of refuge to gather at the Hormisdas Palace and most responded willingly, though Severus himself declined. When they reached Constantinople they presented Justinian with a long petition which emphasized their loyalty. 'We pray God, the bountiful giver, on our behalf to reward your serenity and the God-loving queen with good gifts from on high, and to bestow peace and tranquillity upon you, and to set every rebellious people as a stool beneath your feet.'[14] Long days they had passed in the desert, they said, beseeching God to forgive their own sins and safeguard the wellbeing of the emperor. When they were commanded to come to Constantinople they came, for it was their duty to obey. But on the subject of religious dogma they would not budge. They were brought up in the faith ratified at the Council of Ephesus where Nestorius was condemned and his doctrine rejected as heresy. As they saw it, the Creed which the Council of Chalcedon had adopted in 451 was simply Nestorianism – and indeed the distinction between the two was very subtle. Even convinced backers of Chalcedon did not always find it easy to draw a line between their doctrine and the teachings of the heretic Nestorius.[15]

The dialogue in the Hormisdas Palace continued for a year and climaxed in 533 with a formal debate in the audience chamber of the palace. It lasted three days. The six debaters on the Chalcedonian side were led by the bishops of Ephesus and of Philippi but among their group was Anthimus, bishop of Trapezus,[16] though he preferred to make his home in Constantinople. For some reason, Theodora noticed him. Perhaps his arguments for acceptance of the Chalcedonian Creed were more nuanced than those of his fellows or possibly she had picked up a rumour that, even though he was in the Chalcedonian camp, he was no diehard. She may even have sounded him out in a private conversation and decided to keep an eye on him, for he might be useful in the future.

Yet for the moment Theodora's strategy was to be sweetly reasonable and support Justinian's efforts to reconcile the Chalcedonians and their opponents. The principal clergyman on the anti-Chalcedonian side was the formidable missionary John, bishop of Tella,[17] who had been driven from his see by Justin's persecution and had been quietly ordaining Monophysite clergy along the frontier between Persia and the Roman Empire. Justinian and Theodora tried hard to win his support with but scant success. Yet the first day of the debate went well. Both camps agreed that the father of Monophysitism, Eutyches, had been too extreme. He had been a Monophysite through and through, who believed that Christ never had more than a single nature and that it was divine. None of the debaters in the Hormisdas Palace was willing to go so far as that. No one claimed that Christ had no human nature whatsoever. The anti-Chalcedonian debaters all opted for the doctrines of Peter the Iberian and his disciple, Severus, the exiled patriarch of Antioch, absent though he might be from the conference. They could accept the *Henotikon* that Justin had repudiated but they could not swallow the Chalcedonian Creed nor the hated Tome of Leo, which was a red flag in the theological bullring.

On the second day of the debate, the Monophysites challenged their opponents to show what the difference was between their doctrine and the heresy of Nestorianism. Both the Nestorians and the Chalcedonians preached that during His ministry on earth Christ possessed two distinct natures, one human and the other divine. The Monophysites produced evidence that showed – so they claimed – that what the Chalcedonians preached was nothing other than the Nestorian heresy renamed and, as proof, they pointed out that the Council of Chalcedon had restored two of Nestorius' strongest supporters, Theodoret of Cyrrhus and Ibas of Edessa, to their bishoprics, even though 20 years earlier the First Council of Ephesus had condemned them, along with Nestorius, and defrocked them. Why, the anti-Chalcedonians demanded, had the Council of Chalcedon accepted these defenders of Nestorius back into the fold of orthodoxy and restored them to their bishoprics? Was this not proof that the Chalcedonians found no fault with Nestorius' heretical doctrines?

The Chalcedonians defended themselves as best they could. They pointed out that the Council of Chalcedon had required Theodoret and Ibas explicitly to condemn Nestorius before they were restored to their bishoprics. The anti-Chalcedonians might have replied that the Council of Chalcedon had failed to condemn the *writings* of Theodoret and Ibas, which were clearly Nestorian. Did the rehabilitation of these two supporters of Nestorius mean that what they wrote was considered acceptable? That would have been an embarrassing question for the Chalcedonians but their opponents did not press their advantage. Yet the problem did not go away. It was a chink in the Chalcedonian armour and we shall meet these writings of Theodoret and Ibas again.

Then, as the conference moved into its third day, Justinian himself attended and pushed hard for a solution that was dear to his heart, the so-called Theopaschite formula, which held that one of the Trinity had suffered in the flesh on the cross. There was a whiff of possible heresy about it; yet nothing in the formula violated the letter of the Chalcedonian Creed. It was first broached in Constantinople in 519 by a delegation of four monks from the Roman province of Scythia Minor at the mouth of the Danube River. Justinian had liked it then, and dispatched the Scythian monks to Rome to win over Pope Hormisdas. The pope delayed making any answer but eventually he decided that the Scythian monks were a nuisance and sent them packing. Justinian, however, did not forget the formula and, after the dialogue in the Palace of Hormisdas ended without substantial result, he promulgated it himself as an imperial edict. He then sent a delegation to Rome, led by two bishops who brought with them a statement of faith written in Justinian's own hand asking for papal approval.[18]

In Rome there was a new pope, John II, who had just been chosen in an election tainted by suspicions of simony. He was happy to welcome the delegation from Constantinople and even happier to receive the rich gifts that the delegates brought with them. But on the question of the Theopaschite formula he took time to consider and, while he pondered, Justinian waited with growing impatience. He went so far as to reissue his Theopaschite Edict in November of 533, sending it to the main metropolitan sees, including Thessaloniki where Rome claimed jurisdiction, and even to Rome itself. John overlooked the affront but he would not be rushed. There was nothing that Justinian could do to hurry him, for he had no physical control over Rome – not yet, at least. Finally, on 25 March 534, the pope gave his approval. By then Belisarius had conquered the Vandal kingdom and restored North Africa to the empire and many Romans must have been wondering what Justinian's next military objective would be.

THE YEAR 535 WAS CROWDED WITH IMPORTANT EVENTS. Belisarius conquered Sicily and in Africa Belisarius' successor, Solomon, who held the combined posts of praetorian prefect and Master of the Soldiers, pacified the restive Berber tribes, or so Justinian imagined. Wrongly, as it turned out, for peace in the erstwhile Vandal kingdom was only temporary and among the Byzantine troops in Africa, too, mutiny was simmering. In Italy Amalasuntha was murdered and her young daughter Matasuntha remained as the only descendant of the great Theoderic the Amal. The same year saw the death, on 7 February, of the patriarch of Alexandria, Timothy III, whom Theodora had met during her brief stay there after Hecebolus discarded her. Four months later, Pope John II died and the Roman see became vacant. Then, a month after Pope John, death came to Epiphanius, the patriarch of Constantinople. Fate, blind though it might be, seemed to be hastening change.

It was about this time that the stylite saint Z'ura climbed down from his pillar near Amida, and arrived in Constantinople. We know his adventures because John of Ephesus wrote a short biography of him.[19] Z'ura belonged to the monastery of the blessed Habib close by Amida and many stories were told about his miracles. Once, it was said, a marauding band of Huns invaded the region and Habib and his monks took shelter in a fort, one of the places of refuge which the imperial government built in danger zones. They were without permanent garrisons but their strong walls provided protection for the local population until the raiders got their fill of loot and departed. Thinking the Huns had done their damage and moved on, Habib sent Z'ura to inspect the monastery and see what harm it had suffered. As he was walking along the path carrying a cross, a band of Huns fell upon him and one of them raised an arm to bring his sword slashing down upon him. But the Hun found himself suddenly immobile. He could not move. His sword remained raised above his head, his arm frozen, and Z'ura did not release him until all the rest of the Huns were gone. This was truly a formidable man of God.

When Habib died, Z'ura climbed up on a column and began his career as a stylite saint. Pilgrims crowded to see him, perched on his seat between Heaven and Earth. Disciples flocked to him and the sick and the paralyzed came in throngs to receive the blessings which he pronounced from the summit of his column. But the persecution of the anti-Chalcedonians forced him off his perch and he arrived in Constantinople with ten followers. He was a man of blunt speech and, when he had an audience with Justinian, he spoke his mind with such insolence that Justinian flew into a rage. The Creed of Chalcedon was correct, the emperor asserted with heat, and if Z'ura and his disciples taught the truth when they preached their Monophysite doctrine, then let God send a sign to prove it! Until He did so, Justinian decreed the death penalty for all who anathematized the Creed of Chalcedon!

Z'ura's reply was equally forthright. It is not only we, he declared, who anathematize the Creed of Chalcedon that splits Christ into two parts, but the very angels in Heaven anathematize it, too. True believers needed no sign, but since Justinian wanted one, then the Lord would place a mark upon Justinian's own body that would bear witness to the loathing that He felt for the faith of Chalcedon. Justinian left the audience chamber in high dudgeon.

Next day Justinian fell ill, and became delirious. A fearful tumour appeared on his head. Theodora recognized its meaning and kept it secret. She let no one enter Justinian's bedchamber except for his physicians and a chamberlain. To Z'ura she sent a messenger to request his prayers and invite him to come at once to make peace. Z'ura came and recognized that the tumour was the sign that God had sent. He prayed for Justinian and, within the same hour, Justinian's delirium disappeared. Filled with dread, Justinian assented to all Z'ura requested and Theodora gave him a villa in Sycae, across the Golden Horn. But Justinian was still clung stubbornly to the Chalcedonian Creed. He refused to abandon it.

Yet Theodora was delighted with Z'ura. It did not matter to her that he was rude and malodorous, for she felt that a palpable aura of holiness surrounded him. She chose him to administer the rite of baptism to her. Theodora ceased to be a mere catechumen. At last she could partake of the Body and Blood of Christ as she sat in the gallery of Hagia Sophia that was reserved for women and watched the Eucharist performed in the chancel below.

THEN IN FEBRUARY OF 535 SEVERUS ARRIVED IN CONSTANTINOPLE AFTER A DANGEROUS WINTER VOYAGE FROM ALEXANDRIA. He had changed his mind and decided to come after all. As he had expected, the year-long dialogue that had taken place in the Palace of Hormisdas had been inconclusive, but Justinian's invitation to come to Constantinople was still pressing and Theodora was persuasive. Severus set out from Alexandria a week before Timothy III, the patriarch of Alexandria died, even though winter storms made navigation perilous. He got a warm reception from Theodora and a somewhat cooler one from Justinian, who tried and failed to convert him to Chalcedonianism. Severus found Theodora an eager but naïve theologian: he noted her lack of historical perspective in a letter which is still extant.[20] But he appreciated her assistance and fortune soon gave her a chance to help the anti-Chalcedonians even more. When Epiphanius the patriarch of Constantinople died, Theodora saw a chance to replace him with a more malleable churchman. She secured the election of the bishop of Trapezus, Anthimus.

There was a minor problem that could prove a sticking point. Canon law forbade bishops to transfer from one bishopric to another and thus Anthimus, who was already bishop of Trapezus, was not eligible to become bishop and patriarch of Constantinople. But Theodora smoothed the way. Anthimus was much respected for his asceticism and he appeared to be a stout defender of Chalcedon. In the debate between the Chalcedonians and the anti-Chalcedonians which had taken place in the Palace of Hormisdas almost two years before, Anthimus had been a spokesmen on the Chalcedonian side. Yet Theodora had divined that Anthimus had private doubts and she saw to it that Anthimus and Severus met. They discussed the differences that divided the Chalcedonians and the Monophysites and Severus converted Anthimus.

Severus had never denied the humanity of Christ but he believed that it was distinct from the nature of the Logos or, to use a term that Severus preferred, the *hypostasis* of the Logos. Yet, within Egypt itself, Severus' Miaphysite brand of Monophysitism was losing ground to the Julianists, led by Julian, bishop of Halicarnassus, who had been forced from his see at the same time as Severus and had once been a friend of his. But in Egypt there was a parting of the ways. Julian was an extreme Monophysite, who pushed the Single Nature Doctrine to its logical conclusion, arguing that the divine element in Christ absorbed his human element so much that his body was incorruptible from birth and was never susceptible to decay. Severus could agree that Christ was incorruptible after the Resurrection but before it, during His life on earth, his mortal body was like any other man's. Another controversial point had to do with the expulsion from the Garden of Eden and the consequent Fall of Man. Severus held that Adam was created as a mortal man, with a body that was corruptible and subject to decay after death. Julian argued that Adam was immortal and incorruptible until he sinned and was driven from Eden.

The Julianists were known as Aphthartodocetists: 'believers in the doctrine of incorruptibility'. Their numbers in Egypt had mushroomed and now that the patriarch, Timothy III of Alexandria, was dead, they saw a chance to grab power. Severus must have guessed that there would be trouble as soon as Timothy breathed his last, for one objective of his risky winter voyage to Constantinople, just before Timothy's death, must have been to alert Theodora to the danger in the see of Alexandria. Fortunately for Severus, Theodora's chamberlain Calotychius was on the spot when Timothy died and saw to it that Timothy's secretary, Theodosius, was chosen as the next patriarch of Alexandria. Theodosius was a steadfast Miaphysite and the news of his election must have pleased Severus when it reached him. But, while Theodosius' investiture was in progress, a mob burst into the Great Church of Alexandria, hurled him off the patriarchal seat and enthroned an Aphthartodocetist instead, an archdeacon named Gaianus. Theodosius narrowly escaped with his life. Severus needed Theodora's support as much as she needed him.

It was Theodora who brought Severus and the new patriarch, Anthimus, together and, as she hoped, there was a meeting of minds. Anthimus gave Severus a letter confessing his anti-Chalcedonian belief and sent another to Theodosius in Alexandria. The patriarch of Jerusalem was a fellow traveller. No diehard opposition need be expected from that quarter. Ephraem, the patriarch of Antioch, was a stout Chalcedonian, but he could not hold out if the emperor supported the formula of Anthimus and Severus. The wound that had tormented Christendom seemed on the verge of healing. Everything now depended on Rome.

POPE JOHN II WAS DEAD AND HIS SUCCESSOR, AGAPETUS, WAS AN UNKNOWN QUANTITY. Even before Anthimus announced his conversion, Theodora had sent off letters to him and to the Roman senate, as well as to king Theodahad. Theodahad, anxious to please, wrote back promptly that he had ordered Agapetus and the Senate to reply without delay,[21] and presumably they did what they were told. Neither the popes nor the senators in Italy ever had any stomach for defying their Ostrogothic overlords. But we do not know what they said.

The auguries were not good. Agapetus belonged to one of the great Roman families that had already supplied the church with one pope. He was an old man when he ascended the throne of St Peter and his many years, allied with his aristocratic background, had stiffened his intolerance of deviant churchmen. He had already shown his hand in the African prefecture. Once the Vandal kingdom in Africa was destroyed and Arianism had fallen from grace, some of the Arian clergy switched their allegiance to Catholicism and expected that the Catholics would receive them and integrate them into the Catholic priesthood. It would have been a generous, diplomatic gesture if they had. But the Catholic church in Africa was never generous and Agapetus supported its tough stand. The Arian clergy had shown little compassion for the Catholics in Africa when the Vandals had persecuted them and Agapetus was not ready to forgive and forget.

Agapetus had already received a letter raising the tocsin from Ephraem, the patriarch of Antioch. Ephraem was a former soldier and within his see he enforced the Chalcedonian faith with the mindset of a military man. The agreement between Anthimus and Severus threatened to abort his mission. From the monasteries in Palestine, too, cries of alarm reached the pope. St Sabas, the leader of the community of the holy hermits in Palestine, had died in the last month of 532 but his spirit lived on among the devout men whom he had once led. During his lifetime he had been a doughty defender of Creed of Chalcedon and his intransigence lived on in the Palestinian hermitages.

Hence Agapetus had been made well aware of the dangers which the Creed of Chalcedon faced before he reached Constantinople in March of 536. But in fact, he did not come to deal with the theological crisis, at least, not ostensibly. Theodahad, the Ostrogothic king, was alarmed at the prospect of a Byzantine attack to avenge Amalasuntha's murder. Sicily had already fallen and an invasion of Italy was in the offing. Theodahad ordered Agapetus to go to Constantinople and seek a rapprochement with Justinian and Agapetus obeyed. The Holy See could not afford the travel expenses but Agapetus dared not refuse Theodahad's orders. He arrived in Constantinople with his entourage, among them an ambitious deacon named Vigilius, and Justinian and Theodora received him graciously, Yet, between his arrival in March and his death on 22 April, he destroyed the consensus which Theodora had carefully contrived between Severus and Anthimus and put the Chalcedonians and the Monophysites back on their collision course again. Not for nothing was there a Monophysite tradition that all Constantinople shuddered at the pope's arrival; and both the sun and the moon made an appropriate comment by refusing to shine.[22]

He wasted little time pleading for Theodahad. Justinian had, in any case, by this time made up his mind to invade Italy. Instead Agapetus attacked the apostasy that he found in the capital. Theodora did her best to win him over, while Justinian fulminated and menaced him with exile if he remained unreasonable. Agapetus was unmoved. He refused to recognize Anthimus as patriarch of Constantinople or as anything other than bishop of Trapezus, for his translation from Trapezus to another see was contrary to canon law: a sticking point he would not overlook. Agapetus even accused Justinian himself of giving way to heresy and Justinian had to vindicate himself by signing a certificate declaring that he was a true Catholic of the Chalcedonian faith. Nonetheless, Agapetus refused to accept Anthimus into communion or recognize him as patriarch.

Then Justinian brought the pope and patriarch together and confronted them with each other. Agapetus demanded that Anthimus confess that Christ had two distinct natures as the Chalcedonian Creed mandated. Anthimus refused. Thereupon Agapetus excommunicated him. He also excommunicated Severus and the whole assembly of monks and clergy in the Palace of Hormisdas. Possibly he excommunicated Theodora as well.

Justinian was somewhat unnerved by this tough old bigot. Unlike Theodora, he had been brought up to respect the pope and he believed in the fires of Hell and the fearsome results of excommunication in the afterlife. He was a man without any tincture of scepticism in his makeup who could write in one of his laws that blasphemy caused earthquakes, floods and other natural disasters.

Moreover, there were political as well as spiritual considerations to be kept in mind, for Belisarius was about to fight a war against the Ostrogoths and it was important not to alienate the Italians. The Byzantine invaders wanted the Italians to see them as good Catholics come to deliver Italy from its Arian occupiers. Pope Agapetus had no army to back him but he commanded public opinion in Italy and he could be either a powerful ally or a potent enemy. Justinian wanted him as an ally.

Once Anthimus refused to confess the two natures of Christ, Justinian abandoned him. In his place Agapetus consecrated a new patriarch, Menas, who had been the director of the Hospice of Samson. This hospice, situated between the churches of Hagia Eirene and Hagia Sophia, had been burned to the ground in the *Nika* riot but was being rebuilt. Menas confessed the Chalcedonian faith and Agapetus gave him his approval. Rejected by Justinian, Anthimus took off his pallium, laid it on the altar in Justinian's presence and disappeared. Three successive search parties were sent out to find him but, though they hunted diligently, he was nowhere to be found. Justinian suspected that Theodora had hidden Anthimus in a safe house somewhere outside Constantinople but he did not press the issue. Only years later, after Theodora died, was Anthimus' hiding place discovered. Theodora had concealed him in her private apartments in the imperial palace, where all the attendants were Monophysites and not likely to betray him.[23]

Severus fled and, with Theodora's help, he got away from Constantinople, safely back to Egypt. Two years later he died on the estate of one of his supporters at Xoïs in the Nile Delta. As he was suffering from his final illness, his friends urged him to take a bath to cool his fever. He refused, saying that ever since he had taken up the monastic life he had never looked on his naked body. However, finally his friends prevailed on him to take a bath, fully clothed.

AGAPETUS PRESSED HOME HIS VICTORY. He heard about the holy man Z'ura who was living in the villa which Theodora had given him across the Golden Horn in Sycae and he complained to Justinian that the villa had become a focal point for heresy. Justinian gave him leave to do his worst. Agapetus took a company of soldiers and tried to cross the Golden Horn in a boat. But, according to Z'ura's biographer, John of Ephesus, God intervened to save Z'ura. A gale-force wind blew the ferry-boat backward that was carrying Agapetus and his troops and finally, since Agapetus persisted in trying to cross, a bolt of lightning struck the vessel. But Agapetus still would not cease his fulminations and blasphemies and God showed his hand again. Agapetus' tongue began to swell with an abscess. It was lanced twice but it did no good. The tongue became gangrenous and

Agapetus died on 22 April. He would return to Rome in a lead coffin. John of Ephesus felt no sympathy for him.

The pope's sojourn in Constantinople had been short, but he changed the course of Christendom. Dante, centuries later, would recall Agapetus' achievement with approval. In the *Paradiso*, Justinian appears to Dante in the Afterlife and pays tribute to the doughty pope for revealing to him the True Faith and the reality of Christ's two natures. Thanks to him, Justinian learned to embrace orthodoxy and win a place in Dante's *Paradiso* rather than his *Inferno*.

Dante may have approved but, to Theodora, Agapetus' achievement was an utter calamity. The Monophysites whom she had been sheltering in the Palace of Hormisdas were hustled off to a concentration camp within the fortress of Derkos in Thrace, some 30 miles from Constantinople, distant enough to isolate them. Even Z'ura was not spared. In the see of Antioch, the rigorous patriarch Ephraem commenced persecution again with greater zeal than ever. In Alexandria, law and order broke down but there the struggle was between the Miaphysites, who were Severus' disciples, and the radical Aphthartodocetists. The only comfort Theodora had was that even though Justinian may have deserted to the side of the enemy in the battlefield of theology, his personal devotion to her remained firm.

What if Theodora had won over a pope who was less rigid than Agapetus? Would the growing schism between East and West have been healed? The Greco-Roman world had looked on the East as the 'Other' ever since the Persian Wars in the fifth century BCE but the conflict between East and West in the past had been imperialist rivalry, not a clash of civilizations. Culture and ideas moved freely back and forth between East and West. But now the rivalry was turning into a clash of ideologies. East and West would develop their own belief systems and the victory that Dante hailed in his *Paradiso* can at best be called unfortunate.

Theodora's Riposte

Pope Agapetus had handed Theodora a stinging defeat. In 535, before his arrival in Constantinople, her influence was paramount and her policy of outreach seemed to be bearing fruit. Justinian hailed her in a law that he promulgated in that year as 'our pious consort granted us by God' and acknowledged openly that he sought her advice.[1] She had almost succeeded in finding a formula that was acceptable both to temperate Chalcedonians and those Monophysites who were not locked into stiff-necked inflexibility. In Egypt, Theodosius followed Timothy III on the patriarchal throne and he was Theodora's man. She herself was now baptized, for she had received the rite of Holy Baptism from the hands of the stylite saint Z'ura, the stout foe of Chalcedon, who had come to Constantinople as much to take up cudgels in defence of his faith as for refuge. It had almost seemed possible to heal the schism that split the Christian Church.

Then Pope Agapetus arrived in Constantinople and everything fell apart. Even the weather changed. There were unseasonable storms at sea and a mysterious dust veil enveloped the Mediterranean and blocked out the sun for 14 months![2] Severus was condemned; John of Tella returned to the Persian frontier. Agapetus died on 22 April 536. His tongue, with which he had denounced Severus, intumesced until it dangled out of his mouth. The doctors lanced it twice but it gangrened and the pope died in agony. The Chalcedonians thought that Z'ura had bewitched him, whereas the Monophysites believed that his painful death was punishment visited upon him by God, who had judged him and found him iniquitous. But Theodora could take small comfort from that.

She must have been in a delicate situation but she did not desert her Monophysites. She took care that no harm came to Severus. He escaped from Constantinople with her help and returned to Egypt where he was safe. Yet he was forbidden to dwell in any city of the empire. For the future he was to live in the desert, or some solitary place where he could not corrupt others with his blasphemies. So ordained an edict of Justinian, which also banned the writings of Severus and forbade anyone to possess or copy them.[3]

Menas, who replaced Anthimus as patriarch of Constantinople, convened a synod while Agapetus was on his death bed and Severus' various sins were summed up and denounced in detail. Severus had objected to mosaics and paintings that showed angels clad in robes of imperial purple. Their garments should be white! The council declared him in error. Severus had also faulted the custom of depicting the Holy Ghost as a dove and there were other equally heinous sins. He was accused of being a Manichaean, which was worse than being a Jew in the ranking of theological transgressions; it was alleged that he asserted that Chalcedonians were Nestorian heretics, a charge too close to the truth for comfort; that he had persecuted Chalcedonians – he had, in fact, been very nasty to the Chalcedonians in the see of Antioch while he was patriarch – and so on. But Severus himself was safe in Egypt.

The holy men whom Theodora protected in the Palace of Hormisdas were removed to a fortress at Derkos in Thrace, a safe distance from Constantinople. Yet Theodora herself remained untouchable and she still protected her Monophysite refugees. Justinian preferred not to notice. Did she possess copies of Severus' writings in spite of Justinian's ban? Very likely. Possibly Agapetus had excommunicated her and Menas, Anthimus' replacement as patriarch of Constantinople, must have had qualms about her baptism by Z'ura, who had been shunted off to Derkos along with his fellow Monophysites. But did he dare say so? Was Theodora actually denied the sacraments? We cannot say, but the Anthimus affair illustrates Justinian's determination to protect her. The council meeting in Constantinople in 536 summoned Anthimus to appear before it but he was nowhere to be found. Justinian suspected that Theodora knew his whereabouts but apparently he did not ask and she did not tell. Yet even Justinian, who knew his wife well, must have been mildly surprised when, after her death, Anthimus emerged from the empress' quarters of the imperial palace where Theodora had concealed him for 12 years. Nonetheless, Justinian greeted him with courtesy and did him no harm.

Yet Theodora had suffered a severe defeat and her enemies took note of it. The most bitter and outspoken of them, and the most dangerous, was the praetorian prefect John the Cappadocian, who tried to rouse Justinian's suspicions and even succeeded in creating a transient rift between him and his wife. This was the point in time when John's power was in the ascendant and he had Justinian's ear.[4] Theodora feared and hated him. As for Justinian himself, his moment of flexibility on matters of faith was past, at least for the time being.

Even in Egypt, where Monophysites had been safe so far from persecution, Justinian took a harder line. Imperial revenues from Egypt were vitally important for the economy of the empire but the true faith trumped the economy. Theodosius, who had been chosen patriarch of Alexandria the year before as Timothy III's successor, had quickly run into trouble for his rival, Julian of Halicarnassus, by now had a fanatic following. While Theodosius' investiture was taking place in the Great Church of Alexandria, a mob of Julianist monks broke in, hurled Theodosius off the patriarchal throne and forcibly placed one of their number upon it instead. He was an archdeacon named Gaianus. Theodosius narrowly escaped with his life and Gaianus took over.

Gaianus lasted only 104 days. But his episcopate was long enough to give his name to his party of religious sectarians. Egypt now had Gaianists, Aphthartodocetists and Julianists all preaching much the same dogma with various degrees of intensity. They believed that Christ's godhead allowed no space for human nature, though they did not deny Christ's suffering on the cross. But if He suffered like a human being when he was crucified, it was only because He consented to suffer, for the logical inference of belief in Christ's total divinity was that human pain and anguish never touched him.

When the news reached Theodora that Theodosius was dethroned and his life in danger, she approached Justinian, who was not unhappy to learn that the Monophysites were quarrelling among themselves.[5] However, he did not gloat, for the row threatened law and order in Egypt and he yielded to Theodora's urgent appeal that he grant her leave to intervene. She sent her chamberlain, the able eunuch Narses to Alexandria to support Theodosius, with 6,000 troops at his back, most of them probably recruited within Egypt itself. Narses brought the patriarchate of Gaianus to an abrupt end and packed him off to exile in Sardinia. Theodosius got back the patriarchal throne but holding on to it proved harder than Theodora guessed, even with 6,000 troops under a capable commander to support him.

The Alexandrian mob was not easily cowed. Narses was prepared to be ruthless: at one point he set fire to part of the city to quell the rioters. The street fighting and rioting lasted almost 17 months before Theodosius accepted the inevitable and in the autumn of 536 he left Alexandria for good and sailed to Constantinople. Gaianus, however, was not allowed to return. He died in exile in Sardinia and, though the Coptic Church in Egypt remained split between Theodosians and Gaianists for the next two centuries, it was the Theodosians and the Miaphysitism of Severus that eventually prevailed.

When Theodosius reached Constantinople, he was welcomed by Theodora and, rather more warily, by Justinian. Justinian insisted that Theodosius accept the Creed of Chalcedon as the price of imperial support but Theodosius refused. Justinian coaxed and threatened for a year before he gave up and decided that Theodosius was beyond redemption. He was bundled off to join the recalcitrant

Monophysites at Derkos, where Theodora made them as comfortable as she could, and eventually managed to move them back to the Palace of Hormisdas. But for the moment Justinian was determined to keep them isolated so that their theology could not contaminate the masses.

In Theodosius' place Justinian appointed Paul of Tabennisi, a monk from the mother house of the Pachomian Order in upper Egypt.[6] It was the papal nuncio in Constantinople, Pelagius, who suggested to Justinian that Paul would be a politically correct patriarch with sound religious beliefs, for the Pachomian monks supported the Chalcedonian creed. For 55 years the patriarchs of Alexandria had all been anti-Chalcedonians but Paul's appointment meant that Justinian would no longer tolerate opposition in Egypt. Paul was prepared to be tough. It is no coincidence that Justinian reorganized the imperial administration in Egypt at this time and unified the civil and military commands. The Egyptian church was, in effect, put under military control.

As for Theodosius, whom Paul replaced, when the time was ripe he was allowed to leave Derkos for Constantinople but he remained in the Palace of Hormisdas under Theodora's protection. Yet in exile he gained the acceptance among the anti-Chalcedonians that had eluded him in Alexandria, for apart from the Julianists, the Monophysites looked on him as their leader. They considered him the rightful patriarch of Alexandria, whereas Paul of Tabennisi was one of the Melkite clergy who were the emperor's men, prepared to enforce, with imperial troops if necessary, the doctrines that met with imperial approval. In Alexandria, Paul ousted the Monophysite clergy from their churches, leaving them with only two small places of worship which they built secretly. But in the country villages, the population remained Monophysite and so were the holy men, the hermits and the monks, except for the monasteries that followed the Pachomian rule. A cleavage developed into a deep split between Greek-speakers and Copts in Egypt, between the city and the country villages, and the well-to-do classes and the poor.

WHEN THEODORA SURVEYED THE CALAMITY THAT POPE AGAPETUS HAD WREAKED ON HER PLANS, she realized that not all was lost. She still had political clout as long as Justinian listened to her and protected her. One person who was acutely aware of this was an ambitious deacon named Vigilius who had come from Rome to Constantinople with Agapetus. We do not know whether it was Theodora who made the first contact with him or he with her, but she must have been aware of his background and his ambition to be pope. He had once had the papal throne almost within his grasp, for pope Boniface had once chosen him as his successor. Boniface had announced his decision to a synod held in St Peter's basilica and the clergy at the synod signed an ordinance that put the decision in writing. But Boniface had to recant. The designation of Vigilius was judged contrary to the laws of the church which did not allow a pope to choose his successor and, in the presence of the clergy and the senate of Rome, Boniface burned the ordinance. When he died in 532, it was John II who became pope.[7]

No doubt Vigilius thought he was treated unfairly. He belonged to a family in Rome that was used to power. His father had been a praetorian prefect and his brother an urban prefect of Rome, both in the service of the Ostrogothic realm. But the offices that had real power in the Western Roman Empire were no longer in the imperial civil service. They were in the church and, now that Agapetus was dead and the papal throne was vacant, Vigilius wanted it badly.

He wanted it enough that he made a deal with Theodora. In return for her support, he promised to reverse the excommunication of Anthimus. No one, it seems, doubted that Anthimus was still alive and that Theodora could produce him triumphantly if and when the time was ripe. Vigilius returned to Rome with Theodora's endorsement in his pocket but he arrived too late. Rome already had a new pope. He was Silverius, the son of Pope Hormisdas who had negotiated the end of the Acacian Schism with old Justin I. Hormisdas had been a zealous persecutor of the anti-Chalcedonian clergy and, when he died, his son Silverius had written a triumphal epitaph for his father's tomb which celebrated his conquest of the Greek schismatics. He was not likely to be a malleable pontiff.

He had moved swiftly as soon as he learned that Agapetus was dead and the papal throne was vacant. He approached the Gothic king, Theodahad, whose greed for money was notorious, and offered him a generous bribe. In return, Theodahad intimated to the Roman clergy that he would slay them if they failed to elect Silverius, whereupon any hesitations that they may have had vanished. He became pope in June 536 and when Vigilius reached Rome in September, bringing with him the mortal remains of Pope Agapetus for burial in St Peter's basilica, he discovered that his pact with Theodora was worthless. The papal throne was already occupied.

But Theodora was not to be thwarted. The invasion of Italy was underway. On 9 December 536 the Byzantine army, led by Belisarius, entered Rome. With Belisarius was Antonina, who was ready and willing to act as Theodora's agent, for Theodora was determined either to bend Silverius to her will or get rid of him.

NINE MONTHS EARLIER, IN MARCH OF 536, JUST AS POPE AGAPETUS ARRIVED IN CONSTANTINOPLE and set about undoing the consensus between Anthimus and Severus which Theodora had promoted, Belisarius and Antonina were in Sicily, ready to move across the Strait of Messina into Italy and begin the invasion. Then at the end of the month, disturbing news from Africa reached Belisarius at Syracuse. Solomon, his successor in the African command, arrived and along with him came Procopius, Belisarius' old legal advisor, who now rejoined him. They were anxious men, looking for help. Discontent among the soldiers in Carthage had boiled over into open mutiny. Their pay was in arrears: Justinian and Theodora could find money to build lavish palaces and churches but meeting the payroll of the soldiers was always an irremediable problem. But the core of the mutiny was the Arian contingent in Solomon's army, for Justinian had forbidden the rites of the church to non-Catholics and this ban affected all the Arian troops, including the new Vandal recruits who had been integrated into the Byzantine armed forces. Easter was the customary time for many Christians to have their children baptized, for baptism was administered only between the feasts of Easter and Pentecost, and when Easter of 536 arrived the Arians found themselves excluded. They rebelled.

The mutiny did not go as intended. The ringleaders planned to kill Solomon while he was at church but they hesitated at the last moment, for they feared the wrath of God if they slew a man in a sacred place. Solomon managed to escape to Belisarius in Sicily and begged for help.

Belisarius sailed for Carthage with one ship and a hundred men from his crack unit of guardsmen. The mutineers had chosen as their commander a rebel named Stotzas, who was holding Carthage under siege. It was on the point of capitulating when Belisarius' ship sailed into the harbour and, for the moment, the presence of the great commander shattered the confidence of the mutineers. They fell back but Belisarius pursued them and brought them to battle. Heavily outnumbered though he was, he routed Stotzas and his men, who fled into Numidia and Belisarius returned to Carthage where news reached him of an incipient mutiny in Sicily. He may also have received word that Antonina's lover, Theodosius, had escaped. His presence in Sicily was urgently needed.

Stotzas, meanwhile, rallied his troops in Numidia, modern Algeria, and the Byzantine forces stationed there deserted to him, abandoning their own commanders who had to seek refuge in a church. The situation was extremely serious, so serious that Justinian turned to his cousin Germanus for help. Germanus was one of Justinian's most competent generals and he sailed to Africa and suppressed the mutiny quickly and efficiently. Yet his appointment was a defeat for Theodora. She hated Germanus for he, like Justinian, had been a nephew of the old emperor Justin I but possessed a military reputation, which Justinian lacked. He also had two sons who inherited their father's military ability, whereas Justinian was childless. If Justinian were to die, his obvious heir would be Germanus and then what would happen to Theodora's family and friends? Their interests were very close to her heart. Germanus' selection to deal with the emergency in Africa signalled that, in the aftermath of Pope Agapetus' victory, Justinian was heeding advice from John the Cappadocian more than from Theodora.

She must have been uneasy, all the more so when Germanus accomplished his assignment in Africa brilliantly. But, after the danger was past, he was recalled to Constantinople and Solomon was once again sent out to take command. Justinian may not have doubted Germanus' loyalty but in his empire subordinates should never be too competent.

Meanwhile Belisarius crossed the Strait of Messina and landed at Reggio Calabria, ancient Rhegium. There was no resistance. What Gothic warships there were available to guard the strait were commanded by a son-in-law of Theodahad and he deserted to Belisarius, who in return saw to it that he was made a patrician. From Rhegium, Belisarius advanced up the west coast of Italy to Naples, where he encountered his first serious opposition. The Neapolitans sent him a deputation to urge him to bypass their city and push on to Rome. Belisarius refused; he offered the Gothic garrison safe passage out of the city but he insisted that it surrender first. The citizens debated and decided to resist. The Jewish community was particularly resolute, for they recognized that Justinian was no friend of theirs. Immediately after the conquest of Africa, Justinian had issued an edict proscribing heretics and pagans and he had included Jews among the heterodox that were to be denied religious freedom.[8] Justinian never enforced his edict against the Jews but it was a straw in the wind. Roman law still treated Judaism as a *religio licita*, that is, a religion that had the protection of law – and Justinian respected the law – but in his heart he considered Judaism on a par with heresy.

Belisarius put Naples under siege. It was a difficult task, for the circuit walls of the city were well defended and cutting the aqueduct did not cause any serious water shortage, for Naples had good wells. Belisarius was on the point of giving up and pressing on to Rome. Winter was closing in and it would be one of the coldest winters on record in Italy.[9] Then a soldier who was exploring the aqueduct discovered that where the channel entered the city through the circuit wall it had not been blocked. The aperture was small but the soldiers filed and chipped away the rock until it was large enough for a man to squeeze through. Then, under cover of night, 600 troops entered Naples, killing the sentinels on the northern wall and clearing the way for the rest of the army to scale the battlements. The Neapolitans awoke to find the enemy in their city, who massacred Goths and Romans alike. Men were cut down while their wives looked on, helpless; nuns and priests were killed and even churches were not spared.[10] The Bulgars – 'Huns', as the Byzantines called them – distinguished themselves particularly by their penchant for butchery and booty. Belisarius did not stop the slaughter until his troops had their fill of plunder and bloodshed.

One cannot read the story of Naples' fall as Procopius tells it without feeling that he has used his considerable rhetorical skill to whitewash Belisarius' conduct and make him appear a knight without blemish. The massacre at Naples served a military objective: it made it clear that opposition would be costly. It was a terror tactic, brutal and probably deliberate. But Procopius claimed that the Neapolitans did not blame the Byzantines; rather they pointed the finger at the two men who had urged resistance, Pastor and Asclepiodotus. Pastor died of a stroke when he saw that the city was taken, but a Neapolitan mob crucified his corpse anyway. Asclepiodotus lived long enough to be pardoned by Belisarius but then the mob tore him limb from limb. Belisarius acted properly throughout, according to the loyal Procopius.

It was now early November. While Naples was under siege, Theodahad had lingered in Rome, never lifting a finger to assist the Neapolitans. The Gothic property owners in Rome itself and in Campania south of Rome were utterly disgusted, for they had much to lose. Their estates were in danger. They held an indignation meeting, where they deposed Theodahad and chose in his place an experienced soldier named Witigis, who had not a drop of the royal blood in his veins. Theodahad fled for Ravenna but Witigis sent a soldier in pursuit who bore him a personal grudge. Night and day he rode hard on Theodahad's trail and when he finally overtook him he seized him, hurled him to the ground, and butchered him on the spot. The last male of the Amal royal line came to a miserable end.

Once Witigis was elected king and raised on a shield, according to Gothic custom, amidst warriors with drawn swords, he held a council at Rome to decide what to do next. He faced two threats, one from the south, where Belisarius was advancing, and a second from the north where the Franks threatened invasion, egged on by Justinian. Amalasuntha had been the niece of Clovis, the king of the Salian Franks, who had converted to Roman Catholicism after a victory over the Alamanns in 496, which he believed that the God of the Christians had granted. Clovis was by now dead, but his three sons heard the news of Amalasuntha's murder with a distinct lack of pleasure. To Witigis, the Franks seemed a greater menace than Belisarius, for as long as they threatened attack, the Goths had to keep the bulk of their army in northern Italy to guard against them. Witigis left a force of only 4,000 troops to hold Rome and set out for Ravenna to negotiate with the Franks.

He had a personal objective as well as a strategic one. Witigis did not belong to the old princely house of the Ostrogoths. The only survivor of the Amal royal family was Matasuntha, the young daughter of Amalasuntha, and Witigis was determined to marry her and sire a new line of kings that would carry on the royal line, even though it meant divorcing his own wife. But he did not leave Rome before he extracted oaths of loyalty from Pope Silverius, as well as from the senate and Roman people, and he apparently did not doubt their fidelity. He seems to have been a simple man, unused to the chicanery of emperors and popes. He went to Ravenna, bought off the Franks and married Matasuntha, who made an unwilling and resentful bride. A Byzantine magnate who could introduce her to the splendours of the imperial court would have been to her taste more than a plain Gothic soldier like Witigis.

Meanwhile Belisarius and his army were marching on Rome, with news of the massacre at Naples preceding him. Pope Silverius urged the Romans to forget their oaths of loyalty and open the gates. He reminded them of the horrors of a siege. The Romans needed no great persuasion, for their allegiance laid with their legitimate emperor in Constantinople, not with the heretical Gothic occupiers of Italy. They invited Belisarius into the city and, on 9 December 536, the Porta Asinaria that pierced the south wall of the city close by the papal cathedral of St John Lateran, was opened and the Byzantine army marched in, while in the north the Gothic garrison exited swiftly by the Flaminian Gate. Only the commander of the garrison, Leuderis, remained behind and Belisarius sent him as a captive to Justinian in Constantinople, along with the keys of the city. Rome had fallen without a blow.

IF THE ROMANS THOUGHT THAT THEIR SURRENDER WOULD SAVE THEM FROM THE HARDSHIPS OF A SIEGE, they were sadly mistaken. Witigis quickly realized that he had erred when he trusted the fidelity of the pope and the Romans. He hurried south to retake the city. In the meantime, Belisarius was strengthening the defences of Rome. The great Aurelian Wall that was last used in the Italian Risorgimento of 1870, when Garibaldi's forces broke through it and took the city, is some 18 km long with 18 main gates and 381 towers. It was too long for Belisarius' little army to man properly but, at the same time, its great length made it hard for the besiegers to surround the city and cut it off entirely from the outside. We can only guess the size of Witigis' army. Belisarius reported in a dispatch to Justinian that it numbered 150,000,[11] but that estimate was intended to impress upon an emperor who refused to be hurried just how much reinforcements were needed. Belisarius' own little army numbered a mere 5,000. Yet it endured a terrible siege that lasted a year and nine days and in the end the Goths gave up.

Belisarius and Antonina took up residence in a mansion on the Pincian Hill, just inside the Aurelian Wall. They did not occupy the old imperial palace on the Palatine Hill, though it was habitable – Theoderic the Ostrogoth had paid the stipends of its guards – for if they had, it would have signalled an ambivalent message to Justinian. Yet the *Domus Pinciana* stood on a choice site, with a commanding view of the city.[12] Long ago, in the dying years of the Roman Republic, Lucius Lucullus, whose name became a byword for lavish banquets, had owned a villa there and later Messalina, wife of the emperor Claudius, possessed it. In present-day Rome, the church of St Trinità dei Monti and the Villa Medici crown the Pincian Hill and down its slope cascade the Spanish Steps. Yet tourist guides sometimes point out a section of the Aurelian Wall in that area, which is known as the *Muro Torto* or the *Murus Ruptus*, and tell them that it was the only part of the wall which Belisarius did not fortify against the Goths, for the Romans told him that St Peter himself would act as its defender.

Here was where Antonina and Belisarius, along with Antonina's son Photius, lived during the siege. It was a chilly winter; a bleary sun shone feebly through a dust veil that blanketed much of the Mediterranean that year, and still puzzles climatologists, and the average temperature plunged.[13] Theodosius was absent. Antonina longed for him but he refused to come. Photius knew too much and Theodosius was wary of him. It was here, too, in the *Domus Pinciana* that Antonina carried out a bold mission for Theodora. She dethroned pope Silverius.

IF ANYONE HAD A MOTIVE TO REMAIN LOYAL TO THE BYZANTINES, IT WAS POPE SILVERIUS. He had taken an oath of fealty to Witigis, and then broke it. It was thanks to his treachery that Belisarius' little army had marched, unopposed, into Rome on 9 December 536 and he cannot have been anxious to encounter Witigis again, much less fall into his clutches. Yet rumours began to float about the city that he was planning a second betrayal, this time to the Goths. There can be little doubt that it was Antonina who inspired this gossip.

The *Book of the Pontiffs*,[14] a collection of potted biographies of the Roman popes from St Peter to the late ninth century, is our chief source for the tale of how Silverius was thrust off the papal throne and his life story seems based on a reliable report. It relates that when the news of Silverius' election reached the imperial court, Justinian sent him an invitation to come to Constantinople and reverse the excommunication of Anthimus. It was a remarkable letter to come from Justinian and we can reasonably suspect that its author was Theodora, who may even have written it without Justinian's knowledge. Her hand is easily recognizable: for one thing, the author of the letter was confident that Anthimus was still alive and well and only Theodora and a few of her henchmen knew that. Silverius groaned aloud when he read the letter and foresaw his death, for he did not doubt that it originated with Theodora. He addressed his reply directly to her. 'Lady empress', he wrote, 'to restore a heretic who has been condemned in his wickedness is something I can never bring myself to do'.

Theodora can hardly have been overly surprised at that answer. The son of Pope Hormisdas, who had scuttled the *Henotikon* and pressed old Justin to persecute the anti-Chalcedonians, would not be happy at the prospect of reversing a papal anathema and restoring Anthimus to the ranks of the orthodox. When Vigilius arrived in Rome too late to be elected successor to Pope Agapetus, he had a letter for Belisarius from Theodora in his pocket, which read, 'Seek a chance to oust Pope Silverius from his throne, and send him to us with all due haste. You have with you the archdeacon Vigilius, whom we hold dear, and he has promised us to recall the patriarch Anthimus'. The wording of the letter, which comes from the *Book of the Pontiffs*, and perhaps the letter itself, were probably imaginary, but the instruction was not and Belisarius was prudent enough to heed it. But he took care to absolve himself from sin. It was no trivial matter to dethrone a pope. 'Let him who takes part in the murder of Pope Silverius give an account of his deeds to Jesus Christ', he said, with a presentiment of what would happen.

Probably Theodora also sent a letter to Antonina, telling her how disappointed and angry she was to learn that Silverius had stolen the papal election. He had become an obstacle in Theodora's path that had to be removed. She relied on Antonina to find a way and it was Antonina who managed the plot to bring down Silverius. Her agent was her slave, Eugenius,[15] who had been her accomplice once before, in Sicily, when she inflicted a brutal punishment on the slave girl, Macedonia, who had tattled to Belisarius about her adultery with Theodosius. In Eugenius, Antonina had an assistant who was completely ruthless. They concocted a charge of treason against Silverius.

A letter to Witigis, the king of the Goths, which purported to come from Silverius, was intercepted. It read, 'Come to the gate which is called Asinaria, next to the Lateran Palace, and I shall hand over the city and the patrician Belisarius to you'. It was a forgery, attributed by one source[16] to a lawyer named Marcus and a flunky from the praetorian prefecture called Julian. They are mere names, but no doubt Eugenius knew them and instigated the forged letter which fell into Belisarius' hands. In the background, Antonina wove her web of intrigue.

The letter did not convince Belisarius. He recognized intrigue when he saw it and he was surely aware that his wife was involved. He summoned Silverius to the Pincian Palace and impressed upon him how perilous his position was. It would be prudent, Belisarius intimated, if he yielded to Theodora's wishes. Possibly Antonina was present at the interview and, if so, she must have pushed Silverius hard. But Silverius was not his father's son for nothing. He refused to annul the excommunication of Anthimus. Belisarius pressed him no further and let him go.

Yet by now Silverius recognized what the danger was that menaced him and he moved from his residence in the Lateran Palace to the church of Santa Sabina on the Aventine Hill; for now he understood that it was unwise to live too close to the Asinarian Gate when rumours of treason were floating about. Santa Sabina on the Aventine offered sanctuary and it was not too close to the Asinarian Gate. But his move did not save him. Belisarius may not have believed the persistent reports of Silverius' treason, and he may have known that Theodora and his wife were behind them, but he did not dare cross these two powerful women. Besides, Vigilius had offered him a bribe of 200 gold pounds, payable if he became pope. Belisarius dispatched his stepson, Photius, to summon Silverius a second time to the Pincian Palace. Silverius at first refused, for his attendants warned him not to trust the Greeks no matter how much they swore that he would be safe, but eventually he yielded and left Santa Sabina for the Pincian Palace, accompanied by a retinue of clergy. Once there, the clergy were ordered to remain in the two outer rooms of the audience chamber, while Silverius and Vigilius entered into the presence of Belisarius together. There they saw a tableau symbolic of the relative dominance of Antonina and Belisarius: Antonina was reclining on a couch and at her feet sat Belisarius. It was Antonina who spoke, and her tone was icy.

'Tell me, my lord Pope Silverius, what have we done to you and the Romans that you wish to betray us into the hands of the Goths?'

She did not wait for a reply. While she was still speaking, a subdeacon of one of the regions of Rome, John by name, entered the room, tore the pallium from the pope's shoulders and thrust him into a side chamber, where he was unfrocked and garbed as a monk. Then he was spirited away. Another subdeacon named Xystus came out to the clergy who were waiting in the two anterooms and told them that Silverius was deposed and was now a monk. Panic-stricken, the clergy made a swift exit.

On 29 March Vigilius obtained what he coveted. He was ordained pope. Silverius' deposition had been handled with brutal efficiency. Belisarius was an accomplice but it was his wife, Antonina, who directed the plot and stage-managed the final confrontation with Silverius. No last-minute impulse on Belisarius' part to see justice done was allowed to spoil the proceedings, nor were Silverius' attendants given any chance to protest. Silverius himself was consigned to the pitiless hands of Vigilius, who banished him to Patara in Lycia, on the south coast of modern Turkey.

But the bishop of Patara was shocked at the tragic drama that he saw taking place before his eyes. He made the long journey to Constantinople to complain to Justinian about the brutal treatment that Silverius was receiving: the world had many kings, he told him, but only one pope. Justinian was astonished. He had apparently been unaware of how unceremoniously Silverius had been shoved off the papal throne and what he discovered shocked him. He decreed that Silverius should be returned to Italy. The papal nuncio in Constantinople, Pelagius, protested. The Acacian Schism had interrupted the custom of having a papal nuncio in Constantinople but Agapetus resumed it once he had cleansed the Greek church of heresy, and Vigilius himself had held the appointment briefly until he left for Rome. Pelagius, who took over the post, was a smooth ecclesiastical politician who knew how to navigate through the shoals of court politics, though he could be courageous when courage was needed. At this point in his career he was cultivating Theodora, who did not want Silverius returned to Italy. She may not have known all the details of his brutal deposition but she knew that Antonina had been following her instructions. She must have argued hard with Justinian to keep Silverius in some safe city in the east where he would be out of harm's way, and Pelagius supported her for his own reasons. He knew that Pope Vigilius would not want Silverius back in Rome, where there was room for only one pope.

But Justinian could be pushed only so far. He made up his mind that Silverius should be sent back to Belisarius, who was ordered to investigate the charge of treason. Belisarius, with sublime indirection, entrusted the investigation to pope Vigilius himself and Vigilius took no chances. He banished Silverius to the little island of Palmarola some 40 km off the Italian coast at Anzio, where he subsisted on a diet of bread and water until he perished of hunger and exhaustion. He died in early December 537. Procopius, in his *Secret History*, points to Antonina, with her slave Eugenius as her accomplice, as the mastermind responsible for Silverius' death and the unholy drama that surrounded it, and he was in Rome at the time. He claimed to have inside information that he would reveal in 'later accounts'.[17] He intended to write an account of church politics some time in the future after Theodora and Justinian were dead but he never did. This much is true: Antonina may not actually have overseen the murder of Silverius but she was clearly an accessory. She accomplished what Theodora wanted. Vigilius, Theodora's man, or so she thought, became pope.

The deposition of Silverius took place only two or three weeks after the start of the long siege of Rome by the Goths, which lasted until mid-March 538. What sort of effect did it have on the morale of the Romans, who would be asked to endure terrible hardship in the months to come? We cannot know. Silverius had won the papal throne by bribery and then he forswore an oath of loyalty to Witigis. We need not assume that there was any great fund of sympathy for him in Rome. At the same time Rome must have been full of scuttlebutt about the bargain that Vigilius made with Theodora and Antonina to win their support. He had signalled that he was prepared to be flexible on the Chalcedonian question. One rumour that floated about reported that Vigilius actually wrote letters to the three chief Monophysite churchmen, Theodosius, Severus, and Anthimus, telling them that he endorsed their doctrines, but would they please keep it secret for the moment? At this point in time, Theodosius had just been forced out of Alexandria, in spite of the best efforts of Narses and 6,000 imperial troops to keep him on the patriarchal throne. Severus, banned from living in any city of the empire, was spending his final months on the country estate of a supporter at Xoïs in the Nile Delta and Anthimus was concealed in the women's quarters of the imperial palace. If Vigilius wrote to these three churchmen, who delivered the letters? And how?

Yet the schemers who had raised Vigilius to the papacy were soon disappointed. Vigilius had promised Belisarius a bribe of 200 pounds of gold, which should have assuaged whatever remorse that he might have felt as Silverius starved on his tiny island in the Tyrrhenian Sea. But Vigilius refused to pay.[18] Yet Belisarius' disillusion cannot have been greater than Theodora's. She wrote Vigilius to say, 'Come now, keep the promise about our father Anthimus which you made us of your own free will, and restore him to his office'. But Vigilius had succumbed to an onset of politic scruples. He claimed he could not revoke an excommunication that his two predecessors, Agapetus and Silverius, had endorsed. What had happened was that he had become fully aware of public opinion, not only in Rome but in Africa, newly liberated from the harsh rule of the heretic Vandals and unyielding defenders of the Chalcedonian Creed. The persecution which the African clergy had suffered put steel into their backbones. Vigilius realized that he dared not deviate from the Creed of Chalcedon. The stature and primacy of the Roman papacy and the enduring legacy of Imperial Rome itself were all bound up with it. Anthimus, concealed in the palace, would have to wait for his rehabilitation. Theodora had played her final card and lost. For the moment, she could only choke back her rage and frustration.

THE SIEGE OF ROME, WHICH WAS JUST BEGINNING, WOULD CHANGE THE FACE

OF THE CITY. The sack by Alaric and the Visigoths in 410 and the pillaging of the Vandals in 455 had left great scars but the life-style of classical Rome continued. There was still a Roman Forum, though it was now a pleasant place to ride horseback. The great imperial forums on its edge were still magnificent in decay. Crowds gathered more rarely now in the Flavian Amphitheatre and the Circus Maximus, though every year when one of the empire's two consuls was inaugurated (the other was inaugurated in Constantinople) the games that he offered there were memorable occasions. On the Palatine Hill overlooking the Roman Forum stood the imperial palace, still magnificent though it must have been falling into disrepair. The great Roman baths were open for their clientele but they were the first casualty of the siege. The Goths cut the aqueducts which fed Rome with water and the beleaguered Romans had to make do with wells for their water supply. The aqueducts would never be repaired and baths which they supplied decayed into picturesque ruins.

The aqueducts had also provided the water which powered the mills that ground grain into flour and Belisarius had to replace them with mills which used the current of the River Tiber to turn their wheels. Women, children and non-combatants were evacuated from the city; tradesmen were drafted into the outnumbered Byzantine forces. The Roman civilians, who had counted on Belisarius to defend them, were bitterly disappointed and they would have been more disgruntled than they were if they had known, as some of them may have, that Theodora's protégé, Narses, was supplied with more troops in Alexandria to secure Theodosius on his patriarchal throne than Belisarius had to defend Rome.

Towards the end of June, as the Romans began to feel the warmth of summer, they clamoured for Belisarius to risk a battle. He refused, but he told them that he had news that Constantinople was sending supplies and reinforcements, which were already on their way. He half-believed the report himself for he ordered his secretary, Procopius, to slip out a south gate of the city at night and hurry to Naples to see if the rumour was true. Then he put Antonina in command of 1,000 horsemen and sent her south to Terracina, where the Appian Way passes between a precipitous cliff and the sea. There she set up a base to harry the Gothic supply trains as they moved along the road to Rome. From Terracina, Antonina continued on without escort to Naples, where she found that Procopius had mustered 500 men and prepared a convoy of grain ships. But only in November did the promised reinforcements arrive: 3,000 tough Isaurians from Asia Minor, 800 Thracian horsemen and 1,000 regular cavalry led by John, the nephew of Vitalian, a bold officer who never stood in awe of the great Belisarius. John the Sanguinary, he was called: 'Bloody John'. The

Isaurians and the convoy of grain transports which Procopius had collected sailed for Ostia at the mouth of the Tiber and John himself led the remaining 1,800 mounted troops with a supply train boldly up the Appian Way to Rome.

The tables were turned. Rome had food and the Goths in their camps suffered from starvation and malaria. Witigis began to despair. He negotiated a three-month truce to allow him to send envoys to Justinian in Constantinople and probably it was during this truce that Antonina returned to Rome, for about this time the affair of Praesidius' daggers took place, which resulted in the execution of Constantine.[19] Constantine's insubordination would hardly have led to his death if Antonina had not been at Belisarius' elbow in the Pincian Palace, determined to have her revenge on a man who had counselled her husband to kill her for adultery. The execution damaged Belisarius' stature among his general staff, for Constantine had been a steady soldier and a good officer, no less honest than most of them.

Meanwhile Belisarius had sent 'Bloody John' with 2,000 horse to Picenum to threaten the northern supply lines of the Goths besieging Rome. John moved boldly. He ignored Belisarius' orders to leave no fortresses still in Gothic hands in his rear and advanced confidently to Rimini, a day's march from Ravenna. He guessed that when the news reached Witigis that the capital of the Gothic kingdom was threatened he would rush to protect it, abandoning the siege of Rome, and he was right. The Goths raised the siege and withdrew over the Tiber River by Milvian Bridge where, two and a half centuries earlier the emperor Constantine I had fought a battle that made him master of Rome and marked the victory of Christianity. As the Goths crossed the bridge, Belisarius attacked and inflicted heavy losses.

The following two years, up until the surrender of Ravenna in the spring of 540, were marked by dissension among the Byzantine generals and calamity in Italy. Justinian sent out another army 7,000 strong under the command of Narses, who had returned from Alexandria where he had tried in vain to maintain Theodosius on the patriarchal throne. His Egyptian adventure was a failure, but in Italy he might repair his military reputation. He had no intention of kowtowing to Belisarius. There was soon friction between the ambitious eunuch and the self-important commander of the forces in Italy. Did Theodora bear any responsibility for it? Narses must have had an audience with her before he left for Italy and we can only imagine what she passed between them. At least she did not impress upon him, it seems, that he should respect Belisarius' authority.

One casualty of Narses' refusal to co-operate with Belisarius was the fall of Milan, the second city of Italy, which had gone over to the Byzantine side at the urging of its bishop, Datius, and was promptly besieged by an army of Goths and Franks. A co-ordinated effort could have saved the city. But Narses' officers refused to carry out orders from Belisarius. Delay followed delay and the Milanese, reduced to starvation, finally gave up and surrendered. The inhabitants were massacred. The praetorian prefect of Italy, Reparatus, who was Pope Vigilius' brother, was captured, reduced to mincemeat and fed to dogs. Some 300,000 persons were liquidated by the Goths and Franks. The number comes from Procopius[20] and may be exaggerated but it was great enough to galvanize Justinian, who recalled Narses and left Belisarius in sole command of the Italian campaign. Theodora must have received reports from Antonina which cannot have flattered Narses, but he remained useful.

The countryside was starving. In central Italy, hunger and disease mowed down the population. The weather did nothing to help, for tree ring analysis shows that these were years with cold, dry summers and crops failed.[21] In Tuscany, there was famine; farmers who lived on the mountain slopes made bread from acorns ground up like grain. In Picenum up to fifty thousand died of hunger. There were stories of persons in the last stages of starvation whose skin turned dry and black, so that they looked like charred sticks, with a glint of madness in their eyes. Tales of cannibalism made the rounds: one told of two women who kept a guest house near Rimini, where they killed and ate the customers who sought lodging with them. They had devoured seventeen before the eighteenth awakened in the nick of time, forced them to confess and slew them. Men and women were reduced to eating grass; if they saw a few tufts of grass they would fall to their knees and try to pull them out of the ground, roots and all, and fail, collapsing from weakness and dying, sprawled over the last meal they would ever attempt to eat. Those who survived had to face a plague pandemic in 543 with compromised immune systems. This was a war that would thrust Italy into the Dark Ages.[22] Civilization was dying all over the peninsula. The campaign intended to restore the Roman Empire in the west was, instead, providing the concluding chapter for the classical world and its culture.

But Belisarius was determined to take Ravenna, though Justinian himself would have been happy to cut his losses. The war had gone on long enough and Justinian was ready to accept a peace treaty which would leave Witigis and his Goths in control north of the Po River and end the agony of Italy. Witigis was willing; Justinian's terms were better than he had hoped. But Belisarius would not put his signature to the treaty and if Belisarius did not sign Witigis would not accept it. It was now Belisarius' turn to be insubordinate and his general staff made it clear to him that they were unhappy with him, for they too wanted peace and here was an opportunity which they did not want to lose.

At this point, some of the Gothic notables made Belisarius a secret proposal which allowed him to keep his general staff content and still satisfy his ambition to take Ravenna. The Goths would surrender to him with the secret understanding that he would not return to Constantinople as a loyal subject of Justinian but, instead, would revive the Western Roman Empire with himself as the western emperor. What they wanted was a joint *imperium* in Italy, based on a Gothic-Roman partnership. Witigis did not initiate the proposal but when he learned of it he urged Belisarius to accept. It was, in fact, a feasible plan which could have worked. It would have cut short Italy's agony and brought about what a recent historian[23] has called a 'world that might have been', where Rome's classical heritage could survive. But Belisarius saw it merely as a chance to deceive the Goths and missed an opportunity to end the suffering and destruction.

He pretended to accept. He gave pledges of his good faith. However, one oath he did not swear, thereby fending off the charge of perfidy from his immortal soul with a legalistic argument. He deferred his acceptance of the imperial purple until he was inside Ravenna and could take the oath of office in the presence of Witigis and the Gothic notables. Yet the Goths did not suspect bad faith. The Byzantine army entered Ravenna, as agreed, in May 540 and it must have seemed a glorious moment to Belisarius who may, as yet, have been unaware that two months earlier, in March, the Persians had launched an invasion of Syria. He seized the royal treasury of the Ostrogothic kings. But he made no move to resuscitate the Western Roman Empire and declare himself emperor and, little by little, it dawned on the Goths that he had no intention of keeping his promises to them. The Goths were disconcerted and angry and perhaps they were not alone. Averil Cameron[24] has noted that Procopius' disillusion with Belisarius seems to date from this point. Was Procopius disappointed when Belisarius aborted the revival of the western empire? Or were his sensibilities shocked by his commander's treachery, for which Italy would pay dearly?

Too late Witigis realized that he had been tricked and tried to escape but John, the nephew of Vitalian, captured him and brought back him to Belisarius, who put his royal captive, his wife Matasuntha and the royal treasure on board ship and sailed back to Constantinople. Once there, Justinian received Witigis with honour and made him a patrician as consolation for the loss of a kingdom. Witigis lived only two more years; he died as plague was raging in Constantinople and he may have been a victim.

Justinian may have treated Witigis generously but he received Belisarius with some reserve. The Vandal War had concluded with a great ceremonial triumph but it would not be repeated now. Justinian had no wish to increase the vainglory of his star general. The treasures of the Gothic kingdom were put on display in the palace, where the senators might have a private viewing, but the people of Constantinople were not given a chance to marvel at them. Justinian was prescient enough to realize that Belisarius' victory was hollow and meant trouble in the future. He would have preferred to cut his losses in Italy, for while Belisarius was negotiating Ravenna's surrender a horde of Bulgars and Slavs had swarmed across the Danube River and terrorized Thrace, frightening Constantinople itself. Justinian and Theodora had feared so much for their own safety in the imperial palace that they reinforced the palace gates. All trees and vineyards within some 150 feet of the city walls were levelled, so that the enemy could not use them for cover as they sneaked up with their scaling ladders.[25] The attack did not take place, but Justinian and Theodora were reminded of their own insecurity.

If the imperial couple turned their eyes eastwards, the situation was not much happier. The prefecture of *Oriens*, which together with Egypt supplied most of the imperial revenue, was in deadly peril. Khusro, shah of Persia, had watched Justinian's conquests in the west with apprehension, for they upset the balance of power between Byzantium and Persia. Witigis and his Goths, guessing Khusro's unease, had already sent an embassy urging him to launch an attack and Khusro was ready to listen. So in the same year as Belisarius took Ravenna, Khusro broke the 'Endless Peace' that Justinian had bought at an extravagant price[26] and invaded Syria. Prosperous, tax-paying provinces were plundered, cities were forced to pay ransom and the great city of Antioch-on-the-Orontes, the queen city of the Orient, was utterly destroyed. Justinian was completely unready for the Persian onslaught. It was a calamity for imperial prestige.

But Theodora was glad to see Antonina. She needed her help to bring down her enemy, the praetorian prefect of *Oriens*, John the Cappadocian, who had grown too powerful and menaced her political clout, and perhaps Justinian's throne as well, though Justinian himself was blind to the danger. In the *Nika* riot of 532 the mob had howled for him to be sacked, for he was a ruthless tax collector, and Justinian was too unnerved to refuse. But before the year 532 was out John was back again as praetorian prefect, more powerful than ever. Theodora detested him and he returned the favour. He hated and feared her, for he knew that she would liquidate him if she could. But Justinian valued his efficiency; he knew that if he sought John's counsel he would receive unvarnished advice, possibly unpalatable, but worth heeding nonetheless. He turned a deaf ear to Theodora's complaints and accusations.[27] To bring down John the

Cappadocian Theodora turned to her friend Antonina; and Antonina, who had disposed of pope Silverius swiftly and effectively, was the sort of hardnosed agent that she needed.

The Fall of John the Cappadocian

THE PRAETORIAN PREFECT OF *ORIENS*, WHOSE HEADQUARTERS WAS IN CONSTANTINOPLE, was a grand officer of state who completely overshadowed his colleague, the praetorian prefect of Illyricum, whose headquarters was in Thessaloniki. The title was an ancient one. Five hundred years before Justinian, the emperor Augustus had established a praetorian guard with two prefects in command of it and it rapidly became an elite force with an unhealthy amount of political clout. Three centuries after Augustus, the emperor Constantine disbanded the old praetorian guard and revamped the prefecture. The prefect kept his title but lost his military function and became an administrative official instead. He had a multitude of civil responsibilities: trade, prices, provision of grain, higher education, public construction, the *dromos*, that is, the imperial postal and transportation system, and last but not least, taxation and justice. His only rival in the imperial bureaucracy was the Master of Offices, who directed the secret police as well as the ceremonies at court that grew in importance in the reign of Justinian and Theodora. Praetorian prefects tended not to remain long in office. John the Cappadocian was an exception. He was a survivor who lasted for ten years and his influence grew to rival Theodora's.

John's background was modest. He came from Cappadocia in central Turkey, a hard land that bred tough people: there was a saying that a viper once bit a Cappadocian and it was the viper that died.[1] In 520, when Justinian, still emperor-in-waiting, became one of the two Masters of the Soldiers in the Presence, the commanders of the troops in Constantinople, he found John working as a clerk in his office. For some reason, he noticed him. Once Justinian became emperor himself, John's rise was rapid. He became an accountant – a *logothetes* – in charge of a department, and before the end of April 531 he was appointed praetorian prefect. The *Nika* riot intervened and John was replaced briefly by Phocas, a man more acceptable to the senatorial class. Phocas was reputedly a man of old-fashioned virtue but he was also a pagan and when he was swept up in one of Justinian's witch-hunts against pagans, in 546, he would commit suicide. He did not last long as praetorian prefect. John the Cappadocian was back in office after a hiatus of no more than eight months.

He became consul in 538. Consuls by this time wielded no real power and three years later the consulship would be abolished, but the office still possessed great prestige. Perhaps it is no coincidence that in the year of John's consulship the Arian churches that remained in Constantinople were closed down. The Arians, heretics though they were, had worshipped more or less freely in Constantinople until this time, though Justin had harassed them enough to provoke a protest from the Theoderic in Italy, who was himself an Arian. The Arian churches, however, possessed some wealth and, once Theoderic was dead and his successors were in no position to help, they were vulnerable to John's covetous hands. It is not likely that he cared much about their deviant view of the Trinity, or about Christian dogma in general for that matter, but the property of the Arians was a different matter.[2] Justinian had already helped himself to some scraps of it, and John confiscated what remained for the benefit of the Treasury.

The consulship was the tidemark of his power. Three years afterwards, Theodora brought him down.

John was an efficiency expert and a cost-cutter and such men make government employees nervous. Bureaucrats ordinarily charged fees for their services. *Sportulae* – 'gratuities' or 'bribes', to give the word an unvarnished translation – were extra-legal payments which a client paid an official to get a service performed that he wanted. The law did not sanction them but custom did. Clerks purchased their offices and counted on making a profit from the *sportulae* they would receive. The emperor Constantine I had tried to ban them, pronouncing them beneath the dignity of a public servant, but the ban was not enforced – probably it could not be. John Lydus, a contemporary who knew the praetorian prefect's office from the inside, sketched his own career in his treatise titled *On the Magistracies*, which tells us how profitable a clerkship could be before John the Cappadocian's reforms took effect.[3] John Lydus had arrived in Constantinople in 511, leaving his native Philadelphia some 110 km east of Izmir in modern Turkey, within the region of the ancient Lydian kingdom. Hence John's name, *Lydus* – 'the Lydian'. As luck would have it, the praetorian prefect at this time was Zoticus, a fellow Philadelphian and a relative and family members looked out for each other. Nepotism was no sin in the imperial bureaucracy. Zoticus found a place for John as a shorthand writer in his office.

Zoticus' tenure of the prefecture was brief: little more than a year, but during it, John's fees for services brought him 1,000 *nomismata*, gold coins minted at 72 to a pound. He then got a swift promotion to Chief Accountant, leaping over the heads of the two other accountants, both older men who had purchased their offices for a handsome price, whereas John had paid nothing for his. The annual salary was only 24 *nomismata*, but John could expect many times that sum from extra-legal fees.

John Lydus' promotion may have been due as much to his qualifications as his connections, for those were the days when a good education in the Greek classics and a sound knowledge of legal Latin were the right qualifications for an aspiring civil servant. The emperor himself recognized Lydus' literary competence and command of accurate grammar. He rose rapidly through the ranks. But then John the Cappadocian arrived on the scene and disrupted the traditional procedures in the praetorian prefecture with his craze for efficiency and cost-cutting; thus when Lydus reached the end of his career he was not a rich man. Moderately well-to-do, perhaps, but his more than 40 years of service were rewarded only by an honorific decree and a pension paid in kind. Lydus would have preferred cold cash. The Cappadocian was not the only activist who made the civil service a less satisfying cash cow for bureaucrats, who yearned for a comfortable life. But he was the one whom Lydus hated most.

The Cappadocian's reforms wounded the social stratification of the empire. The emperor Constantius II, the son of the great Constantine, had ruled that a sound knowledge of classical literature was a prerequisite for entry into the civil service and generations of ambitious young men in the cities of the eastern empire studied the prose style of the Greek classics and mastered a working knowledge of Latin, which was still the language of law though it was rarely heard on the city streets of the eastern empire. The lure of a career in the service persuaded boys in schools all over the empire to apply themselves to Latin grammar so that they could study law and prepare themselves to make money as a bureaucrat. Archaeologists have found a cache of sixth- and seventh-century papyri in the village of Nessana[4] in the Negev desert: mostly accounts, wills, private letters and so on, but among them was a student's Latin vocabulary list for Vergil's *Aeneid*, the national epic of Rome! The student was likely an Arab youth who read Vergil in his classroom and looked forward to law school and a fat pocketbook, for a good education in the classics greased the social mobility of late antiquity. But John the Cappadocian considered clarity a greater virtue in law than polished Latin and Justinian followed John's lead. When he promulgated new laws, he used Greek when they were intended for Greek-speaking citizens. No wonder that the prestige which a good command of Latin once conferred on a bureaucrat vanished!

John tried to save money. He cut corners when he could, sometimes with unfortunate side-effects. He curtailed the imperial post. Before Justinian, emperors had maintained a courier service to carry important officials and dispatches across the empire. Along the main roads there were stations where as many as 40 post horses might be stabled. But the service was misused by influential persons, including clergymen who used the imperial post for free trips. The cost of maintaining the stables was enormous and John closed them down. Not all of them, for the service was necessary, but he curtailed it. But these stables had provided a market for grain grown by the local farmers and, once they were closed, the farmers had nowhere to sell their crops. It rotted, unharvested, in the fields. However, the haemorrhage of cash from the treasury had to stop and John was not deterred by the distress of the peasants, who now had no market for their produce.[5]

John Lydus loathed his namesake from Cappadocia. He reported that when the Cappadocian moved into his official residence, which was on the upper floor of the prefecture headquarters, he brought with him a gang of hangers-on, all of whom lived together like animals, in rooms that smelled of urine and faeces. He himself would sprawl naked on his couch, giving orders to his staff and inflicting depraved punishments according to his whim of the moment. His residence already had a bath house but he turned it into a stable and replaced it with another bath built on a higher storey. There, like the debauchee that he was, he bathed with young boys not yet old enough to shave. All of these tales, including the insinuation of homosexuality, were conventional sins attributed to unpopular public figures, but more interesting is the report that he used to dress himself in a burnous resembling the rough cloth cloak worn by some pagan priests and go to a sacred site, where he passed the night mumbling spells and incantations. He may have been a secret adherent of the old religion but the evidence for it cannot have been compelling, for Justinian considered paganism worse than heresy and Theodora would have used the charge of paganism to discredit John if she had found solid grounds. John must have maintained the appearance of Christianity but he had a consuming interest in sorcery and oracle mongering. So, at least, rumour said. If so, he was not the only Christian of his time to find astrology, sorcery and black magic fascinating. The worthy Lydus himself wrote a treatise on astrology and at least one modern scholar has suspected that he nourished a secret allegiance to paganism.[6]

John assembled a staff of cruelly efficient tax-collectors. One his underlings, John Maxilloplumacius,[7] also from Cappadocia, was a bull-necked man whose great jaw was filled with massive teeth and he left a multitude of horrific stories in his trail. A local notable, Petronius by name, from Lydus' home-town of Philadelphia, possessed a valuable jewel which the revenue agents coveted and they seized him, stripped and flogged him, and finally incarcerated him in a stable for mules. The whole populace, including the bishop of the city, protested and were roundly abused for their pains. But Petronius sent for his jewels, and surrendered every one; then, like a true gentleman, he bestowed gratuities on John's minions who had flogged him.[8] It was a magnificently correct gesture, for tax collectors always expected 'a little extra' for themselves and Petronius followed established practice: he remembered a *pourboire* for his tormentors.

Yet people spoke highly of John the Cappadocian. His great enemy, Lydus, reported that all were loud in their praises, particularly whenever Justinian was present. He claimed that it was because they were afraid of the Cappadocian and that judgement may have been a partly true; but it is also true that he was an able administrator and not all sectors of society disliked him. The freeholder farmers in the provinces of Asia Minor found John an ally in their ongoing struggle with the great landowners who tried to appropriate their farms and when, in 540–1, he toured these provinces he was greeted warmly.[9] Procopius, who wasted no love on him, describes him at one point in his *History* as the 'boldest and cleverest of all men of his time'.[10] Theodora assiduously reported all John's misdemeanours to her husband, yet Justinian listened and did nothing. She insinuated that John was aiming at the throne but Justinian remained unperturbed. He valued John's competence and, much as he loved his wife, he knew her capacity for loathing. If Theodora wanted to make a charge of treason stick, she needed an agent who could supply clear and unimpeachable evidence. Antonina was at hand, for in 540 she returned from Ravenna with Belisarius.

Belisarius' victory in Italy in 540 was the only bright spot in an *annus horribilis*, marked by disaster elsewhere in the empire. Everybody esteemed Belisarius and he basked in their admiration. He was the cynosure of all eyes in Constantinople as he left his house each day and made his way to the market-place, escorted by his guard. The tall, blonde Vandals and Goths mingled with dark, wiry Berbers made up a corps of guardsmen that advertised the conquests of the great field marshal. Only John the Cappadocian was unimpressed, though Justinian, too, must have wondered if Belisarius' victory in Italy was really as complete as Belisarius claimed. If so, his doubts were well-founded. However, Justinian had another assignment for his *prima donna* general, for on the eastern frontier the imperial regime was staring disaster in the face.

IN 540 THE SHAH OF PERSIA, KHUSRO, BREACHED THE SO-CALLED 'ENDLESS PEACE' that was only seven years old and invaded Roman Mesopotamia and Syria. He marched up the western bank of the Euphrates following a path well-trodden by earlier invaders from Mesopotamia and then veered west towards Antioch-on-the-Orontes, collecting ransom along the way from Mabbug, and setting fire to Beroea, or Aleppo, as it was later known. In the absence of Belisarius, who was nominally still Master of Soldiers in the Orient, the man in charge of defence was a prudent general named Bouzes, who stayed out of Khusro's path.

Justinian dispatched his cousin Germanus and Germanus' son, Justin, to defend Antioch but they brought with them a force of only 300 troops from Germanus' own corps of guardsmen. Justinian could spare no more, for Constantinople itself was in danger of a Bulgar attack. Germanus urged the Antiochenes to strengthen the circuit wall of their city but they rejected his advice and, when it became clear that no reinforcements were on the way, he abandoned hope. Yet he remained long enough in Antioch to buy silver at bargain-basement prices from the Antiochenes, who preferred to sell it rather than keep it for the Persians to plunder, and then he left the city to its own devices. Germanus' reputation does not emerge well from this episode.[11] With Germanus went the patriarch of Antioch, Ephraem, who had spearheaded the persecution of the Monophysites in the east. He was an old army man and assessed the situation as an experienced soldier would: he judged the defence of Antioch to be hopeless. Ephraem was no steadfast shepherd of his flock. In June, Khusro arrived before Antioch's walls.

Yet Antioch put up a valiant fight. Khusro demanded ransom money but at the last minute 6,000 troops from Palmyra and Damascus arrived and the Antiochenes felt reassured. They hurled taunts at Khusro from the city walls. When he pressed home the assault, citizens and soldiers fought side by side and, after the soldiers retreated, the young men belonging to the Blue and Green parties in the Antiochene hippodrome fought on, though they had no body armour and their only weapons were stones. But for all their desperate bravery they could not save Antioch. Khusro pillaged and burned it and transported some 30,000 Antiochenes to the Persian capital of Ctesiphon to populate a new Antioch which he founded for them in Iraq, near modern Baghdad. Justinian would rebuild Antioch-on-the-Orontes but Khusro had struck a blow at imperial prestige in the east which it would be hard to recoup.

Then Khusro went to Antioch's port city of Seleucia on the coast, some 32 km distant, where he bathed in the Mediterranean, thus placing himself in the long line of Mesopotamian conquerors, beginning with Sargon of Akkad nearly three millennia earlier, who reached the Mediterranean and washed their swords in its water. His next target was Apamea, which possessed a piece of the True Cross When he took the city he helped himself to its wealth but spared the holy relic. But, before he left Apamea, he staged an event to mock Justinian. He presided over a day of chariot races in the city's hippodrome in imitation of an emperor and, when a Blue team pulled ahead, he would not allow it, for he knew that Justinian and Theodora supported the Blues and hence he made a point of showing partiality for the Greens. So a Green chariot had to win, even if it meant holding back the Blue team and making it gallop more slowly.[12]

For the Christians, there was one small victory. Khusro was eager to capture the city of Edessa on his way back home, for it possessed a letter which the Edessenes claimed was written to their king Abgar by Jesus Christ himself. The letter put the city under the protection of God and thus its capture would have been an ideological victory for Persia. But when Khusro and his army advanced on Edessa they lost their way; and when they did at last reach the city, Khusro's face bloated and a boil on his jaw broke and oozed pus. He thought it imprudent to risk God's wrath further by pressing home his attack; yet before he withdrew, he collected 200 pounds of gold from Edessa and, in return, refrained from looting the countryside. It was only a minor setback. On the whole, his raid was a great success. He returned to his capital of Ctesiphon loaded down with captives and plunder, leaving a trail of panic and ruin behind him. The cities of Syria were so devastated that Justinian had to remit their taxes for a year to allow them to recover.

This was the situation awaiting Belisarius and Antonina when they returned to Constantinople from Italy, bringing with them Antonina's secret lover, Theodosius. He was no longer a poor man. He had helped himself to some of the treasure in the palaces in Carthage and Ravenna. But he was uneasy. While Antonina was in Italy, he had refused to join her unless she got rid of her son Photius, for Photius grew jealous when he saw that Theodosius was making a greater profit than himself from Belisarius' conquests. So Antonina sought various ways and means to eliminate her son from Belisarius' staff. Photius grew increasingly bitter but Antonina did not care. Eventually she managed to get rid of him and he returned to Constantinople, hurt and angry.

Then Theodosius had judged it safe to return. Possibly he came to Italy with John, the nephew of Vitalian, and met Antonina in Naples while the siege of Rome was still going on, but we cannot be certain. At some date, however, Theodosius and Antonina were reunited in Italy and the affair continued. Belisarius was a naïve cuckold and easily deceived. Antonina enjoyed her young, vigorous lover once more and when she returned to Constantinople he was in her retinue. But once there, Theodosius became apprehensive again. Antonina made little effort to be discreet and her sexual appetite seems to have been voracious. Theodosius was sure that the affair would be discovered. He left for Ephesus again and became a monk.

Antonina was distraught. She lamented loudly that she had lost her young friend. Even her unsuspecting husband pitied her and entreated Justinian and Theodora to order Theodosius to return, claiming that he was an indispensable member of his household. But still Theodosius would not come. He excused himself, saying that he liked the monastic life. Theodora must have listened to Belisarius' entreaties with some astonishment at the man's simplicity. But she also perceived a way to secure Antonina's co-operation in the unmaking of John the Cappadocian.

In 541 Belisarius was dispatched to the eastern frontier where he managed a cautious offensive against the Persians. Antonina remained behind in Constantinople. That must have aroused comment in court circles, for usually Antonina accompanied her husband on his campaigns, but this time she postponed her departure. The reason was that Theodora planned to set a trap for John and she needed Antonina as an accomplice. Theodosius returned from Ephesus to Constantinople and easily undertook the metamorphosis from monk to stud, with Theodora smoothing the way. Antonina's son Photius, who was by now a man of some wealth and had purchased an honorary consulship for himself in the year 541, was still a fly in the ointment. But he was removed from the scene by the simple expedient of attaching him to Belisarius' staff and dispatching him to the eastern front. As a precaution Antonina spread tales that Photius was paranoid – quite abnormally suspicious. He was a difficult son, she alleged, and a great trial to his poor mother.

Meanwhile, Antonina conspired with Theodora to ensnare John the Cappadocian. John proved a surprisingly easy victim. He was well aware that Theodora hated him and he took careful precautions against assassination. His bedroom was well guarded at night but even so he slept lightly and was always on the *qui vive*. But he did not sense danger from Antonina. He may not have known her well, for during much of his term as praetorian prefect she had not been in Constantinople and their paths can have crossed only seldom. She was the wife of Belisarius, whom John despised as a vainglorious popinjay with an outsized ego that needed constant stroking. Yet he knew that such men could harbour bitter resentment if they feel underappreciated and Justinian was showing scant appreciation for Belisarius' victory in Italy.

In 541 Justinian expected the Persians to launch a second offensive on the eastern frontier and he dispatched Belisarius to take countermeasures. Belisarius was the most acclaimed general of the day, even though he failed to impress John the Cappadocian, and popular expectations were high as Belisarius headed off for Mesopotamia. Antonina promised to follow him later. For the moment, she had other business.

JOHN THE CAPPADOCIAN HAD AN ONLY CHILD, A DAUGHTER NAMED EUPHEMIA, AND HE LOVED HER DEARLY. She was a discreet girl but young and unused to the treachery of the political world. Probably she was also lonely, for John was a watchful father who guarded his daughter carefully. We hear nothing of her mother; very likely she was dead. Euphemia was flattered when an experienced, older woman like Antonina paid attention to her and appeared to enjoy her company. Euphemia and Antonina rapidly became the best of friends.

Soon Antonina began to share secrets with the young girl. Once, when they were alone in Euphemia's room and the time was ripe, she revealed how unhappy she and Belisarius were at the shabby treatment that Justinian had meted out to them. Belisarius had extended the boundaries of the empire and brought two barbarian kings captive to Constantinople, to say nothing of a vast amount of treasure, and yet Justinian was utterly ungrateful. She would speak frankly. The regime of Justinian and Theodora was cruel and unjust, she said, and her body language intimated that Euphemia was mature young woman whom she knew could be trusted with her confidences. Antonina baited her trap with exquisite skill.

Euphemia was elated to hear Antonina's reproaches. Like her father, she feared the empress Theodora and it seems that she also nursed a hearty dislike of the regime. She let Antonina know that a share of the responsibility for the deplorable situation of the empire belonged to Belisarius and Antonina themselves, for they had the power to do something about it and yet they did nothing. It was their failure to defend what was just and right that gave Justinian and Theodora free rein to continue their wicked ways.

This was just what Antonina wanted to hear. Euphemia, she knew, reflected her father's opinions. She seized the opening, pointing out that she and her husband Belisarius could never hope to organize a successful *coup d'état* while they were isolated in army camps far from Constantinople and there was no well-placed accomplice at court to help them. Now, if they had a man of influence and ability as an ally – someone like Euphemia's father, for instance, then they might put together a conspiracy with real hope of success. If they worked together, they could accomplish whatever God willed – and Antonina implied strongly that God willed change at the top. Justinian and Theodora should be removed. Antonina's suggestion fell on fertile soil. Euphemia promised to take it to her father.

Euphemia may have been ingenuous but John was not and it is astonishing that he was so easily duped. He had little love or respect for Belisarius. But he was a devotee of soothsayers and fortune-tellers and they had told him that someday, there would come a time when he would replace Justinian as emperor. Euphemia's message must have seemed the fulfilment of the prophecy. He told Euphemia to make an appointment the next day for him to talk to Antonina.

Antonina was wary. She was not ready to meet John until her snare was ready for its prey and she did not want to appear too eager. She told Euphemia that it was imprudent for her to meet John in the city of Constantinople itself, for the rendezvous would arouse suspicion, but she planned to leave the city momentarily to join Belisarius on the eastern front and no one would think it odd if John met her outside the city to wish her a safe journey. Belisarius had acquired a villa known as the Rufinianae on the Asian shore, where Antonina would pause for a night's rest before she continued on her way. John would come there ostensibly to wish her Godspeed and together they could work out a plot to overthrow Justinian, which she would take with her to Belisarius. Euphemia took the message to John and he agreed. Antonina informed Theodora of her scheme and Theodora approved.

On the day appointed for her departure, Antonina came to the palace to bid the empress farewell and they made last-minute plans. Theodora sent her protégé, Narses, and Marcellus, the commander of the palace guard, along with a contingent of troops, across the Bosporus to the Rufinianae with orders to lie in wait and hear what John said; if he spoke treason, they were to burst out of hiding and kill him. Theodora went to Justinian to denounce John once again and to tell him of the trap that she and Antonina had set for him. Justinian did not try to forbid her but there was a story bruited about that he got in touch with one of John's friends and told him to pass on a message to John not to meet Antonina secretly under any conditions. A less confident man than John might have guessed that Justinian had discovered the clandestine tryst that he was about to have with Antonina, and wondered how much more Justinian knew. But John trusted his prophecies, and his daughter, who was taken in by Antonina's lubricious charm, assured him that Belisarius was ripe for revolution. He ignored the warning and about midnight he met Antonina as arranged. They talked while, behind a wall, Marcellus and Narses lurked with their guardsmen and eavesdropped.

Antonina led the conversation. She laid out a plan for Justinian's overthrow and John consented. Not only did he consent, but he bound himself with great oaths to support the plot. Narses and Marcellus had heard enough. They burst out from behind the wall where they had been listening and tried to seize John. But John had come attended with his usual bodyguard, who rushed to his aid. One of them wounded Marcellus, not knowing who he was, and John got away safely to the city.

Had he gone immediately to the emperor and confessed to him all that had happened, he might have suffered no harm, for Justinian still had confidence in him. If he had pretended that his aim was actually to test Belisarius' loyalty he might have deflected Justinian's suspicions and the plot that Theodora and Antonina devised would have backfired. But John panicked and sought asylum in a church. It was an admission of guilt and Theodora had no trouble convincing Justinian that the charge of treason against John should be taken seriously.

John was removed from the church in Constantinople where he had sought asylum and brought to the Hellespont, where he was taken to another church outside Cyzicus. There, willy-nilly, he was ordained a clergyman, not a bishop but a mere presbyter. Yet he still hoped that Justinian would relent and reappoint him praetorian prefect someday in the future and he took care to remain a clergyman in name only. He refused to perform any priestly duties. His property was confiscated. Yet Justinian returned a portion of it and, what with that and the cache of gold that John had concealed for a rainy day, he could continue to live in luxury. If he had faded into retirement he might have lived a comfortable life.

It turned out otherwise. The bishop of Cyzicus, Eusebius, was a harsh man, disliked by everyone and hated especially by John. The citizens of Cyzicus denounced him to Justinian but Eusebius had too much influence at court for a mere denunciation to bring him down. Thereupon some young thugs attacked him in the marketplace and killed him. John was a well-known enemy of Eusebius and it was natural to suspect his involvement. A commission was sent out to investigate. Unfortunately for John it was made up of senators who had suffered from his reforms and he could expect no mercy from them. They stripped him and flogged him and even though they could find no evidence to convict him of Eusebius' murder they seized his property anyway and put him on board a ship bound for Egypt, naked except for a cheap cloak of rough cloth. Whenever the ship called at a port, John was made to beg for bread or small coins. When he reached Egypt, he was imprisoned at Antinoopolis on the Nile, halfway between Cairo and Luxor.

Theodora neither forgot nor forgave. She continued to look for evidence that would link John incontrovertibly with Eusebius' murder. After four years of searching, she found two young Greens in Cyzicus who were rumoured to belong to the gang which had attacked bishop Eusebius and killed him. By a combination of threats and wheedling, she persuaded one of them to bear false witness against John. But the other resisted all torture. He refused to testify that John planned Eusebius' murder. Disgusted, Theodora ordered the right hands of both youths to be cut off, to punish the one because he refused to bear false witness and discourage the other from revealing her intrigues.

John's immediate successor as prefect was a government employee named Theodotus. Procopius[13] reports grumpily that he was a bad character but still not evil enough for Justinian and Theodora, for they liked officials with a good stench of corruption about them. In any case, Theodora soon found another replacement who was suitably unscrupulous, Peter Bar-Simon, known in Greek as Barsymes, a Syrian banker who had obtained a post in the prefect's office and there attracted Theodora's attention. His career blossomed. First he became Count of the Sacred Largesses, in charge of the mint and the imperial payroll. He continued John the Cappadocian's quest for cutting costs. One ingenious method that he devised was to mint a lightweight *nomisma* and used it to pay public officials, thereby saving gold. The wages of the soldiers were not one of his high priorities; he allowed them to go unpaid, with dire consequences for the morale of the army in Italy. By 542 he was a patrician and next year praetorian prefect.

His boldest and most unlucky venture was to gamble with Constantinople's grain supply. He sold off the reserve of grain in the public granaries. It was a shrewd financial gambit, though it annoyed the cities which were forced to buy this grain at a price which was set by the prefect's office. They found that some of the grain was mouldy and had to be dumped, which made them even more aggrieved. But next year, the crop in Egypt failed and there was no reserve. A grain shortage in Constantinople guaranteed demonstrations in the Hippodrome or worse and Peter had to requisition wheat from Thrace and from across the Bosporus in Asia Minor. Even so, there was not enough and there were bitter complaints in Constantinople about the price of bread.

This was too much for Justinian, who shut his ears to Theodora's objections and dismissed Peter. Yet Theodora remained a loyal supporter. She pressured Justinian to reappoint Peter as Count of the Sacred Largesses and there he continued his double-pronged effort to balance the budget and enrich himself at the same time.[14]

The Theodosius and Antonina Affair Continued

By 541 Photius and his mother Antonina had become bitter enemies. While Antonina was plotting to destroy John the Cappadocian, she used what spare time she had to write a stream of letters to her friends on the eastern front with Belisarius, whining about her paranoid son. He lacked any sense of filial duty or respect for the mother who bore him, she complained. They in turn reproached Photius until he could stand it no longer. The final straw came when a messenger reached him from Constantinople with the news that his mother and Theodosius were reunited and once again were enjoying the raptures of fornication. Photius decided that the cuckolded husband should learn about it. He introduced the messenger to Belisarius and told him to reveal everything.

Belisarius was wild with shock and rage.[1] What tormented him was not only his wounded self-esteem but the threat to his private fortune. It was vulnerable. What if Theodosius returned to Ephesus with a portion of Belisarius' wealth in his saddle-bags? He fell on his knees before Photius and begged his help, reminding him that he had raised him as his own son and it was only right now that he should defend not merely his stepfather but his own fair name as well, for everyone believed that a mother's reputation left indelible stains upon her son's. Yet Belisarius still loved Antonina and insisted that he would do her no harm, so long as he could revenge himself on Theodosius, the scoundrel who had corrupted his house.

Photius was ready to help. In fact, nothing could have made him happier, but he had good reason to be cautious. He remembered what had happened to the slave girl Macedonia, who had informed Belisarius of his wife's adultery while they were in Sicily. He bound Belisarius to him by a solemn oath of fidelity. The two men swore that they would never betray one another. But they thought it prudent not to act right away, but rather to wait until Theodosius returned to Ephesus and Antonina arrived from Constantinople and joined Belisarius. Then Photius himself would travel to Ephesus, and seize Theodosius and his money.

Meanwhile Belisarius had a war to fight against Persia. He prepared for the Persian attack that he thought was imminent but his intelligence was faulty:

Khusro had decided not to invade Mesopotamia again in 541. Instead he led an expedition against Lazica, modern Georgia, and captured the strategic fortress city of Petra on the Black Sea. Belisarius, still expecting to encounter an invading army, sent ahead his ally, al-Harith, sheikh of the Ghassanids, to reconnoitre and plunder Persian territory, while he himself attacked the Persian fortress of Sisauranon. It fell easily, for it lacked provisions and could not stand siege. But al-Harith and his Arabs did not return. The reason – though Belisarius did not guess it – was that they had captured a plentiful haul of loot which they feared they would have to share if they returned to the Byzantine camp. Time passed and al-Harith still did not appear. Belisarius' staff became nervous. They imagined that al-Harith had suffered a disaster, and the way was now open for Persia's allies, the Arab Lakhmids, to raid Syria, where there were no troops to protect it. They were anxious to pull back and Belisarius yielded. So ended the campaign of 541. Belisarius had shown extraordinary timidity, which was out of character, and he missed a golden opportunity to attack Persia while Khusro was not there to protect it. Procopius uses his well-honed rhetorical skills to gloss over the reason for Belisarius' tentative strategy.[2]

He did not tell the whole story, it appears, for the *Secret History*[3] has some important details to add. Just after Belisarius captured Sisauranon, news reached him that Antonina was on her way to join him, and he turned back to meet her. He could not wait. It was true that al-Harith's failure to return from his *razzia* had unnerved the general staff and they wanted to retreat. But it was Belisarius' private motive that decided his strategy and the Byzantines lost a chance to strike a blow that would have avenged the devastation which the Persians had inflicted on the eastern provinces in the previous year and repaired imperial prestige.

When Antonina met Belisarius, she found him beside himself with fury and jealousy. He put her under guard, and even thought of killing her. But he still loved her, and besides there was Theodora to consider. Belisarius did not dare harm Antonina. Theodora would not tolerate an 'honour killing' of her friend. Photius, meanwhile, set out for Ephesus, taking with him one of Antonina's eunuchs, Calligonas by name, who had acted as her go-between, and on the journey Photius forced him under torture to reveal Antonina's secrets. But Theodosius got advance warning that Photius was on his way and he sought refuge in the great church of St John the Apostle in Ephesus. However a judicious bribe softened the scruples of Andrew, the bishop, and he surrendered Theodosius to Photius.

At this point Theodora intervened. She summoned both Belisarius and Antonina to Constantinople. Belisarius had no choice but to obey and he came, leaving his bodyguard to winter in Cilicia on the south-east coast of Asia Minor. When news of the summons reached Photius he guessed what it meant and had Theodosius escorted to Cilicia and handed over to Belisarius' guard. A general's guard – his *bucellarii* – were bound by oaths of loyalty to their general as well as to the emperor and Photius could count on Belisarius' *bucellarii* to conceal Theodosius and resist any effort of the empress to take him. Then Photius and Calligonas came themselves to Constantinople, bringing with them the money that they had seized from Theodosius.

Theodora was merciless. She directed her wrath particularly against the companions of Belisarius and Photius, torturing some and banishing others. One of them, a senator who also bore the name Theodosius, had his property impounded and he himself was thrown into an underground oubliette where he was fettered to a trough with a rock chained to his neck so that he could not lie down and rest. The hapless senator endured four months of sleep deprivation before he went mad. His only sin was that he had accompanied Photius to Ephesus when he was on the trail of Antonina's lover. The unfortunate senator, his mind deranged, died soon after he was set free.

Photius was flogged until his back ran blood from the strokes of the lash, but he refused to reveal the whereabouts of Calligonas or of Antonina's lover, Theodosius. But eventually the secret came out. Theodora handed Calligonas over to Antonina and let her have her revenge. We are not told his fate but no doubt it was unpleasant. Theodosius was brought to Constantinople, where Theodora concealed him in the imperial palace. Then, next day, she invited Antonina to come and marvel at a costly pearl that had just fallen into her hands. Antonina must come and see it! Antonina came, and when the 'pearl' was brought into the room, it was none other than Theodosius in person! Antonina was ecstatic. Theodora was her saviour and benefactor, she exclaimed, and as true an empress as ever lived.

However death soon removed Theodosius from the scene. Theodora kept him in the palace where Antonina could enjoy his talents as a lover and she herself showered him with favours, even promising to make him an army officer, for apparently Theodosius had military ambitions. But before he could display his talents as a field commander he suffered an attack of dysentery and died. In the Mediterranean world of the last century, a summer ailment used to attack tourists and natives alike, known variously as 'Greek stomach', or 'Egyptian', or 'Turkish stomach', depending on the geographical location of the ailment. It has largely disappeared with modern refrigeration, which makes it probable that it was only mild ptomaine poisoning. Probably Theodosius fell victim to a particularly lethal attack of 'Greek stomach'. It is a likelier cause of death than Edward Gibbon's insinuation in his *Decline and Fall of the Roman Empire* that he 'expired in the first fatigues of an amorous interview'.

As for Photius, Antonina's unfortunate son, Theodora wasted no compassion on him. She incarcerated him in one of her oubliettes within the palace, windowless isolated rooms where she kept her enemies imprisoned at her pleasure. Photius escaped, however, and sought asylum in the church of the *Theotokos* – Mary, the Mother of God. But Theodora had him dragged back to his cell. He escaped a second time and this time he fled to Hagia Sophia, where he clung to the baptistery under its magnificent dome and cried for mercy. But Theodora's henchmen dragged him away while the clergy stood by, too frightened to interfere. At last, after three years of confinement, the prophet Zachariah appeared to Photius in a vision and promised help if he tried once again to escape. The prophet kept his word: on his third attempt, he managed to evade the wrath of the terrible empress. He reached Jerusalem where he went unrecognized. He shaved his head and became a monk.

Photius was a tragic example of a failed mother-son relationship. His father died while he was still a babe in arms and Antonina had little time for him. In the typical Byzantine household the mother played a dominant role, but motherhood was a job with little attraction for Antonina and Photius transferred his affection to his stepfather, Belisarius. When he saw him cuckolded, he identified with him as another of his mother's victims. But then Belisarius abandoned him as well. He had sworn an oath to support his stepson; yet, when he saw him persecuted by Theodora, he stood by and made no effort to help. Like everyone else, Belisarius knew better than to incur the enmity of the terrible empress.

Photius was later to resume his military career under Justinian's successor, Justin II, and when the Samaritans rose once again in a last revolt it was he who repressed them – and he was merciless. The unfortunate Samaritans were made to pay for all the bitterness and rage that he had stored up in his unhappy youth.

We can only speculate what went on in Belisarius' mind. Theodora forced a reconciliation of sorts with Antonina and soon Belisarius resumed his old relationship with her. Yet perhaps his secretary Procopius reflected his former employer's mindset at this point in his life, when he complained in his *Secret History* that Theodora's championship of oppressed women made it impossible for men to control their wives: they misbehaved, knowing that Theodora would defend them if their husbands tried to discipline them. Even when they were guilty of adultery, she protected them. She attacked the old double standard for husbands and wives and Belisarius learned from personal experience how hardnosed that attack could be. Yet he must also have reflected covertly on his relationship with his ungrateful emperor. There had been rumours of disloyalty before, once when he conquered the Vandal kingdom, and again when he tricked the Goths into surrendering Ravenna with the pretence that he would make himself emperor of a revived western Roman Empire. But he had been careful to scotch them. Now, however, Belisarius may have begun seriously to reflect that the empire might be better off without the dyarchy of Justinian and Theodora. He cannot have been unaware that there were many disaffected subjects of Justinian who regarded him as the one person who could unseat the regime, and they were disappointed when he chose loyalty instead.[4]

There were dark clouds in the future. In the 530s Justinian had spent money lavishly on an expensive building programme, particularly in Constantinople, where a new Hagia Sophia rose to take the place of the cathedral that was burned in the *Nika* riots. The architecture was daring and the result dazzling, and it was only one of a number of splendid churches and other structures that Justinian and Theodora built. But now Justinian faced the troubled 540s with no reserve fund in the treasury. Rich citizens were less willing to show off their wealth. A sign of the times was the cancellation of the consulship. A consul's inaugural celebration was an expensive affair, subsidized generously by the imperial treasury. In 541 a citizen named Basil the Younger held the consulship in Constantinople and gave his name to the year, the last consul to do so. Justin II would revive the consulship but it had lost its lustre. So ended a tradition that stretched back in Roman history more than a thousand years.

Yet the title of consul was still available for purchase, for the emperor Zeno had established an honorary consulship which could be bought for 100 gold pounds. Selling distinctions was one of the methods by which Justinian raised money, for the imperial exchequer was very needy. The surplus funds that the old emperor Anastasius had left in the treasury had been used up, purchasing the 'Endless Peace' with Persia, which lasted a mere seven years. Meanwhile in Alexandria another cause for anxiety appeared before the year 541 drew to a close. People there were dying of a disease that caused agonizing swellings in their groins and armpits. It would reach Constantinople the next year and thrust the empire into a far grimmer future.

Plague and Intrigue

YERSINIA PESTIS, THE BACILLUS WHICH CAUSES BUBONIC PLAGUE, WAS LIKELY PRESENT IN THE MEDITERRANEAN BASIN LONG BEFORE 524, WHEN IT SMOTE CONSTANTINOPLE, for it is a disease endemic among burrowing rodents that live in large underground colonies. Its closest relative in the bacterial world – and its probable ancestor – is *Yersinia pseudotuberculosis* which causes gastroenteritis and diarrhoea. *Yersinia pestis*, its deadlier cousin, is carried by fleas and has acquired an extra gene which produces an enzyme allowing it to survive in a flea's stomach, so that when the flea finds a host for dinner, it can pass it on. More than one kind of flea can serve as a carrier but the flea of choice is *Xenopsylla cheopis*, a prodigious jumper but wingless, and hence must depend on a rodent host if it is to move any distance. Rats do very well as transporters, particularly *rattus rattus*, the black rat which is now almost extinct in Europe though it still flourishes in places like Hawaii and on the Gulf Islands off the west coast of Canada, where it is known as the roof rat. The flea alights on a rat and takes up residence as its uninvited guest, sucking the rat's blood for nourishment until it is infected by *yersinia pestis* and its sucking tube is blocked by bacteria. When the sick flea tries to suck blood, it fails. Instead, it vomits the contents of its stomach into the rat's blood stream and starves to death, but not before it has passed on the bacteria to the rat which becomes infected with plague and any healthy flea that sucks its blood becomes infected too. In the stricken Algerian town that Albert Camus describes in his novel *The Plague*, the first sign of the epidemic was the appearance of great numbers of infected rats, turning up everywhere in houses or on the roads, dead or dying.[1]

Once the rats die, the hungry fleas must find new victims and humans are acceptable substitutes. Eventually fleas and rats both die, and so do the human victims whose immune systems are not robust enough to fight off the infection. The plague then subsides until there is a new crop of fleas, rats and humans that can serve as its prey. Thus the plague epidemic that appeared in Europe for the first time in 542, when it struck Constantinople, reappeared in regular waves until the mid-eighth century. A scourge in Naples about 767 was its last outbreak before it disappeared from Europe as mysteriously as it came, only to reappear as the Black Death in the mid-fourteenth century.[2]

The earliest description we have of bubonic plague is found in a second-century medical writer dating to the reign of the emperor Hadrian, Rufus of Ephesus, who in turn cited earlier writers, one belonging to the third century BCE, Dionysius the Hunchback, and a couple dating two centuries later, Posidonius and Dioscorides. Rufus used the term *bubon* for the swollen lymph nodes in the groin which are the distinguishing feature of the disease,[3] though he probably did not coin it. He reported that the disease was to be found in the regions of Libya, Egypt and Syria, occurring frequently enough but never as a pandemic.[4] Hans Zinsser,[5] in his classic *Rats, Lice and History*, written before orthodox historians paid much attention to the effect of disease on the course of history, took Rufus seriously and claimed that plague was prevalent in the Near East and the northern coast of Africa three centuries before Christ. Dioscorides, who lived about the time that Julius Caesar was assassinated, investigated a plague in Libya. Probably this Dioscorides should be identified with a physician of that name at the court of Antony and Cleopatra in Alexandria, and we can give our imaginations free rein when we try to conjure up what sort of report he made to that ill-fated pair.

Yet it was not until 541 that plague become epidemic in the Mediterranean basin. The 'Endless Peace' which Justinian had purchased from Persia at a high price had collapsed. The fragile victory in Italy that Belisarius had swindled the Ostrogoths into accepting fell apart. Plague arrived as a third calamity. This is not to suggest that there was any connection among the three, though a Byzantine, who believed in the wrath of God, and that sin causes death, may have thought so.[6] Yet for some mysterious reason the plague was transformed into a pandemic in Justinian's reign. Hans Zinsser thought it may have been the arrival in Europe of the black rat (*rattus rattus)* which, he believed, came as an immigrant from India into the Mediterranean region no earlier than the sixth century. The black rat is a sociable rodent which lives agreeably in urban centres, dwelling alongside humans, unlike the misanthropic and much nastier brown rat, *rattus norvegicus*, a later immigrant into Europe, which eventually displaced its rival. *Rattus rattus* is generally believed to have been the plague carrier in the mid-fourteenth-century pandemic known as the 'Black Death'. It was an efficient carrier of plague, particularly in crowded cities where people and rats shared a congested living space. Unfortunately for Zinsser's theory, however, there is now archaeological evidence for black rats in the classical world, long before the Justinianic plague.[7] Yet though bubonic plague and the black rat both existed in the classical world, plague did not become epidemic until the reign of Justinian.

In any case, the black rat is only an innocent agent in the transmission of plague. The carrier is a flea, and though other fleas can also carry the bacteria, *Xenopsylla cheopis* is particularly efficient, for once it is infected, its sucking tube becomes blocked by colonies of bacteria in less than five days, causing it to inject the infection into its host. Nor is the black rat the only possible carrier: gerbils and marmots[8] can also carry the fleas that transmit plague. In California, ground squirrels were found to be infected in 1900, and they continue to this day to serve as host to the bacillus. *Yersinia pestis* is not so specialized that it cannot exist without an ideal carrier. Yet Zinsser was partly right. Some phenomenon must have taken place in the years immediately before the plague outbreak that caused a population explosion of plague carriers and transformed the plague into a pandemic.

We can only guess what it was. We have already noted that the year of the great siege of Rome, when the Ostrogoths shut Belisarius and his little army up in the city for just over a year, was exceptionally cold and dry.[9] So much we can infer from dendrochronology, the study of the growth rings on trees. Abnormally cold temperatures persisted until the end of the decade; 540 and 541 were both cooler than usual. A dust veil, like a fog without moisture, hung over the Mediterranean for 18 months in 536–7, filtering the sunlight and causing crop failures. An enormous volcanic explosion such as happened at Krakatoa in the late nineteenth century could have caused it, for the dust particles from a volcano can prevent sunlight from penetrating the atmosphere;[10] but we have no record of a great volcanic eruption at this time. Atmospheric dust from comets or asteroids is another possibility, and for that there is some evidence.[11] But whatever the reason for the dust veil, the cooler temperatures that it triggered may have provided an ideal ambience for the flea, causing a population upsurge. Or could the bacillus that caused the Justinianic plague have been a new, mutant strain? DNA analysis may eventually be able to provide some sort of answer, for archaeologists have found pits where plague victims were buried. But what the origin was of the plague bacillus that wandered over Europe from the mid-sixth to the mid-eighth century remains a mystery, though its ultimate source must have been one of the two plague reservoirs that existed at the time, one in north-eastern India and the other in central Africa.

The pestilence appeared first at Pelusium at the north-east corner of the Nile delta, and from there it migrated westwards to Alexandria which it reached in 541. The death toll was heavy. From Egypt, the plague spread up the coast of Palestine into Syria, always starting in the coastal ports and then moving inland.

In 542, in the middle of spring, after the opening of the navigation season, it arrived in Constantinople. The next year it reached Italy, and from there it migrated to Merovingian France. It left behind it a trail of death.

THERE WERE TALES OF GHOSTLY BEINGS AND PHANTASMS that roamed the streets, striking persons they encountered, and these persons immediately took sick.[12] One story told that a black boat was sighted offshore, rowed by men without heads. These were the fearful headless fiends that terrified the popular imagination – the awful attendants of the Evil One himself. It made no difference if people wore amulets bearing magical prayers to ward off devils. Even the houses where copper bells hung over the doorways were not safe, though demons were known to hate the jangle of copper. Nor did it avail to seek sanctuary in a church, or invoke the holy names of the Trinity or the *Theotokos*. Even within churches, men and women died. As time went on, people would lock themselves in their rooms and pay no heed when they heard someone pounding on the door. It might be a friend, but equally likely, it might be a demon that had come to make a terrible visitation.

For most people, the disease came without warning. Suddenly they felt feverish. It was not a high fever, nor particularly alarming. But then on the same day or the next, they developed a swelling in the groin. This was the bubo, the swelling of a lymph node which is the tell-tale symptom of bubonic plague – the word 'bubonic' derives from the Greek *boubon*, meaning 'groin'. When bacteria attack lymph nodes the nodes distend, and since the legs are the area of the body most vulnerable to flea bites, the nodes of the groin are nearest the bite and hence are generally the first to intumesce, though the nodes in the armpits and behind the ears might also become swollen. The Greek doctors, knowing nothing about lymph nodes, thought that the disease was centred in these buboes, and they cut them open on some cadavers to see what was inside. What they found was a kind of hard dark ganglion. It was beyond their comprehension.

After the buboes appeared, some victims fell into a coma, while others became delirious and would run off with loud cries of terror, imagining that some assailant was chasing them. Some, with no one to care for them, simply died of neglect. Still others, who escaped the delirium or the coma, expired when their buboes gangrened and the pain grew unbearable. There were cases, too, where black pustules broke out all over the body. These victims always died quickly. On the other hand, if the buboes suppurated, the victims often survived. Pregnant women were particularly vulnerable. The plague caused either miscarriage, resulting in the death of the mother, or death in childbirth if the mother carried the foetus to term. The caregivers who nursed the ill grew utterly exhausted, for the patients needed constant care and their poor, harassed attendants aroused almost as much pity as the patients themselves.

Procopius' observation[13] that doctors attending plague victims rarely contracted it themselves is fairly good evidence that this was bubonic plague, which kills when the infection enters the bloodstream and results in septicaemia. Without antibiotics to treat it, it can kill from 40 to 70 per cent of its victims. Its deadlier cousin, pneumonic or pulmonary plague, which kills all its victims, occurs when the bacteria invade the lungs and cause plague pneumonia. It is highly contagious, for its bacilli are airborne and, when a victim coughs, he ejects saliva droplets full of thousands of germs. The observation that doctors were not noticeably susceptible shows that this plague was most likely bubonic, not the more terrible pulmonary type.[14] Yet it was terrible enough. It could well have destroyed half the population of Constantinople.

The countryside suffered terribly as well. As *Yersinia pestis* made its way from Egypt northwards along the Mediterranean coast on its way to Constantinople, the Syriac historian John of Ephesus travelled in its wake. He saw villages with only a few people left alive, and they busied themselves removing corpses from the streets; in other villages, all the houses were empty. Fruits ripened in the orchards with no one to harvest them. In Syria, grain in the fields was ready to be reaped but no reapers came to gather in the crops. Sheep, oxen and pigs had no one to tend them and returned to the wild. There were signs of catastrophe everywhere.

The epidemic gripped the city for four months. At first the dead were buried properly, each household looking after its own, but soon the number of deaths overwhelmed the living. In some houses there was no healthy person left to perform funeral rites. Some houses became habitations of the dead, and they were discovered only when the stench of the decomposing bodies behind their closed doors betrayed their presence. Bodies with swollen, gaping mouths sprawled, neglected, on the streets or lay in piles by the seashore, where feral dogs gnawed at them. Animals too: rats, dogs and wild beasts could be found dead with swollen groins.[15] The young toughs belonging to the Blue and Green parties forgot their rivalry and worked together to dispose of the corpses. No one had time for the usual rites of burial.

Streets were deserted. Tradesmen abandoned their shops and there was a shortage of bread and other foodstuffs. Victims who might have recovered from the plague with proper care died of neglect and starvation. The poor died first. There were some who turned to the old religion for help. It was reported that in some cities in Palestine, demons appeared disguised as angels and told the desperate people to worship a bronze image of a pagan god – Apollo, perhaps? – but when they obeyed, death fell upon them.[16] In Constantinople, the population was cut in half, or perhaps more, and it did not easily recover. The plague advanced westwards: in 543, it reached Italy, where the Byzantines were losing ground to a Gothic insurgency, and in the same year, it appeared in southern Gaul and parts of Spain, though it failed to gain a foothold there. Before the end of the century there would be four more onslaughts of plague and it would be two hundred years before Europe got a reprieve.

Most epidemics follow a demographic pattern similar to war: the death rate soars, but so does the marriage rate and the birth rate. Thus the population makes up its losses quickly. But with bubonic plague, pregnant women are particularly susceptible and so, while the marriage rate may go up, the birth rate drops and the population fails to recover swiftly from its losses. At the end of the sixth century, the Byzantine Empire numbered only about 60 per cent of what it was in the year 500.[17]

Justinian ordered an official named Theodore to organize the disposal of the bodies, and he filled all the available tombs, and then ordered pits dug north of the city beyond Sycae, where the bodies might be dumped. John of Ephesus reports that each pit was filled with seventy thousand corpses, piled one layer on top of another. When the diggers could not cope with the great multitude of cadavers, the roofs were torn off the towers on the fortification walls and the bodies were jettisoned there. As they decomposed, a foul miasma spread over the city whenever the wind blew from the north.

Theodora's habit of personal cleanliness stood her in good stead during the plague. Every morning before breakfast she luxuriated in her bath. Fleas were strangers in the women's quarters of the palace and Theodora herself did not rub shoulders with hoi polloi. But Justinian, who was more approachable, fell ill and developed a bubo. For several days, his life hung in the balance. If he died, who would his successor be? In the corridors of the palace there must have been many half-concealed whispers and numerous covert glances.

Theodora knew how perilous the situation was for the regime. She saw to it that Justinian received the best medical attention available and she must have been frightened, though she took care not to show it. If Justinian were to die, her power would vanish overnight. The Chalcedonians would move without mercy against the Monophysite refugees lodged in the Palace of Hormisdas. Theodora herself would have to leave the palace and the hiding place of the excommunicated patriarch, Anthimus would be revealed. The members of the Constantinople Establishment, whom she had antagonized, were lying in wait for revenge. She must have been more grateful than ever to Antonina for engineering the fall of John the Cappadocian the year before the plague reached Constantinople, for he would have been the first to take advantage of her weakness.

However Justinian recovered and applied himself again, with undiminished vigour, to his current theological researches. But Theodora did not forget. Her power was fragile. The Angel of Death had hovered for a moment over the imperial palace and if Theodora was to achieve any security for her Monophysites, she had a precarious space of time in which to do it.

In the long run, the plague may actually have helped the rise of Monophysitism. In times of plague, there is an outmigration from the cities to the rural areas, partly because the cities run short of food and partly to escape the disease, for though the plague struck some villages hard, on the whole the chances of survival were better in the country than the city. Bubonic plague must have contributed mightily to the decline of the cities in the Byzantine Empire, though the evidence is not unambiguous.[18] The Melkite strength in the eastern provinces was in the cities, where the bishops had their seats, whereas the Monophysites drew their support from the rural monasteries and the villages. The plague introduced a subtle shift in the balance of dominance.

It was also, perhaps, a motive for the timing of another crusade against paganism. Plagues punished sin. So good Christians believed. Where were the sinners responsible for this affliction? In what is now Aydin province in south-western Turkey on the Aegean many pagans had survived in the hills around Tralles on the Maeander River, and Justinian commissioned John of Ephesus to convert them. John claimed that he won thousands for the Christian faith, and built twenty-four churches and four monasteries, the largest of which was at a mountain village called Derira above Tralles, where there was a cult centre for the great Mother Goddess of Anatolia.[19] Justinian's chosen missionary, John, was a Monophysite but he was also a friend of Theodora who no doubt recommended him to her husband. In the face of the pagan enemy, Chalcedonians and Monophysites were united. Four years later, John would spearhead another anti-pagan campaign, this time in Constantinople itself.

ONE BY-PRODUCT OF THE PLAGUE WAS A FINAL RECONCILIATION OF BELISARIUS AND ANTONINA. It was engineered by Theodora. In 542 Persia launched another invasion across the Euphrates River. Khusro's objective was Palestine, especially Jerusalem which was full of treasures which devout pilgrims had dedicated there. The outnumbered imperial army, led by Bouzes, a competent but prudent officer, and Justus, Justinian's nephew, retreated to Mabbug and took refuge there. Justinian dispatched Belisarius again, but without an army at his back. Riding hard, using the horses of the imperial post, he reached Dura-Europos on the Euphrates, where there had once been Roman city until the Persians destroyed it years ago, in 256, and summoned the army at Mabbug to come to meet him there. Then, when an envoy arrived from Khusro, Belisarius put on a convincing show of strength. It was pure theatre, for the armed forces that he had were pitifully weak, but the envoy was deceived and reported back to his king that Belisarius commanded a powerful military force. Khusro was impressed enough that he withdrew, though on the way home he captured and razed the border city of Callinicum. It was in the process of rebuilding its fortification wall and when Khusro came upon it, it had no defences.

Then a blunt order came to Belisarius from the imperial court to return to Constantinople. Ostensibly Justinian planned to reassign Belisarius to Italy where the situation was becoming increasingly grim and, in 544, Belisarius did return to the Italian front. But Theodora had not yet produced the concluding act of the Belisarius and Antonina soap opera.

WHEN WORD REACHED THE ARMY ON THE EASTERN FRONT THAT JUSTINIAN HAD FALLEN ILL WITH THE PLAGUE, the officers in Belisarius' general staff began to speculate openly about his successor. If Justinian died, who would follow him on the throne? Some openly expressed their disgust with Justinian and, no doubt, his empress as well. Then the news arrived that Justinian had recovered and the backbiting began. Two generals, Peter, and John, nicknamed the 'Glutton', reported that they had overheard Belisarius and Bouzes vent their unhappiness with the regime. They were overheard saying that they would never put up with another ruler like Justinian. So Peter and John claimed, and perhaps the report was true. Belisarius' relations with Antonina were still cool. A year had not yet passed since Theodora returned Antonina's lover to her, and Photius still lingered in prison. Belisarius remained alienated and embittered. His loyalty had been severely tested.

As soon as the report reached Theodora she acted swiftly, for she knew that one aspect of the regime which Belisarius and Bouzes abhorred was herself. She summoned both the accusers and the accused to Constantinople. Bouzes did not have a great reputation to save him and one day, without warning, Theodora called him into the women's quarters of the palace, where he was arrested and flung into a basement dungeon; there he remained incarcerated for two years and four months. His health never recovered from the ordeal, though he resumed his army career after Theodora released him. Belisarius knew what he could expect, and he was panic-stricken.

No treason was proved against him, however, and even though Justinian was jealous of his star general, he was not prepared to sacrifice him to his wife's paranoia. Yet he did yield to her thus far: he appointed Martin, a general who had served in Africa under Belisarius, Solomon and Germanus successively, to replace Belisarius as Master of the Soldiers in the East. Theodora seized Belisarius' property and his corps of guardsmen was disbanded. The men who had once served on his staff were now forbidden to visit him. He was stripped of any levers of power, purposely isolated.

The great commander who had been smitten so suddenly by Theodora's displeasure was a pitiable sight. He could not bear his misfortune with even the appearance of dignity. Theodora played with him like a cat with a mouse. Finally when Justinian had made up his mind to send Belisarius to Italy, where the Gothic insurgents had recovered most of Italy under the leadership of a new king, Theodora staged a cruel rehabilitation scene with appropriate dramatics. One morning, when Belisarius came to the palace with a tiny escort, he encountered a chilly atmosphere. The emperor and empress were hostile and the courtiers rude. He returned home, a frightened man, convinced that Bouzes' fate or worse awaited him. His nerve broke. He retreated to his room, collapsed on a couch and awaited the end that was surely coming. Beads of sweat stood out on his forehead. Antonina paid him no attention, for she said she had an attack of indigestion and paced up and down outside the room to relieve her discomfort.

After sunset, a courier named Quadratus arrived without notice from the palace and reported that he had been sent by the empress. Belisarius was terrified. He curled up on his couch in the foetal position, numb with fear. But Quadratus sent in a letter addressed to him from the empress, which provided a surprise ending for this tale of the Antonina, Theodosius and Belisarius triangle. Theodora wrote that she was going to be magnanimous and, in spite of Belisarius' ungrateful conduct, she would forgive him for the sake of his wife, to whom she was greatly indebted. She was granting him his life and the return of his property, but at the end of the letter there was both an admonition and a hint of menace. For the future she would monitor Belisarius' treatment of Antonina.

Belisarius was overcome with relief and gratitude. He fell on his face before Antonina and kissed her feet. Henceforth, he said, he would be her slave. Antonina resumed her former place as the senior partner in matrimony with Belisarius. Photius would remain a couple more years in prison before he contrived to escape to Jerusalem. He had become a bitter man, with good reason. He was used to Antonina's malice but he had idolized his stepfather and now he, too, had abandoned him. As for Belisarius, in the spring of 544 he was appointed 'Count of the Stables' (a more important position than it sounds) and he was dispatched to Italy where the Goths were laying siege to Rome once again.

What were Justinian's thoughts as he watched his wife's manoeuvres? We can only speculate. Perhaps he was happy to leave the business of neutralizing any danger from Belisarius to his wife, for he was totally engaged in a theological battle with the see of Rome over an issue that may seem inconsequential to twenty-first-century minds, but in the Byzantine thought-world, theological quibbles had the power to arouse fierce passions. The 'Three Chapters dispute', as it has been named, centred on the question of whether three churchmen, who had been in their graves for a century, should be condemned and labelled heretics.[20] A theological battle was raging in Constantinople, while Belisarius lived in fear of his life, and on the eastern frontier his successor as Master of Soldiers, Martin, prepared for an offensive against Persia. He was supplied with a great army of 30,000 troops. Belisarius had invaded Italy with one-fifth that number or less. The portents for Martin's attack were good. The plague had reached Persia and Khusro was willing to talk about peace. Byzantine intelligence had picked up information that Khusro's son was leading a revolt against his father and that sickness had laid low the whole Persian army. Here was a golden opportunity to take advantage of Persia's weakness and Justinian grasped it. Somehow, in spite of the plague, he found the necessary manpower and ordered an invasion of Persarmenia, where the commander of the Persian garrison had no more than 4,000 troops at his disposal. This should have been an easy victory.

Not so. The Persians dug in at the mountain village of Anglon and, using it as a base, they routed a Byzantine army that was between seven and eight times larger than their own. It was a humiliating defeat. Martin who had replaced Belisarius at Theodora's insistence, had proved utterly incompetent. Justinian must have reflected that the Vandal kingdom had fallen to Belisarius with an army not much greater than half the size of the force that was trounced at Anglon by a mere 4,000 troops and the thought may have occurred to him that it was no easy task to win wars and satisfy his wife's agendas at the same time.

And what covert thoughts did Antonina harbour? She must have appeared outwardly friendly and grateful to the empress, who restored Belisarius' property that she had confiscated, though she skimmed 3,000 pounds of gold off the top as a dividend for Justinian, which must have assuaged any pangs of contrition that he may have felt. It might also have been about this time that Justinian bestowed on Belisarius the palace of John the Cappadocian, which had been expropriated. It was not unfair that Belisarius should profit from John's downfall, since his wife's machinations had brought it about.

Yet Antonina may have nursed some private resentments. She would have noticed that, when Martin replaced Belisarius as Master of the Soldiers in the East, he was given resources the like of which Belisarius himself had never been granted. She may have been unfaithful to her husband's bed, but she had always been his loyal helpmate when it came to furthering his career and increasing his wealth. Belisarius wanted to go back to the eastern front and resume his command but Antonina would have none of it, for she claimed she had been insulted there and would not return. She left unsaid that her husband had suffered an insult there of a different kind: Theodora had chosen Martin, Belisarius' subordinate, as his replacement, and had given him troops enough to guarantee him the victory that rightfully belonged to Belisarius, and so they would have done if Martin had possessed a glimmer of competence. The eastern front was a place where Belisarius had suffered ill treatment as much or more than herself and she did not want to return.

In 544 Theodora and Antonina said goodbye for the last time. Belisarius was leaving to take command in Italy and his constant companion, Antonina was going with him. When she returned to Constantinople, Theodora was already dead. Yet Theodora, who had had her covetous hands on Belisarius' property once and then had to return it, had her acquisitive instincts aroused. She determined to secure Belisarius' wealth for her own family and she laid plans to betroth her grandson, Anastasius, to Belisarius' daughter, Joannina. Belisarius and Antonina were in no position to object. But as Antonina set sail for Italy, we may surmise that her private feelings about Theodora and Theodora's schemes for Joannina's marriage were less than pleasant.

Theodora Fosters an Anti-Chalcedonian Church

IN RETROSPECT, THE GLOOMY DECADE THAT BEGAN IN 540 CAN BE RECOGNIZED AS A TURNING POINT in the history of Late Antiquity. Antioch was destroyed by the Persians and though Justinian rebuilt it the damage to imperial prestige was not easy to repair. The wars in Italy, the Balkans, the eastern frontier and Lazica at the eastern end of the Black Sea all demanded reinforcements, while plague spread desolation across the empire. The imminence of death concentrates the mind, and perhaps for that reason Theodora became more willing to act independently to support her Monophysites, even when her policy subverted her husband's efforts to enforce the Creed of Chalcedon. She knew by now that any attempt that she might make to soften the obduracy of Rome had little chance of success. Vigilius had deceived her. He had promised to annul the excommunication of Anthimus if she made him pope, but once he had the throne of St Peter firmly in his grasp, he stonewalled. He kept his contacts with Constantinople at a minimum. He did not dare honour his pledge, for the Chalcedonian Creed and the prestige of Rome were too closely linked for that. The churches of Italy and Africa saw the struggle for orthodoxy as a contest between East and West, between the subtle theologians of the Orient and the forthright lawgivers of Rome with a thousand years of imperial tradition behind them. Within the city of Rome, the monuments of empire might be dilapidated and plague was pruning its diminished population, but the princes of the Roman church saw themselves as the heirs not only of St Peter but of Augustus, too, and the long line of emperors who succeeded him.

It may have been during one of Theodora's visits to the Hormisdas Palace that she met an elderly presbyter named Julian, who belonged to Theodosius' retinue. Theodosius, exile though he was, remained the rightful patriarch of Alexandria in the hearts and minds of the Monophysites, though in Alexandria itself the see was physically in the hands of the Chalcedonian Melkites – the emperor's men. The plague had already reached Egypt and Julian's mind turned to Nubia, beyond Egypt's southern border. Should not the souls of the Nubians be saved? How could they be brought to the true faith? The faith of the Monophysites?

NOUBADIA, THE NORTHERNMOST OF THE THREE NUBIAN KINGDOMS THAT EMERGED AFTER THE DECLINE OF MEROË, WAS RIPE FOR CONVERSION.[1] Until only a few years before Julian conceived of his mission, pagan and Christian priests had co-existed at Philae, which is now an island rising above the surface of Lake Nasser but until the sixth century it was a thriving pilgrimage centre for the cult of Isis. The cult ended in 537, when Justinian instructed the duke of the Thebaid to close it down. The priests of Isis were arrested, the pagan gods were expelled from the temple, the cult statues and the temple treasures were sent to Constantinople and the temple itself was converted into a church dedicated to St Stephen. The Blemmyes, who lived just beyond the First Cataract, as well as the Noubades to the south of them, used to worship at the Isis temple and they cannot have been pleased when it was closed. Now, with the plague raging, Julian was concerned about the souls of the Noubades and offered himself as a missionary.[2]

Theodora was happy to assist. She did not try to keep the mission a secret from Justinian and perhaps she anticipated no objection from him, for paganism was a common enemy of both the Chalcedonians and the anti-Chalcedonians. It was the stout Monophysite John of Ephesus who was appointed, in the plague year, to root out paganism in the region of Tralles and he may have been working at his holy project at this very time. Paganism was a far more heinous sin than Monophysitism. But Noubadia was a princely Nubian dominion on the southern fringes of Egypt where the Melkite patriarchs of Alexandria sought to impose their authority, and the situation in Alexandria was fragile. Paul of Tabennisi, Justinian's choice as patriarch, had been accused of murdering one of his deacons and fell from grace. At this point in time the patriarch of Alexandria was a monk from Palestine, Zoilus, Egyptian only by adoption. If Justinian were to sanction the conversion of the Noubades by a Monophysite missionary such as Julian, he would undermine Zoilus' shaky authority. He determined to abort his wife's project.

He did not veto Julian or forbid Theodora to do what she was determined to do anyway. He allowed her project to go ahead, while at the same time trying to make sure that it failed: a stratagem which perhaps fitted domestic diplomacy between husband and wife better than outright confrontation. Without delay, he dispatched a Chalcedonian embassy with gifts of gold and baptismal robes to the Noubadian king, Silko, and armed it with a letter to the duke of the Thebaid in Upper Egypt, commanding him to give this embassy his full attention and escort it to Noubadia. But Theodora was not easy to deceive. Her informants let her know what her husband was planning and she moved decisively to thwart him. She sent a swift messenger to the duke of the Thebaid and the message he carried was terse and to the point. She told him two missions were on their way to the Noubadian king, one from herself and the other from Justinian; when Justinian's mission reached him, he must delay it with plausible excuses until her man, Julian, could catch up. If the emperor's envoys reached the Noubades first, she would chop off the duke's head.

The duke took her threat seriously. He had no stomach to face Theodora's wrath. It was safer to abort Justinian's orders and so, when Justinian's mission reached him on the heels of Theodora's letter, he delayed it with an array of excuses. He needed time to find guides and beasts of burden, he explained, but once they were ready, he would send the envoys on their way. Not much later, Theodora's missionaries arrived and without more than a token protest from the duke they commandeered the horses and guides that had been collected for Justinian's deputation.

Then the duke told the Chalcedonians that a mission from the empress had come and requisitioned the beasts of burden that he had prepared for them. He did not dare oppose Theodora's envoys, he explained, for he feared her terrible anger. But let them wait a while, said he soothingly, and he would find guides and horses for them, too.

The Chalcedonian missionaries were wrathful and scolded the duke roundly. But they had no option but to wait until guides and horses were available. They must have guessed the pious fraud which the duke had practised but they could do little about it – except, of course, to give Justinian a full report. We may wonder what Justinian's thoughts were when he received it. Perhaps only a shrug of the shoulders.

Julian and his company, meanwhile, reached the borders of Noubadia and sent word ahead to announce their arrival to the Noubadian king, who sent an armed escort to bring them to his court. He accepted Theodora's gifts and the splendid baptismal robes which she had sent. Her letter was read aloud to him and an interpreter explained its meaning. Silko was delighted. He asked that his court be instructed in the Christian faith, which Julian gladly provided with appropriate partiality. He described the evil Council of Chalcedon to Silko and told how Theodosius, the good anti-Chalcedonian patriarch of Alexandria, had been ejected from his see because he would not accept the iniquitous creed that the Council had ratified, and how he had been welcomed in Constantinople by Theodora, the believing queen. Julian added, too, that a legate from Justinian would soon arrive, who would try to win the Noubades over to the depraved Chalcedonian doctrine, and he told Silko how he should greet him, and what he should say. Silko was well primed for the encounter.

In due time, the emperor's envoy with his missionaries reached Silko's court and was granted an audience. The envoy presented his letters and gifts and delivered his address. He said that the Roman Emperor had sent him so that the Noubades might be instructed in correct Christian belief and not be led into error by heretics who had been expelled from the approved church. Silko heard him out and then replied that his Noubades would willingly accept the emperor's presents but not his doctrine. If they chose Christianity at all, it would be the faith of the patriarch Theodosius, for the emperor's creed was wicked and the Noubades would never adopt it. With that, he dismissed the emperor's legation.

Julian remained two years in Noubadia, where he suffered terribly from the heat. When the sun was at its height, he used to retreat to the coolness of a cave where there was a stream of running water and there he would sit out the torrid hours, dressed only in a loose linen garment. If he ventured out into the open the relentless sun scorched his skin mercilessly. Nonetheless he endured, preaching the faith and baptizing converts and when he left he turned over his little flock to an elderly bishop from southern Egypt named Theodore, who seems to have had little interest in the quarrel with the Chalcedonians. The subtleties of theology were less important in the distant hinterlands than they were in Constantinople or Rome.

Our source for the conversion of Noubadia is John of Ephesus, who was not an impartial reporter. Yet there is no reason to reject it. It reveals that Theodora was feared in the militia of the empire, for she was known to be ruthless and determined to have her way. Justinian, on the other hand, presented the appearance of affability. Procopius called him seemingly good-natured[3] and perhaps the appearance was true, but we should note that after Theodora's death Justinian became more iron-fisted. The contrast between the ruthless empress and the affable emperor was, in part, the window-dressing of absolute rule.

Two of the three Nubian kingdoms accepted Monophysite Christianity. The third aligned itself with the Chalcedonians.

A YEAR OR SO LATER THEODORA FOLLOWED UP THE CONVERSION OF NOUBADIA WITH ANOTHER MOVE THAT UNDERCUT HER HUSBAND'S ROBUST CHALCEDONIAN POLICY MUCH MORE, and unlike Julian's mission, it had far-reaching results. She founded a separate Monophysite church or at least, if she was not its actual founder, she greased the wheels of possibility.

Up until this point, all sides in the dispute remained loyal to the idea of a Christian Romania, professing a single Christian creed. Both the Chalcedonians and the Monophysites, of whatever stripe they might be, wanted their confession of faith to be accepted as orthodox by all subjects of the empire, gathered together in one communion. None of them was willing to contemplate separate denominations. Freedom of religion presupposes that the church and the state can be put into two separate spheres, where each can mind its own business, and that was a concept foreign to the Christian theologians of Late Antiquity, though the emperor Zeno's *Henotikon* was a small step in that direction. However, the *Henotikon* was extinguished by Justinian's uncle, Justin I. Then, Theodora changed the playing field.

By the early 530s the persecution that Justin had begun was hurting the anti-Chalcedonian believers badly. It was aimed at the Monophysite clergy but its effect on the laity was grim. Who was there to administer the rites of the church to them? For they would not accept them from a Chalcedonian priest and men and women were dying without the last rites. Yet the Monophysite bishops in exile were reluctant to ordain priests and form their own hierarchy, for if they did they would break the law and bring the righteous wrath of the empire upon their heads for creating divisions in Christendom. However John, bishop of Tella, whom we have already encountered as one of the Monophysite team that debated with the Chalcedonians in the year-long discussion that took place in the Hormisdas Palace in 532–3, was willing to take the risk.[4] The imperial police had hounded John from his bishopric in 521, and he had returned to the life of an anchorite at his old monastery at Callinicum on the Persian frontier. But the long arm of the police soon reached his monastery and all the monks had to retreat to the desert. Some ten years passed while John watched the ranks of the Monophysite clergy growing thinner. New priests had to be ordained and John rose to the challenge.

After the conference in the Hormisdas Palace achieved nothing and Pope Agapetus destroyed any hope of a softer Chalcedonian posture, John returned to his task of ordaining priests in the eastern provinces. Justinian forbade it but John paid the imperial interdict no heed. The authorities were alarmed and eventually John paid for his boldness with his life, for he was finally captured by the Persian *Marzban* of Nisibis, who sold him to Ephraem, the tough Chalcedonian patriarch of Antioch. Once John fell into Ephraem's pitiless hands, he was imprisoned and tortured and finally put to death.

Yet John's mission was continued by another John, the bishop of Hephaestopolis in Egypt, who had accompanied the patriarch Theodosius to Constantinople.[5] During his brief period on the patriarchal throne in Alexandria, Theodosius had noticed John and ordained him bishop. Thus he was one of the anti-Chalcedonian holy men who were taken along with Theodosius to the fortress of Derkos in Thrace and interned there. Theodora saw to it that they had some of the comforts of life at Derkos but they were forbidden to ordain priests; if they did, and were caught, even Theodora could not save them.

John would not endure his confinement. He asked Theodosius for permission to leave Derkos and to go to Constantinople to see a physician and in fact he did seem genuinely ill. Theodosius allowed him to go and when the empress heard of his coming she assigned him living quarters in Constantinople and an allowance. What Theodora did not know, or preferred not to know, was that he secretly received Monophysite believers in the quarters she had provided for him, consecrated altars for their use and made clandestine ordinations.

The Chalcedonian clergy in Constantinople soon guessed what John was doing and demanded that Theodosius restrain him. But Theodosius replied that he was powerless: he could not leave Derkos himself and anyway, while John was in Constantinople, he was under the supervision of the empress, who was well aware that John had no instructions to ordain priests. With that, Theodosius washed his hands of the matter. But the Chalcedonians were determined to rid the city of this maverick bishop and they forged a petition to Theodora that purported to come from John, which was a request to depart from Constantinople for a short while for rest and recuperation. Theodora took the petition at face value and gave John permission to leave the city. Then the Chalcedonians passed on Theodora's mandate to John with an emendation: Theodora, they claimed, had ordered him to depart from Constantinople forthwith. If he tried to see her; he would be put to death.

John pretended to obey. But instead he slipped past the Chalcedonian watchdogs, went boldly to the palace where he found Theodora and complained to her that he had suffered wrong. Who had wronged him? Theodora wanted to know and John replied that it was she herself who had ordered him to leave Constantinople. So the truth came out. But when Theodora threatened John's deceitful accusers with the punishment they deserved, John spoke up on their behalf. Yet his wiles did not deceive Theodora. She ordered him to remain within the palace and make no more ordinations.

John promised to follow her wishes. But he was a man who enjoyed constant ill-health and, citing his various maladies, he begged for a month's respite at a villa outside the city. Once there, he slipped away furtively and journeyed through Asia Minor as far as Tarsus, never staying longer than a single day in any one place. Yet everywhere, when Monophysite believers learned of his coming, they gathered and he ordained priests. He planned to go beyond Tarsus but the authorities discovered his presence and he had to slip back to Constantinople in disguise. But the patriarch of Antioch, Ephraem, wrote to Justinian to complain that an anti-Chalcedonian bishop, whom he could not identify, had come secretly from Constantinople, made ordinations and performed the rites of penance and absolution. Ephraem and his bishops wanted him stopped.

Suspicion fell on John. But Theodora herself spoke up in his defence. She testified that he was lying sick in her villa outside Constantinople and had been in touch with her only a few days before. So word was sent back to Ephraem that no Monophysite bishop had left Constantinople. The renegade bishop had come from somewhere else and Ephraem was instructed to find him and arrest him.

John continued his covert mission. He got permission to visit hot springs for his health, a short journey from Constantinople, but instead he travelled as far as Cyprus and the coast of Phoenicia. Then he visited Rhodes. At Tralles on the Maeander river, he secretly ordained more than fifty priests in one of the city churches, while watchmen guarded the door against imperial spies. At Ephesus, he ordained more than seventy men in a single night, using the open courtyard of a house. John came and went like a will-o'-the-wisp, while Theodora remained unaware of what he was doing.

And yet she knew. We can hardly believe otherwise. While Justinian was, to all intents and purposes, enforcing the orthodoxy that Pope Agapetus had laid down, Theodora was subverting it. To the men on the streets of Constantinople who witnessed the performance, Justinian and Theodora seemed to be a team that pulled in opposite directions in matters of Christian faith and they could make no sense of it. This was a wedlock which contradicted the norms of ordinary married life, where the husband was the head of the family. Evagrius,[6] writing after both Justinian and Theodora were long dead, speculated that either they genuinely held different beliefs, or that they had agreed secretly that the one should support the Chalcedonians and the other the anti-Chalcedonians. Procopius' *Secret History*[7] put forward a malevolent rationalization: Justinian and Theodora were partners collaborating in a scheme to set the Christian world at loggerheads. They were the instruments of the Evil One himself, and worked according to his plan.

That was an explanation which reflected the views of an embittered underground opposition in Constantinople, who might be Chalcedonian, Monophysite, or even pagan sympathizers. They thought that Justinian and Theodora were fomenting discord for their own purposes, whatever they were. There was no doubt in their minds that the imperial office had grown into an outright autocracy and its goal was the ultimate destruction of Romania. Justinian stood revealed as the very antithesis of an ideal Byzantine emperor.

Yet there is another rationalization with greater appeal to modern-day historians. It is that Justinian and Theodora were anxious that the religious contention which divided the empire should never impair loyalty to the emperor. The emperor was more than a political leader; he was also God's deputy and it was his duty to sustain the link between God and His people. Italy and Africa were solidly Chalcedonian and if Justinian was to bring them back into a unified empire he could not deviate far from Pope Leo the Great's sharp definition of orthodoxy. In the east both the Chalcedonians and the Monophysites had constituencies but the prevailing sentiment was anti-Chalcedonian and Pope Leo's *fatwa* was detested. It suited Justinian's statecraft that the foes of Chalcedon should know that they had a friend at court and it was all the better that their friend was his wife, whose loyalty to him was above suspicion. Theodora reached out to the outsiders, who needed a voice to speak for them. In Heaven, the Virgin interceded for sinners. Should she not have a counterpart on earth to intercede with God's deputy?.

There was perhaps another reason, too, for this odd dyarchy of Chalcedonian and Monophysite. Theodora was at best an amateur theologian with a sketchy education but about her faith she felt no uncertainty. She was a true believer. She had not learned her doctrine from books but from the holy men she encountered in a life that took her from the theatre to the imperial palace, and she found the Monophysite believers more congenial than the Chalcedonians who spoke with the intonations of imperial Rome. Justinian, on the other hand, was a skilled student of theology but he lacked Theodora's conviction. He had doubts. Was he ever completely convinced that the Chalcedonian Creed totally embodied orthodoxy? It was a question that he spent nights pondering and, as he grew older, the task of defining orthodox belief became an obsession. He worked on the problem late into the night by the uncertain light of candles and oil lamps. On the eve of his death he arrived at last at the definition that he sought – and it was not the Chalcedonian Creed; it was the extreme anti-Chalcedonian faith taught by Julian of Halicarnassus, the credo of Aphthartodocetism.

Theodora was by then long dead and we can only guess what sort of intellectual odyssey brought Justinian, at the end of his life, to the conclusion that the Chalcedonian Creed was wrong after all. Perhaps long conversations with Theodora in the private chambers of the palace had planted the seeds of uncertainty, which germinated with time and grew. It seems more than possible that Justinian had not merely a political motive for tolerating his wife's advocacy of Monophysitism. There was also his own nagging doubt.

JUSTINIAN'S REORGANIZATION OF THE EASTERN FRONTIER DEFENCES AT THE START OF HIS REIGN included the recognition of al-Harith ibn Jabala as phylarch of the Saracen allies, with the status of king.[8] Al-Harith was the sheikh of the

Ghassanid tribe, Christian Arabs who drove their flocks of sheep and goats along the borders of Palestine. At Rusafa, ancient Sergiopolis, which marked the northern limit of his territory, the ruins of his great audience hall can still to be seen. He was an invaluable ally, for he guarded the southern sector of the frontier and allowed the Byzantines to concentrate their defences further north where the provinces were more exposed to Persian incursions. The Persians countered by making allies of the Ghassanid rivals, the Lakhmids, led by their formidable sheikh, al-Mundhir, whose flocks claimed grazing rights that clashed with those of the Ghassanids.

In 542, the year of the plague, al-Harith came to Constantinople and was honoured with patrician status. At this time in particular his friendship had to be carefully cultivated, for the empire was vulnerable and his requests could not be ignored. Perhaps during this visit, if not earlier, he asked Theodora for a bishop for his tribe. Al-Harith's Arabs were Monophysites and the scarcity of Monophysite clergy caused them anxiety. As men and women died of the plague, they had no priests to administer the last rites. Theodora was sympathetic and willing to help.

She turned to Theodosius, the exiled patriarch of Alexandria,[9] and at her urging he consecrated two bishops, Theodore as bishop of Bostra and Jacob Baradaeus as bishop of Edessa. Neither dared set foot in Bostra or Edessa, for those cities were not safe for Monophysite bishops. Instead Theodore followed the Ghassanid nomads as they ranged with their flocks from north to south along the desert fringes of Syria and Palestine, whereas Jacob made the whole Orient his diocese.

JACOB HAD BEEN ONE OF THE ANTI-CHALCEDONIAN MONKS who flocked to Constantinople to seek Theodora's protection when Justinian and Theodora came to the throne.[10] He had spent 15 years in a cell, presumably most of them within the Hormisdas Palace. Now he emerged and flung himself into his new mission with astonishing energy. He was a tireless apostle. Travelling on foot, he ranged from Constantinople throughout the prefecture of the Orient, going east as far as the Persian frontier and south as far as Alexandria. The Chalcedonian bishops were wild with frustration and wanted him arrested, and Justinian himself offered a reward to anyone who captured him. But Jacob was a master of disguise. He would stay in one place for only a day and a night and then the next night he would find a place to sleep 30 miles or more further along the road.

Everywhere he ordained priests and bishops. The patriarchate of Antioch, which spread over the Near East and Asia Minor, had a Melkite patriarch who enforced the Chalcedonian faith but the Monophysites did not recognize him.

They considered the patriarchal throne of Antioch vacant ever since Severus died, an exile in Egypt. Jacob ordained a patriarch to fill the vacancy, a Syrian named Sarkis (the Greeks called him Sergius), an old comrade of Jacob, who had accompanied him to Constantinople to seek Theodora's protection. Sarkis did not dare enter Antioch itself; instead he directed a Monophysite hierarchy in Syria from the monasteries in the countryside that gave him refuge. But among Syriac speakers he was recognized as the rightful patriarch of Antioch.

Two parallel hierarchies emerged in the sees of Antioch and Alexandria. One was Chalcedonian; its patriarchs lived Antioch or Alexandria and the tongue of its clergy was Greek. The other was anti-Chalcedonian and its languages were Syriac in Syria and Coptic in Egypt. These languages would develop Christian literatures of their own, which would challenge the dominance of Greek. The Chalcedonian Church was city-based, whereas the Monophysites were strong in the rural villages. Without Theodora's intervention none of this would have happened – or, at least, it would not have happened when it did. For better or worse, the anti-Chalcedonian churches that separated from the Greek Orthodox faith were Theodora's achievement. She assured Monophysitism a future.

The Agony of Italy

IN THE GRIM DECADE OF THE 540S THE PLIGHT OF ITALY GREW MORE DESPERATE and Belisarius bore a large part of the blame for it. He had wanted to crown his five-year campaign in Italy with the capture of Ravenna, followed by a triumphal return to Constantinople and fresh honours from the emperor. When he could not take Ravenna by military force he won it by duplicity: he allowed the Goths to believe that if they handed over Ravenna to him he would revive the western Roman Empire in partnership with the Goths. But a month after the surrender of Ravenna Belisarius loaded the Gothic royal family and the royal treasury on board ship and prepared to sail away to Constantinople. It dawned upon the Goths that Belisarius had tricked them.[1]

Their reaction was bitter. They chose a new king named Ildibad, a nephew of the Visigothic ruler in Spain, and at his urging they made a last effort to win over Belisarius before he left Italy. As he got ready to embark for Constantinople, the Goths sent him a deputation and upbraided him for his perfidy, but he shrugged off their reproaches. As long as Justinian was alive, he told them, he would never aim at the imperial throne. He knew that well-founded rumours of disloyalty could end his career and he wanted to scotch them before they spread to the imperial palace. Not entirely successfully. Justinian never completely trusted his *prima donna* commander again. He was wealthier and more popular than a loyal, honest army officer should be. Justinian and Theodora suspected that he had skimmed off an inappropriate share of the spoils of victory for himself, and no doubt they were right.

Ildibad had no more than one thousand troops but he quickly took control of the region north of the Po River. Justinian's attention was focused elsewhere. Italy must have seemed comparatively peaceful and Belisarius no doubt gave Justinian an optimistic report when he returned to Constantinople. No one foresaw the gathering storm. However, paranoia was a constant ingredient of life at court and Justinian decided not to appoint another commander-in-chief in Italy who might dream of a revived Western Roman Empire. Instead he appointed a cadre of generals with equal authority: in Venetia, Vitalius was in command, in Ravenna, Constantian, Justin in Florence, Conon in Naples, Cyprian in Perusia and Bessas, in Perugia. None of them concentrated a dangerous amount of power in his hands. But the lack of an overall command in Italy meant no co-ordinated action and discipline in the Byzantine army grew lax under this fragmented power structure. The officers plundered the Italians and the troops followed their example.

But if the Byzantine military was negligent, the tax collectors were not. A *logothetes*, a comptroller of revenues, named Alexander arrived at Ravenna and set about collecting taxes. He rapidly became the most detested bureaucrat in Italy. Italians who had served in the Ostrogothic administration were required to account for all receipts that they had handled during their years of service and make good any shortfalls out of their own pockets. Alexander acted on the premise that during the years that the Goths ruled Italy it remained part of the Roman Empire, and thus Romans who served as officials of the Gothic kings were ultimately responsible to the emperor. The soldiers, too, abominated Alexander, for their pay was always in arrears and whenever it did reach them, Alexander arrived with a bill for taxes. *Logothetai* took a cut of 12 per cent of the revenue they collected but Alexander went beyond the usual commission: he would even clip the edges of the gold coins that passed through his hands. His skill as a clipper earned him the nickname *Psalidion* – 'Scissors'.

Ildibad did not live long enough to exploit this administrative muddle, for he was assassinated by a royal guardsman who hated him. The plot has overtones of Grand Opera. Ildibad owed his election as king to the nephew of Witigis, Uraias, who had refused the crown himself, saying that any nephew of the luckless Witigis would be unlucky himself, whereas Ildibad was young, vigorous and well-connected. But one day Uraias' wife, expensively dressed and followed by a train of attendants, met Ildibad's queen in the public baths and snubbed her. Ildibad was a comparatively poor man and his wife's garb was cheap and ordinary. The queen was hurt and angry and demanded vengeance.

Ildibad was willing. First he slandered Uraias with a rumour that he was planning to desert to the Byzantines and then engineered his murder. The Gothic nobles were incensed, for Uraias was well liked. Yet none of them would have avenged his death themselves. But there was a royal bodyguard, Velas by name, who nursed a private grudge, for he had once returned from a campaign to discover that during his absence, Ildibad had given another warrior his bride-to-be. He saw a chance for revenge. At dinner one day, while Ildibad was reclining on his couch and stretching out a hand to take some food, Velas lopped off his head, imagining that the Goths would applaud the murder of their unpopular king. They did not. So ended the winter of 541.

THE AGONY OF ITALY

In the chaos that followed, a company of troops known as the Rugians pushed forward one of their own as king. The Rugians were a barbarian tribe that had served in the heterogeneous army of the warlord Odoacer, who had dethroned the last western emperor in 476. After Odoacer was in turn liquidated they transferred their services to the Goths, though they refused to intermarry, for they were determined to remain a separate people. The Rugian king, Eraric, lasted five months before the Goths could stomach him no longer – he was, in fact, plotting secretly to betray them – and they looked about for a more worthy leader, Their choice fell upon a nephew of Ildibad named Baduila,[2] who commanded the garrison in the town of Treviso.

Baduila had almost given up. He despaired of the Gothic cause so much that he was already negotiating secretly with the Byzantines to turn over Treviso to them and he had even agreed upon a day for the surrender when a deputation of Gothic nobles arrived to offer to him the crown. Baduila made one condition: he gave the Goths a date before which Eraric must die – it was, in fact, the date when he had agreed to surrender Treviso. Whereupon Eraric was eliminated, the surrender of Treviso did not take place, and in the fall of 541 Baduila became king of the Ostrogoths.

He lost no time. In 542, while Constantinople was distracted by the plague, he defeated the Byzantines in two battles and sent their generals scurrying back to the safety of the fortified towns that served as their bases. He then made the shrewd decision not to challenge the imperial forces in central Italy where they were safely ensconced behind the walls of their towns, but instead moved to the south of the peninsula, where the Byzantine garrisons were small and the takings were easy. He captured Benevento and levelled its walls, and then laid siege to Naples which was guarded by only 1,000 troops. A few kilometres west of Naples lay Cumae where the Cumaean Sibyl once gave her oracles in the distant past. Its citadel had now become a Byzantine base where treasure was stored for safekeeping and a number of Roman senators' wives had taken refuge there as well. Baduila seized the base and its treasure as well as other strongholds in the vicinity, always taking care to treat women captives with consideration. He then collected the taxes owed to the imperial treasury from the large Roman estates in southern Italy and the rents owed to their proprietors, many of whom must already have fled to Constantinople for safety. Hence the revenues which should have gone to pay Justinian's troops went to the Goths instead. Pay fell more and more in arrears, and the troops grew increasingly disaffected.[3]

Justinian was alarmed, but the plague had hollowed out his forces[4] and recruits were hard to find. Persia was a greater threat to the wellbeing of the empire than the Goths. The imperial treasury could manage without whatever tax revenues it got from Italy but the income from the eastern provinces was vital. Justinian could muster 30,000 troops in the Orient for an ill-fated offensive against Persia in 543, but for Italy the best he could do was to appoint a praetorian prefect with a modest force of Thracian and Armenian troops and a few Bulgars and dispatch him to Italy to give some coherence to the Italian administration.

The praetorian prefect was a timid bureaucrat named Maximin, who set out for Italy but got only as far as Epirus. There he stayed and dithered, trying to decide what to do next. Then Justinian dispatched one of Belisarius' veterans, who made two attempts to relieve the beleaguered city of Naples which the Goths held in a vice grip. In the second attempt, the Byzantine supply ships were caught in a storm in the bay of Naples and driven ashore conveniently close to the Gothic camp. Their cargoes helped feed the Goths. The Neapolitans held out as long as they could but by spring 543 they were starving and had no choice but to surrender.

Had a better man than Maximin been appointed praetorian prefect, he might have retrieved the situation. But who? Belisarius' relations with Antonina were rancorous and until they improved he was in Theodora's bad books. He wouldn't do. Justinian's cousin Germanus was immensely able but Theodora would not hear of him. Her enmity was so well known that Germanus could not find marriage partners for his children. As Justinian watched the situation in Italy deteriorate he must have grown a little impatient with his wife's grudges that got in the way of good government. Theodora would never be reconciled to Germanus, but with Belisarius an entente was possible. Theodora claimed that she forgave Belisarius and restored his fortune for the sake of her good friend Antonina, but we may suspect pressure in the background from Justinian. Moreover, Belisarius was anxious to leave Constantinople and return to Italy: so anxious that he agreed to recruit his own troops. So once again he was yoked to Antonina and they were sent back to Italy in 544 to cope with the Gothic insurgency.

In Constantinople there was now a growing colony of displaced Italian landowners, who had fled the horrors of war in Italy. Among them was one well-known notable, Cassiodorus Senator, who had served as praetorian prefect for Theoderic the Ostrogoth and, after him, kings Theodahad and Witigis. He was one of a small cadre of Romans who continued to foster Latin culture in Italy. We may speculate what his thoughts were as reports of plague and warfare reached him from Italy. It must have seemed that the lights that once illuminated the past were going out; and darkness was gathering, jeopardizing the legacy of classical civilization. Cassiodorus watched the decline with foreboding. When he eventually returned to Italy after some 15 years in Constantinople, he founded a monastery called Vivarium on his ancestral estate in southern Italy at Squillace, where the monks worked at copying books, pagan as well as Christian, in an effort to preserve what they could of Rome's ancient culture. Other monasteries would follow the example of Vivarium and thanks to them much of Latin literature survived, though it was severely pruned by the ravages of time and neglect.

Among these refugees there were some who expected that, once Belisarius was in Italy again, he would renounce his allegiance to Justinian and their hope may have resonated with a number of the Chalcedonians in the capital, who would have preferred a pope who was free of Justinian and his heretical empress. The Goths had offered Belisarius their fealty once. If a western Roman Empire were revived with combined Roman and Gothic support, might it bring peace, order and good government to the ravaged peninsula? Would the Goths be willing to renew their offer?

It was too late. The Goths now had an able king and his aim was to revive the kingdom of Theoderic, not to support Belisarius as a breakaway emperor in the west. In any case, if Belisarius ever contemplated rebellion, he must quickly have realized that it was impossible, for he lacked a cadre of loyal troops in Italy upon whom he could rely. Yet, back in Constantinople, many of Belisarius' old companions were bitterly disappointed and many of the Italian refugees, too, who had to watch the agony of Italy from the sidelines, must also have become disenchanted with the great general. As for Antonina, she settled into her role as Belisarius' loyal wife and supporter and followed him from place to place in Italy for the next four years, as he pursued the victory that always eluded him. And as for Justinian, he seems to have hoped that Belisarius would either perform a miracle in Italy or else tarnish his reputation indelibly. He was ready to accept either outcome; the empire had higher priorities than Italy.

Yet the idea of a revived western empire did not die. Years later, in 550, after Theodora was dead and her enmity for Germanus no longer mattered, Justinian put him in charge of a revitalized Italian campaign and his first act was to marry Theoderic's granddaughter, Matasuntha, the last of the Amal royals. Their son, named Germanus after his father, might have become the emperor of a Romano-Gothic empire in the west, which could have brought a degree of security to Italy and revived the traditions of the Latin empire. But the scheme remained only one of history's 'might-have-beens'. Germanus never got to Italy. While he was making preparations for his expedition he took sick and died. His son was born after his death and left no mark on history.

THE CONVENTIONAL WISDOM ABOUT JUSTINIAN'S POLICIES WHICH IS EMBALMED IN TEXTBOOKS is that he neglected the Orient and poured his resources into the reconquest of the west. Nothing could be further from the truth. Justinian always planned to reconquer the west with minimal risk and expense. Belisarius took an army of no more than 16,000 men against the Vandal kingdom and he began the reconquest of Italy with a force barely half as large. Justinian refused to commit large-scale resources to the Italian campaign until he was left with no alternative except defeat and withdrawal from Italy. Yet Justinian's generals made poor use of the forces they did have. They alienated the Italians while Baduila, by contrast, was careful to treat them well. An Italian from Calabria complained that one of Baduila's guardsmen had raped his daughter. Baduila put the man to death and gave his property to his victim. The Goths were shocked to see one of their own punished so severely but they acquiesced once they understood that, if they were to win over the Italians, Gothic justice would have to be even-handed. Baduila continued his charm offensive when he moved from southern Italy to a camp near Rome and began siege operations. But first he smuggled messages into the city promising the Romans no harm and reminding them of the warm relations they once had with the Goths in the past, when Theoderic and Amalasuntha were alive. Why, he asked, had they deserted the Goths for the Byzantines who only exploited them? Justinian's commanders warned him that the situation was becoming very grave. What if Rome fell?

The loss of Rome to the Goths would do more than damage imperial prestige. There was a theological dimension as well, as both Justinian and Theodora must have been aware. Pope Vigilius was physically within their grasp as long as Byzantine troops held Rome. Vigilius had deceived Theodora once and he was keeping his head low, trying to have as little to do with Constantinople as possible. But now Justinian was ready to launch the major theological initiative of his reign. In 542 while the plague was raging and wars were being fought on the frontiers, Justinian was hard at work on a major treatise on theology and he expected to bend the artful pope to his will. That would be possible only while Justinian's forces still occupied Rome, for when Italy was ruled by Theoderic the Ostrogoth the popes had been free to defy the emperor with no fear of reprisal. Theoderic had watched the pope quarrel with the old emperor Anastasius with some satisfaction.

So in 544 Belisarius and Antonina arrived in Ravenna to retrieve the situation in Italy. Belisarius was officially back in imperial favour but he had not won back Justinian's trust. When Belisarius had enjoyed the full glow of imperial good will he had supported a huge bodyguard of some 7,000 *bucellarii*; but when Theodora ordered him back from the eastern front to Constantinople, they stayed behind. The imperial pair was not prepared to be generous. Belisarius wanted to return to Italy and dreamed of another victory there; so now, they must have thought, let us see what he can do. He was left to recruit troops at his own expense in the provinces of Thrace and Illyricum.

But in the aftermath of the plague, there were few volunteers to be had. Belisarius managed to enlist only about four thousand but some of them soon deserted. In Bologna, which one of Belisarius' officers had recovered from the Goths, all the troops from Illyricum withdrew secretly one night and returned home. Their excuse was that the news had reached them that a horde of Bulgars had invaded Illyricum and were enslaving the women and children. The Illyrians wanted to defend their homes. What was more, they had given long service in Italy and received no regular pay or supplies. Meeting the payroll for the troops in the west was never high among Justinian and Theodora's priorities.

BELISARIUS SOON REALIZED THAT THE SITUATION IN ITALY WAS MORE DESPERATE THAN HE HAD IMAGINED. The army which he found in Italy was disgruntled and discouraged and his fresh recruits were too few. He had been so eager to get back to his old field of glory in Italy that he underestimated the resources he would need. He sent 'Bloody John', the nephew of Vitalian, back to Constantinople to bring home to Justinian how serious the crisis was and find more troops. John had served under Belisarius in his first campaign in Italy and relations between the two men had been rancorous, but now Belisarius bound John with an oath to press Justinian hard for reinforcements and come back to Italy himself as speedily as he could.

Yet once John reached Constantinople he was in no great hurry to return. Instead he used his time to acquire a bride, Justina, daughter of Justinian's cousin Germanus. The betrothal exasperated Theodora, whose hatred of Germanus extended to his family, nor would Germanus himself have assented to it under normal circumstances, for John lacked the status that Germanus wanted for his son-in-law. But Justina was 18 and still unwed, for no upper-crust suitor dared to propose an alliance with Germanus' family and find himself in Theodora's bad books. John, at least, was not frightened away by Theodora's hostility.

Theodora was livid and tried to break the marriage compact, but John and Germanus had bound themselves by a great oath to maintain it. Theodora directed most of her firepower against John, for he was more vulnerable than Germanus. She threatened to destroy him and John took the threat seriously, for he knew what Theodora was capable of doing. He also knew that Antonina acted as her agent, for Antonina's role in the fall of John the Cappadocian was common knowledge among the upper crust of Constantinople. So when John did, at last, return to Italy with reinforcements he was wary, for he suspected that Antonina had instructions from Theodora to murder him. Yet he could not elude Antonina without also avoiding Belisarius and thus he tried to keep his distance from them both. No co-ordinated strategy was possible as long as Antonina was in Belisarius' headquarters.

While Belisarius waited in Ravenna for John to return, Baduila drew the noose more tightly around the city of Rome. By now, Belisarius realized that Ravenna was a poor base for operations in Italy and, leaving a garrison there, he and Antonina crossed the Adriatic Sea with a detachment of troops and made their way south along the Dalmatian coast to Durazzo, where he sent Justinian another dispatch to repeat to him how desperately Italy needed reinforcements. Roused at last, Justinian sent a mixed force of Roman soldiers and barbarian allies to join Belisarius at Durazzo. The commanders were John and Isaac, an Armenian from Persarmenia who had defected to Byzantium and been taken into the officer corps of the army. Baduila, meanwhile, had assumed personal command of the siege of Rome and began to beleaguer it in deadly earnest.

If Belisarius had had his way he would have moved immediately to relieve Rome with the troops that reached him at Durazzo, but 'Bloody John' thought otherwise. He preferred to drive the Goths from southern Italy first and then march on Rome. John had logic on his side, for the Goths had relatively few troops in the south and, once the great estates of the Romans in southern Italy were recovered, the taxation revenue they provided would pay the wages of the soldiers. The disagreement resulted in compromise. Belisarius, with Isaac and half the army, sailed for *Portus Traiani*, 'Trajan's Harbour', which was north of the port of Ostia at the Tiber River mouth and firmly in Byzantine hands, whereas Ostia itself was not. With Belisarius went Antonina, to the great relief of John, who took the troops that were left and drove the Goths out of Calabria, Apulia and Bruttium in the Italian south.

John should then have rejoined Belisarius at Portus. But he did not come. Instead he continued to campaign in southern Italy, where he was a safe distance from Antonina. If John were shut up in Portus with her, she would have a chance to wreak Theodora's vengeance by making his new bride a widow. He stayed clear of her and left Rome to its fate.

WHILE ITALY ENDURED ITS AGONY, Justinian's passion for theology continued unabated. Before the Ostrogothic noose around Rome was drawn so tight that all escape routes were blocked, pope Vigilius was taken into custody. Justinian sent instructions to Bessas, the commander of the Roman garrison, to seize the pope and send him to Constantinople. Whilst he was celebrating mass in the church of Santa Cecilia within the Trastevere region of Rome, a company of troops stationed itself outside the doors while an officer entered and presented his orders. Vigilius went willingly. He did not even linger long enough to finish the mass, though at the riverbank he paused for a few minutes to pronounce the blessing that concluded the liturgy. The Romans lining the shore of the Tiber watched as the boat floated downriver and, as it dawned on them that Vigilius was deserting Rome and escaping the rigours of the siege, they hurled stones at him and filled the air with their taunts and jeers. But war or no war, Justinian's quest for the reconciliation of the Chalcedonians and Monophysites had to go on.

What moved Justinian to snatch pope Vigilius from Rome with so little ceremony was the great ecclesiastical drama known as the 'Three Chapters' controversy, which was to occupy the middle decade of Justinian's reign. To understand its background, we must turn back to the year 536 when Pope Agapetus arrived in Constantinople, where he routed the anti-Chalcedonians and recalled Justinian to the Chalcedonian camp. One result of that memorable year was that Justinian appointed a stoutly Chalcedonian monk, Paul of Tabennisi, as Melkite patriarch of Alexandria to replace Theodora's protégé, Theodosius, whom the Gaianists had forced to flee to Constantinople.[5] Paul was ordained by Menas, the patriarch of Constantinople, and sailed to Alexandria in 536 with a mandate to clear Egypt of its heretical anti-Chalcedonian bishops. The Augustal Prefect of Egypt, Rhodon, was instructed to support him. With Paul came Arsenius, a Samaritan who had adopted Christianity to advance his career and who, once converted, became an enthusiastic student of Christian theology. In the past he had made himself useful to Theodora and, thanks to her patronage, he had become a senator, but at this point in his career he was, for some reason, *persona non grata* in the imperial palace. He hoped that by supporting the Melkite patriarch Paul he would win back imperial favour.

Paul promptly closed the Monophysite churches in Alexandria and though the city remained quiescent, anger simmered under the surface. Theodosius, the Monophysite patriarch whom Paul replaced, was incarcerated in Thrace along with the other holy men who had sought refuge in Constantinople and could do nothing to help, but a deacon in Alexandria named Psoes spoke up for the beleaguered anti-Chalcedonians. Paul determined to stamp out this nucleus of resistance. He turned Psoes over to the Augustal Prefect, Rhodon, who tortured him to death. Arsenius was involved somehow; perhaps he was the over-enthusiastic torturer. But when word of Psoes' death by torture reached Theodora's ears she rose in furious defence of her Monophysites.

She browbeat Justinian into making an investigation. It was Justinian himself who had instructed Rhodon to support Paul but at this juncture he preferred to forget about his complicity. An official of long experience, Liberius, was appointed to succeed Rhodon as governor of Egypt. Liberius had once been a Roman senator who had served Odoacer in Italy. After Odoacer's murder, he had transferred his services to his murderer, Theoderic the Ostrogoth, and after him, his daughter Amalasuntha. But Theodahad had been too much for him to stomach and he transferred his services to Justinian. He was by now an old man but as able as ever, and he set about his task in Egypt with dispatch.

Paul was brought before a synod of clergy which met at Gaza in 540 to investigate Psoes' death. Paul's guilt was not proved but it was revealed that, for an ex-monk, he had developed a remarkable talent for self-enrichment. He was deposed and replaced by another former monk, Zoilus who came from a monastery in Palestine. He was as stalwart a Chalcedonian as Paul but a kindlier man. Rhodon fled to Constantinople, where he pleaded that he was only following imperial orders when he incarcerated Psoes, which was at least half-true, but he was beheaded anyway. The career of Arsenius ended abruptly. Theodora ordered Liberius to crucify him. His crime was failure to navigate through the shoals of court politics with adequate skill.

THE CLERIC WHO PRESIDED OVER THE SYNOD IN GAZA THAT CONDEMNED PAUL OF TABENNISI was the papal nuncio in Constantinople, Pelagius, who had recommended Paul to Justinian in the first place as a suitable Melkite patriarch of Alexandria. Nonetheless, he was a contented man as he left Gaza, for he knew that Paul's fate would gratify Theodora. On his return journey he passed through Jerusalem and there he met some monks who were on their way to Constantinople to urge Justinian to condemn Origenism. This was a doctrine that harked back to the third-century philosopher and theologian Origen, a brilliant professor in the Alexandrian School that operated at that time under the control of the patriarch of Alexandria. He was excommunicated in 231 and fled to Caesarea in Palestine, where he continued to teach. In the sixth century, his doctrines got new life thanks to a monk from Edessa, Stephen bar-Sudaili, who migrated to Palestine after his beliefs made him unpopular at home. He soon won disciples in the Palestinian convents and Origenism became a bone of contention there, pitting one monastery against another. Origenism injected a dose of mysticism into Christian theology – an unhealthy dose, in the eyes of the Catholic theologians. Pelagius watched with disquiet as the popularity of Origenism grew.

He was particularly alarmed at the malign influence at court of two disciples of this renascent Origenism, Theodore Ascidas and Domitian. They had come to the notice of the emperor, who liked what he saw and he made both of them bishops. A theological tug-of-war developed at court between the Origenists, led by Theodore, and the unadulterated Chalcedonians, led by Pelagius and the patriarch of Constantinople, Menas. Hence Pelagius was very pleased to encounter in Jerusalem the party of monks who were setting out for Constantinople to warn Justinian of the dangers of Origenism. He went along with them.

Justinian was convinced by the warnings he received from the monks and produced a long edict against Origen and Origenism, which was as much a theological treatise as a legal pronouncement. It was a *tour de force*; evidence, if evidence is needed, that Justinian was a skilful theologian and it also embarrassed the Origenist leader at court, Theodore Ascidas, as Pelagius intended that it should. If Ascidas remained loyal to his beliefs and refused to countersign the imperial edict condemning Origenism, he would forfeit his bishopric and his influence at court. After searching his conscience, he opted in the end to retain them both. He signed, with bitter resentment in his heart. But he had his revenge. Once Pelagius returned to Rome, laden with the wealth he acquired in Constantinople, Ascidas suggested to Justinian a subtle tactic for conciliating the Monophysites, which he believed that Pelagius could never support. Pelagius had embarrassed him; now he would embarrass Pelagius. Justinian rose to the bait.

To understand the strategy which Ascidas proposed we must go back to the Council of Chalcedon almost a hundred years earlier, which produced the uncompromising Chalcedonian Creed. That same council had rehabilitated three supporters of the heretic Nestorius, who by now had been well demonized. They were Theodore of Mopsuestia, Theodoret of Cyrrhus and Ibas of Edessa, the first of whom was the spiritual father of the Nestorian heresy. Ascidas persuaded Justinian that if he condemned Theodore posthumously he would remove a barrier that prevented the Monophysites from accepting Chalcedon. His argument seemed reasonable enough, for a common accusation that Monophysites hurled at the Chalcedonians was that they were really Nestorians masquerading in the robes of orthodoxy and, as proof, they pointed to the case of Theodore of Mopsuestia. The Council of Chalcedon had actually accepted this founding father of the Nestorian heresy back into the fold of the Catholic Church! Theodore was long since dead but his writings had survived and, by condemning them, Justinian would correct a mistake of the Council of Chalcedon and would demonstrate for all to see that no trace of Nestorianism infected Chalcedonian theology! Theodora supported Ascidas' idea, and Justinian was convinced. In 546 he issued his Edict on the Three Chapters.[6]

The edict itself has not survived but we know its contents. Under three headings, or 'chapters', it condemned Theodore of Mopsuestia and his writings, some works of Theodoret of Cyrrhus that attacked the great Cyril, patriarch of Alexandria, and a letter written by Ibas. In the eastern empire, the Three Chapters Edict was received without enthusiasm. The patriarchs in the eastern sees hesitated, for the men whose writings were condemned had died years ago, at peace with the church. Yet they followed the lead of Menas, the patriarch of Constantinople, who had serious qualms at first, but the pressure from Justinian and Theodora was intense and he yielded and countersigned the edict with the proviso that he could retract his signature if the pope refused to sign. In due time, however, he would move from hesitation to co-operation and become an advocate of the edict.

In the Roman Catholic west, the edict encountered intense antagonism. Pope Vigilius would not sign.

Theodora cannot have had high hopes for the Three Chapters Edict. She was enough of a realist to know that the opportunity to heal the schism was by now past. She had already helped to launch a separate anti-Chalcedonian church and there was no easy path for retreat now. Yet there were two reasons why she must have liked the edict. First, it modified the Council of Chalcedon and acknowledged that the bishops who had assembled at Chalcedon had made an error. That was a significant concession which should please the moderate Monophysites and might be a step forward on the long road to some sort of reconciliation. Second, and equally important: the edict embarrassed Vigilius. He was a slippery prelate who had once deceived Theodora but now he would have to choose between angering Justinian or accepting Justinian's right to define church doctrine. Theodora must have felt some satisfaction as she watched him wriggle.

In fact, Justinian was on solid theological grounds. His condemnation was sound, for the writings listed in the Three Chapters Edict were indeed tainted by Nestorianism, which was rejected by Chalcedonian and Monophysite alike. On that score, Justinian was right. If all the Latin bishops who objected to the Edict of the Three Chapters with such fury had been sufficiently fluent in Greek to read what Theodore, Theodoret and Ibas had written, they might well have developed grave doubts about their orthodoxy. But bilingualism was disappearing in the empire. In the Latin west churchmen competent in Greek were becoming scarce, whereas in the east Latin was fading and Greek was the tongue of the educated classes. It was the language of theology, philosophy and literature and, even in the field of law, it was making inroads.

But when the Latin bishops rose in wrathful defence of Theodore, Theodoret and Ibas, it had little to do with their writings. Instead they were resisting the claim of an emperor in Constantinople to decide what correct church doctrine should be. That, they believed, was the prerogative of the Church of Rome and they defended the rights of Rome with all the fervour they could muster. The churchmen from Africa, which Belisarius had brought back into the empire, were particularly valiant combatants. They had survived the persecution of the Vandals and they knew what it was like for Roman Catholics to be beleaguered by heretics. They expected Pope Vigilius to put up a stout fight and, if he did not, they would desert him even if he was the successor of St Peter to whom Christ had given the Keys of the Kingdom. If necessary, they would break off communion him and condemn the pope himself as a heretic.

Vigilius was not by nature a stubborn diehard. When he made his promise to Theodora to undo Pope Agapetus' excommunication of the patriarch Anthimus in return for her support he may even have intended to keep it, but once he became pope himself and took stock of the situation, he realized how limited his options were. But he tried to avoid a confrontation. He kept his contacts with Justinian and Theodora at a minimum, until Justinian decided that the time had come for some arm-twisting and ordered him arrested. But Vigilius was in no rush to reach Constantinople. His voyage took him from Rome to Sicily and there he stayed, making his home in Catania throughout the winter and into the following summer. While he was there he took the measure of the Catholic clergy. Italy and Africa were solidly opposed to Justinian's Three Chapters Edict and the support for it in the east was soft. Whether Vigilius wanted it or not, a confrontation with the emperor was in the offing.

WHILE VIGILIUS WAS ENJOYING THE COMFORTS OF CATANIA he did not forget Rome, where Baduila was tightening his vice around the city and hunger stalked the streets. He collected a convoy of grain transports and sent it to Rome. It never arrived. As it neared Trajan's Harbour, the Goths spotted it and prepared an ambush. The Byzantine garrison on the harbour battlements could see the trap awaiting the grain ships and tried to signal to them to turn back. They shouted and took off their cloaks and waved them over their heads, trying desperately to alert the cargo ships to the danger. But the sailors misunderstood; they thought the garrison was cheering their arrival and they sailed all the more confidently into the ambush. The ships were captured and all the sailors killed, except for a bishop named Valentine whom Vigilius had sent to act as his proxy in Rome. Baduila cut off his hands but spared his life.

Rome was left to starve. The Byzantine garrison commanded by Bessas had a small store of grain, which they sold at a high price to those Romans who still possessed some wealth, but those who were penniless were reduced to subsisting on the meagre nourishment of boiled nettles and they became walking skeletons, as ashen as ghosts. One Roman, the father of five, was driven to such desperation by his children tugging at his clothes and asking for something to eat that he told them to follow him and he would take them to food. When they reached a bridge over the Tiber, he covered his face with his cloak and leaped to his death in the river before his children's eyes. Most of the Romans tried to escape from the city, but even if they evaded the Goths they were too weak to go far. Those whom the Goths captured were killed.

Meanwhile, Belisarius and Antonina had made their way to Trajan's Harbour and along with them came Isaac the Armenian and half the reinforcements that Isaac and John had brought to Italy. The plight of Rome was desperate and Belisarius had only one option, for his force was too small to risk a battle with the whole Gothic army. He had to try to bring food up the Tiber River to Rome. Baduila had blocked the channel by bridging it, where the river narrowed, with long timbers stretching from one bank to the other and upon these timbers he had built a rampart, so that no ships could pass through. Belisarius improvised a tactic that might have broken the blockade if it had been given a chance. He took two barges, lashed them together and built a tower on them, which was loftier than the Gothic rampart. Over this tower he suspended a little boat filled with pitch and other flammable materials. His plan was approach the Gothic barrier as nearly as possible, set the little boat ablaze and drop it down on top of the Gothic rampart. With luck, the rampart would ignite and burn fiercely.

Next, he took around two hundred small boats, built for speed, and on both their starboard and port sides he built parapets pierced with apertures, which would allow the boatmen to shoot missiles at the enemy without exposing themselves. These vessels he loaded with cargoes of grain. To protect Trajan's Harbour in his absence, he stationed infantry and cavalry troops in outstations near the mouth of the Tiber and, behind the walls of the Harbour itself, he left Antonina along with a garrison commanded by Isaac the Armenian. He gave Isaac strict orders not to leave the shelter of the Harbour under any circumstances, even if he heard that Belisarius had been killed. He also smuggled in orders to Bessas, the torpid commander of the garrison in Rome, to make a sally to distract the Goths as the little flotilla made its way up the Tiber. Bessas, however, did nothing. He was a Goth himself and though he was a career soldier in the Byzantine army he felt very limited compassion for the suffering of the Romans.

Yet the attack began well. At first Belisarius met no opposition. Before his boats reached the bridge, they encountered a chain stretched across the Tiber but the sailors lifted it and routed the sentries who tried to protect it. The Goths were now alerted and rushed to defend their barrier. Yet the Byzantines managed to set a Gothic bastion near the riverbank ablaze. The Goths lost about two hundred men in the fire and they began to lose heart as the Byzantines pushed home their assault.

At Trajan's Harbour, news came to Isaac that the battle was going well. The chain had been taken and the barrier across the river was on fire. Victory seemed certain and Isaac wanted a part of it for himself. He took a hundred horsemen and attacked a Gothic stockade and captured it, killing a number of Goths and wounding the Gothic commander, Ruderic. But once Isaac's troops penetrated the Gothic camp and turned to plunder the Goths counterattacked. Isaac was taken and many of his troops were killed. A few horsemen escaped to tell Belisarius that Isaac had been captured.

Belisarius' nerve snapped and he panicked. He imagined that Trajan's Harbour had been taken and Antonina was in enemy hands. He did not pause to ask questions and discover exactly what had happened. His first priority was to recover his wife and his base of operations. He ordered an immediate withdrawal to Trajan's Harbour where he discovered the truth. The harbour fortifications were safe and so was Antonina, though Isaac was captured and two days later, when Ruderic died of his wounds, Baduila put him to death. The opportunity to relieve Rome was lost for good. Belisarius was so chagrined that he fell sick.

His illness may have been malaria, for he developed a fever and for a while was close to death. The mouth of the Tiber was silting up and the lowlands were a breeding ground for mosquitoes. But it is also true that Belisarius exhibited some of the symptoms of a manic depressive. Victory had just been snatched from him by his hasty action and the realization plunged him from the peak of excitement into a crippling bout of depression. At any rate, while Antonina nursed him back to health, there was nothing he could do to help Rome, which was reaching the end of its long agony.

Inside the city, Bessas became increasingly careless. The grain he sold from the garrison's stores to Romans who could pay for it was making him rich but the troops guarding the walls were left without supervision. Finally four soldiers of the garrison approached Baduila with an offer to betray the city. Baduila was cautious – almost too cautious, for Bessas and his fellow commander Conon got wind of the plot, but they paid no heed. Baduila was finally convinced that the offer was genuine and sent four Goths to scale the wall near the Asinarian Gate where the quisling soldiers stood guard, and chop through the wooden beams that secured the gates. The portal swung open and the Goths entered warily, while the Byzantine troops fled through another gate.

Then Baduila sent two envoys to negotiate with Justinian: Theodore, a Roman lawyer, and the deacon Pelagius, whom we have already met as the papal nuncio in Constantinople. He had returned to Rome in time to share the rigours of the siege and used the wealth that he accumulated in Constantinople to relieve the hardships of the Romans. Pope Vigilius himself was by now in northern Greece, making his way overland at a snail's pace to Constantinople – he would arrive on 25 January 547 – and Pelagius was left to speak for the Romans. He had already trudged once from the beleaguered city to negotiate with Baduila and now that it was fallen he interceded once again. When Baduila went to pray at St Peter's basilica on the Vatican mount while the Goths plundered the city, Pelagius came to meet him with a Bible clasped in his hands and entreated him to spare the Romans.

Baduila's reply was a sneer; but Pelagius did not give up. He reminded Baduila that it was God who had put the Romans at his mercy. It behoved him to be merciful to his subjects, both now and in time to come, and somewhere in his makeup Baduila was touched. He gave his Goths orders not to slaughter the Romans, though they were free to pillage their property after he had set aside the choicest plunder for himself. There were particularly rich pickings to be found in Bessas' lodgings, for he had not had time to remove his ill-gotten gains. Then Baduila assembled the senators and reproached them bitterly. He reminded them that the Ostrogoths had always treated the Roman senatorial class well and yet, in return, they gave the emperor in Constantinople their loyalty. But Pelagius spoke up for them once again. These were people who had suffered great tribulation, he pleaded, and in the end he persuaded Baduila to promise them mercy. Pelagius' courage won Baduila's respect. He chose him to go along with Theodore as his emissary to Justinian.

The proposal which Pelagius and Theodore took to Justinian invited him to renew the association which the emperor Anastasius once had with Theoderic the Amal, the king of the Ostrogoths who now slept in his tomb at Ravenna. Theoderic had been an independent ruler who did not take orders from Constantinople; yet he acknowledged the suzerainty of the emperor. Baduila proposed a similar entente with Justinian, and he warned the two envoys to do their best to persuade him, for if Justinian denied him the peace he wanted he would massacre the senators, raze Rome to the ground, cross over the Adriatic Sea and invade northern Greece – the hinterland of Constantinople itself. It was a threat that the emperor should have taken take seriously. If the Goths could win a secure base in Italy, northern Greece would be vulnerable.

Yet, Justinian merely replied that Belisarius held supreme command in Italy and Baduila should negotiate directly with him. The war in Italy continued.

MEANWHILE IN SOUTH ITALY, A ROMAN LANDOWNER NAMED TULLIANUS RAISED A MILITIA OF TENANT FARMERS and blocked the Goths from entering Lucania to plunder. Tullianus offered John, the nephew of Vitalian, his support if John pledged that the imperial troops would do the Italians no harm. He seized a pass that gave access to Lucania in south-west Italy and defeated a scratch force which Baduila raised to retake it. Baduila realized that he could linger no longer in Rome. He decided to leave most of his army in camp at Ceraso, beside Mount Algidus, some 32 km southeast of Rome, while he hurried south to deal with Tullianus.

Tullianus' militia of tenant farmers soon fell apart. Baduila had only to promise them ownership of the lands that they were tilling for their landlords. In southern Italy where most of the land was held by great magnates and their tenants were virtually serfs, a whiff of land reform was enough to snuff out the allegiance of the peasants to the imperial regime. Baduila recognized the soft underbelly of the Roman social structure. If he promised freedom to slaves and serfs he might lose the support of the landowners, including some Goths who were proprietors themselves, but he would win over the underclass. John could never hope to counter a peasant uprising that had Gothic support. He hastily sought refuge in Otranto.

Rome had by now become a ghost town. All its inhabitants had evacuated, and Baduila had, in fact, been about to raze the empty city to the ground before he withdrew his army to Ceraso. But Belisarius, whom Antonina was nursing back to health at Trajan's Harbour, learned what Baduila purposed to do and wrote him a remarkable letter, pleading for Rome in the name of civilization. Humanity would suffer an irretrievable loss if a city that had lasted a thousand years was wiped off the face of the earth. Baduila read and reread the letter and in the end he was persuaded. He knocked down parts of the wall and removed the gates but he spared Rome. He then moved south, recovered southern Italy and was about to move up the Adriatic coast against Ravenna, when he received startling news.

Belisarius had recovered his health and reoccupied Rome. His soldiers filled in the gaps in the wall with stone ramparts and brought food up the Tiber from Trajan's Harbour. Nothing now blocked cargoes of Sicilian grain from reaching the city and the Romans who had taken refuge in neighbouring towns returned and reoccupied their houses. However, before the gates could be replaced Baduila reappeared and attempted to retake the city.

Rome might be without gates but Belisarius blocked the entrances with his best men who inflicted such heavy losses on the Goths when they tried to force their way in that they withdrew. The next day Baduila threw his whole army against the city but failed again. His troops retired to their camp to lick their wounds, only to return a few days later for a third assault. This time, Baduila's standard bearer was mortally wounded as he led the Goths forward and he fell from his horse, dropping the standard on the ground. The front ranks of both armies joined in fierce battle over his corpse. The Goths grabbed the fallen standard, cutting off the standard bearer's left hand to save the gold bracelet on his wrist from falling into enemy hands, but once they retrieved the standard they fell back in disorder. Baduila gave up the siege and retired with his disgruntled Goths to Tibur,[7] destroying all the bridges over the Tiber River before he left, except the Milvian Bridge which was too close to the walls of Rome for the Goths to approach safely.

Then a message reached Baduila from the Gothic army besieging Perugia. The defenders of the fortress were short of food and it could be easily taken if Baduila led his whole army against it. The fiasco at Rome had diminished the Gothic confidence in their king but they let themselves be persuaded. They need not expect any attack from the rear, Baduila told them, for not only had he destroyed the bridges over the Tiber but 'Bloody John', Vitalian's nephew, refused to co-operate with Belisarius. Antonina was the reason, though Baduila can hardly have known it. As long as Belisarius had Antonina in his headquarters, John was wary. If he were to join Belisarius, could he guard himself against a knife in the dark?

But John threatened Baduila nonetheless, for while Baduila besieged Perugia, John moved into Campania, the region north of Naples where the Goths were holding an assortment of hostages, including the wives of many Roman senators. John freed them and sent them to Sicily for safety. Baduila had planned to use these hostages as pawns when he negotiated a peace treaty with the Byzantines and their loss was a setback. He countered by moving an army of 10,000 men surreptitiously from Perugia south to Lucania, where John was encamped, and made a surprise night attack. John's little force was outnumbered ten to one, but John, with about nine hundred troops, escaped under cover of darkness.

The emperor was dribbling only a few soldiers into Italy but at least by now he understood the importance of holding Calabria in the heel of Italy, for otherwise the Byzantines could not secure the route between Italy and the Balkans. He sent a dispatch to Belisarius in Rome saying that he intended to send out a large army across to Calabria, where Belisarius should join it. So Belisarius put Rome in charge of a subordinate officer, Conon, while he and

Antonina sailed for Sicily, taking with them 900 men, 700 cavalry and 200 infantry. From Sicily they set sail for Taranto but, half way there, a storm forced them into the harbour of Cotrone on the shore of Calabria. While his ships rode at anchor, Belisarius ordered the cavalry to ride inland to forage, thinking that if they met the Goths in the mountain passes they could at least defend themselves. They did meet a Gothic army that was besieging Rossano, now Rossano Stazione at the southwest end of the Gulf of Taranto, and defeated it but when they retired to camp, overconfident after their victory, 3,000 Gothic horsemen made a surprise attack and nearly wiped them out.

Belisarius and Antonina fled back to Sicily with the infantry. A good wind filled the sails of their ships and they reached Messina in a single day.

SPRING 548 CAME AND MORE REINFORCEMENTS DRIBBLED IN. But not enough. Italy, ravaged by war and pestilence, was in desperate straits. It was by now clear to both Belisarius and Antonina that Justinian had no intention of committing an adequate force to Italy's deliverance. He did not want to lose Italy; but neither did he want Belisarius to win a victory. There was another important consideration that weighed heavily with him as well, and that was his dispute with the pope over the Edict of the Three Chapters. If Pope Vigilius and the stubborn bishops from Italy and Africa had been more co-operative Justinian might have taken pity on the Italians, for in his thought-world theology was as important as military campaigns – perhaps more important. The battle for orthodoxy had to be fought, for the emperor was responsible for a healthy relationship between Heaven and the earthly kingdom. It suited Justinian's policy to prolong the war in Italy and Belisarius' reputation did not matter.

Antonina decided to play her last card. She would return to Constantinople and appeal directly to Theodora. Theodora was a realist and she would listen. She would know what it meant to lose Italy. If Antonina could persuade her to use her influence with Justinian to support the Italian campaign, Belisarius might yet snatch success from the morass of the Gothic war. But without the empress to nudge her partner into action he would continue to dribble reinforcements into Italy, never enough for victory but large enough to avoid complete defeat. Italy would continue to slide into the abyss of misery and disorder.

Antonina held one trump card. Theodora wanted her daughter, Joannina, as a bride for her grandson Anastasius. The two women had already corresponded about Joannina's betrothal to Anastasius and Antonina must already have explained to Theodora that, until the campaign in Italy improved, the wedding would have to wait. For Theodora, however, the marriage was a top priority; as for Italy, she knew little about it except that it was full of stiff-necked

Chalcedonians led by Vigilius, who refused to countersign the Edict of the
Three Chapters while all the time urgently beseeching Justinian to help Italy.
She did not tell Antonina that she felt death dogging her footsteps and closing
in upon its prey more nearly as each week passed. As Antonina set off for
Constantinople, she probably thought that in return for consenting to the
marriage of her daughter and Theodora's grandson she could secure Theodora's
support.

But Theodora was already dead when Antonina reached Constantinople. The
cause of death, mentioned by only one source, was cancer.[8] If the Latin word
'cancer', meaning 'crab', describes a medical condition like our 'cancer', then she
must have passed her last weeks of life dying slowly and painfully.[9] Justinian
was at her side in her final hours and on her death bed she remembered her
Monophysite refugees in the Palace of Hormisdas and asked Justinian to protect
them after her death. Justinian promised. Probably it was he, too, who closed
her eyes after she breathed her last breath and bound her mouth shut. These
were the final services to the dead, usually done by a close relative and they
were important, for the soul departed through the mouth at the moment of
death and, after the moment had passed, it was important that the mouth be
bound shut so that no evil spirit might slip inside. Antonina must have learned
of Theodora's death with ambivalent emotions.

ONCE ANTONINA LEFT ITALY, JOHN THE NEPHEW OF VITALIAN CAME WILLINGLY
TO DISCUSS TACTICS WITH BELISARIUS. They first tried to break the siege of
Rossano but Belisarius abandoned it after their first effort failed and sailed for
Rome, leaving John behind. He attempted a diversionary ploy to save the city
but Baduila would not be diverted from the siege and Rossano was left with no
way out. It capitulated.

When Belisarius reached Rome he found that the garrison had mutinied and
killed Conon, the officer in charge. The mutineers had then dispatched some
clergymen to Justinian to demand a pardon for their misdeed and the payment
of the wages due to them; otherwise they would hand over Rome to the
Goths. Justinian accepted their terms. He had little choice. However, Belisarius
restored order and saw to it that the city had a good supply of provisions in case
it was put under siege again. Then orders came from Constantinople recalling
him. Early in 549 he handed over the command of the garrison to one of his
retainers, Diogenes, and left Italy forever.

He owed his recall to Antonina. Once she found that Theodora was dead,
she took stock. As she assessed the situation, she now had no advocate at court
and Belisarius was isolated. She asked Justinian to recall him, possibly hoping

that Justinian would refuse and, if he did, then she would press the case for reinforcements. But Justinian agreed. He had no further use for Belisarius and scant compassion for Italy.

Perugia fell soon after Belisarius left Italy and, when summer came, Rome fell too. The garrison in Rome fought well but the city was betrayed again by soldiers guarding the Ostian Gate, which gave on to the road leading past the Church of St Paul outside-the-Walls. Their wages had not been paid for years.

Belisarius returned to Constantinople with his reputation in tatters. He arrived to find that Antonina had already taken her revenge on Theodora's memory. Feeling death approaching, Theodora had grown impatient with Antonina's endless postponements of the marriage of Joannina and Anastasius. She arranged a tryst between the two. Joannina was unwilling but Theodora insisted. Not to put too fine a point on it, Theodora schemed to have her grandson rape Joannina or at least, so the scuttlebutt in the capital reported. Then, when the girl was compromised, Theodora arranged a marriage; when Antonina reached Constantinople, she discovered that her daughter and Theodora's grandson had been living in wedded bliss for eight months. Theodora's cold-blooded scheming notwithstanding, the two had fallen deeply in love.

Antonina was incensed. Not only had Theodora paid no heed to the desperate struggle that Belisarius and Antonina had waged in Italy but she had connived at the rape of their daughter. Then she had hijacked Joannina's wedding, shutting Antonina out of the arrangements. Theodora was beyond Antonina's reach but she descended on the two lovers like an avenging angel. It did not matter that they had developed a real affection for each other. She forced them to separate.

Belisarius must have met a tearful daughter when he returned to Constantinople. The *Secret History* of Procopius, which probably was written only a few months after Belisarius' return, reports that he did not interfere with his wife's arrangements, even though Joannina was compromised and her legal status dubious. Was she not now an adulterer? The secret historian reports that everyone was amazed to discover how supine Belisarius was.[10] The general opinion before Theodora's death was that Belisarius yielded to Antonina because he feared Theodora; now it was clear that he feared Antonina too. Procopius was disgusted with his old commander, who could not stand up to his wife, even when her teeth were pulled and she had no power to harm him.

Yet Antonina probably relented eventually and the young lovers resumed their marriage. The law was on their side. Justinian's laws did not allow divorce by mutual consent and the reasons for divorce that he did recognize did not include a resentful mother-in-law. Sometime after Procopius finished his *Secret History*, Joannina and Anastasius were probably reunited.

But Belisarius' fortune did not fall into the eager hands of Theodora's grandson, as Theodora planned. When Belisarius died in March of 565, Justinian appropriated his estate. The imperial treasury rather than his daughter Joannina was the heir to Belisarius' fortune.

13

Postlude: The Ending of the Era of Reconquest

ONCE DEATH REMOVED THEODORA, HER ENEMIES TOOK HEART. John the Cappadocian, in exile in Egypt, received the news with renewed hope. Time had blunted his ambition but the fire was still warm. He trusted that Justinian would remember him and bring him back into his service once Theodora was no longer at his side. He was not entirely disappointed. Justinian did remember him and recalled him from exile, but the years had passed him by. He had been ordained a priest and Justinian allowed him to remain one. There was no longer a place for him in the emperor's inner circle.

In Jerusalem, Antonina's son, Photius, realized that he need no longer conceal his identity. His lines of communication with the imperial court reopened. Perhaps Belisarius put in a good word for him and possibly even Antonina felt some stray maternal instincts stirring in her bosom. Within a few years, Photius became the abbot of the New Monastery in Jerusalem and Justinian surely approved. The New Monastery had been a hornets' nest of Origenist heretics and a man like Photius with his wealth, contacts and military experience had the mettle to handle them.

The Chalcedonian lobby in Constantinople thought that it was safe at last to mount an attack on the refugees whom Theodora had protected in the Hormisdas Palace. They persuaded Justinian to move them to a less upscale establishment, the House of Urbicius, and having accomplished that they unsheathed the weapon of sexual temptation. Both canon and civil law ruled that male monasteries were off-limits to women. But among those who took refuge in the House of Urbicius were some married couples, for it was not uncommon for a man and woman who were linked in wedlock to embrace a life of asceticism together. Yet the practice could raise questions. So God, Monophysite tradition claimed, purified the House of Urbicius by burning it down and in the conflagration some women of suspect chastity lost their lives.[1] However, Justinian built a monastery on the site and kept the promise that he made Theodora on her deathbed. He continued to shelter the anti-Chalcedonian refugees and Theodosius lived on in Constantinople under his protection, recognized as their leader by the Monophysites who were not seduced by the extremes of Aphthartodocetism.

Then, while Justinian was mourning Theodora's death and distracted by the Three Chapters dispute, a plot was formed to kill him. It failed, but it cast suspicion on the emperor's cousin, Germanus. The ringleader was Arsaces, an Armenian who had a private grudge, for once he had been caught carrying on correspondence with the shah of Persia and Justinian had him whipped and paraded through the streets on a camel's back. Arsaces found an accomplice in Artabanes, also an Armenian, who had planned to wed Justinian's niece until Theodora forced him to remain faithful to the wife whom he had married in his youth back in Armenia. Once Theodora was dead he rid himself of his unwanted Armenian wife, but he still harboured a secret rage.

Another man with more power also had a grievance, Germanus. His brother Boraïdes made him his heir when he died, leaving his own daughter only as much as the law required. Justinian intervened on the daughter's behalf. He had acted, probably, at the instigation of Theodora, who detested Germanus and pitied Boraïdes' daughter. Germanus was incensed. So Arsaces thought it safe to approach the elder son of Germanus, Justin, and test the waters.

Justin told his father, who told Marcellus, the Count of the Excubitors. Marcellus was an austere, upright man who wanted proof of the conspiracy before he involved the emperor, whose time was fully occupied with the Three Chapters controversy. Germanus complied. He and Justin talked with one of the conspirators while one of Marcellus' men listened from a hiding-place. The plot called for the murder of Belisarius, Marcellus and Justinian himself. That was enough.

Marcellus put the information before Justinian, who summoned the senate to the palace to judge the case. All agreed that Germanus and his son were guiltless. But when they entered the emperor's chamber, they found him in a paranoid mood. He burst out angrily against Germanus. His wrath may have been fuelled by disappointment. Now that Theodora was dead and he did not have to take account of her prejudices, he had Germanus in mind to replace Belisarius in Italy. That plan would have to be put on hold as long as Germanus was under suspicion.

Germanus might have suffered incarceration or worse, except that Marcellus spoke up for him and took the blame for the delay in reporting the conspiracy to the emperor. Justinian cooled down. He did the conspirators no harm other than keeping them under surveillance in the palace for a time. Artabanes was soon afterwards appointed Master of the Soldiers in Thrace and sent to defend Sicily from the Goths as best he could.

SICILY WAS IN DESPERATE NEED. The Goths were plundering it at will. Had it not been for the conspiracy, Justinian might have sent Germanus to the Italian front immediately, but he hesitated. Instead he appointed old Liberius, now past 80 but a man with roots in Italy. Then, upon reflection, Justinian changed his mind. While Byzantine dominion in Italy was collapsing, Justinian was trying to coerce the Latin west into accepting his Three Chapters Edict and he knew that, as long as the Goths ruled Rome, he could never control the papacy. He overcame his hesitation and appointed Germanus generalissimo of the campaign in Italy.

Germanus moved swiftly to recruit an army with the help of his two sons, Justin and Justinian, whose career prospects had brightened after Theodora's death. Volunteers drawn by Germanus' military reputation came from Thrace and Illyricum and the Danube regions. But his strategy included conciliation as well as force. His first wife, Passara, was dead and for his second wife he chose Matasuntha, the granddaughter of Theoderic the Amal and the last of the Gothic royal family. He was reaching out to those Goths who felt no enthusiasm for Baduila's regime, for Baduila's policy of freeing slaves and tenant farmers from their lords and masters hurt not only the Roman well-to-do landowners but also the Goths, who had occupied one-third of the land of Italy when the great Theoderic ruled the peninsula. The union of Germanus and Matasuntha promised a restoration of the good old days when there was a Roman Empire in the west and that was what the propertied classes wanted, whether they were Roman or Gothic.

Germanus' new approach might have worked. We can only surmise what the outcome might have been, for in the autumn of 550 Germanus took sick and died. After his death, Matasuntha gave birth to a son, named Germanus after his father but we lose track of him unless we can identify him with a senator named Germanus, whose daughter married the eldest son of the emperor Maurice in 601 and a year later, after Maurice was overthrown, hoped briefly for the imperial throne himself. He was executed for treason.[2]

Justinian now turned to Narses, the ageless eunuch who had been Theodora's protégé. He was on the point of abandoning public life and withdrawing to a monastery which he had built, intending to retire there.[3] When the summons from Justinian came his rejoinder was blunt: either find adequate resources to defeat the Ostrogoths or give up Italy. At last Justinian listened. In April 551 Narses departed for Italy with 30,000 troops and enough money to pay the soldiers their back wages. He reached Ravenna in early June and not much later met the Goths with an army that outnumbered them two-to-one. The Goths were routed near modern Gualdo Tadino, north of Rome, on a battlefield called

'Busta Gallorum' ('Tombs of the Gauls'), for the Romans had once wiped out a horde of Gallic invaders there.[4] The defeat of the Goths was as complete as that of the Gauls centuries before. Baduila fled and was killed in flight. But there was still mopping up to do. Under Baduila's successor, Teias, the Goths fought a final battle against the backdrop of Monte Lattari in southern Italy and went down to defeat.

Yet, for the unfortunate Italians, the war in Italy, with its carnage and destruction, was not yet over. There was a new invasion. The Goths had begged the Franks to help them but the Franks saw no reason to comply. They wanted Italy for themselves. They remained neutral while the Goths went down to defeat but two brothers, Leutharis and Buccelin, launched their own freelance invasion of Frankish and Alemann adventurers, which did not turn out as they hoped. Leutharis and much of his army died of plague, and Narses annihilated Buccelin's force in a pitched battle. It was his third great victory in Italy and it consolidated his reputation as a great tactician. By 562 he had secured all of Italy and then, for a few brief years, the land was at peace.[5]

No ancient source tells us what Belisarius and Antonina thought when they learned of Narses' victory. Narses had been given resources the like of which Belisarius never had. It must have seemed to both of them that their glory days were over. It was all quite unfair. Yet fate would give Belisarius one last chance to shine on the battlefield.

THE VICTORY IN ITALY OVER THE GOTHS AND JUSTINIAN'S VICTORY OVER POPE VIGILIUS WERE NOT DISCONNECTED EVENTS. It had been almost nine years since he had been snatched from Rome and when he set out on his return journey, an old man suffering from kidney stones, he perhaps hoped that he might undo the terrible damage that the two wars, one on the battlefield and the other in the arena of religion, had wrought. He died on the way home. But Justinian did grant him his reward for accepting the Three Chapters Edict. On 13 August 554 he issued his 'Pragmatic Sanction' that tried to re-establish the old social order in Italy. Tenant farmers and slaves whom Baduila had freed were restored to their masters. In the city of Rome itself honorariums were established once again for the professors at the University of Rome and funds were to be set aside for public works. In each province of Italy the bishops and notables were granted the right to elect their governor from among themselves. The colony of Italian refugees in Constantinople who had been petitioning Justinian for succour got what they wanted.

But in the Byzantine world, the laws that were promulgated by the emperors rarely meshed completely with what actually happened. Power in Italy remained in the hands of the army. Narses was generalissimo and officers took orders from him. He became immensely rich and remained *de facto* ruler of Italy until after Justinian's death, when Justinian's successor, Justin II, dismissed him.[6] Even so, he did not return to Constantinople, for he had no stomach for an encounter with Justin's wife, the empress Sophia, who was Theodora's niece and as tough as her aunt. Instead he remained in Rome, watching from the old imperial palace on the Palatine Hill as Byzantine rule in Italy crumbled under the onslaught of a new invasion that began in 568, this time by the Lombards. He was there when the time came at last for him to meet his Maker. He made his final voyage home to Constantinople in an immensely expensive casket and was laid to rest in the monastery where he had intended to live out his years of retirement.

Belisarius lived on quietly with Antonina in Constantinople, rich and respected but retired from public office. The years pressed on. On 17 December 557, at midnight, a great earthquake shook Constantinople, damaging the new church of Hagia Sophia, and on 7 May of the following year, while the stone masons were repairing the damage, the dome collapsed. About the same time, bubonic plague returned to Constantinople to carry off a new crop of victims. And the following year, Constantinople found itself in deadly danger from a new invasion.

A HORDE OF KUTRIGURS AND SLAVS, LED BY THE KUTRIGUR KHAGAN, ZABERGAN, took advantage of a cold snap in March 559 to cross the frozen Danube and sweep down into Thrace. There it split into three spearheads: one advanced into Greece as far as the pass of Thermopylae where it was stopped, another made for the Gallipoli peninsula, and a third, under Zabergan himself with 7,000 horsemen at his back, galloped for Constantinople. The Master of Soldiers in Thrace was an old protégé of Theodora, Sergius, whom she had once favoured, in spite of his manifest incompetence, because he was a suitor of Antonina's granddaughter. Age and marriage alliance with Antonina's progeny had not increased his military competence. Zabergan took him prisoner.

Justinian sent out a force of new conscripts, strengthened by the Scholarians, to stop the horde at the Long Wall, or Wall of Anastasius I, which stretched across the Thracian peninsula some 65 km west of Constantinople. Anastasius had built it as an advance line of defence, but the earthquake of December 557 that had damaged Hagia Sophia had toppled parts of the wall and it was not yet repaired. The recruits sent to guard it were ineffective and the Scholarians were not much better than toy soldiers. When the Kutrigur horde threatened them with a real battle they retired at high speed, with the raw recruits following their example. In desperation, Justinian turned to Belisarius.

Ten years had passed since Belisarius fought his last campaign and they had not been kind. He was no longer the robust soldier of his younger years but he was still a competent general. He put on his armour again, raised a scratch force with a core of 300 of his old veterans and with it he advanced to a village a few kilometres west of Constantinople, where he made camp. His effective troops were few but he had a crowd of peasants who had been driven out of the Thracian countryside by the Kutrigur horde. Belisarius set a careful trap. He concealed 200 mounted troops in a valley where they loosed a volley of arrows against the Kutrigur horsemen as they rode past. Then, before they could recover from this unexpected flank attack, Belisarius charged them with his motley force of peasants and recruits, all of them making as much noise as they could. The Kutrigurs thought they were facing a much larger army than they were, and they fled in panic.[7]

Once the immediate danger was over, Justinian recalled Belisarius and he himself moved with his court to Selymbria on the Sea of Marmora, the southern terminus of the Long Wall, and oversaw its reconstruction in person. He was 77 years old but he evidently felt the need to show himself a vigorous defender of his capital. Then, having stayed at Selymbria from April to mid-August, he proceeded back to Constantinople, returning as a conquering hero and making a ceremonial advent into the capital city with all the customary solemnities that advents demanded. But as he passed near the Church of the Holy Apostles where Theodora lay in her sarcophagus, he stopped and left the cheering crowds for a moment to enter, light candles before her tomb and kneel to say a prayer.

Belisarius made his last appearance in the theatre of history three years later. In October of 562 a plot against Justinian's life was uncovered. The motive is unclear but the chief mover was a money-changer and a banker and it is probable that Justinian's monetary policies at the end of his reign were squeezing bankers like him hard. One of the conspirators was captured in the church of the Virgin in Blachernae where he had sought asylum and under torture he revealed names of other confederates: two silversmiths, who were also bankers, Belisarius' domestic comptroller who managed his household and Belisarius himself. They were arrested and brought before the urban prefect.

The urban prefect was named Procopius[8] and it would have been an ironic twist of fate if this were Belisarius' former legal advisor, Procopius the historian, who is our chief source for Belisarius' life. But no contemporary witness identifies the two men and the name was not uncommon. The urban prefect took the information against Belisarius seriously. He was put under house arrest and his attendants were removed from him. Presumably Antonina also found her movements restricted. But on the first of April the next year the urban prefect was dismissed from office and, not three months later, Justinian restored Belisarius' honours. In March 565 the great general died.

His fortune, which Theodora had coveted for her grandson, was appropriated by Justinian for the treasury which needed it and Antonina was left to seek solace in a convent where she might make her peace with God, whose capacity for mercy should be great enough to forgive her sins. As the years went by, a legend grew up that an ungrateful Justinian blinded his great general in his old age and reduced him to beggary, and it developed into a full-fledged romance. Eight centuries after Belisarius' death, a nameless versifier produced a poem on the subject. The roots of the legend must be early. Perhaps Antonina herself planted the seeds from which it sprouted.

Justinian himself had not long to live. He died in his sleep on the night of 14 or 15 November 565. But before he died, he realized at long last what orthodoxy was, the Holy Grail which he had pursued throughout his entire reign. It was not the Chalcedonian Creed. Whether it was his arguments with Theodora or with himself that convinced him or because he attained at last the certainties of a senile mind, he became a Monophysite. Not a moderate Monophysite, accepting the Miaphysite doctrine that Theodora followed, but rather an extreme Monophysite, following the teachings of Severus' rival, Julian of Halicarnassus. Theodora would have told him that he had gone too far but she was dead. Justinian became an Aphthartodocetist, believing that Christ's body had been so completely assimilated to his divine nature that it escaped corruption and His suffering on the cross was an illusion. If He suffered, it was because He consented to suffer. Justinian's unexpected vision may have owed as much to incipient dementia as to his investigation of the Scriptures. Yet towards the end of 564 he issued an edict proclaiming that Aphthartodocetism was orthodox and requiring the assent of the five great sees of the church.

He was now a dogmatic old man and in no mood to trifle with churchmen who got in his way. The patriarch of Constantinople, Eutychius, refused to sign the edict and was arrested while he was in the midst of a church service and hustled off to a monastery. The other patriarchs were steeling themselves for a new theological conflict when Justinian died. His successor Justin II immediately cancelled the offending edict and if Justinian ended his life a heretic, it was not considered a sin deserving of eternal damnation. It was said that a holy man, upon Justinian's death, had a vision of a great plain and in its midst a furnace with flames rising to Heaven, which had been set alight for Justinian because he had introduced corruption into the True Faith. But because he had shown mercy to the poor and had built many churches, he had escaped its fire.[9]

And Antonina? If she ever went to a convent, I cannot believe that she remained there for long. She was not the sort of woman who found the ascetic life appealing, even when she reached an age when she lacked the physical vigour to sin. A tradition found in a late source reports that she went to live with Vigilantia, the sister of Justinian and mother of the emperor Justin II, and when fire destroyed Vigilantia's palace chapel, Antonina persuaded her to replace it with a church dedicated to St Procopius. He was an early Christian martyr, who was beheaded in Caesarea in Palestine during the persecution of the Christians under the emperor Diocletian. He was also the name saint of the historian, Procopius of Caesarea.

Was it a coincidence? Probably. But let us say a final goodbye to Antonina by conjuring up a purely imaginative picture of this lusty old lady in her declining years. Time has taken its toll. Men and women were considered old between 50 and 60 years of age,[10] and she had lived far beyond those limits. Her joints have grown stiff and her hair thin, but she still has some remnants of the allure that once fascinated Belisarius. Let us imagine her enjoying the warmth of the sun as she sits in a balcony of Vigilantia's palace and listens to young slave reading from a codex which had only recently chanced to fall into her hands. It was written by her old comrade-in-arms, Procopius, who had composed it at the same time as copies of his great *History of Justinian's Wars* were appearing for sale in the bookstalls around the Basilica, where the lawyers practised their learned trade. Antonina had half-forgotten what Procopius looked like. He was dead now. His last published work was a laboured panegyric on Justinian's building programme, full of insincere flattery, but it had pleased old Justinian, who thought squandering money on buildings showed how much he cared for his subjects. And all the time Procopius had belonged to an underground cell of malcontents who met secretly to vent their spleen! He had turned their grumbling into this little surreptitious essay which he pretended was a supplement to his *History of the Wars* and he was scheming to bequeath it to posterity! It was an irreverent and rather shocking piece of writing, Antonina thought; yet it was really rather enjoyable, all the same.

What a lot a gossip he had gathered about Theodora's life in the theatre! Everyone assumed that actresses were prostitutes and, of course, most of them were. Poor girls had to make a living. But, Antonina reflected, Theodora always had dreams of respectability. She wanted to be a great lady, generous to her friends and feared by her enemies. She had taught herself to read, and write a little too: she could do more than write her own name, which was as much as most actresses could do. But she was a quick learner when it came to languages. She learned enough Latin to hold a conversation in it. Latin was her husband's native tongue, and he liked Latin-speakers. She mastered some Syriac too, for when a person in the theatre world was sick and needed God's mercy, it was a Monophysite holy man who would offer help, and often his native tongue was Syriac. The Chalcedonians had no use for theatre trash.

As for herself, Procopius was unkind, and if only she were younger, she would have made Procopius pay for it; but it was too late to hold grudges. Yet she smiled as her little slave read that everyone suspected she used sorcery to keep Belisarius in thrall. Sorcery had its place and there were many simple souls, including holy men, who feared its power, and rightly so, but she had never used it to cast a spell on Belisarius. No spell was necessary to keep him in thrall. Belisarius needed her too much. Poor man! What would he have been without her to manage his career? It was thanks to her that Theodora opened doors for him. It was she who steadied him in his moments of panic. She cared for him on his campaigns, nursed him when he was ill, and saw to it that he got the portion of the booty from his victories that they both deserved. What Belisarius wanted out of life was wealth, glory and the public's admiration. He liked to go through the streets of Constantinople attended by a great bodyguard of blonde Germans and swarthy Berbers, and he basked in the admiration of the onlookers.

And what an admirable lover Theodosius was! Inexperienced at first, but with a natural talent. Why should women be expected to live lives of tedious chastity while men could take their pleasure with courtesans as much as they wished? Conventional, male chauvinist morality, which seemed to appeal to poor old Procopius, was merely an exercise in masculine hypocrisy.

What was more, she had always been loyal to Belisarius in her own way. The wives of other generals remained at home when their husbands were on campaigns, wasting their time with gossip and needlework, surrounded by the paraphernalia of respectability. She had stayed at her husband's side to help him when he need help and nurse him when he was ill. He was a brilliant general but never secure, and he invited the jealousy of his colleagues-in-arms. Even Justinian was jealous; there were already stories being told of the emperor's ingratitude.[11] The war against the Ostrogoths may have been the graveyard of his reputation; yet posterity would remember him as a great military commander and for that he could thank two accidents of history: first, he had his secretary, Procopius, who wrote the story of his campaigns in good, classical Greek that would meet the approval of the toughest schoolmaster, and second he had Antonina as his wife and his manager. The second was the more important reason, for few people could read Procopius' Greek, though those that could were the opinion-makers, whereas everyone could hear the tales about Belisarius that passed from one storyteller to another, adding details along the way. Belisarius would always have his defenders, but much as Antonina was reluctant to admit it, Narses was a better tactician, shrewder both as a courtier and a general, and better at siphoning off a personal fortune than Belisarius ever was, even with his wife's help.[12]

She had outlived most of them: Justinian, Theodora, Belisarius, Theodosius and the scribbler, Procopius. Narses had so far avoided death; dismissed by Justinian's successor, Justin II, he was living in Rome in the old imperial palace, watching new invaders of Italy, the Lombards, undo his conquests. Photius was still alive but he had always been a difficult son, whining for his mother when he was a boy and tattling on her when he became an adult. He had suppressed another Samaritan revolt without mercy, but mercy was an overrated virtue in real life, at least as it played out in the imperial service. Antonina had no regrets, even now when the morality of old age was the only fun left in life. She and Theodora had played the power game well, as well as fortune allowed.

She signalled to the slave to put the codex aside. Slowly, she rose to her feet and, moving with the unhurried dignity that the stiff joints of advancing age forced upon her, she made her way towards the new church of St Procopius that Vigilantia had built. There she lit a candle for St Procopius and for the indignant soul of his namesake, the historian who made it possible to reconstruct the lives of Antonina and Theodora. She may even have said a little prayer that Heaven would remember her virtues and forget her many sins, and that posterity would judge her kindly.

Regrettably, this picture of Antonina in her old age is purely imaginative. The passage of time and human forgetfulness have shrouded Antonina's final days in obscurity.

Appendix

TWO CONTEMPORARY WITNESSES: PROCOPIUS AND JOHN OF EPHESUS

For much of what we know about the private lives of Antonina and Theodora we are dependent on two sources, John of Ephesus and Procopius of Caesarea, and particularly on the latter's *Secret History* (*Anekdota*), an invective written for a clandestine group of disaffected members of the Constantinople élite and unpublished during his lifetime – hence the name *Anekdota*. John of Ephesus had no interest in Antonina, but on Theodora he provides almost as much information as Procopius. Procopius wrote in classical Greek, which was accessible to a very small minority in a society where only about 10 per cent were literate, even if we count those who could write little more than their names. John wrote in Syriac, the language of the Christian East. Procopius knew Antonina well, but there is no reason to think that he had much personal acquaintance with Theodora. John did know Theodora personally; for him she was 'the believing queen', the defender of the Monophysites, but the inner workings of government concerned him only so far as they affected his fellow churchmen. Both are biased, but how much does bias affect their evidence? Let us look at Procopius first.

It would be helpful if we knew more about him. The tenth-century lexicon called the *Souda* has an entry under his name which calls him a *rhetor* and an *illustris*, a lawyer and a senator. We cannot be sure that he ever did attain the rank of senator, for *illustris* was now a purely honorary title, but he was very likely a product of a law school, and the two schools that he could have attended were in Constantinople and Beirut. He chose a career path that was not uncommon for law-school graduates: he became *adsessor* or legal advisor to a public official.[1] The man whose staff Procopius joined was the young Belisarius, who was newly appointed duke of the troops at Dara, evidently in the four-month period when Justin and Justinian shared the throne.[2] He followed Belisarius on his Vandal campaign and joined him in Italy for the war against the Goths until the surrender of Ravenna in 540. Three years later, when Belisarius fell from favour, Procopius must have been among Belisarius' friends who were forbidden to visit him, and we do not know if Procopius ever returned to Italy.

His writings betray little personal information.[3] We can only guess the year of his birth, or for that matter his death. Like his exemplar, Thucydides, he did not let autobiography intrude. He came from Caesarea Maritima in Palestine – 'my Caesarea', he calls it in a passage in his *Secret History*, where he reports that Caesarea's population included many Samaritans who prudently abandoned their 'senseless belief' and became nominal Christians to avoid persecution.[4] The passage suggests compassion for the Samaritans but there is no reason to think that Procopius himself was one of them.[5] He must have attended a school that offered a solid education in the classics. Near Caesarea was Gaza, which had a famous school, and at one time I thought that Gaza was an obvious place for the young Procopius to seek a higher education.[6] Since then, Anthony Kaldellis[7] has shown how greatly he was influenced by contemporary Neoplatonist philosophy and hence we cannot rule out study in Alexandria, where Neoplatonism had made peace with Christian belief, or even at the Neoplatonic School in Athens, where it had not. In 529 Justinian either closed down the School of Athens or left it mortally wounded.[8] Whatever Procopius' school was, he learned some Latin, which was necessary for a legal career, and read the standard classical Greek authors. When he turned to writing history himself, he wrote as if his readership were in classical Greece a thousand years before his time, for whom the Christian world was a foreign country. Herodotus and Thucydides were his models and, like Thucydides, he claimed to rely on eye witnesses for his sources, though as Ian Colvin[9] has argued, for battles in the Caucasus region, he may have used military dispatches in the imperial archives that were tucked into the bowels of the Hippodrome. He wrote from behind a kind of classical mask, which gave him a degree of freedom to imply criticisms that it would have been imprudent and perhaps dangerous to voice openly. But only the tiny sliver of society that had an education similar to his would have understood them.

Was he a pagan or a Christian,[10] or was he a spiritual dual citizen, inhabiting both thought-worlds without any sense of contradiction? Anthony Kaldellis has argued that Procopius belonged to a circle of pagan thinkers and writers that included John the Lydian, Agathias of Myrrhina, who continued Procopius' *History of Justinian's Wars*, and Hesychius of Miletus.[11] There were still pagans in the public service in Justinian's empire, though paganism was dangerous. We can cite the case of Phocas,[12] a man of recognized integrity who replaced John the Cappadocian during the *Nika* riots. Procopius' circle admired him as the ideal praetorian prefect. He was suspected of paganism in Justinian's first anti-pagan pogrom in 529 but he satisfied his interrogators. However, in the second pogrom of 545–6, orchestrated by Theodora's friend John of Ephesus, he preferred suicide.[13] Procopius would know well enough how prudent it was to avoid any suspicion of paganism, whatever his private beliefs were, for the second pogrom hit Constantinople's literate elite hard and Procopius must have known some of the victims personally. Yet my own opinion is still that Procopius was a Chalcedonian Christian,[14] though he was without sympathy for the holy zeal with which Justinian tried to enforce orthodoxy. He thought the Christian clergy were a corrupt, self-seeking lot and he censured Justinian for favouring them whenever there was a dispute between them and laymen.[15] He disliked the new age of intolerance that began when the *Henotikon* was cancelled and he detested the trappings of the tyranny that Justinian and Theodora initiated.[16]

He published nothing while Theodora was still alive, though probably he followed the custom of presenting readings of portions of his *History of the Wars* to select groups while it was still a work in progress. One passage, which describes the great siege of Rome in 537–8, retains an indication of the date of its presentation.[17] It tells how an arrow struck a soldier in the face and disappeared entirely into his head but the soldier lived on, feeling no discomfort until five years later when the arrow tip began to emerge and, writes Procopius, 'this is now the third year that it has been slowly but steadily coming out'. The third year is 544, or perhaps 545, after Belisarius returned to Italy to deal with the Gothic insurgency. Another passage, which may have been first published orally describes how 'Jesus the Son of God' cured Abgar, the ruler of Edessa, of gout and gave him a letter promising to keep Edessa safe from capture.[18] Procopius takes off his classical mask to refer to Jesus in terms that marked him as a devout Christian and if this gobbet was presented in about 545, at the height of the pagan witch-hunt of that year which swept up some of Procopius' friends, it shows that Procopius was a prudent man, albeit with Christian leanings. The description of the climax of the *Nika* riots, when Theodora told the frightened men in Justinian's council that the imperial purple made a good winding sheet, is a well-honed passage which would have made a good public presentation, beginning as it does with contrasting speeches, one by a senator advising caution and the other by Theodora urging boldness, and with the massacre in the Hippodrome as its conclusion.[19] If we give free rein to our imaginations we may picture Procopius presenting the passage as a public recitation at court, to an audience that included the emperor and empress.

After Theodora's death, there was a burst of creativity. Seven books of the *Wars* were published in 551 and I presume that copies appeared in the bookstalls of Constantinople in that year. At the same time, Procopius produced his unpublished *Secret History* as a clandestine supplement to his *Wars*.[20] When he wrote it, 32 years had passed since Justinian took control of the empire and Procopius was counting from the year when Justin I appropriated the throne, in 518. It was also 32 years since the new age of intolerance had begun. In the seven books of the *History of the Wars*, Procopius' outlook had grown darker, but not enough to suggest its bitter coda, the *Secret History* which must have been intended as a clandestine eighth book, for when a few years later Procopius did publish an eighth book to conclude his *Wars*, he borrowed its opening words from the introduction to the *Secret History*. It was not a standard invective, distorting the truth. Rather it was intended as a palinode that revealed news which could not be circulated openly, even after Theodora was dead.

Yet it did have an audience, for it survived, and we may guess that it consisted of a small, disaffected circle whom Procopius could trust, like-minded men with a similar education, cultural dual citizens of the Christian present and the pagan past. They were members of a chattering class that was afraid to chatter. Some may have been clandestine pagans, some nominal Christians and others may even have had a real interest in Christian theology, but they were out of tune with the bigotry of the age. They were unnerved by the harsh anti-pagan intolerance of the Justinianic regime. I believe – but I cannot prove – that this was the very select audience that heard Procopius read excerpts from the *Secret History*, and it survived because it was circulated among them as a *samizdat* publication.

The *Secret History* falls into two parts. The first part starts with a section on the evil deeds of Belisarius, abetted by his wife, Antonina, and it segues into a second, longer section on the even more iniquitous deeds of Justinian and Theodora.[21] It presents Justinian as the antithesis of an ideal emperor, responsible not only for the maladministration that injured his subjects but for the natural calamities as well.[22] True emperors were God's representatives on earth and if the empire was ruled rightly it mirrored the Heavenly Kingdom. But with Justinian and Theodora the order sanctioned by Heaven was turned upside down. Justinian carried absolutism to its ultimate extreme; he claimed not merely to be the source of law but incarnate law itself.[23] Like Louis XIV of France, he was the state.

The first part concludes with the allegation that Justinian and his empress were, in fact, not human at all, but *anthropodaimones* – 'demons appearing as humans'.[24] Justinian's mother claimed that it was not her husband – nor, indeed, a human being at all – but a devil who sired him, and Theodora's lovers claimed that when they spent the night with her a demon would descend like an outraged husband and drive them from the room. A holy man admitted into the imperial presence claimed to see Satan on the throne, and there were other reports that Justinian would sometimes change into a headless spirit, like one of the dreaded headless demons that spread death.[25] Was this the 'End of Times', foretold in St Mark's *Gospel*,[26] when there would be wars and persecutions and the sun would be darkened and the moon hide its light? We would not have expected such speculation from the rational Procopius, the imitator of Thucydides. But he may not have been as detached as he appears to be in his *Wars*. He planned to write a history of the theological controversies of his day. He indicated his intention to write one in his *Secret History* and he repeated it in the eighth book of his *Wars*.[27] But it remained unwritten. If he had written it, it might have revealed an aspect of Procopius' character that was fascinated by eschatology more than we have suspected. Yet we need not be surprised for his contemporary, John the Lydian, who belonged to his circle, could write a handbook on divination.[28]

The second part is an indictment of Justinian's administration and according to Anthony Kaldellis[29] it was written later – though not by much – than the first part. It begins with a vision that came to a notable in Constantinople when Justin became emperor. He dreamed he saw a man standing in the Bosporus, who drank up all the water in the sea, and when it was replaced by sewage, he drank that, too. The vision defines the topic. This section will show how Justinian's administration drained the empire of its wealth. Here we can check Procopius' trustworthiness against Justinian's *Novels*; fortunately that is a task that has already been done.[30] Procopius gets good marks for reliability as far as facts go. However, his standard for judging Justinian's laws is how much they injured established practices[31] or affected the economy and social order. His is a 'worm's eye-view' but he does not fabricate.

What then of the first section, particularly the lurid details about Theodora's early years in the theatre? Some of it was based on malicious gossip and stock jokes about whores, one of them recycled from a speech of Demosthenes.[32] But we have some independent evidence. John of Ephesus refers to her casually as 'Theodora *ek tou porneou*' – 'Theodora from the whorehouse'.[33] These are Greek words inserted into John's Syriac text and hence they were probably not his invention. He had heard them on the streets of Constantinople and repeated them without intent to denigrate. All actresses were deemed to be prostitutes, and the street would have considered Theodora a harlot even if she were the exception to the rule. Yet she had a bastard daughter when she married Justinian, for whom she found a husband in the house of the old emperor Anastasius, and we know of two grandsons.[34] Solid evidence that Theodora was an ex-actress comes from the Justinianic Code as well. Procopius reports that the emperor Justin had to promulgate a new law to make the marriage of Justinian and Theodora legal and in the code the new measure appears. It wipes away all blemishes of a penitent actress and opens the way for marriage between her and a man of senatorial rank. The law fits the marriage of Justinian and Theodora too closely to be coincidence.[35]

We know nothing about the interlude in Theodora's life when she was Hecebolus' mistress in Libya. However, her visit to Alexandria on her way back to Constantinople from Libya may have left a mark on Coptic tradition. The *History of the Patriarchs of the Coptic Church*[36] reports that Theodora originally came from Alexandria. No tradition makes Alexandria her native city and hence the report must be based on her visit there. She later referred to the Alexandrian patriarch, Timothy III, as her spiritual father,[37] which suggests a meeting of the two. We do not know how she met Justinian. I have suggested that the go-between was one of Justinian's spies in Antioch,[38] a dancing girl named Macedonia. But Justinian's life before his uncle became emperor is a closed book for us; for all we know, he may have been a fan of the theatre and seen Theodora perform on stage. Theodora's career as an actress cannot have been a secret.

Once Theodora became empress, she made a determined effort to repress the sex trade. She founded a convent for ex-prostitutes and Procopius' panegyric on Justinian's building programme[39] treats the foundation as a righteous achievement. It would have appealed to a woman who had first-hand knowledge of the trade. Did Theodora arrange the murder of the Ostrogothic princess, Amalasuntha, as the *Secret History* claims?[40] We cannot be certain, but Procopius' report, which the great Italian scholar Domenico Comparetti[41] once called a malicious afterthought of the historian's old age, may simply reflect the 'buzz' roused by the relatively recent publication of Cassiodorus' letters, where there is a missive from the Gothic queen Gudeliva to Theodora, mentioning an unnamed affair that should make the empress happy.[42] It must have provoked suspicion in those circles that were prone to it.

We must approach the *Secret History* with our critical faculties alert, ready to recognize that it reflects the climate of opinion in Procopius' circle in the mid-sixth century and to discount bias – but we must do that with any ancient source. When Procopius wrote the *Secret History*, Constantinople had lost half its population to plague which brusquely terminated a period of prosperity.[43] It had just endured another anti-pagan pogrom that entrapped large numbers of the educated elite to which Procopius belonged, and the war in Italy seemed lost. Even God was angry, for why otherwise would He allow the numerous earthquakes that shook the cities of the east? The outlook of the *Secret History* is black, but it is not mere libel.

But what about Antonina and Belisarius? Procopius knew both of them well and I believe that he had enough integrity as an historian not to fabricate defamatory tales about them. The report of how pope Silverius was deposed is corroborated by the *Book of the Pontiffs*. His portrayal of Antonina's unloved son, Photius, is congruent with that of John of Ephesus,[44] who reports that he accompanied his stepfather on a number of campaigns and then, for some reason other than piety, he became a monk under an assumed name. Then he changed course. John does not cite Theodora's death as the reason – in fact he gives no reason at all for why Photius offered his services to Justinian, who dispatched him with full powers to Syria to suppress a revolt of the Samaritans, and his terror tactics frightened Samaritans and Christians alike. The torrid romance between Antonina and Theodosius is not attested elsewhere But nothing about it contradicts the report that Procopius gives in his *History of the Wars*.

Between Procopius and John of Ephesus, the difference is enormous. Procopius was the product of a good school, wherever it was, and wrote correct, classical Greek which could be read easily only by persons with an education like his own. John wrote for an entirely different audience. He was born in a Syriac-speaking village close to Amida and was educated in a Monophysite monastery. None of his brothers had lived as long as two years, but when John fell ill with the same sickness at the age of two his parents brought him for help to Maro, the local holy man who perched on top of a column on the summit of windy hill, and he prescribed cooked lentils. Three times the lentils were inserted into the infant's mouth on a finger tip, and the third time he opened his eyes.[45] John survived, and in return for the cure, he was put into Maro's care and prepared for life in a monastery at Amida. He became a monk.

When the age of tolerance ended with Anastasius' death, the monks were driven from the Amida monasteries. They sought shelter where they could find it until Justinian relaxed the persecution in 532 and sponsored a dialogue between Chalcedonians and Monophysites.[46] For a brief period, until pope Agapetus destroyed the entente between Anthimus and Severus, the persecution ceased, but then it broke out again more fiercely than before. The monks at Amida had once again to leave their monasteries. It was probably at this point that John made his way to Constantinople and was sheltered by Theodora and, Monophysite though he was, he won the confidence of Justinian.[47] In 542, the year that the plague smote Constantinople, Justinian sent him on a mission to suppress paganism in the hilly country around Tralles in south-west Asia Minor and, when that task was completed, he spearheaded a witch-hunt in Constantinople.[48] He then made his base at Sycae (Galata) across the Golden Horn from Constantinople, where the imperial eunuch Callinicus provided him with a property which he transformed into a monastery.

After Justinian died his successor, Justin II, at first attempted to reconcile the Monophysites and the Chalcedonians, but discussions broke down. Justin lost patience with the Monophysites and the persecution began again. John spent his last years in prison and at least part of his *Church History* was written there. What survives is his *Lives of the Eastern Saints*, 58 biographies of Monophysite ascetics in Mesopotamia and Syria and the third part of his *Church History*. The first part, covering the years from Julius Caesar to the death of Theodosius II, is completely lost. The second part was used by the author of the chronicle of Pseudo-Dionysius of Tel-Mahre[49] and later by Michael the Syrian. The third part was found among a group of manuscripts bought by the British Museum from the convent of St Mary Deipara in Egypt. It covers the years from when the persecutions recommenced under Justin II up to 585. It is a rambling narrative which occasionally sheds light on the period of Justinian.

John was an uncompromising Miaphysite. In his eyes, Theodora was 'the believing queen', a generous and courageous defender of the faith.' She was a gracious and courageous defender of the faith. For that matter, he seems to have respected Justinian as well. Yet John nowhere contradicts the *Secret History*. He knew that people called her behind her back – never, I feel sure, to her face – 'Theodora from the brothel'. John saw her as a tough, devoted defender of the Monophysites who restrained her husband, who belonged to the dark side, though he was God's deputy on earth. She was a woman who knew how to wield power and get what she wanted. She was defeated in the end, but the final weapon that brought her down was cancer.

Notes

Notes to Preface

1 Anthony Kaldellis (Kaldellis, 2007a, 82–119) argues that it had evolved into a true nation state, which is not inaccurate. However, contemporaries still thought of Romania as an 'imperium' that inherited traditions from the Roman past. The name 'Romania' came into popular use in the proto-Byzantine period

2 For a succinct description of the church-state relationship, see Moorhead, 1994, 116–20

3 *Secret History* 24.7; cf. *Wars* 4.27.38

4 Ps.-Dionysius of Tel-Mahre, pt. 3, 76 (TTH # 22, trans. Witakowski, 71)

5 John of Ephesus, *Ecclesiastical History, Third Part,* 3.26–30

6 See Bagnani 1949, for Justinian's view of divine right

7 Cassiodorus, *Variae 10.20.2*

8 *Secret History,* 2.33–6

9 Amida is modern Diyarbakir on the Tigris River, in eastern Turkey. For John of Ephesus, see the Appendix; also Michael Whitby, LA *Guide,* 526–7

10 See Carney, 1971, which includes the first translation into English of John Lydus' *De Magistratibus*

11 18.33; 23.1; 24.29; 24.33

12 See Evans, 1972, 41–6. The only evidence for connecting the dates of the *Secret History* to the *Buildings* is a cross-reference: SH 18.38 to *Buildings* 2.7.2–16 re the flood of the river Scirtus at Edessa

13 Kaldellis, 2009. See also Greatrex, 1994, Evans, 1996b, and Croke, 2005

Chapter 1: The Scum of Society

1 The emperor was heir to two traditions of kingship: one that went back to Hellenistic monarchy which held that the emperor was above the law, and the other that was a legacy of the early empire, particularly the Augustan settlement of 27 BCE, that the emperor was bound to respect existing statutes. See Oost, 1968; Bagnani, 1949; Downey, 1968; Downey, 1940. Under Justinian, the first

emperor to refer to himself as 'law incarnate', and hence the source of law, the Hellenistic legacy became dominant and the emperor became a *de facto* despot

2   Cf. Bassett, 2004, 121. See also Cecily Hennessy, OHBS, 202–16

3   Marcellinus Comes, *Chronicle, sub anno* 527

4   *Novel* (CIC) 22.12, 536. If we apply the rule that laws are never promulgated to prohibit a deed that never happens, this edict of Justinian may be evidence that wives *did* sometimes attend the theatre or the races

5   Cekalova, 1991, 16

6   For the factions, see Alan Cameron, 1976; Roueché, 1993, 44–7. Cameron has argued, correctly, that the old view which claimed that the Blue party supported the Chalcedonian Creed whereas the Greens were anti-Chalcedonian is wrong: see Alan Cameron, 1974. This is not to say, however, that the parties could not be politicized. Barry Baldwin (1978) points out that, *pace* Cameron, John Malalas seems to have thought that the parties had political agendas

7   Cf. Bagnall, 1993, 104. Gymnasiums remained in use into the fifth century, but we lack evidence for their survival into the sixth century. Instead, athletic culture centred on professional shows in the circus

8   Treadgold, 1997, 169. For the *venationes*, see O'Donnell 2008, 52–3

9   *Nov.* 105.1

10 Procopius, *Secret History* 26.12–14. Perhaps the plague was also a motive for the abolition of the consulship. In 541, the epidemic had reached Egypt and the Near East, and if there had been a consul in 542, he would have presided over a plague year. Bagnall et al., 1987, 11–12, suggest that it was Justinian's fear of rivals which motivated the abolition

11 *Secret History* 9.2. For Procopius' tale of Theodora's beginnings, see *Secret History* 9.2–3; 42–59

12 *On Mimes*, 114–17. The father of St Theodore of Sykeon was an acrobat in the Hippodrome who performed with camels. See Dawes and Baynes, 1948, 88

13 Re: The meaning of the term *demos*, plural, *demoi*: Edward Gibbon took it to refer to the populace of the city, and Alan Cameron has revived his hypothesis (Alan Cameron, 1976). However the *demos* in the classical and Hellenistic cites never referred to the total population but only to the male citizen body. After 212, when Roman citizenship was extended to everyone, the situation in the Greek cities changed, but it appears that the *demoi* were still a distinct social stratum of the populace, not the mass of city dwellers. See Zuckerman, 2000; Gascou, 1976

14 Roueché, 1993, 29–30. When the Blue fans rioted in the cities of the East in Justin's reign, their dancers were banished except in Alexandria: Malalas 14.12 [417]

15 On claques in theatres and the influence of dancers, see Browning, 1952, 13–20, esp. 17–19

16 PO XVII, 1, 189
17 http://sor.cua.edu/Encyclicals/PatrEnc000212.html
18 *Chronicle* 9.20
19 ODB I, 444, s.v. 'Chronicle of 819'
20 In fact, we know nothing of Justinian's military career as a young man in the reign of Anastasius and it is possible that he was posted to the east. The qualification 'as far as we know' should be taken seriously
21 *Patria*, 3.93. Holmes, 1912, 343–4, makes the fanciful suggestion that on her way back from Libya, she stopped off in Paphlagonia, which was known for its Puritanism, and there she turned her back on her old way of life
22 For the traditions about Theodora's birthplace, see PLRE IIIb, s.v. 'Theodora 1'
23 An English translation has been published by Gorgias Press, Piscataway, NJ, in 2007. For a list of all references on Theodora's youth, see PLRE IIIB, s.v. Theodora 2, 1240–1
24 Diodorus 14.8.5; cf. Evans, 1972, 33
25 Clive Foss (2002) has already written a life of the empress that does not rely on the *Secret History*. I have relegated my defence of the *Secret History* as a reliable source to the Appendix
26 Rubin, 1960, 109
27 The 12 folios of the *Annales Ecclesiastici* were published between 1588 and 1607
28 See my remarks in Evans, 2002, 108–9
29 Procopius seems to accept that Justinian's theology was sound enough; it was his ferocious determination to make all Christians adhere to the same creed that he could not stomach. See *Secret History* 13.4–13.7. He gives Theodora no credit for trying to promote toleration for the Monophysites
30 Its designation in *Novel* (CIC) 105.1; cf. Rubin, 1960, 100
31 *Secret History* 1.12–14
32 See in general, Richard Lim, 'Christianization, Secularization and the Transformation of Public Life', in Rousseau, 2009, 497–511, esp. 499. Yet there was more mobility than we might expect from the law codes. Actors and actresses could be the sons and daughters of fig or grape merchants, butchers, saddlers, blacksmiths, etc., as John Chrysostom noted in one of his homilies (cf. Ceran, 1970, 199) and as A. H. M. Jones pointed out, a daughter of an actress could refuse to go on stage if she was a woman of exceptional piety (1964, 1020)
33 There is a series of laws in the Theodosian Code designed to degrade entertainers, whether actors, actresses or charioteers, and actresses seem to have been especially targeted, either because of prejudice against them based on gender or because they sought escape from their profession more frequently than men. *Cod.Theod.* 15.7.1 denied actresses the sacraments unless death was imminent; *Cod.Theod.* 15.7.4, 380, ruled that they must perform on stage unless they

adopted a holy life; *Cod. Theod.* 15.7.9, 381, conscripted women from the dregs of society for the stage, unless they were nuns. *Cod. Theod.* 15.7.11, 393, regulated their dress – no figured silk or gems. Stars of the theatre did sometimes appear in public richly dressed, perfumed and bare-headed, which no respectable woman would do .

34 *Secret History* 1.11–12, reports that she was one of those 'who had prostituted themselves in the orchestra'. Dewing, *Anecdota*, LCL translates as 'one of the prostitutes attached to the theatre'

35 See Evans, 1977

36 On women in public, see Beaucamp, 1998 and, in church, Taft, 1998; Fisher, 1984, 256. On the status of actresses, French (1998) is a thorough examination. On women in Byzantium in general, see Clark, 1993

37 For the separation of the sexes in Hagia Sophia, see Procopius, *Buildings* 1.1.56–8

38 On the topography of Constantinople, see Hennessy, 2008 (OHBS, 202–16)

39 Cf. Krueger, 2005, 300–2

40 Carney, 1971, 121–2; Jones, 1964, 911

41 Jones, 1964, 904–10. Town councils in some parts of the empire, such as Egypt, still existed under Justinian who attempted to enforce the duties of the *curiales*

42 For the *Brumalia*, see F. R. Trombley, ODC, s.v. *Brumalia*; for the *Maiouma*, see MacMullen, 1997, 30. On the lingering death of paganism, Trombley (1985) is particularly valuable

43 See Hodgkin III, 1967, 454–5; Mitchell, 2007, 293; Averil Cameron,1993, 24–5

44 See Marinus (7), PLRE II, 726–8

45 The see of Antioch nominally covered the whole of the Roman diocese of *Oriens*, but north of the Tauris Mountains the patriarchate of Constantinople took over much of its territory, and the Council of Chalcedon of 451 detached Jerusalem from the Antiochene see and made it a separate patriarchate. For historical reasons, the Armenian Church was independent of Antioch. See Witakowski, 1987, 48–9

46 Holum, 1982, 114–21, argues convincingly that Athenais was a native of Antioch, not Athens

47 For Hypatia's death, see Watts, 2006; Rist, 1965

48 Cf. Treadgold, 1997, 126–32. For a good general survey of religious beliefs and schisms in early Byzantium, see Richard Lim, in Bowersock, Brown and Grabar (1999), 196–218; see also Zemov, 1961 *passim*, and Evans, 1996a, 71–8

49 As Sidney Griffith pointed out in his paper, 'Imperial Theology and Church Unity: Justinian and Theodora in the Christological Crises of the Sixth Century', at the 'The Age of Theodora' Conference held 7 October 2000, at Connecticut College. Reported in *Hugoye* 4/1 (2001)

50 Zemov, 1961, 74–5

51 Cf. remarks of Peter Brown (Brown, 1971, 147–50)

52 For a good recent survey of the rise of monasticism, see Daniel F. Caner, "'Not of this World": The Invention of Monasticism', in Rousseau (ed.), 2009, 588–600

53 Evagrius, 3.14, preserves a copy of the *Henotikon*. Michael Whitby, *Ecclesiastical History of Evagrius Scholasticus*, TTH #33, 147, remarks with some cynicism that the *Henotikon* was 'moderately and cautiously phrased: this ensured its ultimate failure ...'

54 These were the so-called 'Acephaloi', the 'Headless Ones', since they did not acknowledge either the patriarch or the emperor as their head, with the authority to define belief

55 The term 'Monophysite' appears first in the seventh century as a term referring to all Christians who rejected the two-nature doctrine of the Chalcedonians. They ranged from the Miaphysites or 'Hesitants' who did not deny Christ's human nature, and could accept the *Henotikon*, to the Aphthartodocetists who claimed that He was all divine nature. However, I use the term here as a synonym for 'anti-Chalcedonian', even though it is anachronistic

56 I cannot accept the view of Walter Goffart (Goffart, 1980) that the Goths took over one-third of the revenues from the land, and not the land itself. Goffart argues the case well, but it takes too much ingenuity to make it fit the evidence. The Goths were not simply immigrants into Italy who could eventually be assimilated. They were foreign conquerors, and their rule was comparable to that of the British in India. Theoderic's Italy was never a 'World that Might Have Been' as James O'Donnell put it (O'Donnell, 2008, 107–74)

57 Cf. Evagrius, *Ecclesiastical History* 4.10. The emperor Anastasius' family was one of those divided between Chalcedonianism and Monophysitism: see Alan Cameron, 1978

58 Procopius, *Secret History* 26.26–7, notes that Theoderic paid the stipends of the palace staff

59 For the war on the eastern frontier against Persia, see Greatrex, 1997, 73–119; Greatrex and Lieu, 2002, 62–77

60 Dara was some 30 km from Nisibis, which had been ceded to Persia in 363, after the defeat of the emperor Julian expedition against Persia. See de'Maffei, 1986, 237–8

61 Sarris, 2006, 11, who cites M. Hendy, *Studies in the Byzantine Monetary Economy*, Cambridge, 1981

62 The law forbade marriage between a freedwoman and a man of senatorial rank and we can only guess how Justin evaded it when he married Lupicina. Daube suggests that Justin made Lupicina not only free but freeborn, i.e. born again, which the law allowed (Daube, 1967, 385–6.) It seems more likely to me that the

marriage took place early in Justin's career, before he acquired senatorial rank. Once he did acquire it, the marriage should have ended, but this legal technicality was easily ignored

Chapter 2: The Scum of Society

1 For the theatre, see LaPiana, 1936; R. Lim, 'Theater'. LA *Guide*, 719-21; Cottas, 1930; Mango, 1980, 63–5; cf. Mango, 1984. For women in the theatre, see French, 1998. Webb, 2008, is a new and excellent account of theatre in Late Antiquity

2 Jones, 1964, 691; 1283, n. 8

3 *The Greek Anthology*, 16.8

4 Webb, 2008, 101, notes that apart from Theodora there is only one other morsel of evidence for mime actresses stripping themselves naked: Valerius Maximus relates that mime actresses stripped naked in the *Floralia* festival. But many of the favourite subjects for mimes, e.g. 'the Birth of Venus', 'Aphrodite's Affair with Ares', 'Leda and the Swan', etc. required a striptease: cf. Beck, 1986, 75. Note that even the exaggerated report in the SH does *not* claim that Theodora stripped completely naked

5 For the story of Pelagia, see Brock and Harvey, 1987, 40–62

6 *Secret History* 9.26. The details of Theodora's early life in the theatre are entirely dependent on the *Secret History*

7 *Secret History* 1.13

8 Cf. Debidour, 1877, 17–22; Evans, 2002, 36–8

9 Alan Cameron, 1978, 269–71, dates the birth of Theodora's daughter to about 515

10 So Daube, 1967, 390

11 *Cod. Theod.* 15.7.5

12 *Novel* (CIC) 8.1

13 21.9.13

14 Alternatively, Theodora could have left her daughter in Constantinople with her mother, if she was still alive, or with one of her sisters

15 Malalas 16.22

16 On Hypatius' inglorious military career, see Greatrex, 1996a

17 Malalas 17.2. Thunder and lightning were regarded as signs of divine displeasure. 'Malalas' comes from a Syriac word meaning 'eloquent' and was used to translate the Greek word *rhetor* (lawyer). Yet Syriac also borrowed the word *rhetor* from Greek and used it as an exact translation. See Witold Witakowski, in Jeffreys (ed.) with Croke and Scott, 1990, 306, n. 108. For the suggestion that Malalas had access to official sources, see Scott, 1985. For John of Ephesus, see Ps.-Dionysius of Tel-Mahre, [17]; TTH #22, 18

18 PLRE II, 67–8. s.v. 'Amantius'. He was the chief eunuch at Anastasius' court and a well-known Monophysite

19 *Wars* 1.11.1

20 *Secret History* 6.26

21 6.18; 8.1–3. The *Secret History*'s report that Justin used a wooden stencil to sign decrees (6.15–16) does not prove illiteracy, for imperial signatures were works of art, difficult for an untrained calligrapher to produce

22 For overviews of the period, see Averil Cameron, 2000, and Evans, 1996a; Evans 2008

23 Cf. Daube, 1967, 385–6. Daube speculates that Lupicina may have been 'born again', which wiped out the stain of slavery. This was a legal ploy which had crept into Roman law by the second century CE

24 *Novel* (CIC) 131.3, 545

25 The first edition no longer survives

26 See entry 'Monophysites' (Dietmar W. Winkler) in LA *Guide*, 586–8

27 See Dietmar W. Winkler, 'Monophysites' in LA *Guide*, 586–8 for a brief, authoritative guide to the controversy

28 See Gray, 2005, 224–6

29 On Vitalian's revolt, see Ruscu, 2008. Vitalian had two demands: one was for the restoration of the subsidies for the federate troops which Anastasius had cancelled, and the other was that Anastasius should defend the 'True Faith'

30 John of Ephesus notes that she intervened on behalf of the Chalcedonians: Ps.-Dionysius of Tel-Mahre, *Chronicle*, pt. III [16–17], (TTH #22, 18)

31 The best study of Justin's reign is Vasiliev, 1950

32 John of Nikiu, 90.87–9 and note 74. See ODB, s.v. 'John of Nikiu.' (D. W. Johnson). Cf. *Patriarchs of the Coptic Church*, PO I, 459, which claims Theodora for Alexandria: a reference, I believe, to her brief visit there

33 Hardy, 1968, 31–2, points out, rightly, I believe, that Theodora's experience in Egypt made a lasting impression and helps to explain her Monophysite beliefs

34 Evans, 2002, 17–18; cf. Angold, 1996, 31: '[Theodora's] introduction into the circles where she met Justinian was through the Blues network'

35 See Cameron, 1974; cf. Alan Cameron, 1976. Cf. Baldwin, 1978, who points out that Malalas seems to have considered the differences between the factions to be rooted in religion.

36 For speculation at this time about the coming of the Antichrist, see Alexander, 1985, 194 ff. esp. 203

37 Novel (CIC) 74.4

Chapter 3: The Rise to Power

1 PO I, 187–9. For the return of Mare's remains to Amida, see 198–9
2 *Cod.Just.* 5.4.23
3 Browning, 1987, 41
4 See Jenkins, 1967, 141, for the sin of innovation
5 For St Polyeuctus, see Harrison, 1989; Evans, 1996a, 216–17; cf. Joseph D. Alchermes in Maas, 2005, 364–5; Bardill, 2004; 2006. Jonathan Bardill's study of Constantinople brick-stamps (Bardill, 2004, 62–4, 111–16) has shown that Anastasius was still alive when the construction of St Polyeuctus began. On Anicia Juliana as a patron of the arts, see Connor, 2004, 105–16; cf. Garland 1999, 19–21. Bardill, 2006 presents a cogent argument that St Polyeuctus did not have a brick dome and was not, as suggested by Harrison, a model for Hagia Sophia
6 Malalas 17.16
7 Modern Yalova. The spa itself is called 'Termal' after the Greek *thermos,* which refers to a gentle heat
8 Malalas 18.25. See Evans, 2002, 29–30
9 Procopius, *Buildings* 5.3.16–19
10 *Cod.Just.* I. 14. 4 (429 CE) Cf. Oost, 1968
11 Cf. Oost, 1968, 120; also Bagnani, 1949, 51–9. See also Evans, 1972, nn. 21–2
12 *Novel* (CIC) 105.2.4. See Geanakoplos, 1966, esp. 185–6; also Downey, 1968, who shows the degree to which Justinian's view of the imperial office broke with past tradition. The term 'caesaropapism' is used to describe Justinian's concept of his role as emperor, but we should remember that however much Justinian intervened in theological matters, he was not a priest
13 *Secret History* 15. 24–5. The choir implied that the old man's scrotum was swollen. Cf. Beazley, 1945, 12. Kaldellis, 2004a, 140–1, points out that the language which Procopius uses in this passage leaves little doubt that Theodora was treating the old patrician to a parody of a church service
14 *Novel* (CIC) 74.4
15 *Yiayia* is modern Greek for 'grandmother', who is a force to be reckoned with in the Greek family. Procopius (*Secret History* 17.28) reports that Theodora regulated marriages with 'grandmotherly' authority, and though the word he used for 'grandmotherly' is not found elsewhere, its meaning is clear
16 *Secret History* 17.32–7
17 *Wars* 4.27–28; 7. 31.1–16
18 Cf. Evans, 1996a, 176
19 17.7–15. See Garland, 1999, 15–18 for Justinian's laws which improved the status and legal rights of women in contemporary society

20 *Secret History* 17.25. Justinian did enact a clutch of laws that improved the rights of women (Cf. Evans, 1996a, 209–10) and perhaps Theodora inspired them. Almost certainly she was consulted

21 On the position of women see Beaucamp, 1998; 2000a, 87–103

22 *Secret History* 16.7–17; cf. Malalas 18.43, who dates Priscus' arrest to 529, the year of an anti-pagan witch hunt

23 *Secret History* 16.18–28

24 *Novel* (CIC) 14.1

25 *Secret History* 10.1–2. Procopius' class prejudice is showing

26 Evagrius, 4.10, suggests two possibilities: either they did sincerely hold opposing religious views, or they agreed that Justinian should be the Chalcedonian proponent and Theodora his Monophysite counterpart. Procopius, *Secret History* 10.13–15; 27.12–13, suggests malign influence

27 *Secret History* 22.27–8

28 *Secret History* 12.28. Procopius (*Secret History* 12.14), describing Justinian's property confiscations after the *Nika* revolt of 532, calls both Justinian and Theodora *anthropodaimones* – demons in human form. The harm suffered by the propertied class put an edge on Procopius' hatred

Chapter 4: *The Remarkable Career of the Young Belisarius*

1 *Secret History* 1.12

2 *Wars* 5.5.5

3 On Ildiger, see PLRE IIIA, 615–16.

4 On *bucellarii*, see C. R. Whittaker, s.v. 'Bucellarii', LA *Guide*, 348–50

5 Guilland, 1971 accepts the tradition; see also Sayre, 1986. A. P. Kazhdan, ODB, s.v. '*zosté patrikia*' expresses doubt. Cf. PLRE IIIA, s.v. Antonina 1, 91–3

6 *Iliad* 24, line 348

7 Cf. Greatrex, 1998, 147–50

8 See Greatrex, 1998, 120–2

9 Justinian seems to have made two attempts to fortify the border, first at a site south of Nisibis called Tamurin or Thannuris which resulted in a Roman defeat, after which Justinian ordered Belisarius to build a fort at Minduos north of Nisibis, which the Persians forced him to abandon. See PLRE IIIA, 183; Greatrex, 1998, 150; Greatrex and Lieu, 2002, 86–7, who seem to regard Thannuris and Minduos as the same place. Malalas 18.26, reports that Belisarius fled from the battle. Minduos was probably on the site of the village called Durak Basi in Turkish or Kasir Srgehan in Syrian (de'Maffei, 1986, 240–2)

10 His undistinguished career is examined in Greatrex, 1996a

11 Malalas 18.34

12 On Harith, see PLRE IIIA, 111–13, s.v. 'Arethas'

13 In Evans, 1996a, 117, I wrote that the battle of Dara was fought some 3.5 km
    from the fortress of Dara, basing my calculations on Procopius' account. I
    was immediately challenged on this and retreated. (In the paperback edition,
    I removed the 3.5 km.) However, now Christopher Lillington-Martin has
    identified a ditch some 3 km from the fortress, which he suggests is what
    remains of the trench that Belisarius' forces dug. See Lillington-Martin, 2007,
    310. Lillington-Martin's article is the best examination of the topography of the
    battle available, but see also Greatrex, 1998, 168–85

14 I have followed Stein, 1949, 55, 145 and 307 (supported by Brian Croke) in
    identifying Mundo with Mundus. For Mundus, see PLRE III B, s.v. 'Mundus',
    903–5; for Mundo, see PLRE II, 768–8. Mundo is identified by the three sources
    that name him as a Hun, whereas Mundus was a Gepid, but 'Hun' is a treach-
    erous designation; many barbarians called 'Huns' belonged to tribal groups that
    were subject to Attila's horde. See also Evans, 2005, 91–2

15 Malalas 18.46; see Croke, 1980. Mundo had been in the service of Theoderic the
    Ostrogoth until Theoderic's death in 256

16 Zachariah of Mytilene, 9.4–6, mentions the wind. He also notes that Justinian
    held Belisarius responsible for the defeat

17 The report in Malalas 18.60 [463–4] differs significantly from that of Procopius.
    Malalas praises the skilful manoeuvring of the exarchs Sounikas and Simmas,
    and implies some criticism of Belisarius' performance. Procopius seems to
    exhibit bias against al-Harith, possibly, as suggested in Kawar, 1957, because he
    was Monophysite and Theodora liked him

18 On Constantinus, see 'Constantinus 3', in PLRE IIIA, 341–2

19 John the Lydian (*On the Magistracies* 3.70.1–6) and Ps.-Zachariah of Mytilene
    9.14, name John's depredations as the cause of the riot)

20 This point is made by Bury, LRE II, 42, note 1. See also Bury, 1897, a classic
    description of the *Nika* revolt, not altogether replaced by Greatrex, 1997, or
    Meier, 2003. See also Evans, 1996a, 119–24; Evans, 2002, 40–7

21 See the remarks of Angold, 1996, 30–1: 'Various reasons [for the street violence]
    have been put forward. The most plausible is that in the absence of any effective
    municipal organization their mindless violence filled a vacuum …' 'Mindless
    violence' on the streets, however, has a history of assuming a mind of its own

22 *Secret History* 11.34–6

23 Malalas 17.18 [422]

24 AM 6024. (*Chronicle*, trans. Mango and Scott, 276–9). The so-called *Chronichon
    Paschale* (Easter Chronicle) also quotes from the dialogue, but the quotation was
    a later interpolation and appears to have been borrowed from Theophanes. Cf.
    Mango and Scott, 281, n. 8

25 According to Agathias, 1.12, he was short and very thin, but remarkably clever. Castration was outlawed in the Roman Empire and hence eunuchs were imported from beyond the imperial borders, such as from the portion of Armenia that was controlled by Persia. There is no clear evidence that the Greens were referring to Narses, for he may have been the only *spatharius* at the time. We should also note Hunger's suggestion that Kalopodius was the imperial herald who relayed Justinian's replies to the crowd. See Hunger, 1986, 9

26 The text of the dialogue has been preserved in full in Theophanes the Confessor, *Chronographia*, 181.32–184.3, and partially in the *Easter Chronicle*, 620. Theophanes' text is translated in Bury LRE, II, 71–4; see also the translation of Theophanes by Mango and Scott, 277–9

27 Bury, LRE II, 72, raises the possibility that the dialogue has nothing to do with the revolt. Maraval, 1999, 33, makes the same point. The general tone of the dialogue, however, seems to point to a period just prior to the revolt. Meier (Meier, 2003; 2004), does not consider the *Nika* riots a popular revolt with broad support. He suggests that Justinian chose to appear weak as a ruse to tempt his enemies to come out of hiding so that he could destroy them. This view is hard to accept, though Justinian did emerge stronger after the bloodbath that ended the revolt

28 On Hagia Eirene, the old patriarchal church, see George, 1912. Rebuilt after the riots, it is still standing and is now a military museum

29 Procopius, *Wars*, 1.24.6

30 See Alexander, 1985, 95–6. On the other hand, he had rescinded the value-added tax known as the *chrysargyron*, which was the first time a late Roman emperor rescinded a tax

31 According to the *Chronicon Paschale* [622] (Whitby and Whitby, 119–20), a contingent of loyal troops arrived from Thrace at this point and, if so, Justinian's position was not as desperate as he may have thought. His reason for ordering Hypatius and Pompeius out of the palace does not appear to be rational

32 Bury, 1897, 93, thought so

33 *Wars* 1.24.32–7

34 In Evans, 1984, I suggested that Theodora's literary ancestor was Artemisia (Hdt. 8.68) who spoke up to advise Xerxes before the battle of Salamis. But note also Percy Neville Ure's remarks (Ure, 1951), 202–3, who suggests that Theodora's 'magnificent arrogance ... recalls Clytaemnestra in her superbest mood, and the words "yonder is the sea" may be an intentional reminiscence of the words of the Mycenaean queen in the *Agamemnon*'

35 There is a sting to the words with which Theodora concludes her speech. The adage that she quotes, incorrectly, says that the purple made a good shroud for a tyrant, not an emperor, and the tyrant to whom it was said was Dionysius the

Elder, tyrant of Syracuse in the early fourth century BCE. See Evans, 1984; also Evans, 1972, 33. Is this a subtle hint that the regime of Justinian and Theodora was closer to a tyranny than an ideal kingship?

36 According to Ps.-Zachariah of Mytilene (9.14), Theodora objected angrily when Justinian seemed inclined to show mercy

37 Alan Cameron, 1978, 264–7, argues that only the body of Pompeius was recovered. Hypatius' corpse was lost

Chapter 5: Antonina in Love

1 *Secret History* 1.15–17

2 Jones, 1964, 270 states this baldly, and the theme, adapted with wisdom obtained from experiencing the presidency of George W. Bush, reappears in O'Donnell, 2008, 247–68. Moorhead, 1994, 63–4 is sensibly cool to the idea

3 See Barnwell, 1992, 114–24; Jones, 1964, 259–60. For the number of Vandal invaders, see Goffart 1980, 231–4, who concludes that the evidence from Procopius and Victor of Vita is unreliable and we can only guess how many they were

4 Malalas 14.44 (who reports that Basiliscus took a bribe from Gaiseric); cf. John Lydus, *De Mag.* 3.43.3–5; cf. Fisher, 2004, 51

5 Procopius *Wars* 3.10.1–22 is modelled on Hdt. 7.10–18. For St Sabas' visit, see Millar, 2008, 63–4

6 *Ecclesiastes* 1.2

7 *Ecclesiastes* 3.16

8 Jones, 1964, 273–4; Salama, 1981, 503–10

9 The gold coin known as the *solidus* (Gk. *nomisma*) minted at 72 coins to the gold pound, was introduced by Constantine I

10 Malalas 18.24; cf. Evans, 2002, 30–2. In 535, Justinian promulgated a law that expelled procurers from Constantinople and freed prostitutes from their control: *Novel* (CIC) 14. The law was probably inspired by Theodora

11 *Secret History* 17. 5–6. Theodora's crusade against harlotry is circumstantial evidence that she had first-hand knowledge of it herself. Her crusade had Justinian's full support

12 *Secret History* 17.5–6

13 *Buildings* 1.9.1–6

14 John of Ephesus, *Third Part of the Ecclesiastical History* 1.10. John reports that some of these convents had more than three hundred nuns in the reign of Justin II

15 *Novel* (CIC) 14.1

16 Cf. Treadgold, 1997, 189

17 For a general overview of the Italian campaign, see Moorhead 1994, 72–86; Evans 1996a, 136–51; Bury LRE II, 159–216, and the detailed account in Hodgkin IV, 1967, 15ff.

18 Cassiodorus, *Variae* 10.3, trans. S. J. B. Barnish, TTH XII, 13

19 Cassiodorus, *Variae* 10.21

20 *Secret History* 16.1–5

21 In my appendix on Procopius (see pages 00) I suggest that Gudeliva's letter to Theodora, included in Cassiodorus' *Variae*, which he was collecting about 538, was known in Procopius' circle of friends and was the basis for the rumour that Theodora was responsible for Amalasuntha's death

22 Cf. Brock and Harvey, 1987, 23–4

23 PLRE IIIA, s.v. 'Agapetus 1', 23. His father's name raises the suspicion that he was related to Pope Felix III (483–92), who produced the 'Acacian Schism' by excommunicating Acacius, the author of the *Henotikon*, in July 484

24 Cf. Cassiodorus *Variae* 12.20 – a graceful letter to the pawnbrokers asking for the return of the treasures

25 *Secret History* 1.21–30. If the *Secret History's* reporting of the affair is accurate, it must have bred resentment among the officer corps in his army. The *Secret History* reports that Justinian himself shared this dislike of Belisarius

26 *Wars* 6.8.1–3; cf. *Secret History* 1.28–30

Chapter 6: Victory and Defeat in the Ecclesiastical Arena

1 The best general account of the religious controversy is still Frend, 1972. Meyendorff, 1968, is still a useful overview.

2 Cf. Gray, in Maas (ed.), 2005, 225–7

3 The quotation comes from the Syriac biography of Severus by John of Beith-Aphthonia, CSCO II, 238–9. A second Life of Severus, by Zacharias Scholasticus states that Anastasius, not wanting to depart from the *Henotikon*, and at the same time combat the Nestorians, ratified Severus' election as patriarch of Antioch

4 *Novel* (CIC) 45

5 Malalas 18.47 [451]. Malalas mentions an order sent by Justinian to Athens in 529 banning the teaching of philosophy or expounding the laws. What happened has been much debated. See ODB, s.v. 'Academy of Athens'; see also Blumenthal, 1978, and Watts, 2004. No law directing that the Academy be closed is to be found in Justinian's law code. Watts argues, convincingly I think, that the date when the Academy ceased teaching was 531, and that Malalas' report that instruction in law was banned in Athens does not show that there was ever a law school there. Hällström, 1994 provides the clearest review of the evidence.

6 John of Ephesus, *Ecclesiastical History, Third Part*, I.10, refers to convents in Constantinople and its neighbourhoods which 'the late queen, Theodora' built for refugee nuns who had been driven from Antioch, Isauria, Cilicia, Cappadocia and Roman provinces in the east'

7 Michael the Syrian, 9.24. (*Chronique*, ed. J.-B. Chabot)

8 Ps.-Dionysius of Tel-Mahre, pt. III, 49 (TTH, #22, 46–7). The Chalcedonian source is Evagrius, HE, 4.5

9 Matthews, 1971, 42–7. The church no longer stands but Matthews thinks it was south of SS Sergius and Bacchus, the south wall of which served as the north wall of the earlier church. Justinian's letter to Hormisdas is preserved in *Collectio Avellana* II, 187.5, 645

10 On the Hormisdas palace as monastery, see Croke, 2007. Croke argues that the Hormisdas palace did not come into its own as a refuge for Monophysites until after the failure of the synod of 536, for 531–536 was a period of truce between the Chalcedonians and anti-Chalcedonians. However, after the failure of the synod of 536, most of the anti-Chalcedonians in the Hormisdas Palace were sent off to exile in Thrace and the number of refugees in the Hormisdas palace was probably reduced. It is true that, in 531, Justinian ended the muscular persecution of the Monophysites begun under Justin I, but it is likely that low-level persecution continued and refugees probably trickled into the Hormisdas Palace. It may have been because of the palace's reputation as a refuge that it was chosen as the venue of the Synod of 536. It was a place where Monophysites did not fear to come

11 'Concerning the Holy Communities which Theodora the Queen gathered together in Constantinople, Communities from every place in the Royal City which were gathered together in the Royal Mansion called [the house of] Hormisdas by the believing Queen Theodora whose soul is at rest.' PO XVIII, 676–84

12 On this incident, see Millar, 2008, and Croke, 2007. Though I believe that Croke underestimates the severity of Justin's persecution of the anti-Chalcedonians, this article is the best examination of Theodora's Monophysite refuge in the Hormisdas Palace and the church of SS Sergius and Bacchus

13 See Bardill, 2000. Croke, 2007, suspects that Justinian built SS Sergius and Bacchus to rival Anicia Juliana's church of St Polyeuctos, which was the largest church in the city before Justinian built Hagia Sophia. Croke rejects the argument, first put forward by Cyril Mango, that SS Sergius and Bacchus was built for the use of anti-Chalcedonians

14 Quoted from Zachariah of Mytilene, 9.15

15 Cf. Millar, 2008, 69–70

16 Modern Trabzond on the Black Sea coast of north-east Turkey

17 On John of Tella, see Andrade, 2009

18 *Liber Pontificalis* 58, 1–2 (TTH #6, 50–51). No doubt a scribe did the actual writing

19 PO XVII, 18–35; cf. Michael the Syrian, 9.22

20 Garland, 1999, 23. A letter of Severus dated to 537, addressed to a deacon and palace chamberlain, mentions a mistake in theology that Theodora made, due to her ignorance of church history

21 Cassiodorus, *Variae*, 10.20

22 Michael the Syrian, *Chronicle* 9.23. The darkening of the sun and the moon is a reference to the mysterious dust veil that covered the Mediterranean at this time

23 The attendants in the empress' household were still Monophysites when Theodora's niece, Sophia, wife of Justin II, ascended the throne: John of Ephesus: *Third Part of the Ecclesiastical History*, 2.9

Chapter 7: Theodora's Riposte

1 *Novel* (CIC) 8

2 Cf. Zachariah of Mytilene, 9.19. To Zachariah, a Monophysite, the earth seemed to protest the pope's actions

3 *Novel* (CIC) 42.1, 536

4 Cf. John Lydus, *De. Mag.* 3.69.2–3. John, writing shortly after the Cappadocian's fall, refers very delicately to this period when the Cappadocian replaced Theodora as Justinian's chief consultant

5 According to the chronicler of the Alexandrian Patriarchs, Severus of Asmounein, Justinian was glad to hear of the quarrel; yet he gave Theodora permission to do what she wished. PO I, 459

6 On Tabennisi, see ODB, s.v. 'Tabennisi' (A. Kazhdan)

7 *Liber Pontificalis* 57.3–4, (TTH #6, 50)

8 *Novel* (CIC) 37

9 Tree rings for 536 are the second narrowest in the past 1500 years and indicate a cold, dry summer. Sallares 2007, 284

10 *Liber Pontificalis* 60 (TTH #6, 53); cf. Procopius, *Wars*, 5.10

11 *Wars* 5.24

12 Torsten Jacobsen (Jacobsen, 2009, 98) points out the strategic position of the *Domus Pinciana*. The general reader will find Jacobsen's account of the siege of Rome particularly valuable

13 Ps.-Dionysius of Tel-Mahre (quoting John of Ephesus), 65 (Witakowski trans.); Procopius, *Wars* 4.14.56; cf. Arjava, 2005

14 *Liber Pontificalis* (TTH, #6). Cf. also Liberatus, *Breviarium* 2; Victor of Tunnena, *sub anno* 542; Procopius, *Wars* 5.25.13. See also Bury, LRC II, 378–80; Evans, 1996a, 145–6

15 So the *Secret History* reports (1.27)

16 Liberatus, *Breviarium*, 22

17 Procopius refers to the murder of Silverius twice in the *Secret History*, at 1.14, and 1.27, and promises to reveal more later: a promise he failed to keep. It cannot be proved that Antonina's slave assassinated Silverius at her orders, but there may have been a rumour to that effect circulating in Rome

18 Liberatus, *Breviarium*, 22

19 See above, pp. 101–02

20 *Wars* 6.21.39–40

21 Cf. Arjava, 2005 on the climate in these years

22 I am aware that the term 'Dark Ages' is no longer in style; yet if we compare Italy under Theoderic the Ostrogoth with Italy in the last years of Justinian and under Justin II, it must appear that darkness descended with the Byzantine invasion.

23 O'Donnell, 2008, 107–74

24 Averil Cameron 2000, 74, cf. Averil Cameron 1985, 188–9. Yet it is at this point that Procopius inserts a eulogy of Belisarius. Both the soldiers and the peasants in Italy loved him, he claims: see Evans, 1972, 73. In Evans, 1972, 106, I suggested that it was the sack of Antioch in the same year as the surrender of Ravenna that made a deep impression on the historian and helped form the gloomy, disillusioned outlook that we find in the later years of the war

25 Ps.-Dionysius of Tel-Mahre, *Chronicle*, (trans. Witakowski), 83

26 See above, page 84

27 Cf. John Lydus, *De Magistratibus* 3.69.2

Chapter 8: *The Fall of John the Cappadocian*

1 I have borrowed this quotation from Van Dam, 2002, a splendid account of ancient Cappadocia

2 The Arians surviving in Constantinople by this time must have been, for the most part, federate troops in the army. For the closure of the Arian churches, see Greatrex, 2001, 79–81, who connects the closure with the suppression of Arianism in Africa after Belisarius recovered it for the empire

3 *On the Magistracies* 3.26.1–3.30.10

4 LA *Guide*, s.v. 'Nessana' (Yoran Tsafrir)

5 Cf. Haldon, 2005, 51 and footnotes; Jones, 1964, 830–4

6 Kaldellis, 2003

7 PLRE IIIA, s.v. Ioannes 'Maxilloplumacius' 10 (626–7). He was most likely a *tractator*, whose job was to supervise tax collection, or perhaps a *discussor*, who audited accounts. Maraval, 1999, identifies him as vicar of the diocese of Asia

8 *On the Magistracies*, 3.59.1–3.59.8

9   Cf. Maraval, 1999, 87–8

10 *Wars* 3.10.7. We should, however, remember the context of this flattering passage.
    Procopius here has taken Herodotus as his model, and John the Cappadocian
    has the role of a wise advisor who gives advice at a critical moment; usually, but
    not always, negative advice. That is not to say, however, that Procopius misrep-
    resented John's fears about the Vandal expedition. On John's administrative
    reforms, see Jones, 1964, 279–83

11 See Downey, 1953. Downey argues that Procopius' account of the fall of Antioch
    was biased in favour of Germanus and seeks to excuse his hasty withdrawal from
    Antioch before the Persian army arrived

12 Procopius, *Wars* 2.11.16–20; 31–35; Evagrius, *Ecclesiastical History* 4.25–26

13 *Secret History* 22.2

14 On Peter, see PLRE IIIB, 999–1002

Chapter 9: The Theodosius and Antonina Affair Continued

1   The source for what follows is Procopius, *Secret History* 1.31–2.26; 3.1–20

2   Procopius, *Wars* 2.19.15–46; cf. Averil Cameron, 1985, 160–2

3   2.17–19, cf. *Wars* 2.19.24

4   Cf. *Secret History* 4.40. Procopius states that he was *erotoleptos*: i.e. 'captured
    by lust' for Antonina, 'even though she was already sixty years old'. It is more
    likely Belisarius' loyalty was based on a realistic assessment of his power to do
    otherwise. Without his corps of *buccellarii*, he lacked a power base

Chapter 10: Plague and Intrigue

1   Albert Camus' novel, *La peste*, (*The Plague*) was published in 1947. It describes
    an outbreak of bubonic plague in an Algerian town during World War II

2   Stathakopoulos, 2007, 104–5; cf. Horden, 2005, 134–9. The intervals between
    plague outbreaks averaged 11.6 years

3   Hooker, 1958, 81, argued that the plague in fifth-century BCE Athens described
    by Thucydides was bubonic plague, claiming that when Thucydides used the
    word *helkos* he referred to the bubo of bubonic plague. In 2006, fossilized dental
    pulp from the time of the Athenian plague yielded the bacterium that causes
    typhoid fever, *Salmonella enterica*. See Rosen, 2007, 191

4   Sallares, 2007, 251, n. 79, prints the relevant passage from Rufus, reporting that
    Posidonius and Dioscorides investigated plague in Libya

5   Zinsser's book was published in 1935 and went through 31 printings by 1965.
    His eleventh chapter on rats is worth reading. Little, 2007a, is a collection of
    papers presented (with one exception) at an interdisciplinary conference at the

American Academy in Rome in 2001, published under the title *Plague and the end of Antiquity*. It has put the study of the Justinianic plague on a new footing. Rosen 2007 is also an invaluable contribution – a reminder of how far the study of plague has come since Zinsser

6   For reactions to the plague, see the excellent article by Kaldellis, 'Piety and Plague' (Kaldellis, 2007b)

7   Rosen, 2007, 186

8   The genes of the plague strain that infects marmots differ from those that infect rats, but the flea that transmits the disease can play host to both. Cf. Orent, 2001, 75. See McNeill, 1976, 163–8, who mentions a plague originating with Manchurian marmots that might have spread world-wide in 1894–1921 except for the intervention of modern medical techniques

9   See page 137, above

10 Keys, 1999, suggests a dust-veil event in 536, causing severe drought in east Africa, followed by increased rainfall that caused a population explosion of plague-bearing rodents. This might have triggered a plague epidemic which was carried north by trading vessels bringing ivory from Zanzibar. Rosen, 2007, 200–3 argues that the drop in average temperature allowed the flea to move north overland from east Africa. See also Sallares, 2007, 284–6; cf. Arjava, 2005

11 Procopius, *Wars* 2.4.1, reports a great comet in the year 539. Halley's comet appeared on 27 September, 530 and cannot be the comet that Procopius reports

12 The main sources for the Justinianic plague are Procopius, *Wars* 2.22.1–23.21, John of Ephesus, whose description was copied by Ps.-Dionysius of Tel-Mahre, *Chronicle Part III*, 74–98, and Evagrius, *Ecclesiastical History* 4.29. Corippus describes the plague in North Africa: *Iohannis* 3.343–400. Michael the Syrian's account (*Chronicle*, 9.28) is dependent on John of Ephesus

13 *Wars* 1.22.23

14 There is one morsel of evidence from John of Ephesus that may indicate pulmonary plague. He reports that for some, none of the signs of bubonic plague was apparent, but 'as [persons] were looking at each other, they [began to] totter and fell, either in the streets or at home, in harbours, on ships, in churches and everywhere' (Ps.-Dionysius of Tel-Mahre, *Chronicle Part III*, 96, trans. W. Witakowski). Sudden death of this sort is more symptomatic of pulmonary than bubonic plague. Allen, 1979, in her valuable study of the plague, thinks that pulmonary plague played a major role, but Procopius' evidence does not support her view

15 Ps.-Dionysius (see n. 176) who reproduces John of Ephesus, reports 'cattle … even rats' dying with the tell-tale swellings (Witakowski trans., 87)

16 Michael the Syrian, *Chronicle*, 9.28

17 The estimate is taken from Russell, 1958, 42. Turtledove, 1983, also makes the

case for a precipitous population decline after Justinian, which he attributes to the effects of plague and the war in the west

18 The pattern varies: some urban communities in Syria and Palestine flourished up until the Arab conquest; others began to decline as early as the fourth and fifth centuries. Clearly local factors were often at work. See Rouché, 1989, xxvi. Roueché dates the beginning of Aphrodisias' decline to the plague

19 *Ecclesiastical History, Third Part*, 3.36–7.

20 See above page 100

Chapter 11: *Theodora Fosters an Anti-Chalcedonian Church*

1 The other kingdoms were Makuria and Alodia, all in modern Sudan. Noubadia and Alodia were converted to Monophysitism while Makuria opted for Chalcedon. Meroë was the capital of the Kushite kingdom, an important source of iron and cotton cloth in the ancient world. See Tomas Hägg, 'Nubia' in LA *Guide*, 613–14

2 John of Ephesus, *Ecclesiastical History*, III, 4.6–8. John reports that Justinian paid a subsidy to the tribes south of the border to prevent them from raiding imperial territory. The date of Julian's mission is uncertain. Bury, 1958, LRE II, 328, puts it at 'about AD 540'. I think that the context of John's story fits a somewhat later date

3 *Secret History* 15.17

4 See above, page 112. John of Tella's biography is included in John of Ephesus' *Lives of the Eastern Saints*, PO XVIII, 511–25. Cf. Andrade, 2009, a fine study of a second life of John in Syriac. (*Vita Iohannis Episcopi Tellae*, CSCO III, 25, 7–8)

5 Ibid., 527–39

6 *Ecclesiastical History* 4.10

7 10.15

8 On Harith, see PLRE III.i, s.v. Arethas

9 The year when the exiles incarcerated in the Derkos fortress were allowed to return to the Hormisdas palace is not certain. The incarceration cannot have been long

10 Jacob's biography is included in John of Ephesus' *Lives of the Eastern Saints*, PO XVIII, 690–7

Chapter 12: *The Agony of Italy*

1 Cf. Bury's remark, 'It is disappointing that the historian [Procopius] does not describe the scene in which Belisarius undeceived the Gothic king and nobles as to his intentions.' Bury, LRE II, 213

2 'Baduila' is the name that appears on his coins. Procopius' name for him is 'Totila'

3 For a particularly vivid description of Baduila's war, see O'Donnell, 2008, 261–7. Goffart, 1974, 384 (citing Procopius, *Wars* 7.6.5–7) sees Baduila's interception of the tax revenues and rents from the estates in southern Italy as evidence that he, in effect, 'nationalized' the land in Italy. *Wars* 7.22.20, reports that he gave the estates in Lucania to their *coloni*, but that was a move made to forestall a peasants' revolt on behalf of the imperial forces

4 Teall, 1965, analyzes the effect of the plague on the armed forces. Justinian increasingly had to rely on barbarian recruits

5 See above, page 124

6 For the edict, see Sotinel, 2005 in Maas, 2005, 279–89, and Gray, 2005 in Maas 2005, 215–38.

7 Modern Tivoli

8 Victor of Tonnena, *sub anno*, 549

9 James Fitton (1976), points out that the word 'cancer' was used by Celsus for illnesses like gangrene, erysipelas and septic ulcerations

10 *Secret History* 5.23–7

Chapter 13: Postlude: The Ending of the Era of Reconquest

1 John of Ephesus, PO XVIII, 683–4

2 PLRE IIIA, s.v. 'Germanus 11', 531–2; also 'Constantina 1', 337–9

3 John of Ephesus, *Ecclesiastical History, Third Part*, I, 38. Like his patron, Theodora, Narses was Monophysite and in his monastery he sheltered a group of Monophysite monks, some 70 in all, who had been driven from Cappadocia by persecution

4 ODB, s.v. 'Busta Gallorum'. Jacobsen 2009, 282–7, gives a good description of the battle

5 Bury, LRE II, 274–81; Evans, 1996a, 177–82. Agathias is our chief source for the invasions of Buccelin and Leutharis

6 On Justin II, see my contribution to the on-line encyclopedia, *De Imperatoribus Romanis*

7 The story is told in Agathias (5.15.7–19.12), who makes a comparison with the Battle of Thermopylae in 480 BCE, when king Leonidas of Sparta, no longer a young man either, defended the pass to the death. Theophanes (AM 6051) gives a somewhat different account of Belisarius' victory. Cf. Averil Cameron, 1970, 49–50

8 Theophanes AM 6055. The *Chronicle* of John of Nikiu, trans. Charles, 92, in the late seventh century, indicates that the historian Procopius was a patrician

and prefect but does not identify him with the urban prefect of 562. Cf. Averil Cameron, 1985, 12

9 The story is told in Michael the Syrian, *Chronicle*, 9.34

10 Dennis, 2001, 2; cf. Talbot, 1984, 267–78

11 The legend that Belisarius in his old age was blinded and forced to beg for a living at the central crossroads of Constantinople appears in the *Patria of Constantinople* in the twelfth century and in the fourteenth century a versified *Romance of Belisarius* tells the same story. See ODB I, 278

12 The latest appreciation of Belisarius is Hughes, 2009, a highly flattering portrait

Appendix: Two Contemporary Witnesses: Procopius and John of Ephesus

1 On legal training in Late Antiquity, see Schiller, 1969

2 *Wars* 1.12.24–13.1

3 Geoffrey Greatrex has attempted to revive a theory first put forward by J. Haury that Procopius was the son of Stephanus, the proconsul of First Palestine who lost his life in the Samaritan insurrection of 556 (Greatrex, 1996b). However there is not enough evidence to make a secure identification. See Evans, 1972, 136, note 35

4 *Secret History* 11.25. See Evans, 1972, 30–41, for Procopius' life. See also Howard-Johnston, 2000

5 As suggested by Adshead, 1996

6 Evans, 1972, 31–2; cf. Downey, 1963, 99–116

7 Kaldellis, 2004a, 94–117. In Evans, 1972, 125–6, I attempted to draw a parallel between his treatment of free will and predestination in Boethius and Procopius and suggested that both may have been influenced directly or indirectly by Neoplatonic teachings in Alexandria. The School at Alexandria was not ideologically non-Christian, whereas the Neoplatonic School at Athens was. See Blumenthal, 1993, who suggests that the Alexandrians deliberately distanced themselves from the pagan Athenian School. But I do not believe that Procopius' concept of the historian's task was greatly influenced by philosophy

8 Cf. Watts, 2004; Blumenthal, 1993; 1978

9 Colvin, 2011

10 Averil Cameron, 1985, 131–3: 'not much of a religious thinker ... nevertheless a strongly Christian impression comes over from his work'; Kaldellis, 2004a, 58: 'Procopius ... was no Christian, and therefore did not subscribe to any Christian theory of kingship ...'; Evans, 1972, 125: 'Procopius owes many of his basic concepts to pagan historical thought, but they have been brought within a teleological Christian framework'

11 Kaldellis 1999; 2003; 2004b; 2005a

12 PLRE II, 881–2. Procopius (*Secret History* 21.6) and John Lydus (*De Magistratibus* 3.72) both admired him

13 For the pogrom, see Ps.-Dionysius of Tel-Mahre [76] (trans. Witakowski, TTH #22, 71). The chronicler's source was John of Ephesus. There were three anti-pagan pogroms in Constantinople in Justinian's reign, in 528–9, 545–6, and 562. *Secret History* 11.31–3, refers to the pagan persecution (specifically, probably, to the persecution of 545–6), and reports that even those pagans who made a pretence of Christianity were caught as they made secret sacrifices to the gods. Procopius' sympathies were clearly with the persecuted pagans, for the educated élite to which Procopius belonged was hit hard by the pagan persecutions

14 Cf. Evans, 1971; Evans, 1972, 111–27. Procopius found Justinian's theology sound enough (*Secret History* 13.4) but he condemned his excessive zeal. In his review of Kaldellis' *Procopius of Caesarea*, William Edmund Fahey (2005) points out that Kaldellis does not explain away the one passage in *Wars* 2.12, where Procopius 'gives a bold and clear statement about "Jesus, the son of God", his life in Palestine, his sinlessness, etc.' It is not impossible that this passage was inserted for self-protection after the anti-pagan pogrom of 545–6, which must have caused apprehension in Procopius' circles

15 *Secret History* 13.7–8; 13.4–6. At 13.4, he concedes that Justinian's faith was orthodox, which indicates that he did not quarrel with Chalcedonianism. When Procopius states at *Secret History* 24.18 that he will relate Justinian's dealings with the Christian clergy in his later writings, it does not necessarily mean that he intended to write an ecclesiastical history. It may indicate that he planned to show how Justinian promoted the greed of the clergy

16 *Wars* 2.12.26

17 *Wars* 6.5.24–7

18 *Wars* 2.12.20–30. If this passage belongs to 545, it may be proof of Procopius' prudence rather than Christian belief

19 *Wars* 1.24.22–41

20 Croke, 2005, provides an excellent overview of the controversy about the date of the *Secret History*. See also Greatrex, 1994; Evans, 1996b; Greatrex 2003, and finally Kaldellis, 2009, who has, I believe, settled the date of the *Secret History*. I continue to believe that it was in 557 that Procopius published his eighth book of the *Wars*, with its markedly more critical tone than the earlier books. However, most students of Procopius follow Stein II, 1949, 720, and place it some three years earlier. Procopius' panegyric on Justinian's building programme was finished in 560, though the first book seems to have been written before the collapse of the dome of Hagia Sophia in 558. Kumaniecki (1929–30) suggests that a monody on the collapse of the dome of Hagia Sophia found in a Vatican

Library document was from Procopius' hand, for the author was familiar with the description of the dome in the *Buildings* before the collapse. It may have been written by someone in Procopius' circle

21 *Secret History* 1.10–11. I had almost forgotten that I once suggested a comparison of the first part of the *Secret History* with the Milesian Tale until K. Adshead credited me with the theory (Adshead, 1993, 7–10) and developed it more than I ever did; I meant by the suggestion merely that one motive that Procopius had for writing the *Secret History* was to amuse the little circle of acquaintances who might read it. His accuracy was not necessarily affected thereby. Reality can be quite comic if viewed from the right angle

22 *Secret History* 18.36–45. At 18.45, Procopius makes it clear that he saw the reigns of Justin I and Justinian as an unbroken string of calamity

23 Cf. Bagnani, 1949

24 *Secret History* 12.14–32; cf. Rubin, 1960, 442–54; Adshead, 1993, 16–17

25 *Secret History* 12.13.18–28. John of Ephesus reported headless demons in bronze boats spreading plague in Palestine: see Ps. Dionysius, trans. Witakowski, 77

26 *The Gospel According to St Mark*, 13.7–27

27 8.25.13; cf. Kaldellis, 2009, 607–9. Earlier statements of Procopius' intention are found in the *Secret History* 1.14; 11.33; 26.18

28 *On Omens*, a survey of divination. For John's friendship with Procopius, see Kaldellis, 2004b, who argues that John was one of the intended readers of the *Secret History*

29 Kaldellis, 2009, 604

30 Kaldellis 2004a, 150–4, 223–8; cf. Kaldellis 2009. 592: '… this section of the work was an innovative historical commentary on Justinian's laws'

31 Justinian himself acknowledges the charge that appears in *Secret History* 11.1–2, that he kept introducing new laws, and he defended himself in the preface to *Novel* 60. The picture that Procopius presents of Justinian as the Lord of the Demons (*Secret History* 12.26; 18.1) was not his alone, for Evagrius (*Ecclesiastical History* 4.32) hints at a similar view: 'Justinian possessed another quality which surpassed the character of any beast – whether this was a defect of nature or the product of cowardice and fear …' TTH, #33, trans. Michael Whitby, 236; cf. Frend, 1972, 255. Evagrius' choice of words recalls the two beasts of the *Apocalyse* of St John, ch. 13

32 The 'joke' at *Secret History* 9.18, comes, directly or indirectly, from the speech *Against Neaera*, which dates from the fourth century BCE, whether it was by Demosthenes or not. The 'joke' was mentioned as an example of vulgarity in the rhetorical handbook by Hermogenes which could have been used in the school that Procopius attended. See Wilson, 1983, 16–17. Cf. also Evans, 1996a, 99–100

33 PO XVII, 1, 189. See above, page 7

34 *Secret History* 17.16–23 cf. John of Ephesus, *Ecclesiastical History, Third Part*, I, 30, who mentions her grandson Athanasius, an advocate of Tritheism
35 *Secret History* 9.47–54; cf. *Cod.Just.* 5.4.23 (probably dating to 523). Cf. Daube, 1967
36 PO I, 459
37 John of Nikiu, 87
38 See above, page 46.
39 *Buildings* 1.9.4–10; cf. *Secret History* 17.5–6, where Procopius takes a more cynical view
40 *Secret History* 16.2–5
41 Comparetti, 1925, 76. Comparetti believed – wrongly – that Procopius wrote the *Secret History* in 559.
42 *Variae* 10.21
43 See Russell, 1968, who argues that the plague began a period of decline which lasted until after the Arab conquest of the east
44 *Ecclesiastical History, Third Part*, I. 32
45 John describes the cure in his *Lives of the Eastern Saints*, PO XVII, 56–83
46 See above, pages 111–13. The details of the persecution are told by John in his *Lives of the Eastern Saints*, PO XVIII, 607–23
47 Michael Whitby, LA *Guide*, s.v. 'John of Ephesus', 526–7, suggests that he reached Constantinople by 540. Probably he arrived a little earlier
48 Ps.-Dionysius of Tel-Mahre, pt. 3, 76–7 (TTH #22, 71)
49 Dionysius of Tel-Mahre was the Jacobite (Monophysite) patriarch of Antioch, 818–45. The chronicle, however, was written not by the patriarch but by a monk in the monastery at Zuqnin; hence its alternative title *Chronicle of Zuqnin*, and the prefix 'Pseudo' attached to Dionysius' name

Sources

'Acts of the Council of Constantinople of 536', CSCO II, 336–50

Acts of the Council of Constantinople of 553, with related texts on the Three Chapters Controversy, translated by Richard Price, TTH #51 (Liverpool, 2009)

Agathias, *The Histories*, translated by Joseph D. Frendo, (Berlin/New York, 1975)

Book of the Pontiffs (Liber Pontificalis), translated by Raymond Davis, TTH 6, 3rd edn (Liverpool, 2010)

Bury LRE, II – J. B. Bury, *History of the Later Roman Empire from the Death of Theodosius I to the Death of Justinian* (New York: Dover, 1958)

Cassiodorus Senator – *Variae*, translated by S. J. B. Barnish, TTH 12 (Liverpool, 1992)

Choricius of Gaza, *On Mimes* – Choricii Gazaei *Opera*, ed. Richard Foerster, xxxii = Oratio 8 (Stuttgart, 1972)

Chronicon Paschale 284–628 AD – translated by Michael Whitby and Mary Whitby, TTH 7 (Liverpool, 1989)

Cod.Just. – *Codex Justinianus*, in Corpus Iuris Civilis, vol. 2, eds T. Mommsen, P. Krueger et al. (Berlin, 1928–9)

Cod.Theod. – *The Theodosian Code, and the Novels and the Sirmondian Constitutions*, translated with commentary by Clyde Pharr, with the collaboration of Theresa Sherrer and Mary Brown Pharr (New York, 1969)

Collectio Avellana – Episulae imperatorum pontificum aliorum inde a. CCCLXVII usque ad a. DLIII datae Avellana quae dicitur collectio, ed. O. Guenther, 2 vols. 1895–8

Corippus, *Iohannidos: De Bellis Libycis, Libri VIII* – Flavius Cresconius Corippus, *Iohannidos des De Bellis Libycis Libri VIII*, eds J. Diggle and D. Goodyear (Cambridge, 1970)

Evagrius Scholasticus – *Ecclesiastical History*, translated by Michael Whitby, TTH 33 (Liverpool, 2000)

Greek Anthology, Loeb Classical Library, edited with translation by W. E. Paton (London: Heineman; New York: Putnam, 1916–18)

John of Beith-Apthonia – *Life of Severus*, translated into French by M.-A. Kugener, CSCO II, 205–64 (1904)

John of Ephesus – *Lives of the Eastern Saints*, edited and translated by E. W. Brooks, PO 17, 1–307, (1923); 18, 513–609, (1924); 19, 153–285 (1926)

John of Ephesus – *The Third Part of the Ecclesiastical History*, translated by Robert Payne Smith (Oxford, 1860); and by E. W. Brooks (into Latin), CSCO 106 (1936)

John of Nikiu – *The Chronicle of John, Coptic Bishop of Nikiu* (c. 690 AD) translated by Robert Henry Charles, (London, 1916, repr. Amsterdam)

Liberatus, *Breviarium causae Nestorianorum et Eutychianorum*, PL, 68, cols. 963–1052

Malalas – *The Chronicle of John Malalas*, translated by Elizabeth Jeffreys, Michael Jeffreys and Roger Scott, *Byzantina Australiensia* 4 (Melbourne, 1986)

Marcellinus Comes – *The Chronicle of Marcellinus*, text with translation and commentary by Brian Croke (Sydney, 1995)

Michael the Syrian – *Chronicle* (*Chronique de Michel le Syrien, patriarche jacobite d'Antioche, 1166–1199*, edited and translated by J.-B. Chabot (Paris, 1902)

Patria of Constantinople – in *Scriptores originum Constantinopolitanarum,* ed. T. Preger, II (Leipzig, 1901–07)

Patriarchs of the Coptic Church – Severus of Ashmounein, *History of the Patriarchs of the Coptic Church of Alexandria,* pt. 2, translated by B. Evetts, PO, vol. 1

Procopius of Caesarea, *History of the Wars, Anecdota* or *Secret History, Buildings.* LCL, Translated by H. B. Dewing (London and Cambridge, Mass., 1921–61)

Pseudo-Dionysius of Tel-Mahre, *Chronicle* Part 3, translated by Witold Witakowski TTH 22 (Liverpool, 1996)

Pseudo-Dionysius of Tel-Mahre, *The Chronicle of Zuqnin,* Parts 3 and 4, A.D. 488–775, translated with notes, Amir Harrak (Toronto: Pontifical Institute, 1999)

Theophanes the Confessor, *Chronographia*, translated by Cyril Mango and Roger Scott, with the assistance of Geoffrey Greatrex, with the title *Chronicle of Theophanes. Byzantine and Near Eastern History, A.D. 284–818* (Oxford, 1997)

Victor of Tunnuna – *Chronicle,* ed. Th. Mommsen, MGH *AuctAnt XI*, 178–206

Victor of Vita – *Historia persecutionis Africanae provinciae,* ed. C. Halm, MGH *AuctAnt* 3.1

Zachariah of Mytilene – *Chronicle of Pseudo-Zachariah Rhetor, The Church and War in Late Antiquity,* translated by Geoffrey Greatrex, Robert R. Phenix and Cornelia B. Horn, TTH 55 (Liverpool, 2010)

Zacharias of Mytilene – *Life of Severus*, translated into French by M.-A. Kugener, PO II.1, 7–115 (Paris, 1903)

Zacharias of Mytilene – *The Syriac Chronicle known as that of Zacharias of* Mytilene, translated by F. J. Hamilton and E. W. Brooks (London: Methuen, 1899)

Bibliography

Katherine Adshead, 'The *Secret History* of Procopius and its Genesis', *Byzantion* 63, 5–28 (1993)

—'Procopius and the Samaritans', in Pauline Allen and Elizabeth Jeffreys (eds) *The Sixth Century: End of Beginning? Byzantina Australiensia 10*, 35–41 (Brisbane, 1996)

Paul J. Alexander, *The Oracle of Baalbek: the Tiburtine Sibyl in Greek Dress* (Washington, DC: Dumbarton Oaks, 1969)

Paul J. Alexander (ed.) with introduction by Dorothy deF. Abrahamse, *The Byzantine Apocalyptic Tradition* (Berkeley: University of California Press, 1985)

P. Allen, 'The "Justinianic Plague"', *Byzantion* 49, 1–20 (1979)

Pauline Allen and C. T. R. Hayward, *Severus of Antioch* (London & New York: Routledge, 2004)

Nathaniel J. Andrade, 'The Syriac Life of John of Tella and the Frontier *Politeia*', *Hugoye: Journal of Syriac Studies* 12.2, 199–233 (2009)

Irina Andrescu–Treadgold and Warren Treadgold, 'Procopius and the Imperial Panels of S. Vitale', *Art Bulletin* 79, 708–23 (1997)

Michael Angold, 'Procopius's portrait of Theodora', *ΦΙΛΕΛΛΗΝ, Studies in Honour of Robert Browning*, 21–34 (Venice, 1996)

Léonie J. Archer, Susan Fischler and Maria Wyke (eds) *Women in Ancient Societies. An Illusion of the Night* (New York: Routledge, 1994)

Antti Arjava, 'The Mystery Cloud of 535 C.E. in the Mediterranean Sources', DOP 59, 73–94 (2005)

Roger Bagnall, Alan Cameron, Seth Schwarz and K. A. Worp, *Consuls of the Later Roman Empire*, APA Monograph 36 (Atlanta: Scholars Press, 1987)

—*Egypt in Late Antiquity* (Princeton: Princeton University Press, 1993)

Gilbert Bagnani, 'Divine Right and Roman Law', *Phoenix* 3, 51–9 (1949)

Barry Baldwin, 'A Note on the Religious Sympathies of Circus Factions', *Byzantion* 48, 275–6 (1978)

Jonathan Bardill, 'The Church of Sts. Sergius and Bacchus in Constantinople and the Monophysite Refugees', DOP, 54:1–11 (2000)

—*Brickstamps of Constantinople* (Oxford Monographs on Classical Archaeology) (Oxford: Oxford University Press, 2004)

—'A New Temple for Byzantium: Anicia Juliana, King Solomon, and the Gilded
   Ceiling of the Church of St Polyeuktos in Constantinople', in William Bowden,
   Adam Gutteridge, Carlos Machado (eds) *Social and Political Life in Late Antiquity*,
   339–70 (Leiden/Boston: Brill, 2006)

P. S. Barnwell, *Emperors, Prefects and Kings. The Roman West, 395–565*, (Chapel Hill
   and London: University of North Carolina Press, 1992)

Sarah Bassett, *The Urban Image of Late Antique Constantinople* (Cambridge:
   Cambridge University Press, 2004)

Joëlle Beaucamp, 'Les femmes et l'espace public à Byzance', DOP 52, 129–45 (1998)

—'Exclues et Aliénées: les Femmes dans la Tradition Canonique Byzantine', in
   Dion C. Smythe (ed.) *Strangers to Themselves: The Byzantine Outsiders*, 87–103
   (Aldershot: Ashgate, 2000a)

—'Le droit successorial relative aux curiales: Procope et Justinien', in S. Puliatti and
   A. Sanguinetti (eds) *Legislazione, culture giuridica, prassi dell'impero d'oriente in
   età giustinianea* (Milan: A. Guiffrè, 2000b)

J. D. Beazley, 'The empress's joke', *Classical Review*, 59:12 (1945)

Hans-George Beck, *Kaiserin Theodora und Prokop* (Munich: Piper, 1986)

H. J. Blumenthal, '529 and After. What Happened to the Academy?' *Byzantion*,
   48:369–85 (1978)

—'Alexandria as a Centre of Greek Philosophy in Later Classical Antiquity', *Illinois
   Classical Studies*, 18:307–25 (1993)

H. Börm, *Prokop und die Perser. Oriens et Occidens*, 16 (Stuttgart: Steiner, 2007)

G. W. Bowersock, *Hellenism in Late Antiquity* (Ann Arbor, MI: University of
   Michigan Press, 1990)

G. W. Bowersock, Peter Brown, Oleg Grabar (eds), *Late Antiquity. A Guide to the
   Postclassical World* (Cambridge, MA: Harvard University Press, 1999)

Sebastian P. Brock and Susan Ashbrook Harvey, trans., *Holy Women of the Syrian
   Orient* (Berkeley: University of California, 1987)

D. Brodke, *Die Geschichtsphilosophie in der spätantiken Historiographie. Studien zu
   Prokopios von Kaisareia, Agathias von Myrina und Theophylaktos* (Frankfurt am
   Main: Peter Lang, 2004)

Peter Brown, *The World of Late Antiquity, from Marcus Aurelius to Muhammad*
   (London: Thames and Hudson, 1971)

T. S. Brown, 'The Interplay between Roman and Byzantine Tradition and Local
   Sentiment in the Exarchate of Ravenna', *Bisanzio, Roma e l'Italia nell'alto
   Mediaevo*. Settimane di Studio del Centre Italiano di Studie sull'alto Mediaevo, 34,
   2 vols. (Spoleto), I, 127–60 (1988)

Robert Browning, 'The Riots of A.D. 387 in Antioch. The Role of the Theatrical
   Claques in the Later Empire', *Journal of Roman Studies*, 42:13–20 (1952)

—*Justinian and Theodora*, second edn (London: Thames and Hudson, 1987)

Leslie Brubaker, 'Sex, lies and textuality: the *Secret History* of Prokopios and the rhetoric of gender in sixth–century Byzantium', in Leslie Brubaker and Julia M. H. Smith (eds) *Gender in the Early Medieval World, 300-900*, 83–101 (Cambridge: Cambridge University Press, 2004)

—'The Age of Justinian: Gender and Society', in Maas (ed.), *The Cambridge Companion to the Age of Justinian*, 427–47 (2005)

Leslie Brubaker and Helen Tobler, 'The Gender of Money: Byzantine Empresses on Coins (324–802), *Gender and Society* 12/3, 572–94 (2000)

J. B. Bury, 'The Nika Riot', *Journal of Hellenic Studies*, 17:92–119 (1897)

—*History of the Later Roman Empire from the Death of Theodosius I to the Death of Justinian* (London, St Martin's Press, 1923, repr. New York: Dover, 1958)

Alan Cameron, 'Heresies and Factions', *Byzantion*, 44:92–120 (1974)

—*Circus Factions. Blues and Greens at Rome and Byzantium* (Oxford: Oxford University Press, 1976)

—'The House of Anastasius', GRBS 19:259–76 (1978)

Averil Cameron, 'The 'Scepticism' of Procopius', *Historia*, 15, 466–82 (1966)

—*Procopius* (Great Histories series) (New York: Washington Square, 1967)

—*Agathias* (Oxford: Oxford University Press, 1970)

—*Procopius and the Sixth Century* (Berkeley/Los Angeles: University of California Press, 1985)

—'Eustratius' *Life* of the Patriarch Eutychius and the Fifth Ecumenical Council', ΚΑΘΗΓΗΤΡΙΑ in J. Chrysostomides (ed.) *Essays presented to Joan Hussey for the 80th Birthday*, 225–47 (Camberley, Surrey: Hellenic Institute, 1988)

—*The Mediterranean World in Late Antiquity AD 395-600* (London/New York: Routledge, 1993)

—*Cambridge Ancient History* xiv, second edn, 63–258 (Cambridge: Cambridge University Press, 2000)

T. F. Carney, *Bureaucracy in Traditional Society* (Lawrence, KS: Coronado Press, 1971)

Paavo Castrén (ed.), *Post-Herulian Athens.* Papers and Monographs of the Finnish Institute at Athens, I (Helsinki, 1994)

A. A. Cekalova, 'Der Nika–Aufstand', in F. Winkelman (ed.) *Volk und Herrschaft im frühen Byzanz. Methodische und quellenkritische Probleme*, 11–17 (Berlin: Akademie Verlag, 1991)

W. Ceran, 'Stagnation and Fluctuation in Early Byzantine Society', *Byzantinoslavica*, 31, 192–203 (1970)

Gillian Clark, *Women in Late Antiquity. Pagan and Christian Lifestyle* (Oxford: Oxford University Press, 1993)

Graeme Clark (ed.), *Reading the Past in Late Antiquity* (Rushcutters Bay, NSW: Australian National University Press, 1990)

Ian Colvin, 'Reporting Battles and Understanding Campaigns in Procopius' and
Agathias: Classicizing Historians' Use of Archives Documents and their Sources'
forthcoming in *War in Late Antiquity,* volume 7 of *Late Antique Archaeology*
(Leiden: Brill, 2011)

Domenico Comparetti, 'Maldicenze procopiane', *Raccolta Lumbroso,* 68–76 (1925)

Carolyn L. Connor, *Women of Byzantium* (New Haven: Yale University Press,
2004)

Vénétia Cottas, *La Théâtre à Byzance* (Paris: Paul Guenther, 1931)

Brian Croke, 'Justinian's Bulgar Victory Celebration', *Byzantinoslavica,* 41, 188–95
(1980)

—'Procopius' *Secret History*: Rethinking the Date', GRBS 45, 403–31 (2005)

—'Justinian, Theodora and the Church of Saints Sergius and Bacchus', DOP, 60,
25–63 (2007)

Gilbert Dagron, 'Rome et l'Italie vues de Byzance (IVe – VIIe siècles', *Bisanzio,
Roma e l'Italia nell'alto Mediaevo. Settimane di Studio del Centro Italiano di Studie
sull'alto Mediaevo,* 34, 2 vols. (Spoleto), I, 43–64 (1988)

David Daube, 'The Marriage of Justinian and Theodora', *Catholic University of
America Law Review,* 16/4, 380–99 (1967)

Elizabeth Dawes and Norman H. Baynes, *Three Byzantine Saints,* translated from
the Greek (Oxford: Blackwell, 1948; repr. Crestwood, NY: St Vladimir's Seminary
Press, 1977)

Fernanda de'Maffei, 'Fortificazione di Giustiniano sul limes orientale: monumenti
e fonti', *The Seventeenth International Byzantine Congress. Major Papers,* 237–63
(New Rochelle, NY: Aristide D. Caratzas, 1986)

A. Debidour, *De Theodora Justiniani Augustae Uxore* (Paris: Andegavi, 1877)

George T. Dennis, 'Death in Byzantium', DOP 55, 1–7 (2001)

Glanville Downey, 'The Pilgrim's Progress of the Byzantine Emperor', *Church History,*
9, 207–17 (1940)

—'Paganism and Christianity in Procopius', *Church History,* 18, 89–102 (1949)

—'The Persian Campaign in Syria in A.D. 540', *Speculum,* 28, 340–8 (1953)

—'The Christian Schools of Palestine: A Chapter in Literary History', *Harvard
Library Bulletin,* 12, 297–319 (1958)

—*Gaza in the Early Sixth Century* (Norman, OK: University of Oklahoma Press,
1963)

—*Justinian and the Imperial Office,* Lectures in Memory of Louise Taft Semple, 2nd
series, delivered at the University of Cincinnati (1968)

H. A. Drake (ed.), *Violence in Late Antiquity. Perceptions and Practices* (Aldershot:
Ashgate, 2006)

M. A. Elferink, 'TÚXH et Dieu: Procope de Césarée', *Acta Classica,* 10, 111–34
(1967)

J. A. S. Evans, 'Procopius and the Emperor Justinian', *Canadian Historical Association: Historical Papers,* 126–39 (1968)

—'Christianity and Paganism in Procopius of Caesarea', GRBS 12, 81–100 (1971)

—*Procopius* (New York: Twayne, 1972)

—'The Walls of Thessalonica', *Byzantion,* 47, 61–2 (1977)

—'The "Nika" Rebellion and the Empress Theodora', *Byzantion,* 54, 380–2 (1984)

—*The Age of Justinian: The Consequences of Imperial Power* (London/New York: Routledge, 1996a)

—'The Dates of Procopius' Works: A Recapitulation of the Evidence', GRBS 37, 301–13 (1996b)

—*The Empress Theodora: Partner of Justinian.* Austin, TX: University of Texas Press, 2002)

—*The Emperor Justinian and the Byzantine Empire* (Westport, CT: Greenwood, 2005)

—'Justinian', Anthony A. Barrett (ed.) *Lives of the Caesars,* 280–303 (Malden, MA/ Oxford: Blackwell, 2008)

William Edmund Fahey, Review of Kaldellis, *Procopius of Caesarea, Bryn Mawr Classical Review,* 2005.10.11, http://bmcr.brynmawr.edu/2005/2005-10-11.html (2005)

Elizabeth A. Fisher, 'Theodora and Antonina in the Historia Arcana: History or Fiction', in Peradotto and Sullivan, *Women in the Ancient World,* 287–313 (1984)

Greg Fisher, 'Rome's Desert Frontier', BASOR, 336, 49–60 (2004)

James Fitton, 'The Death of Theodora', *Byzantion,* 46, 119 (1976)

C. Foss, 'The empress Theodora', *Byzantion,* 63, 5–28 (2002)

Elizabeth Key Fowden, *The Barbarian Plain: Saint Sergius between Rome and Iran* (Berkeley: University of California Press, 1999)

Dorothea R. French, 'Maintaining Boundaries. The Status of Actresses in Early Christian Society', *Vigiliae Christianae,* 52, 293–318 (1998)

W. H. C. Frend, *The Rise of the Monophysite Movement* (Cambridge: Cambridge University Press, 1972; repr. 1979)

Lynda Garland, *Byzantine Empresses. Women and Power in Byzantium, AD 527–1204* (London/New York: Routledge, 1999)

Jean Gascou, 'Les institutions de l'hippodrome en Égypte byzantine' *Bulletin de l'Institut français de l'archéologie oriental,* 76, 185–212 (1976)

Deno John Geanakoplos, 'Church Building and "Caesaropapism", A.D. 312–525', GRBS 7, 167–86 (1966)

Walter George, *The Church of Saint Eirene in Constantinople* (Oxford: Oxford University Press, 1912, repr. 1993)

Walter Goffart, *Caput and Colonate: towards a History of Late Roman Taxation* (Toronto: University of Toronto Press, 1974)

—*Barbarians and Romans A. D. 418–584. The Techniques of Accommodation*
    (Princeton: Princeton University Press, 1980)
Patrick T. R. Gray, 'The Legacy of Chalcedon. Christological Problems and their
    Significance', in Maas (ed.), *The Cambridge Companion to the Age of Justinian*,
    215–38 (2005)
Geoffrey Greatrex, 'The Dates of Procopius' Works', BMGS 18, 101–14 (1994)
—'Flavius Hypatius, *quem validum Parthus sensitque timendum.* An Investigation of
    his Career', *Byzantion*, 66, 120–42 (1996a)
—'Stephanus, the Father of Procopius of Caesarea?' *Medieval Prosopography*, 17/1,
    125–45 (1996b)
— 'The Nika Riot: A Reassessment', *Journal of Hellenic Studies*, 117, 60–86 (1997)
—*Rome and Persia at War, 502–532* (Leeds: Francis Cairns, 1998)
—'Procopius the Outsider?' in Dion C. Smythe, *Strangers to Themselves: The
    Byzantine Outsider*, 215– 28 (Aldershot: Ashgate, 2000)
—'Justin I and the Arians', *Studia Patristica*, 34, 72–81 (2001)
—'Recent Work on Procopius and the Composition of Wars VIII', BMGS 27, 48–67
    (2003)
Geoffrey Greatrex and Samuel N. C. Lieu, *The Roman Eastern Frontier and the
    Persian Wars*, Part II: A.D. 363–630. *A Narrative Sourcebook* (London/New
    York:Routledge, 2002)
Ruth Evans Grubbs, *Women and Law in the Roman Empire. A Sourcebook on
    Marriage, Divorce and Widowhood* (London/New York: Routledge, 2002)
R. Guilland, 'Études sur l'Hippodrome de Byzance', *Byzantinoslavica*, 26/1, 1–39 (1965)
—'Études sur l'Hippodrome de Byzanance. Les Spectacles de l'Hippodrome',
    Byzantinoslavica, 28, 262–77 (1967)
—'Études sur l'Hippodrome de Byzance', *Byzantinoslavica*, 31, 1–11 (1970)
—'Contribution à l'histoire administrative de l'empire Byzantine. La patricienne à
    ceinture.' *Byzantinoslavica*, 32, 269–75 (1971)
F. K. Haarer, *Anastasius I: Politics and Empire in the Late Roman World*, ARCA 46
    (Cambridge: Francis Cairns, 2006)
John F. Haldon, 'Economy and Administration: How did the Empire Work?' in Maas
    (ed.), *The Cambridge Companion to the Age of Justinian*, 28–59 (2005)
Gunnar Hällström, 'The Closing of the Neoplatonic School in 529: An Additional
    Aspect', in Paavo Castrén (ed.), *Post–Herulian Athens. Aspects of Life and Culture
    in Athens, A.D. 267–529*, 141–60 (Helsinki: Finnish Institute at Athens, 1994)
Edward R. Hardy, 'The Egyptian Policy of Justinian', DOP 22, 21–41 (1968)
R. M. Harrison, *A Temple for Byzantium* (London: Harvey Miller; Austin: University
    of Texas Press, 1989)
Susan A. Harvey, 'Theodora, the 'Believing Queen': A Study in Syriac
    Historiographical Tradition', *Hugoye* 4.2, 1–32 (2001)

J. Haury, *Procopiana* (Augsburg: Haas and Grabherr, 1890–91)

—'Zu Prokops Geheimgeschicte', *BZ* 34, 10–14 (1934)

Cecily Hennessy, 'Topography of Constantinople', OHBS, 202–16 (2008)

Patrick Henry III, 'A Mirror for Justinian: The *Ekthesis* of Agapetus Diaconus', GRBS 8, 281–308 (1967)

Thomas Hodgkin, *Italy and her Invaders*. I–V. 1880–1889 (Reprint, New York: Russell and Russell, 1967)

William Gordon Holmes, *The Age of Justinian and Theodora. A History of the Sixth Century A.D.* (London: G. Bell, 1912)

Kenneth G. Holum, *Theodosian Empresses: Women and Imperial Dominion in Late Antiquity* (Berkeley: University of California Press, 1982)

E. M. Hooker, 'Buboes in Thucydides', *Journal of Hellenic Studies,* 78, 78–83 (1958)

Peregrine Horden, 'Mediterranean Plague in the Age of Justinian', in Maas (ed.), *The Cambridge Companion to the Age of Justinian*, 134–60 (2005)

James Howard–Johnston, 'The Education and Expertise of Procopius', *Antiquité Tardive,* 8, 19–30 (2000)

Ian Hughes, *Belisarius: The Last Roman General* (Yardley, PA: Westholme, 2009)

Herbert Hunger, 'Der Kaiserpalast zu Konstantinopel', Jahrbuch der Österreichischen Byzantinistik, 36, 1–11 (1986)

Torsten Cumberland Jacobsen, *The Gothic War. Rome's Final Conflict in the West* (Yardley, PA: Westholme, 2009)

Liz James, 'Men, Women, Eunuchs: Gender, Sex and Power', in John Haldon (ed.), *A Social History of Byzantium* (Malden, MA/Oxford: Blackwell-Wiley, 2009)

Elizabeth Jeffreys (ed.) with Brian Croke and Roger Scott, *Studies in John Malalas. Byzantina Australiensia*, VI (Sydney: Australian Association for Byzantine Studies, 1990a)

—'Malalas' Use of the Past', in Clarke (ed.) (1990b)

Romilly Jenkins, *Byzantium and Byzantinism,* Lectures in Memory of Louise Taft Semple delivered at the University of Cincinnati, 1st Series, 137–78, delivered at the University of Cincinnati (1967)

A. H. M. Jones, *The Later Roman Empire, 284–602 (*Norman, OK: University of Oklahoma Press, 1964)

Heinz Kähler, translated by Ellyn Childs, with a chapter on the mosaics by Cyril Mango, *Hagia Sophia* (London: A. Zwemmer; New York: Praeger, 1967)

Anthony Kaldellis, 'The Historical and Religious Views of Agathias', *Byzantion,* 69, 206–52 (1999)

—'The Religion of Ioannes Lydos', *Phoenix,* 59, 300–16 (2003)

—*Procopius of Caesarea: Tyranny, History and Philosophy at the End of Antiquity* (Philadelphia: University of Pennsylvania Press, 2004a)

—'Identifying Dissident Circles in Sixth-Century Byzantium: the Friendship of Prokopios and Ioannes Lydos', *Florilegium*, 21, 1–17 (2004b)

—'The Works and Days of Hesychios of Miletos', GRBS 45, 381–403 (2005a)

—'Republican theory and political dissidence in Ioannes Lydos', BMGS 29, 1–16 (2005b)

—*Hellenism in Byzantium. The Transformations of Greek Identity and the Reception of the Classical Tradition* (Cambridge: Cambridge University Press, 2007a)

—'The Literature of Plague and the Anxieties of Piety in Sixth-Century Byzantium', in Franco Mormando and Thomas Worcester (eds), *Piety and Plague from Byzantium to the Baroque. Sixteenth Century Essays and Studies* 78, 1–22 (Kirksville, MO: Truman State University Press, 2007b)

—'The Date and Structure of Prokopios' *Secret History* and his Projected Work in Church History', GRBS 49, 585–616 (2009)

I. Kawar, 'Procopius and Arethas', *Byzantinische Zeitschrift*, 50, 39–67; 362–82 (1957)

David Keys, *Catastrophe. An Investigation into the Origins of the Modern World* (London: Century; New York, Ballantine, 1999)

Derek Krueger, 'Christian Piety and Practice in the Sixth Century', in Maas (ed.), *The Cambridge Companion to the Age of Justinian*, 291–515 (2005)

K. Kumaniecki, 'Eine unbekannte Monodie aus den Einsturz der Haghia Sophia im Jahre 558', *ByzZeit*, 30, 35–43 (1929–30)

George LaPiana, 'The Byzantine Theatre', *Speculum*, 11, 171–211 (1936)

Samuel N. C. Lieu, *Manichaeism in the Later Roman Empire and Medieval China*, second edn (Tübingen: J. C. B. Mohr, 1992)

Christopher Lillington-Martin, 'The Late Roman Army in the Near East from Diocletian to the Arab Conquest', in Ariel S. Lewin and Pietrina Pelligrini (eds), *Proceedings of a Colloquium held at Potenza, Acerenza and Matera, Italy*, 299–311 (May, 2005)

Richard Lim, 'Christian Triumph and Controversy', in Bowersock, Brown and Grabar (eds), LA *Guide*, 196–218 (1999)

—'Converting the unchristianizable: the baptism of stage performers in Late Antiquity', in K. Mills and A. Grafton (eds), *Conversion in Late Antiquity: Seeing and Believing*, 84–126 (Suffolk: Boydell and Brewster; Rochester, NY: University of Rochester Press, 2003)

Lester K. Little (ed.), *Plague and the End of Antiquity. The Pandemic of 541–750* (Cambridge: Cambridge University Press, 2007a)

—'Life and Afterlife of the First Plague Epidemic', in Little, *Plague and the End of Antiquity*, 3–32 (2007b)

Michael Maas, *John Lydus and the Roman Past* (London: Routledge, 1992)

Michael Maas (ed.), *The Cambridge Companion to the Age of Justinian* (Cambridge: Cambridge University Press, 2005)

Ramsay Macmullen, *Christianity and Paganism in the Fourth to Eighth Centuries* (New Haven, CT: Yale University Press, 1997)

Rowland J. Mainstone, *Hagia Sophia. Architecture, Structure and Liturgy of Justinian's Great Church* (London: Thames and Hudson, 1988)

Cyril Mango, *Byzantium. The Empire of New Rome* (London: Weidenfeld and Nicolson, 1980)

--'Daily Life in Byzantium', *Jahrbuch der Österreichischen Byzantinistik*, 31/1, 1981, 337–53 (1984)

Pierre Maraval, *L'empereur Justinien* (Paris: Presses universitaires de France, 1999)

Thomas F. Matthews, *The Early Churches of Constantinople. Architecture and Liturgy* (University Park and London: Pennsylvania State University Press, 1971)

A. McClanan, 'The empress Theodora and the tradition of women's patronage', in June Hall McCash, *The Cultural Patronage of Medieval Women*, 50–72 (Athens, GA: University of Georgia Press, 1996)

William H. McNeill, *Plagues and Peoples* (New York: Anchor Press, 1976)

Mischa Meier, 'Die Inszenierung einer Katastrophe: Justinian und der Nika Aufstand', *Zeitschrift für Papyrologie und Epigrafik,* 142, 273–300 (2003)

--*Justinian: Herrschaft, Reich und Religion* (Munich: Beck, 2004)

John Meyendorff, 'Justinian, the Empire and the Church', DOP 22, 21–41 (1968)

Fergus Millar, 'Rome, Constantinople and the Near Eastern Church under Justinian', *Journal of Roman Studies,* 98, 62–82 (2008)

Stephen Mitchell, *A History of the Later Roman Empire, A.D. 284-641* (Oxford: Blackwell, 2007)

Arnaldo Momigliano, 'Cassiodorus and Italian Culture of his Times', *Proceedings of the British Academy,* 41, 207–36 (1955)

John Moorhead, *Justinian* (London: Longman, 1994)

James J. O'Donnell, *The Ruin of the Roman Empire* (New York: HarperCollins, 2008)

S. I. Oost, 'Galla Placidia and the Law', *Classical Philology,* 53, 114–21 (1968)

Wendy Orent, 'Will the Black Death Return?' *Discover,* 22, 72–7 (November, 2001)

Charles Pazdernik, '"Our Most Pious Consort Given Us by God". Dissident Reactions to the Partnership of Justinian and Theodora. AD 525–548', *Classical Antiquity*, 13, 251–81 (1994)

John Peradotto and J. P. Sullivan (eds), *Women in the Ancient World. The* ARETHUSA *Papers (*Albany, NY: SUNY Press, 1984)

Richard Price, *Acts of the Council of Constantinople of 553, with related texts on the Three Chapters Controversy*, (Liverpool: University of Liverpool Press, 2009)

J. M. Rist, 'Hypatia', *Phoenix,* 19, 214–25 (1965)

William Rosen, *Justinian's Flea. Plague, Empire and the Birth of Europe* (New York: Viking Penguin, 2007)

Charlotte Roueché (with a contribution from J. M. Reynolds), *Aphrodisias in Late Antiquity*, JRS Monographs, V (London: Society for the Promotion of Roman Studies, 1989)

––*Performers and Partisans at Aphrodisias*. JRS Monographs VI (London: Society for the Promotion of Roman Studies, 1993)

––'Entertainment, Theatre and the Hippodrome', in OHBS, 677–98 (2008)

Philip Rousseau, 'Procopius' *Buildings* and Justinian's Pride', *Byzantion*, 68, 122–30 (1998)

Philip Rousseau (ed.), *A Companion to Late Antiquity* (Malden, MA/Oxford: Blackwell, 2009)

Berthold Rubin, *Das Zeitalter Iustinians,* I (Berlin: De Gruyter, 1960)

Dan Ruscu, 'The Revolt of Vitalianus and the "Scythian Controversy"', *ByzZeit*, 101/2, 773–85 (2008)

J. C. Russell, *Late Ancient and Medieval Population. Transactions of the American Philosophical Society,* n.s., XLVIII, pt. 3 (1958)

P. Salama, 'Part II: From Rome to Islam', in G.Moktar (ed.) *General History of Africa,* II, 499–560 (London/Berkeley: University of California Press, 1981)

Robert Sallares, 'Ecology, Evolution and Epidemiology of Plague', in Little, *Plague and the End of Antiquity*, 231–89 (2007a)

Peter Sarris, *Economy and Society in the Age of Justinian* (Cambridge: Cambridge University Press, 2006)

––'Bubonic Plague in Byzantium. The Evidence of the Non–Literary Sources', in Little, *Plague and the End of Antiquity*, 119–132 (2007a)

Pamela G. Sayre, 'The Mistress of the Robes. Who was She?' *Byzantine Studies/ Études Byzantines*, 13/2, 229–39 (1986)

A. Arthur Schiller, 'The Courts are no More', *Studi in onore di Edoardo Volterra* (Milan: A. Giuffrè, 1969)

Roger Scott, 'Malalas, the Secret History, and Justinian's Propaganda', DOP 39, 99–109 (1985)

Claire Sotinel, 'Emperors and Popes in the Sixth Century. The Western View', in Maas (ed.), *The Cambridge Companion to the Age of Justinian*, 267–90 (2005)

Dionysios Stathakopoulos, 'Crime and Punishment. The Plague in the Byzantine Empire, 541–749', in Little, *Plague and the End of Antiquity*, 99-118 (2007a)

E. Stein, *Histoire du Bas–Empire. II. De la disparition de l'Empire d'Occident à la mort de Justinien (476–565)* (Paris: Desclée de Brouwer, 1949)

Robert F. Taft, 'Women at Church in Byzantium: Where, When – and Why?' DOP 52, 27–87 (1998)

A.-M. Talbot, 'Old Age in Byzantium', *BZ* 77, 267–78 (1984)

John L. Teall, 'The Barbarians in Justinian's Armies', *Speculum* 40, 294–322 (1965)

Warren Treadgold, *A History of the Byzantine State and Society* (Stanford, CA: Stanford University Press, 1997)

--*The Early Byzantine Historians* (New York: Palgrave Macmillan, 2007)

Frank R. Trombley, 'Paganism and the End of Antiquity', *Harvard Theological Review,* 78, 327–52 (1985)

Henry Turtledove, 'The True Size of the Post–Justinianic Army', *Byzantine Studies/ Études Byzantines,* 10/2, 216–22 (1983)

Percy Neville Ure, *Justinian and His Age* (Harmondsworth: Penguin, 1951)

Raymond Van Dam, *Kingdom of Snow. Roman Rule and Greek Culture in Cappadocia* (Philadelphia, PA: University of Pennsylvania Press, 2002)

A. A. Vasiliev, *Justin the First. An Introduction to the Epoch of Justinian the Great,* DOS I (Cambridge, MA: Harvard University Press, 1950)

Bryan Ward–Perkins, *The Fall of Rome and the End of Civilization* (Oxford: Oxford University Press, 2005)

Edward Watts, 'Justinian, Malalas and the End of Athenian Philosophical Teaching', JRS 94, 168–84 (2004)

--'The Murder of Hypatia; Acceptable or Unacceptable Violence', in Drake (2006) 333–42

Ruth Webb, *Demons and Dancers. Performance in Late Antiquity.* Cambridge, MA/ London: Harvard University Press, 2008)

N. G. Wilson, *Scholars of Byzantium* (London: Duckworth, 1983)

Witold Witakowski, *The Syriac Chronicle of Pseudo–Dionysius of Tel–Mahre. A Study in the History of Historiography. Acta Universitatis Upsaliensis,* Studia Semitica Upsaliensia, IX (1987)

David Womersley (ed.), *Edward Gibbon – The History of the Decline and Fall of the Roman Empire,* 3 vols. (London: Allen Lane, 1994)

Nicolas Zemov, *Eastern Christendom. A Study of the Origins and Development of the Eastern Orthodox Church* (London: Weidenfeld and Nicolson, 1961)

Constantin Zuckerman, 'La Cirque, l'Argent et le Peuple à propos d'une inscription du Bas–Empire', *Revue des Études Byzantines,* 58, 69–96 (2000)

Index